First World War
and Army of Occupation
War Diary
France, Belgium and Germany

42 DIVISION
Divisional Troops
Divisional Signal Company
1 March 1917 - 31 March 1919

WO95/2651

The Naval & Military Press Ltd
www.nmarchive.com
Published in association with The National Archives

Published by

The Naval & Military Press Ltd

Unit 10 Ridgewood Industrial Park,

Uckfield, East Sussex,

TN22 5QE England

Tel: +44 (0) 1825 749494

www.naval-military-press.com

www.nmarchive.com

This diary has been reprinted in facsimile from the original. Any imperfections are inevitably reproduced and the quality may fall short of modern type and cartographic standards.

Contents

Document type	Place/Title	Date From	Date To
Heading	42nd Division Divl Signal Coy R.E. Mar 1917-Mar 1919.		
Heading	42nd Divisional Signal Coy. R.E., (T) War Diary. Chapter V. From March 1st to March 31st 1917. Vol 1.		
War Diary	Hallencourt	01/03/1917	15/03/1917
War Diary	Pont Remy		
War Diary	Caours		
War Diary		15/03/1917	31/03/1917
War Diary	Hamel	15/03/1917	25/03/1917
War Diary	Frise	25/03/1917	25/03/1917
War Diary	Dompierre	29/03/1917	30/03/1917
War Diary	St Saveur	31/03/1917	31/03/1917
War Diary	Hamel	31/03/1917	31/03/1917
Diagram etc	Circuit Diagram. 42nd Divisional Communications. March 1917.		
Heading	War Diary of 42nd Divisional Signal Coy. R.E. (T) From April 1st to 30th 1917. Vol. IV.		
War Diary	Hamel	01/04/1917	01/04/1917
War Diary	Mericourt-Sur-Somme	02/04/1917	03/04/1917
War Diary	Peronne	06/04/1917	06/04/1917
War Diary	Morecourt	07/04/1917	11/04/1917
War Diary	Peronne	13/04/1917	29/04/1917
Miscellaneous	Plans to accompany War Diary of 42nd Divnl Signal Coy for April 1917.		
Diagram etc	Circuit Diagram 42nd Divisional Communication		
Diagram etc	Diagram. Communications. April 1917. Appendix "A".		
Diagram etc	Circuit Diagram 42nd Divisional Communications.		
Diagram etc	Circuit Diagram 42nd Divisional Communications. Appendix "C".		
Miscellaneous	Appendix "C". Honours and Awards.		
Miscellaneous	Appendix "D". Weekly Strength.		
Heading	42nd Div Sig Co. R.E. War Diary Chap 7. May 1. Vol 3.		
War Diary	Roisel.	02/05/1917	17/05/1917
War Diary	Ytres.	17/05/1917	17/05/1917
War Diary	Lechelle	19/05/1917	19/05/1917
War Diary	Brusle.	19/05/1917	19/05/1917
War Diary	Ytres.	23/05/1917	31/05/1917
Miscellaneous	Appendix "A". Description of Routes-Roisel.	03/06/1917	03/06/1917
Miscellaneous	Appendix "B" Description of Routes-Ytres.	03/06/1917	03/06/1917
Miscellaneous	Appendix "C". Honours and Awards.	03/06/1917	03/06/1917
Miscellaneous	Appendix "D". Weekly Strengths, Casualties, Reinforcements.	03/06/1917	03/06/1917
Diagram etc	Messages Graph. 42nd Divisional Signal Company May 1917. Appendix E.		
Heading	War Diary 42nd Divisional Sig Coy R.E. (T.F.) Chapter VIII June 1917. Vol 4.		
War Diary	Ytres.		
Diagram etc	Diagram of Communications. 42nd Div. Signal Coy., R.E. Appendix "A".		

Diagram etc	Appendix "B" Diagram of Buried Route.		
Diagram etc	Messages Graph 42nd Divisional Signal Company. June 1917. Appendix E.		
Miscellaneous	War Diary Description of Buried Cable Scheme. Appendix "B".	04/07/1917	04/07/1917
Miscellaneous	War Diary. Honours and Awards. Appendix "C".	04/07/1917	04/07/1917
Miscellaneous	War Diary. Weekly Strengths, Casualties, Reinforcements. Appendix "D".	04/07/1917	04/07/1917
Miscellaneous	Effects of Thunder Storms of Communications. Appendix "F".	04/07/1917	04/07/1917
Miscellaneous	Signalling to Kite Balloons. Appendix "C".	04/07/1917	04/07/1917
Heading	War Diary 42nd Div Sig Coy R.E. (T.F.) Chapter 9. July 1917. Vol 5.		
War Diary	Ytres.		
War Diary	Achiet-Le-Petit.		
Diagram etc	Diagram of Communications. 42nd Divisional Signal Coy., R.E. July 1917.		
Miscellaneous	War Diary Recreational Training. Appendix "B".		
Miscellaneous	Event.		
Heading	42nd Signal Coy. R.E. Mounted Sports.		
Miscellaneous	Training Scheme. Appendix "C".	06/08/1917	06/08/1917
Miscellaneous	Nth Divisional Signal Order No. 3059, by Major "Y" O.C. Signals, "N" Division.		
Miscellaneous	G.S.5/82	12/07/1917	12/07/1917
Miscellaneous	Report on Signal School. Appendix "D".	05/08/1917	05/08/1917
Miscellaneous	Honours and Awards. Appendix "E".	06/08/1917	06/08/1917
Miscellaneous	Weekly Strengths, Casualties, Reinforcements. Appendix "F".	06/08/1917	06/08/1917
Diagram etc	Diagram of Communications. 42nd Divisional Signal Coy.		
Diagram etc	Major. 42nd Div. Sig. Coy. R.E. May 10th 1917.		
Diagram etc	Circuit Diagram of Communication 42nd Divisional Signal Coy. R.E.		
Diagram etc	Diagram of Communications Divisional Signal Coy. R.E. Appendix "C".		
Diagram etc	Diagram of Communications. 42nd Divisional Signal Coy.		
Diagram etc	Diagram of 42nd Div. Signal. Appendix "A".		
Diagram etc	Diagram of Communications Signal Co. R.E.		
Diagram etc	Diagram 'B'		
Diagram etc			
Diagram etc	Major O.C. 42nd Divisional Signal Coy. R.E. September 1917.		
Diagram etc	Message Graph. 42nd Divisional Signal Company. July 1917.		
Heading	42nd Divisional Signal Co. (R.E.) War Diary. Chapter 10. August 1917. Vol 6.		
War Diary	Achiet-Le-Petit.	20/08/1917	20/08/1917
War Diary	Beaucourt	21/08/1917	22/08/1917
War Diary	Watou	23/08/1917	31/08/1917
Miscellaneous	Appendices to this diary.	09/09/1917	09/09/1917
Miscellaneous	War Diary. Appendix "A".	09/09/1917	09/09/1917
Miscellaneous	Signalling Certificate. 42nd Divisional School of Signalling.	09/09/1917	09/09/1917
Miscellaneous	War Diary. Appendix. "B". Honours and Awards.	09/09/1917	09/09/1917

Miscellaneous	Weekly Strengths, Casualties, Reinforcements. Appendix. "C".	09/09/1917	09/09/1917
Heading	Messages Graph. 42nd Divisional August 1917.		
Diagram etc	Message Graph. August 1917. Signal Company.		
Heading	War Diary. Monthly Message Chart. August 1917. Appendix "D".		
Heading	42nd Divisional Signal Coy War Diary. Chapter XI September 1917. Vol 7.		
War Diary	Erandhoek.	01/09/1917	18/09/1917
War Diary	Poperinghe.	13/09/1917	21/09/1917
War Diary	Wormhoudt	22/09/1917	22/09/1917
War Diary	Poperinghe.	22/09/1917	22/09/1917
War Diary	La Panne Bains.	23/09/1917	25/09/1917
War Diary	St Idesbalde.	25/09/1917	25/09/1917
Operation(al) Order(s)	42nd Divisional Signal Company. R.E. Order No.6.	24/09/1917	24/09/1917
Operation(al) Order(s)	42nd Divisional Signal Company. R.E. Order No.5.	21/09/1917	21/09/1917
Operation(al) Order(s)	42nd Divisional Signal Company. R.E. Order No.4.	16/09/1917	16/09/1917
Heading	Appendix A Diagram A		
Map			
Diagram etc	Diagram 'A'		
Diagram etc	42nd Divisional Signal Coy. R.E. September 1917.		
Miscellaneous	Diagram A.		
Miscellaneous	Notes on Communications in the Ypres Sector. Appendix. "B".		
Heading	Appendix "C"		
Diagram etc	Diagram 'C' Power Buzzers A Amplifiers		
Miscellaneous	War Diary. Honours and Awards. Appendix. D.	03/10/1917	03/10/1917
Diagram etc	War Diary. Weekly Strengths, Casualties, Reinforcements. Appendix. E.	03/10/1917	03/10/1917
Diagram etc	Messages Graph, 42nd Divisional Signal Company. September 1917. Appendix F.		
Miscellaneous	Appendix "F"		
Heading	War Diary. 42nd Div. Signal Coy. R.E. October, 1917. Chapter 12. Vol 8.		
War Diary	St. Idesbalde	01/10/1917	07/10/1917
War Diary	Coxyde Bains.	07/10/1917	31/10/1917
Operation(al) Order(s)	42nd Divisional Signal Company. R.E. Order No.7.	06/10/1917	06/10/1917
Miscellaneous	Communications. A. Telephone Communications in Divisional Sector. (Diagram A.)		
Miscellaneous	B. Visual Communications in Divisional Sector. (Diagram B.)		
Miscellaneous	C. Wireless Communications. (Diagram C).		
Miscellaneous	D. Despatch Riders and Runners.		
Miscellaneous	E. Pigeons.		
Miscellaneous	F. Rockets.		
Miscellaneous	War Diary. Honours and Awards. Appendix "D".	04/11/1917	04/11/1917
Miscellaneous	War Diary. Weekly Strengths, Casualties, Reinforcements. Appendix "E".	04/11/1917	04/11/1917
Diagram etc	Diagram of Communications 42nd Div. Signal Coy. R.E. October 12th 1917. Appendix "A".		
Diagram etc	Message Graph 42nd Division Signal Company October 1917. Appendix B.		
Diagram etc	Wireless and Power Buzzer Communications. Diagram "C".		
Diagram etc	Visual Communications 42nd Division. Diagram "B".		

Heading	War Diary. for November 1917. 42nd Div. Signal Coy. R.E. Chapter XIII. Vol 9.		
War Diary	Coxyde Bains.	01/11/1917	19/11/1917
War Diary	Aire.	19/11/1917	29/11/1917
Operation(al) Order(s)	42nd Divisional Signal Company. R.E. Order No. 8	18/11/1917	18/11/1917
Operation(al) Order(s)	42nd Divisional Signal Company. R.E. Order No. 9.	28/11/1917	28/11/1917
Miscellaneous	War Diary. Honours and Awards. Appendix "C".	04/12/1917	04/12/1917
Miscellaneous	Weekly Strengths, Casualties, Reinforcements. Appendix "D".	04/12/1917	04/12/1917
Diagram etc	Local Route Chart. Appendix "A".		
Diagram etc	Messages Graph 42nd Divisional November 1917. Appendix "B".		
Diagram etc	Message Graph November 1917. Signal Company.		
Heading	War Diary 42nd Div., Signal Co., R.E. Chapter XIV. December 1917. Vol 10.		
War Diary	Locon.	01/12/1917	01/12/1917
War Diary	Near Bethune.	09/12/1917	09/12/1917
Miscellaneous	War Diary. Part 1. Methods of Communication. Appendix "A".		
Miscellaneous	Part 2. "A"-Telegraph and Telephone.		
Miscellaneous	B-Wireless Communications. (Diagram "C").		
Miscellaneous	C-Despatch Riders and Runners.		
Miscellaneous	E-Visual Communications in the Divisional Sector. (Diagram "D").		
Miscellaneous	Part 3. Signalling Instructions for Gas Cloud Attack.		
Diagram etc	Chart Shewing Responsibility for Repeating Gas Attack Warnings. Diagram. "X".		
Miscellaneous	List "A". 42nd Divisional Exchanges. D.H.Q. Exchange.		
Miscellaneous	Advanced D.H.Q. (Le Quesnoy) Exchange.		
Miscellaneous	Left Infantry Brigade Exchange.		
Miscellaneous	Right Group R.F.A. Exchange.		
Miscellaneous	War Diary. Honours and Awards. Appendix "D".	04/01/1918	04/01/1918
Miscellaneous	War Diary. Weekly Strengths, Casualties, Reinforcements. Appendix "E".	04/01/1918	04/01/1918
Diagram etc	Wireless. Power Buzzer, & Amplifier Communications in 42nd Division Area.		
Diagram etc	Visual Communications in 42nd Divisional Area.		
Map	Route Chart of Communications in 42nd Divisional Area.		
Diagram etc	Diagram "A".		
Diagram etc	Messages Graph 42nd Divisional Signal Company R.E. December 1917.		
Heading	War Diary. 42nd Div., Signal Co., R.E. Chapter XV. Vol 11.		
War Diary	Locon. (X.7.c.8.8)	01/01/1918	01/01/1918
War Diary	Nr Bethune. (W.28.d.8.8)	06/01/1918	31/01/1918
Miscellaneous	War Diary. Part 1. Methods of Communications. Appendix "A".		
Miscellaneous	A Telegraph and Telephone.		
Miscellaneous	B Wireless Communications. (Diagram "J2).		
Miscellaneous	C-Despatch Riders and Runners.		
Miscellaneous	E Visual Communications in the Divisional Sector. (Diagram "J3".)		
Miscellaneous	War Diary. 42nd Division. Appendix "D".	11/01/1918	11/01/1918

Miscellaneous	Signalling Certificate. 42nd Divisional School of Signalling.	10/01/1918	10/01/1918
Miscellaneous	War Diary. 42nd Division. Appendix "E".	21/01/1918	21/01/1918
Miscellaneous	42nd Divisional Signal Class. Results of Third Wireless Course.		
Miscellaneous	Nominal Roll of Signallers Trained in Wireless Power Buzzer and Amplifier Work.		
Miscellaneous	War Diary. Honours and Awards. Appendix "F".	03/02/1918	03/02/1918
Miscellaneous	War Diary. Weekly Strengths, Casualties, Reinforcements. Appendix "G".	03/02/1918	03/02/1918
Diagram etc	Circuit Diagram of Communications		
Diagram etc	Appendix B		
Heading	War Diary. 42nd Divisional Signal Coy., R.E. February 1918. Chapter XVI. Vol 12.		
War Diary	Locon. (X.7.c.8.8)	01/02/1918	01/02/1918
War Diary	Locon.	12/02/1918	12/02/1918
War Diary	Locon-Lenglet.	15/02/1918	15/02/1918
War Diary	Chocques.	15/02/1918	15/02/1918
War Diary	Hinges.	15/02/1918	15/02/1918
War Diary	Nr. Bethune. (W.28.d.88)	15/02/1918	17/02/1918
Operation(al) Order(s)	Corrigendum to 42nd Divisional Signal Company. R.E. Order No.10.	13/02/1918	13/02/1918
Operation(al) Order(s)	42nd Divisional Signal Company R.E. Order No.10.	12/02/1918	12/02/1918
Diagram etc	Forecast Diagram of Communications of 42nd, Div., at 10-0 am., on 15.2.18.		
Miscellaneous	Lenglet. Appendix. A.		
Miscellaneous	Wireless Training. 42nd Divisional Signal Co. R.E.		
Miscellaneous	Training-Mounted and Dismounted Linemen.		
Miscellaneous	Chocques.		
Miscellaneous	Hinges.		
Miscellaneous	Report of Training and Results of the Eighth (Refresher) Course 42nd Divisional Signal School. Appendix "B".	24/02/1918	24/02/1918
Miscellaneous	War Diary. Honours and Awards. Appendix "C".	03/03/1918	03/03/1918
Miscellaneous	War Diary. Weekly Strengths, Casualties, Reinforcements. Appendix "D".	03/03/1918	03/03/1918
Diagram etc	Message Graph. 42nd Divisional February 1918. Appendix "E".		
Diagram etc	Message Graph. February 1918 Signal Co., R.E.		
Heading	42nd Divisional Engineers 42nd Divisional Signal Company R.E. March 1918 Attached:- Appendices A.B.C&D. O.O. No. 11. Diagrams of Communications.		
War Diary	Hinges	01/03/1918	01/03/1918
War Diary	Lenglet	01/03/1918	01/03/1918
War Diary	Chocques	01/03/1918	01/03/1918
War Diary	Nr Bethune. (W.28.d.8.8).	17/03/1918	17/03/1918
War Diary	Lenglet.	23/03/1918	23/03/1918
War Diary	Adinfer.	24/03/1918	24/03/1918
War Diary	Monchy-Le-Bois.	25/03/1918	25/03/1918
War Diary	Bucquoy.	26/03/1918	26/03/1918
War Diary	Fonquevillers	27/03/1918	27/03/1918
War Diary	St. Amand.	28/03/1918	28/03/1918
Miscellaneous	Report on Training and Results of the Ninth (Beginners) Course, 42nd Divisional Signal Class. Appendix "A".	21/03/1918	21/03/1918
Miscellaneous	Report on Training and Results of the Tenth (Refresher) Course. 42nd Divisional Signal Class. Appendix "A".	02/04/1918	02/04/1918
War Diary		23/03/1918	31/03/1918

Miscellaneous	War Diary. Honours and Awards. Appendix "C"	04/04/1918	04/04/1918
Miscellaneous	War Diary. Weekly Strengths, Casualties, Reinforcements. Appendix "D".	04/04/1918	04/04/1918
Heading	Order No. 11. Diagrams of Communications.		
Operation(al) Order(s)	42nd Divisional Signals Company. R.E. Order No.11.	04/03/1918	04/03/1918
Diagram etc	Forecast Diagrams of Communications of Units of 42nd Division.		
Diagram etc	Diagram 1		
Diagram etc	Diagram 2		
Diagram etc	Diagram 3		
Diagram etc	Diagram 4		
Diagram etc	Diagram 5		
Diagram etc	Diagram 6		
Diagram etc	Diagram 7		
Heading	IV. Corps. Third Army. War Diary 42nd Divisional Signal Company, R.E. April 1918 Attached: Appendices "A", "B", "C" & "D".		
Heading	War Diary. 42nd Divisional Signal Co. R.E. Chapter XVIII. Vol 14.		
War Diary	St. Amand.	01/04/1918	01/04/1918
War Diary	Henu.	03/04/1918	03/04/1918
War Diary	Pas.	07/04/1918	07/04/1918
War Diary	Couin.	16/04/1918	30/04/1918
Miscellaneous	Appendices to this diary.	05/05/1918	05/05/1918
Heading	Appendices "A", "B", "C" & "D".		
War Diary	Diagram 1.	01/04/1918	01/04/1918
War Diary	Diagram 2.	02/04/1918	02/04/1918
War Diary	Diagram 3.	03/04/1918	06/04/1918
War Diary	Diagram 4.	07/04/1918	09/04/1918
War Diary	Diagram 8.	09/04/1918	09/04/1918
War Diary	Defence Scheme.	09/04/1918	17/04/1918
War Diary	Diagram 9.	17/04/1918	17/04/1918
War Diary	Diagram 11.	17/04/1918	17/04/1918
War Diary	Map 2.	17/04/1918	17/04/1918
War Diary	Diagram 12.	17/04/1918	17/04/1918
War Diary	Sub-Appendix A 2.	21/04/1918	25/04/1918
War Diary	Diagram 13.	30/04/1918	30/04/1918
War Diary	Map 2.	30/04/1918	30/04/1918
War Diary	Diagram 1.		
Diagram etc	Diagram 2.		
Diagram etc	Diagram 3.		
Diagram etc	Diagram 4.		
Diagram etc	A.8 Diagram of Communications 42nd Division.		
Diagram etc	Telephone Line Communications 42nd Division Hebuterne Sector.		
Diagram etc	Diagram 11.		
Diagram etc	Diagram 12.		
Diagram etc	Diagram 13 Central Division's Communications		
Diagram etc	Diagram 13		
Map	France		
Operation(al) Order(s)	Sub Appendix A.1.	14/04/1918	14/04/1918
Diagram etc	Diagram "A" Communication while 42nd DHQ remain at Pas		
Diagram etc	Diagram "B" Communication while D.H.Q remain at Pas Visual & Wireless		

Diagram etc	Diagram "C" Communications when 42nd D.H.Q. moves to Orville.		
Diagram etc	Diagram "D" Visual & Wireless Communications when D.H.Q. moves to Orville		
Miscellaneous	42nd Divisional Defence Scheme. Communications in the Gommecourt Sector. Sub-Appendix. A.2.		
Miscellaneous	Communications.		
Diagram etc	Diagram "A" Appendix "D".		
Diagram etc	Diagram "B".		
Diagram etc	Diagram "C".		
Miscellaneous	Appendix I. 42nd Divisional H.Q. Exchange.		
Miscellaneous	Souastre Exchange.		
Miscellaneous	D.R.L.S. Time Table. 42nd Division. Appendix II.		
Miscellaneous	War Diary. Honours and Awards. Appendix. "B".		
Miscellaneous	War Diary. Weekly Strengths, Casualties, Reinforcements. Appendix. "C".		
Diagram etc	Messages Graph. 42nd Divisional Signal Co., R.E. April 1918. Appendix D.		
Miscellaneous	Appendix War Diary.		
Heading	War Diary. 42nd Divisional Signal Coy. R.E. Chapter XIX. May 1918. Vol 15.		
War Diary	Couin.	01/05/1918	01/05/1918
War Diary	Pas.	06/05/1918	31/05/1918
Operation(al) Order(s)	42nd Divisional Signal Company Order No.16.	05/05/1918	05/05/1918
Miscellaneous	Special Detail of Transport.	06/05/1918	06/05/1918
Operation(al) Order(s)	42nd Divisional Signal Company. R.E. Order No. 17. on Receipt of Order "Battle Positions".	10/05/1918	10/05/1918
Miscellaneous	War Diary. Communications. Appendix "A".	03/06/1918	03/06/1918
Diagram etc	Diagram 1 Communications 42nd Division		
Diagram etc	Communications 42nd Division Diagram "2".		
Miscellaneous	Notes on Communications During Scheme, 18/5/18. Appendix "A".	18/05/1918	18/05/1918
Miscellaneous	Communications for Left Division Holding the Red Line. Appendix "B".		
Diagram etc	Diagram "B".		
Diagram etc	Diagram "C".		
Miscellaneous	War Diary. Honours and Awards. Appendix "C".	03/06/1918	03/06/1918
Miscellaneous	War Diary. 6 Weekly Strengths, Casualties, Reinforcements. Appendix "D".	03/06/1918	03/06/1918
Diagram etc	Diagram "E" Message Graph.		
Miscellaneous	Message Appendix "E".		
Heading	War Diary. 42nd Divisional Signal Coy. R.E. Chapter XX 4th July 1918. Vol 16.		
War Diary	Pas.	01/06/1918	01/06/1918
War Diary	Bus.	07/06/1918	07/06/1918
War Diary		01/06/1918	30/06/1918
Diagram etc	Diagram. "D" Wireless Communications 42nd Division.		
Diagram etc	Diagram "A" 42nd Division.		
Diagram etc	Diagram "B" Communications 42nd Division.		
Operation(al) Order(s)	42nd Divisional Signal Company. R.E. Order No. 18.	06/06/1918	06/06/1918
War Diary		01/05/1918	06/05/1918
War Diary		07/05/1918	07/05/1918
War Diary		14/06/1918	14/06/1918
War Diary		18/06/1918	18/06/1918
Diagram etc	Visual Communications 42nd Division		
Diagram etc	Diagram "C" Visual Communications 42nd Division.		

Diagram etc	Wireless Communications 42nd Division.		
Miscellaneous	War Diary. Honours and Awards. Appendix 'C'.	04/07/1918	04/07/1918
Miscellaneous	War Diary. Weekly Strengths, Casualties, Reinforcements. Appendix 'D'.		
Diagram etc	Message Chart Appendix "E".		
Heading	War Diary 42nd Divisional Signal Coy Chapter XXI August 1918. Vol 17		
War Diary	Bus.	01/07/1918	01/07/1918
War Diary	Halloy.	04/07/1918	05/07/1918
War Diary	Beaurepaire.	06/07/1918	10/07/1918
War Diary	Sarton.	15/07/1918	15/07/1918
War Diary	Authie.	16/07/1918	31/07/1918
Operation(al) Order(s)	42nd Divisional Signal Company. R.E. Order No.19.		
Operation(al) Order(s)	42nd Divisional Signal Company. R.E. Order No.20.		
War Diary		01/07/1918	31/07/1918
Diagram etc	Diagram "B" Communications.		
War Diary		01/06/1918	31/07/1918
Diagram etc	Diagram "C" Visual Communications 42nd Division.		
Diagram etc	Visual Communications 42nd Division.		
Diagram etc	Diagram "D" Wireless Communications 42nd Division		
Diagram etc	Diagram "A" Communications 42nd Division.		
Diagram etc	Diagram "D" of Wireless Communications 42nd Division.		
Miscellaneous	Report on Training and Results of the Twelfth (Beginners) Course. 42nd Divisional Signal Class. Appendix "C".	12/07/1918	12/07/1918
Miscellaneous	War Diary. Honours and Awards. Appendix 'D'.	04/08/1918	04/08/1918
Miscellaneous	War Diary. Weekly Strengths, Casualties, Reinforcements. Appendix 'E'.	04/08/1918	04/08/1918
Diagram etc	Message Chart		
Miscellaneous	Appendix 'F'		
Heading	War Diary. 42nd Divisional Signal Coy. R.E. Chapter XXII Sept 1918. Vol 18.		
War Diary	Authie.	01/08/1918	01/08/1918
War Diary	Bus-Les-Artois.	15/08/1918	24/08/1918
War Diary	Colincamps.	25/08/1918	27/08/1918
War Diary	Bucquoy.	28/08/1918	30/08/1918
War Diary	Grevillers.	31/08/1918	31/08/1918
War Diary		01/08/1918	31/08/1918
War Diary		01/08/1918	30/08/1918
War Diary		18/08/1918	31/08/1918
Diagram etc	Communications 42nd Division		
Miscellaneous	Communications 42nd Division		
Diagram etc			
Diagram etc	Communications 42nd Division		
Diagram etc	Straight Line Diagram of Communications		
Operation(al) Order(s)	42nd Divisional Signal Company. R.E. Order No. 21. Appendix 'C'.		
Operation(al) Order(s)	42nd Divisional Signal Company. R.E. Order No. 23. Appendix 'C'.	27/08/1918	27/08/1918
Miscellaneous	Appendix 'D'. War Diary. Honours and Awards.		
Miscellaneous	Appendix 'E'. War Diary. Weekly Strengths, Casualties, Reinforcements.	10/09/1918	10/09/1918
Diagram etc	Communications 42nd Division		
Miscellaneous	Message Chart		

Heading	War Diary 42nd Divisional Signal Company R.E. Chapter XXIII. 4th Oct 1918. Vol 19.		
War Diary	Grevillers.	01/09/1918	03/09/1918
War Diary	Nr Reincourt les-Bapaume.	04/09/1918	20/09/1918
War Diary	Velu Wood.	21/09/1918	30/09/1918
Diagram etc	Straight-Line Diagram of Communications 42nd Division.		
Diagram etc	Communications 42nd Division Diagram 2.		
Diagram etc	Communications 42nd Division Diagram 3		
Diagram etc	Communications 42nd Division Diagram 4.		
Diagram etc	Communications 42nd Division Diagram 5.		
Diagram etc	Artillery Communication 42nd Division. Diagram 6.		
Diagram etc	Communications 42nd Division Diagram 7.		
Operation(al) Order(s)	42nd Divisional Signal Company. R.E. Order No.24. Appendix "A".	20/09/1918	20/09/1918
Miscellaneous	42nd Division. Battle Instructions No.1 Signal Communications. Appendix B.	25/09/1918	25/09/1918
Diagram etc	Tactical Communications 42nd Division Appendix 1.		
Diagram etc	Wireless & Visual Communications 42nd. Division. Appendix 2.		
Miscellaneous	War Diary. Honours and Awards. Appendix C.	04/10/1918	04/10/1918
Miscellaneous	War Diary. Weekly Strengths, Casualties, Reinforcements. Appendix D.	04/10/1918	04/10/1918
Diagram etc	Sectional Diagram. Appendix IV.		
Diagram etc	Sectional Diagram. Appendix V.		
Diagram etc	Sectional Diagram. Appendix VI.		
Diagram etc	Message Chart. Appendix E.		
Miscellaneous	Appendix "E".		
Diagram etc	Diagram "J".		
Diagram etc	1:20,000 First Army Front. Map Q.		
Heading	War Diary 42nd Divisional Signal Coy. R.E. Chapter XXIV 4th Nov. 1918. Vol 20.		
War Diary	Velu Wood.	01/10/1918	07/10/1918
War Diary	Q.10. Central.	08/10/1918	08/10/1918
War Diary	Esnes.	09/10/1918	11/10/1918
War Diary	Beauvois-En-Cambresis	12/10/1918	31/10/1918
War Diary	Hautmont.	01/12/1918	01/12/1918
War Diary	Move to Binche, Belgium.	14/12/1918	14/12/1918
War Diary	Move to Charleroi	16/12/1918	16/12/1918
Miscellaneous	War Diary. Honours and Awards. Appendix A.	16/01/1919	16/01/1919
Miscellaneous	War Diary. Weekly Strengths, Casualties, Reinforcements, etc. Appendix B.	16/01/1919	16/01/1919
Operation(al) Order(s)	42nd Divisional Signal Company. R.E. (T.F.). Order No. 25. Appendix 'A'.	11/10/1918	11/10/1918
Miscellaneous	42nd Division. Battle Instructions No.1. Signal Communications. Appendix 'B'.	19/10/1918	19/10/1918
Diagram etc	Appendix IX.		
Diagram etc	Appendix I.		
Diagram etc	Appendix IV		
Diagram etc	Appendix III.		
Diagram etc	Sectional Diagram Showing Contours Between Points D.22.a.4.4. & E.10.d.8.0. Appendix V.		
Miscellaneous	War Diary. Weekly Strengths, Casualties, Reinforcements. Appendix 'C'.	04/11/1918	04/11/1918
Diagram etc	Communications 42nd Division. Diagram 1.		
Diagram etc	Communications 42nd Division. Diagram 2.		

Diagram etc	Communications 42nd Division. Diagram 3.		
Diagram etc	Communications 42nd Division.		
Diagram etc	Communications 42nd Division		
Diagram etc			
Diagram etc	Message Graph. Appendix 'D'.		
Miscellaneous	Appendix "D"		
Miscellaneous	War Diary. Map 2 Communications		
Heading	War Diary 42nd Div. Signal Coy R.E. Chapter XXV November 1918 Vol 21.		
War Diary	Beauvois en Cambresis.	01/11/1918	05/11/1918
War Diary	Potelle Chateau.	05/11/1918	08/11/1918
War Diary	La Haute Rue.	08/11/1918	09/11/1918
War Diary	Hautmont.	09/11/1918	30/11/1918
Diagram etc	Diagram 1		
Diagram etc	Diagram 2		
Diagram etc	Diagram 3		
Diagram etc	Diagram 4		
Diagram etc	Diagram 5		
Diagram etc	Diagram 6.		
Miscellaneous	War Diary. Honours and Awards. Appendix 'A'.	04/12/1918	04/12/1918
Miscellaneous	War Diary. Weekly Strengths, Casualties, Reinforcements, etc. Appendix 'B'.	04/12/1918	04/12/1918
Operation(al) Order(s)	42nd Divisional Signal Company R.E. (T.F.). Order No. 26. Appendix. D.	04/11/1918	04/11/1918
Diagram etc	Diagram of Communications 42nd Division Feb 1919.		
War Diary	Charleroi	01/01/1919	31/01/1919
War Diary		17/01/1919	20/01/1919
War Diary	Charleroi.	01/02/1919	28/02/1919
War Diary		05/02/1919	05/02/1919
War Diary		03/02/1919	21/02/1919
War Diary	Charleroi.	01/03/1919	31/03/1919
War Diary		05/03/1919	25/03/1919
War Diary		19/03/1919	31/03/1919
Miscellaneous	G.18/35.	17/01/1919	17/01/1919
Diagram etc	Message Chart. Appendix "C".		

42ND DIVISION

DIVL SIGNAL COY R.E.

MAR 1917 - MAR 1919.

Secret.

Vol 1

42nd Divisional Signal Coy. R.E., (T)

WAR DIARY.

Chapter V.

From March 1st to March 31st 1917.

Army Form C. 2118.

WAR DIARY
or
~~INTELLIGENCE SUMMARY~~

(Erase heading not required.)

Instructions regarding War Diaries and Intelligence Summaries are contained in F. S. Regs., Part II. and the Staff Manual respectively. Title Pages will be prepared in manuscript.

Place	Date	Hour	Summary of Events and Information	Remarks and references to Appendices
			42. DIVISIONAL SIGNAL COY. RE (T.F)	MAPS. REF FRANCE 1/100,000 Sheets 14, 16, 17
MARCH 1917			CHAPTER V MARCH 1917.	
	1/3/17 – 16/3/17		The concentration of the 42nd Division near ABBEVILLE took place during the period 1 March 17 to 15th March 17. During this period the Divisional Signal Company were stationed at	
HALLENCOURT			HALLENCOURT. The work of the unit during this time was not very heavy the communications were established on the existing lines which were lent by 4th ARMY. A detailed Diagram of the communications established is given in APPENDIX A	APPENDIX "A"
			These communications were established gradually as the units arrived in the country. It was found that the HQ office at HALLENCOURT was not suitably placed to deal with all the telephone work required and so as to work the communications	

Instructions regarding War Diaries and Intelligence Summaries are contained in F. S. Regs., Part II. and the Staff Manual respectively. Title Pages will be prepared in manuscript.

WAR DIARY
or
INTELLIGENCE SUMMARY

(Erase heading not required.)

Army Form C. 2118.

Place	Date	Hour	Summary of Events and Information	Remarks and references to Appendices
PONT REMY			in a more satisfactory manner a telephone exchange was established at PONT REMY which was the Divisional Railhead.	
CAOURS			The establishment of this office very greatly effected the communications, by allowing the R.T.O. and 4th ARMY MUSKETRY CAMP (who were put on our exchange) to give us their line to ABBEVILLE EXCHANGE by which means we were able to communicate with the HQ Divisional Artillery who were stationed at CAOURS.	
			During this period the Company was issued with much of the necessary new equipment including rifles and steel helmets. Horses riding and Draught were drawn from Remounts and the AHTD respectively. Several waggons were repaired or replaced. The Brigade section transport was altered from 1 limbered RE waggon and two pack animals to one limbered RE and one Maltese Cart, the pack animals being handed in.	

2449 Wt. W14957/M90 750,000 1/16 J.B.C. & A. Forms/C.2118/12.

Instructions regarding War Diaries and Intelligence Summaries are contained in F. S. Regs., Part II. and the Staff Manual respectively. Title Pages will be prepared in manuscript.

WAR DIARY
or
INTELLIGENCE SUMMARY
(Erase heading not required.)

Army Form C. 2118.

Place	Date	Hour	Summary of Events and Information	Remarks and references to Appendices
	~~15~~ 9/3/17 to 31/3/17		This period was occupied in completing the equipment of the unit and establishing communications with the different Brigades who were moved forward into the III CORPS AREA.	
HAMEL	15/3/17		The 125th Bde ~~[illegible]~~ moved to HAMEL by train from PONT REMY on 15th march communication with them was then established via III Corps and 4th ARMY.	
FRISE	25/3/17		The 125 Brigade moved by route march from HAMEL - to - FRISE ~~by route march~~ Communication was then obtained ~~to~~ with them through 48th Division who were at CAPPY	
DOMPIERRE	29th		The 127 Brigade moved on this date by train from PONT REMY to DOMPIERRE where they established communication with the ~~[illegible]~~ 1st Division at CHUIGNOLLES	
	30th		On the 30th the Headquarters & No 1 Section transport started by march Route for MERICOURT - SUR - SOMME. they were billeted	

2449 Wt. W14957/M90 750,000 1/16 J.B.C. & A. Forms/C.2118/12.

Army Form C. 2118.

Instructions regarding War Diaries and Intelligence Summaries are contained in F. S. Regs., Part II. and the Staff Manual respectively. Title Pages will be prepared in manuscript.

WAR DIARY
or
INTELLIGENCE SUMMARY
(Erase heading not required.)

Place	Date	Hour	Summary of Events and Information	Remarks and references to Appendices
ST SAVEUR			at ST SAVEUR.	
			The route followed was SOREL – FONTAINE – HANGEST – PICQUIGNY – ST SAVEUR arriving at the latter place at 6. p.m.	
HAMEL	31st	0900	at 0900/31st the march was resumed the column marching via AMIENS – VECQUEMONT – FOUILLOY – HAMELET to HAMEL arriving at the latter place at 4.0 pm where the party was billeted for the night. At this place the distance to the watering place was about 2 Kilos.	
			The march was resumed on the next day.	
			S. Gordon Thurston Capt. O C. 42 Div Sig Coy RE	

2449 Wt. W14957/M90 750,000 1/16 J.B.C. & A. Forms/C.2118/12.

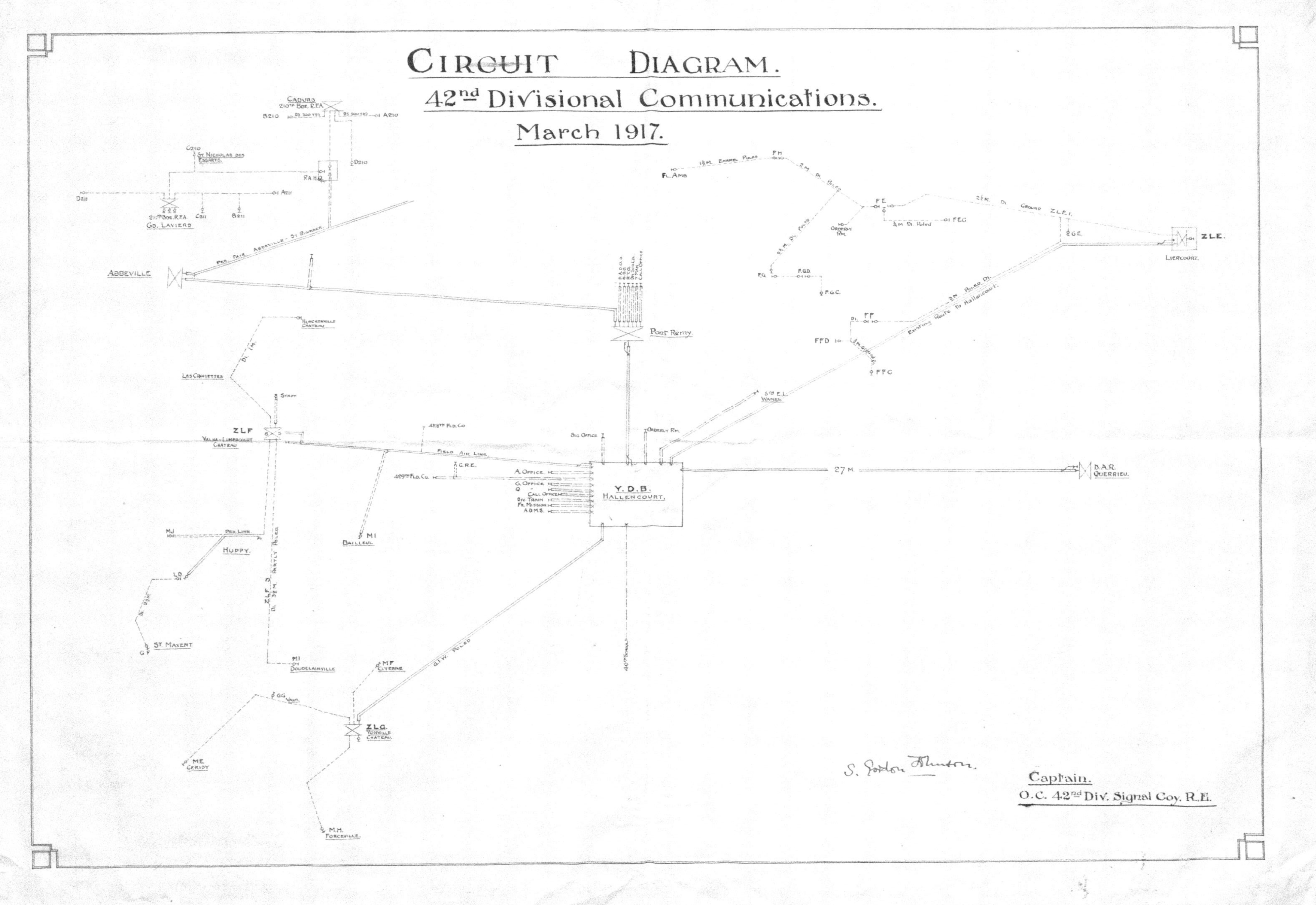

Circuit Diagram.
42nd Divisional Communications.
March 1917.
Abbeville
Port Remy
Y.D.B.
Hallencourt.
A. Office
G. Office
Q
Call Offices
Div. Train
Fr. Mission
A.D.M.S.
Sig. Office
Orderly Rm.
27 M.
D.A.R.
Querrieu.
ZLE.
Liercourt.
ZLF
Field Air Line
C.R.E.
Staff
Les Caulettes
Huppy.
Per Line
St. Maxent
Doudelainville
Bailleul
Citerne
ZLG.
Forceville.
Ceroy
Go. Laviero
Caours
Fl. Amb
Existing Route to Hallencourt
S. Gordon Thurston
Captain.
O.C. 42nd Div. Signal Coy. R.E.

Vol 2

WAR DIARY

of

42nd Divisional Signal Coy. R.E. (T.)

From April 1st to 30th

1917.

Vol. IV

Army Form C. 2118.

WAR DIARY
or
INTELLIGENCE SUMMARY

(Erase heading not required.)

Instructions regarding War Diaries and Intelligence Summaries are contained in F. S. Regs., Part II. and the Staff Manual respectively. Title Pages will be prepared in manuscript.

Place	Date	Hour	Summary of Events and Information	Remarks and references to Appendices
			-42 Divisional Signal Company R.E. (T.F.)	
			CHAPTER 6 REFERENCE MAPS) FRANCE 1/40000) sheets) 62d 62c.	
			APRIL 1917.	
HAMEL	1/4/17	0945	The transport details of this unit resumed the march to MERICOURT)-SUR-SOMME) via CERISY and MORECOURT. the march was finished by 1 pm .	SEE APPENDIX (A) FOR CIRCUIT DIAGRAM.
			On arrival at MERICOURT the party immediately started to take over the signal office which was being run by the corps operators . The circuits in use were as follows.	
			(A)Telegraph and two telephone circuits to Third Corps.	
			(B) Telephone circuit to the 125 Brigade at FRISE.	
			A telegraph circuit was superimposed on this latter, this composed the only communication to FRISE during the period that the division was stationed at MERICOURT.	
			Communication was established by telephone with the 127 Brigade at HERBECOURT; a sounder was afterwards superimposed on this line .	
MERICOURT-SUR-SOMME	2/4/17		The party left behind at HALLENCOURT (FRANCE 1/100000 DIEPPE sheet 16)arrived having been delayed through a breakdown of the motor lorry.	
	3/4/17		Communication was kept up with the 126 Brigade who were still at HALLENCOURT through the corps and army signal offices using the same lines as ~~were~~ were formerlyused by the divisional office as described in CHAPTER 5 of this Diary.	

Army Form C. 2118.

WAR DIARY
or
INTELLIGENCE SUMMARY
(Erase heading not required.)

Instructions regarding War Diaries and Intelligence Summaries are contained in F. S. Regs., Part II. and the Staff Manual respectively. Title Pages will be prepared in manuscript.

PAGE 2

Place	Date	Hour	Summary of Events and Information	Remarks and references to Appendices
PERONNE	6/4/17		On this date tht CRE and the 125 Brigade on to whose exchange the CRE had been put moved from FRISE toPERONNE where communication was established by telephone and telegraph .The CRE being again put on to the 125 Brigade exchange. The H Q R.A. arrived at BOIS OLYMPE from ~~CAIEUX~~ CAOURS (FRANCE 1/100000ABBEVILLE SHEET 14) . Communication was established with them by telephone and telegraph . The D A C were connected to divisional H Q by ~~telegraph~~ telephone. Their position being Sheet 62d R3	SEE APPENDIX (A) FOR CIRCUIT DIAGRAM.
MORECOURT	7/4/17		The 126 Brigade moved from HALLENCOURT to MORECOURT where communication was established by telephone and telegraph .	
	9/4/17		Bl cable detatchment which had been left behind at HALLENCOURT to assist the 126 Bde and the R.A. arrived back at the company H Q having picked up all cable at HALLENCOURT and CAOURS . The detatchment came by march route: taking the same route as that described in the previous chapter .	
	11/4/17		The 126 Brigade march from MORECOURT to FRISE. Communication as for the 125 Bde previously.	

2449 Wt. W14957/M90 750,000 1/16 J.B.C. & A. Forms/C.2118/12.

Instructions regarding War Diaries and Intelligence Summaries are contained in F. S. Regs., Part II. and the Staff Manual respectively. Title Pages will be prepared in manuscript.

WAR DIARY
or
INTELLIGENCE SUMMARY
(Erase heading not required.)

Army Form C. 2118.

Place	Date	Hour	Summary of Events and Information	Remarks and references to Appendices
			The 125 Brigade were attatched to the 48 division for tactical purposes and communic--ation was through them ;the brigade H Q being at VILLERS FANCON.	
PERONNE	13/4/17		Orders were received to move divisional H Q from MERICOURT to PERONNE and a small a advance party was sent on to prepare the signal office .	
	14/4/17		D.H.Q. moved to PERONNE . The main body of the company moved by march route via CHUIGNES -DOMPIERRE- HERBECOURT -BIACHES to PERONNE.	
			A small office was left at MERICOURT to deal with the traffic of the R A ;D A D O S; and part of the supply column which remained in their old positions.	
			These units could not immediately be connected up to the new office on account of the great shortage of lines running into PERONNE from the west at that time.	
			The office left at MERICOURT was composed as under. 1 NCO; & 7 OR 1 telephone exchange and two sounder sets.	

2449 Wt. W14957/M90 750,000 1/16 J.B.C. & A. Forms/C.2118/12.

Instructions regarding War Diaries and Intelligence Summaries are contained in F. S. Regs., Part II. and the Staff Manual respectively. Title Pages will be prepared in manuscript.

WAR DIARY
or
INTELLIGENCE SUMMARY

(Erase heading not required.)

Army Form C. 2118.

Place	Date	Hour	Summary of Events and Information	Remarks and references to Appendices
	15/4/17		The 125 Brigade returned to the division from VILLERS FANCON and were billeted in PERONNE . they were put on to the divisional exchange and were also connected by a superimposed sounder .	FOR NEW CIRCUIT DIAGRAM SEE APPENDIX (B)
		16/4/17	The 125 Brigade and the 126 brigade changed places the 125 Brigade returning to FRISE which was then connected direct to the new H Q at PERONNE.the 126 Brigade did not work sounder to us as they were going on next morning and the distance was short enough to use orderlies.	
	17/4/17		The 126 Brigade came under the orders of the 48 division on this date and communication was kept with them through that division .the headquarters were established at VILLERS FANCON . the D.R.L.S. was still kept up direct with them as this was thought to be quicker for administrative work.	
			H.Q. RA. move up to PERONNE and are connected direct on to the Divisional exchange as the distance was short they did not work telegraph.	

2449 Wt. W14957/M90 750,000 1/16 J.B.C. & A. Forms/C.2118/12.

Instructions regarding War Diaries and Intelligence Summaries are contained in F. S. Regs., Part II. and the Staff Manual respectively. Title Pages will be prepared in manuscript.

WAR DIARY
or
INTELLIGENCE SUMMARY
(Erase heading not required.)

Army Form C. 2118.

Place	Date	Hour	Summary of Events and Information	Remarks and references to Appendices
			PAGE 5	
		17/4/17	The 210 Brigade R F A take over the R A H Q at BOIS OLYMPE using the telephone back to MERICOURT . This was found to be unsatisfactory and this brigade the D A C and supply	
	18/4/17		officer R A were put on a party line to the 125 Brigade at FRISE this finally removed all the divisional lines from MERICOURT.	
	19/4/17		The 125 Brigade moved from FRISE to PERONNE and were put direct on to the division by sounder and telephone. the party line of the R A was then put through direct on to the divisional exchange .	
			The 127 brigade moved from DOMPIERRE to PERONNE and were put direct on to the divisional exchange.	
	21/4/17		The 210 Brigade R F A moved up from BOIS OLYMPE and came under the orders of the 48 Division through whom communication was maintained to them.	

Instructions regarding War Diaries and Intelligence Summaries are contained in F. S. Regs., Part II. and the Staff Manual respectively. Title Pages will be prepared in manuscript.

WAR DIARY
or
INTELLIGENCE SUMMARY

(Erase heading not required.)

Army Form C. 2118.

PAGE 6

Place	Date	Hour	Summary of Events and Information	Remarks and references to Appendices
	29/4/17		The 127 Brigade came under the orders of the 48 Division on this date, taking the place of the 126 Brigade who went back to LONGAVESNES.	
			Warning was received that the divisional H Q would move to ROISEL in the near future and that the Division would take over from the 48 Division : with this in view an advance party of one N C O and four linesmen were sent forward to learn the lines.	

APPENDICES TO THIS DIARY.

(A) Circuit diagram

(B) " " "

(C) Honours and awards

(D) Strength, Casualties, Reinforcements.

30/4/17

S. Gordon Johnston, Major.
O. C. 42 Div: SIGNAL Coy
R.E.

2449 Wt. W14957/M90 750,000 1/16 J.B.C. & A. Forms/C.2118/12.

Plans to accompany War Diary of 42nd Divnl. Signal Coy for April 1917

CIRCUIT DIAGR
42nd Divisional Communicatio
REFERENCE
Permanent Lines
Cable Lines (Onground)
Buried Lines
German
Field Airline
Exchange (Telephone)
Sounder S.C.
D.C.
Fullerphone
Magneto Telephone
Buzzer Exchange
Eclusier
N10
N1
Cappy
D.A.C.
Froissy
P.C.
Y.D.B.
Mericourt
ZLF
Mericourt
C.B.M.
V.C.M.
Bayon
Merignolles
Y.A.
N2
Chuignolles
N2 – N20
Supply C
Chuign
P.J.
3rd Corps
Foucaucourt

APPENDIX "A"

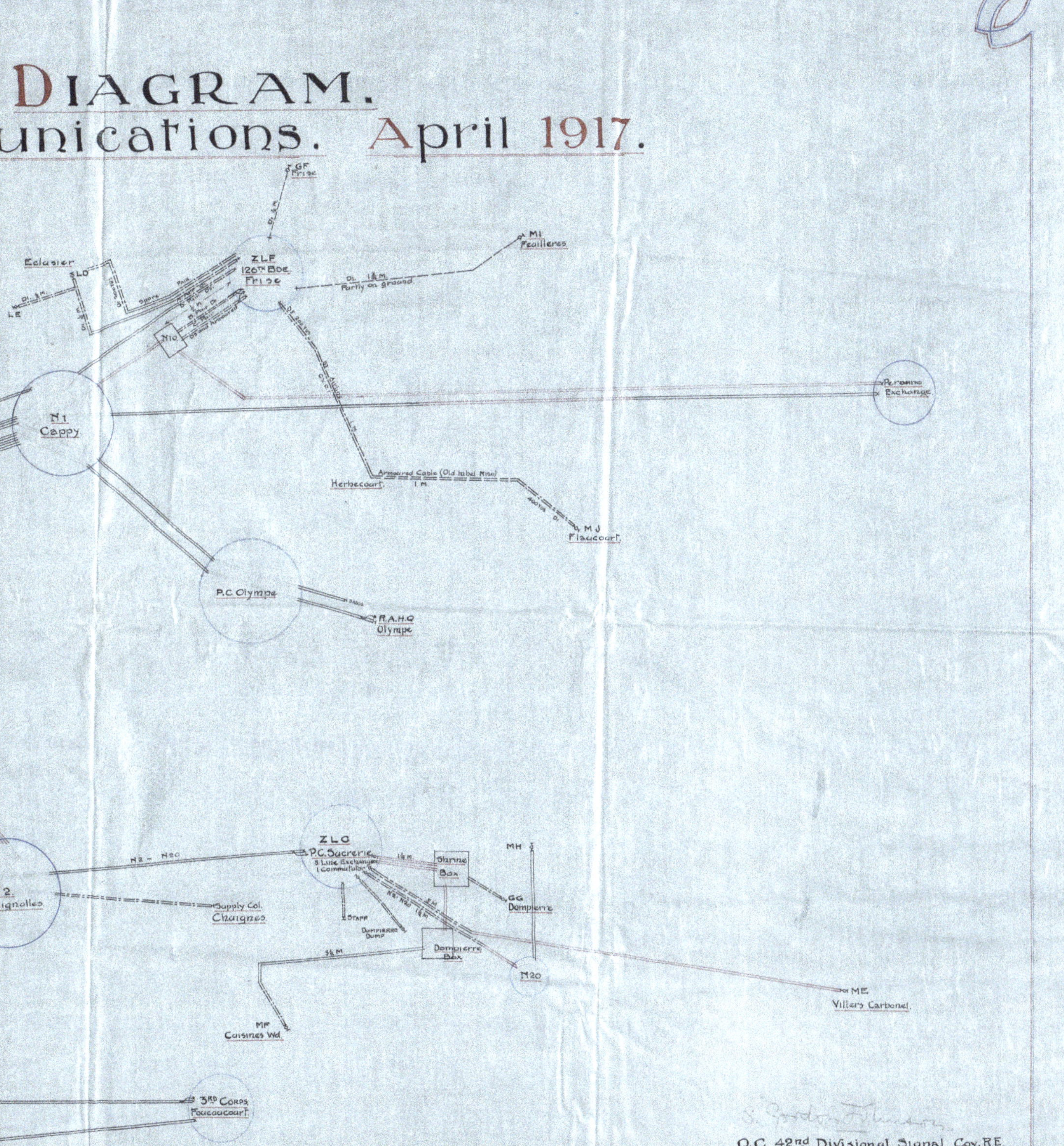
DIAGRAM.
unications. April 1917.
GF Frise
Eclusier
LO
LE
ZLE 126th Bde. Frise
MI Feuilleres
DL 1¾M Partly on ground
N10
N1 Cappy
Peronne Exchange
Armoured Cable (Old label Rte) 1 M.
Herbecourt
MJ Flaucourt
P.C Olympe
R.A.H.Q Olympe
ZLG P.C. Sucrerie
MH
Sunne Box
GG Dompierre
N2 – N20
12 ugnolles
Supply Col. Chaignes
Staff
Dompierre Dump
Dompierre Box
N20
ME Villers Carbonel
MF Cuisines Wd.
3rd Corps Foucaucourt
O.C. 42nd Divisional Signal Coy. R.E.

Circuit Diagram
42nd Divisional Communications.

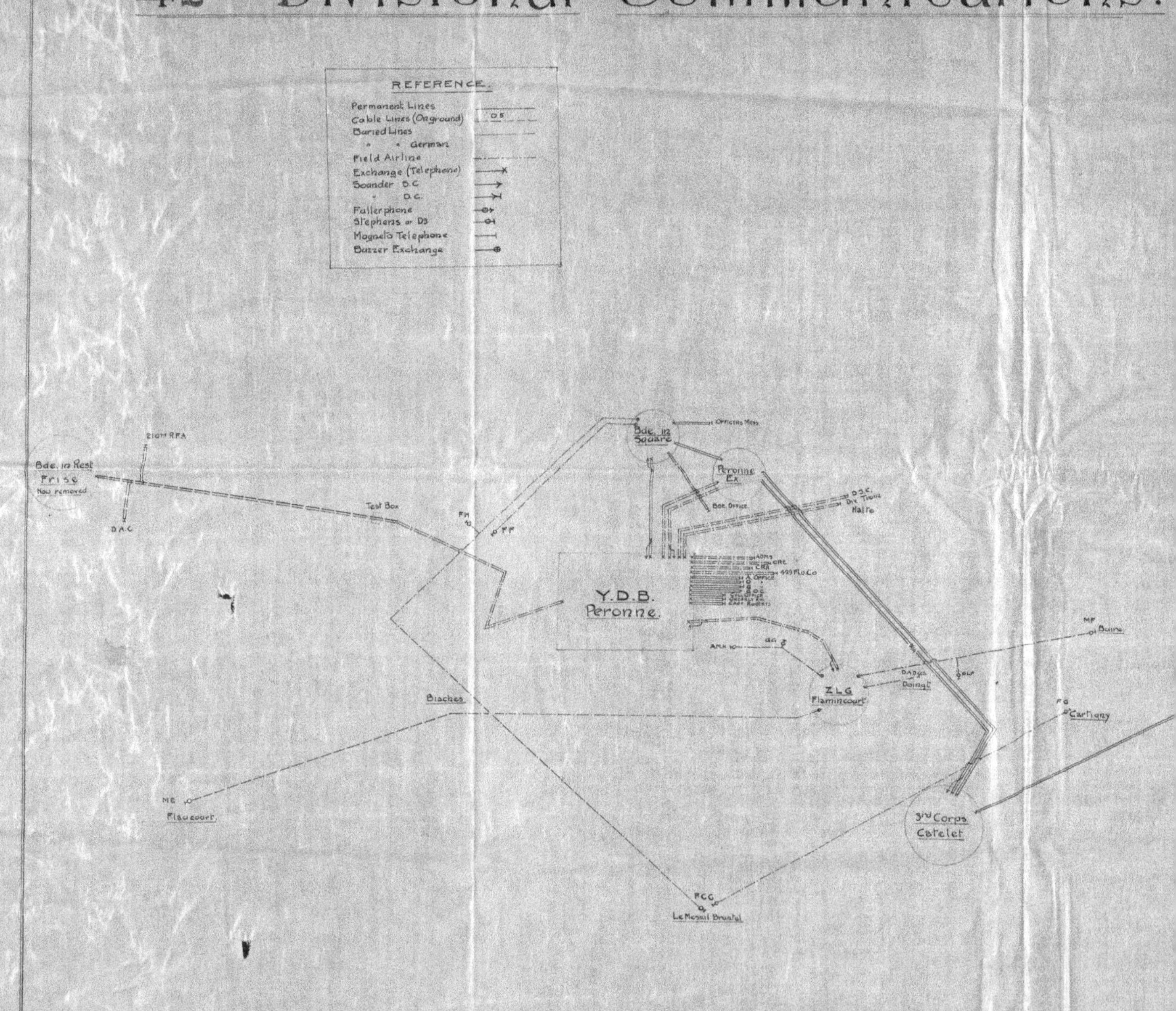

APPENDIX "B".

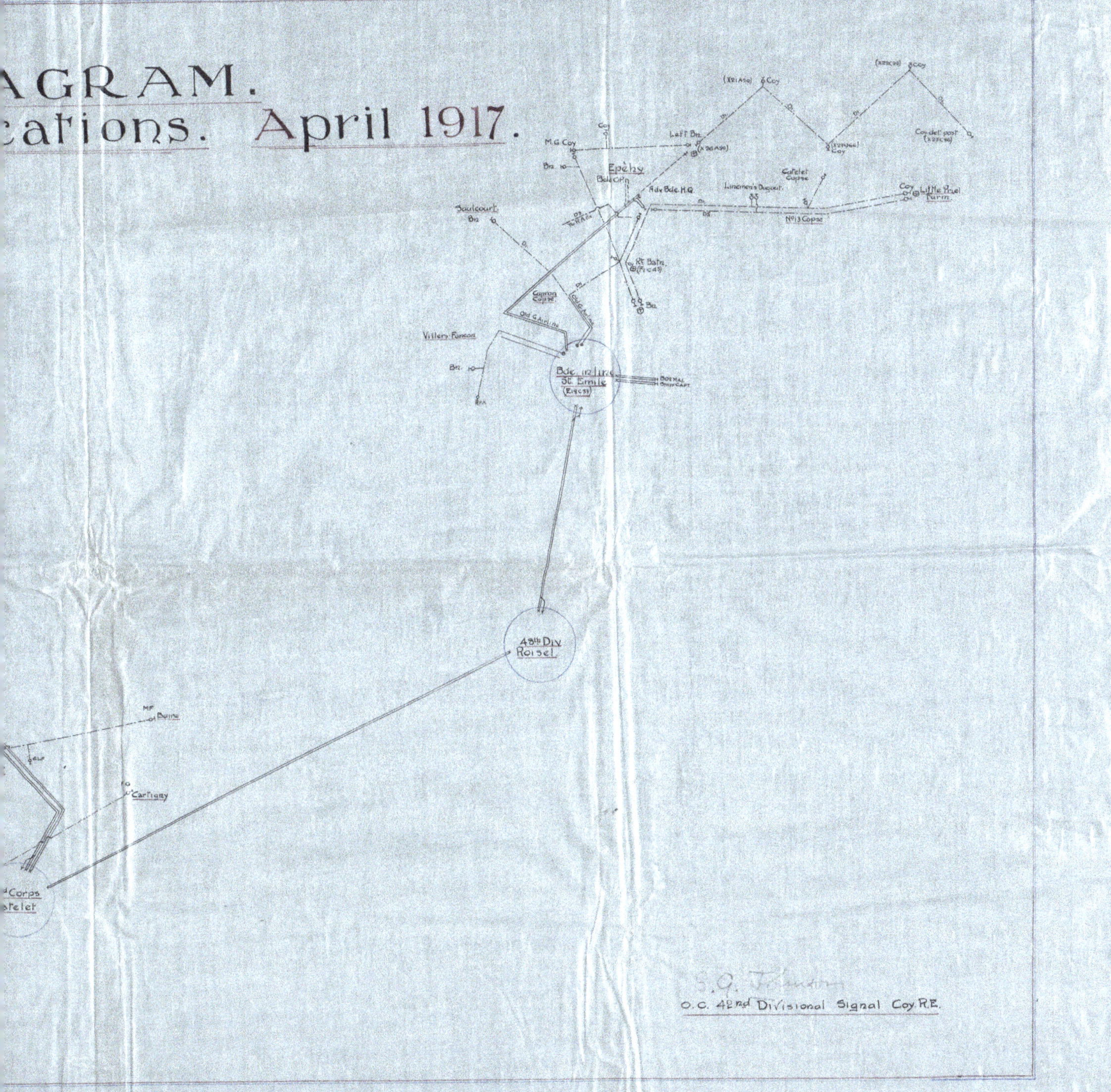

AGRAM.
cations. April 1917.
(X21A50) Coy
(X29C99) Coy
Coy
M.G. Coy
Left Bn.
(X26A90)
(X27A60) Coy
Coy det post (X27C90)
Bn.
Epèhy
Bde OPn
Adv Bde. H.Q.
Linemen's Dugout.
Catelet Copse
Coy
Little Priel Farm.
Saulcourt
Bn.
No. 13 Copse
Rt Batn. (F1 c 43)
Bn.
Capron Copse
Old G Airline
Villers-Faucon
Bn.
Bde in line St. Emile (E19c33)
48th Div Roisel.
Bouvincourt
Cartigny
Corps
atelet
O.C. 42nd Divisional Signal Coy. R.E.

W A R   D I A R Y

APRIL 1917.   APPENDIX "C".

HONOURS AND AWARDS.

The Field Marshall Commanding-in-Chief, under authority granted by HIS MAJESTY THE KING, has been pleased to confer upon No. 444312 Corporal Samuel Eccles, 42nd Divisional Signal Company, the

MERITORIOUS SERVICE MEDAL

for the following action :-

" For courage and endurance in carrying out his duties as despatch rider. Whilst carrying despatches he fractured his ankle and, though in considerable pain, repaired his bicycle without assistance and proceeded on duty, delivered his despatches, and returned with fresh ones for the Division - in all he went 35 kilometres and did four hours duty after the accident, afterwards being admitted to Hospital".

The KING has been pleased to approve of the award of the

DISTINGUISHED CONDUCT MEDAL

to the following N.C.O's for acts of gallantry and devotion to duty in the field.

No. 444594, Sergt. Mallalieu, J., R.E.
No. 444038, 2nd Corpl. Moores, H. J., R.E. (Now Corpl.)

W A R   D I A R Y.

APRIL 1917.   APPENDIX "D".

Weekly Strength.

April 7th.	8 officers,	219 other ranks.
" 14th,	8 "	218 " "
" 21st,	8 "	220 " "
" 28th,	8 "	221 " "

Casualties.

Killed.	Nil.
Wounded.	Nil.
Sick.	9 other ranks to Hospital.
Total.	9 O.R.

Reinforcements.

From Hospital.	8 other ranks.
From Depot.	1 officer, 5 other ranks.
Total.	1 officer, 13 other ranks.

Vol 3

SECRET

42nd DIV SIG Co R.E.

WAR DIARY

Chap 7.

May 1

S. Gordon Johnston
Major

Instructions regarding War Diaries and Intelligence Summaries are contained in F. S. Regs., Part II. and the Staff Manual respectively. Title Pages will be prepared in manuscript.

WAR DIARY

or

~~INTELLIGENCE SUMMARY~~

(Erase heading not required.)

Army Form C. 2118.

Place	Date	Hour	Summary of Events and Information	Remarks and references to Appendices
			42nd Divisional Signal Company, R.E. (T.F.)	
			CHAPTER 7. MAY, 1917. Reference Maps, FRANCE - 1/40,000 Sheets, 62c and 57c.	
			The month of May was spent by the 42nd Divisional Signal Company, in constructing air line routes in the areas occupied by the 42nd Division. This was necessitated by the Division being placed in the front line in areas in which no permanent systems had been established since the advance in March. The main portion of this chapter sets out the various localities where the Signal Company was stationed, with the dates of reliefs. The full descriptions of the lines constructed together with the diagrams, are set out in APPENDICES A and B of this chapter, which will be referred to in their proper places.	SJ
ROISEL.	2/5/17.		The R.A. Headquarters took over from the 48th Division, R.A. at ROISEL. The lines taken over were very incomplete, and required a great deal of work carrying out before xxxx xxxx satisfactory communication could be obtained.	SJ
	3/5/17		The Division took over the area formerly commanded by the 48th Division. Schemes were immediately started for building air line routes. These were decided upon and constructed as described in appendix "A". Attached to appendix "A" is a diagram shewing the lines as finally handed over on relief of the division.	APPENDIX "A". SJ
	11/5/17		Orders were received that the Division would be relieved by the 2nd Cavalry Division.	SJ
	12/5/17		Orders were received that the reliefs would probably take as follows:- Right Sub-section, both brigades, night 17/18th, May. Left " right, brigade. " 18/19th, May. " " left " " 19/20th, May.	SJ
YTRES.	17/5/17.		An advance party was sent on this date to the 20th Divisional Signal Company, whom we had been instructed, that we should relieve. The party consisted of one Signal Office relief and linemen to learn the routes. The 20th Division were stationed near YTRES, (FRANCE, 1/40,000, sheet 57.c.)	SJ

2449 Wt. W14957/M90 750,000 1/16 J.B.C. & A. Forms/C.2118/12.

Instructions regarding War Diaries and Intelligence Summaries are contained in F. S. Regs., Part II. and the Staff Manual respectively. Title Pages will be prepared in manuscript.

WAR DIARY
or
INTELLIGENCE SUMMARY
(Erase heading not required.)

Army Form C. 2118.

Page. 2.

Place	Date	Hour	Summary of Events and Information	Remarks and references to Appendices
LECHELLE	19/5/17.		On this date the main body of the Signal Company moved to Lechelle, (France, 1/40,000, sheet 57.c.) after having been relieved by the Signal Squadron of the 2nd Cavalry Division.	SG
BRUSLE.			A party of one officer and 10 men moved from ROISEL to BRUSLE, (1/40,000, sheet 62.c.) where Division Headquarters were established until the 23rd. The communications there consisted of two pairs to the Cavalry Corps Exchange. All messages were dealt with by the Cavalry Corps Signal Office and carried by D.R. to Divisional Headquarters.	
YTRES.	23/5/17.		Divisional Headquarters moved from BRUSLE to YTRES, and took over from the 20th Division.	SG
	24/5/17.		The remainder of the Company moved from LECHELLE to YTRES, and were encamped close to Divisional Headquarters.	SG
	26th to 31/5/17.		This period was spent by the Signal Company in building routes in the new area. These routes are shewn in the diagram and fully described in Appendix "B"	SG Appendix "B"

APPENDICES TO THIS DIARY.

(A) Circuit diagram and description of routes, ROISEL.

(B) Circuit diagram and description of routes, YTRES.

(C) Honours and Awards.

(D) Weekly strengths, casualties and Reinforcements.

(E) Message chart for month ending, May 31st, 1917.

3.6.17.

S. Gordon Thurston
Major.
O.C., 42nd Div'l Signal Coy., R.E.

2449 Wt. W14957/M90 750,000 1/16 J.B.C. & A. Forms/C.2118/12.

APPENDIX "A".

DESCRIPTION OF ROUTES - ROISEL.

The main system of communication as taken over from the 48th Dixixi Division, consisted of two routes as follows:-

(a) A route of light hop poles with two four-way arms and bobbin insulators carrying 8-60 lb G.I. wires from Division Headquarters to Villers Faucon, a pair being extended to the Right Brigade, Ronssoy, a pair to the left brigade at E.13.c.3.1. (France, 1/40,000, sheet 62c) a pair to the 211th Brigade R.F.A. at E.18.c.3.4. (Sheet 62c), and a pair to the 427 Field Coy. R.E. and R.E. Dump, working as a party line.

(b) A route as above with two pairs to the Reserve Brigade, Longavesnes, one pair being spare, a pair to Tincourt to the 42nd Divisional Train and on to the left Division, working as a party line, and a spare pair to Villers Faucon.

In view of a forward move, this system was considered inadequate, so it was decided to increase "A" route by the addition of another four way arm and extend the six pairs to a point outside Villers Faucon, whence the remains of a French civil route, ran. The idea of this being, that with the material left behind by the enemy it was possible to run a four pair route from this point to Longavesnes and so join up with "B" Route. Also it was proposed to place a test dug-out at the junction of "A" route and the Civil route.

The scheme also included a four pair route from the proposed test dug-out to Epehy, the advanced position of the left brigade, then to Ronssoy and back to the test dug-out, Ronssoy being the position of the right brigade, thus having two triangles, the apex of each being in the test dug-out and Division Headquarters in one corner.

It can be seen from the above that by means of crossing the lines, at the test point, it was possible to still be in communication with all three brigades should any one route, be put completely out of action.

The material left behind by the enemy consisted of a portion of a first class route from Longavesnes to E.14.Central (Sheet 62c) all the poles were in good condition complete with 12 insulators and the greater portion of the wire, which was five strand G.I., the only damage to the route being that the lines were cut in various spans. It took a gang of 10 men three days to put this route in complete working order.

From E.14 Central to Villers Faucon ran the remains of a French civil route, complete with insulators on which was run four pairs of 60 lb. G.I. completing the route from Longavesnes to Villers Faucon.

S. Gordon Johnston, Major.

3.6.17. O.C., 42nd Div'l Signal Coy. R.E.

APPENDIX "B"

DESCRIPTION OF ROUTES - YTRES.

The system of communication adopted here consists of a main route of hop poles with two four way arms bobbin insulators and cap wire, and 60lb G.I. wire from LittleWood, Ytres, to the S.E. corner of Havrincourt Wood, there the lines are terminated and provision is being made for a test point.

From this point a nine wire route has been constructed along the W.side of the wood tp the Left Brigade P.10.a.8.8. (France 1/40,000 sheet 57 c) and Left Group R.F.A. and a nine wire route is being constructed from the same point along the East side of the Wood to the Right Brigade P.18.d.1.3.(Sheet 57c) and Right Group R.F.A.

The lines will be allocated as follows:-

1 pair from Divisional Headquarters to the Left Brigade
1 " " " " " " Left Group, R.F.A.
1 " " " " " " Right Brigade
1 " " " " " "Right Group.R.F.A.
1 " for lateral communications between Brigades
1 " " " " " R.F.A. Brigades.

The two Infantry Brigades in the Line and the two Artillery Brigades will be connected to Divisional Headquarters and to the Reserve Brigade by the cap wire, so that in the event of a CQ message it can be transmitted with the minimum delay.

S. Gordon Johnston.

Major.

3.8.17. O.C. 42nd Divisional Signal Co. R.E.

WAR DIARY. MAY, 1917.

APPENDIX "C".

HONOURS AND AWARDS.

No. 444104, Sgt. ELLWOOD, J., 42nd DIVISIONAL SIGNAL COMPANY, R.E., awarded the MEDAILLE MILITAIRE. List No. 272, dated G.H.Q., E.E.F., 30.3.17.

-----0-----

The G.O.C., 111 Corps, has been pleased to confer upon:-
No. 444371, Sapper, J. WALSH, 42nd DIVISIONAL SIGNAL COY., R.E., the

MILITARY MEDAL,

for the following action.

"He successfully laid a most important telephone line under heavy shell-fire. He remained on duty for two days and nights, (22nd-24th April, 1917) under shell fire and frequently repaired the line when cut by intense barrage".

S. Gordon Johnston Major.

3.6.17. O.C., 42nd Div'l Signal Coy, R.E.

WAR DIARY.

APPENDIX "D". MAY, 1917.

WEEKLY STRENGTHS; CASUALTIES; REINFORCEMENTS.

Strength, week ending, May 5th,	7 officers.	231 other ranks.
" " 12th,	7 "	239 " "
" " 19th,	7 "	239 " "
" " 26th,	7 "	242 " "

Casualties.

Killed.	Nil.
Wounded.	Nil.
Sick.	14 O.R. to Hospital.
Total.	14 O.R.

Reinforcements.

From Hospital.	2	O.R.
From Depot.	19	O.R.
Total.	21	O.R.

S. Gordon Johnston Major.

3.6.17. O.C., 42nd Div'l Signal Coy., R.E.

Appendix E.

Message Graph

42nd Divisional Signal Company. May 1917.

Total
D.R.L.S.
A
B
C

Reference

1 2 3 4 5 6 7 8 9 10 11 12 13 14 15 16 17 18 19 20 21 22 23 24 25 26 27 28 29 30 31

600 560 480 400 320 240 160 80 0

S. Gordon Johnson
Major,
O.C. Signals 42nd Division.

Secret

Vol 4

WAR DIARY

42nd Divisional Sig Coy

R.E. (T.F.)

Chapter VIII

June 1917.

Instructions regarding War Diaries and Intelligence Summaries are contained in F. S. Regs., Part II. and the Staff Manual respectively. Title Pages will be prepared in manuscript.

WAR DIARY
or
~~INTELLIGENCE SUMMARY~~
(Erase heading not required.)

Army Form C. 2118.

Place	Date	Hour	Summary of Events and Information	Remarks and references to Appendices
			42nd Divisional Signal Company, R.E. (T.F.) Page 1.	
YTRES.			CHAPTER 8. JUNE, 1917. Reference maps, FRANCE, 1/20,000 Sheets, 57C S.E. and N.E.	
			During the month of June the Headquarters of the Signal Company were stationary at YTRES.	
			The Scheme of communications described in Appendix "B" of chapter 7 of this diary, was completed.	
			Experiments in signalling to Kite Balloons were carried out. The results obtained and the methods used are fully laid out in appendix "G" of this chapter.	APPENDIX "G"
			A system of buried cable was commenced. The route diagram of this system, together with a description of it, are contained in appendix "B" of this chapter.	APPENDIX "B"
			The only large alteration in the existing communications was occasioned by the move of the 127th Infantry Brigade Headquarters and the 210th R.F.A. Brigade Headquarters from RUYAULCOURT (P.10.a Central) to Q.1.a. This necessitated the entire brigade to battery lines being relaid in this group. At the same time the Battery lines to O.P's were re-laid and brought through an O.P. exchange. The full details of these changes are	

Army Form C. 2118.

Instructions regarding War Diaries and Intelligence Summaries are contained in F. S. Regs., Part II. and the Staff Manual respectively. Title Pages will be prepared in manuscript.

WAR DIARY
or
~~INTELLIGENCE SUMMARY~~

(Erase heading not required.)

Place	Date	Hour	Summary of Events and Information	Remarks and references to Appendices
			Page. 2.	
YTRES.			best seen by comparing Appendix "A", chapter 7 with Appendix "A" of this chapter (both circuit diagrams). The changes in the Infantry Brigade lines were not very great owing to their being laid from the rear headquarters through the new headquarters.	
			During this month, the Divisional Wireless Section was formed out of the Wireless Personnel previously attached to the division..	
			A notable feature of the month were the severe thunderstorms which were experienced. The effect of these on the signal communications is described in detail in Appendix "F".	APPENDIX "F".
			Work was still carried on by the Signal School in training men of the Division.	
			APPENDICES TO THIS DIARY.	
			(A) Circuit diagram.	
			(B) Diagram and description of buried Cable Scheme.	
			(C) Honours and Awards.	
			(D) Weekly strengths, Casualties and Reinforcements.	
			(E) Monthly message chart.	

2449 Wt. W14957/M90 750,000 1/16 J.B.C. & A. Forms/C.2118/12.

aR

Army Form C. 2118.

Instructions regarding War Diaries and Intelligence Summaries are contained in F. S. Regs., Part II. and the Staff Manual respectively. Title Pages will be prepared in manuscript.

WAR DIARY
or
~~INTELLIGENCE SUMMARY~~
(Erase heading not required.)

Place	Date	Hour	Summary of Events and Information	Remarks and references to Appendices

APPENDICES TO THIS DIARY, (CONT'D)

(F) Effect of Thunderstorms on the communications.

(G) Signalling to Kite Balloons.

A Roberts Capt RE
for Major,

4.7.17. O.C., 42nd Divisional Signal Company, R.E.(T)

2449 Wt. W14957/M90 750,000 1/16 J.B.C. & A. Forms/C.2118/12.

APPENDIX "A"

DIAGRAM OF COMMUNICATIONS.
42nd Div. Signal Coy., R.E.

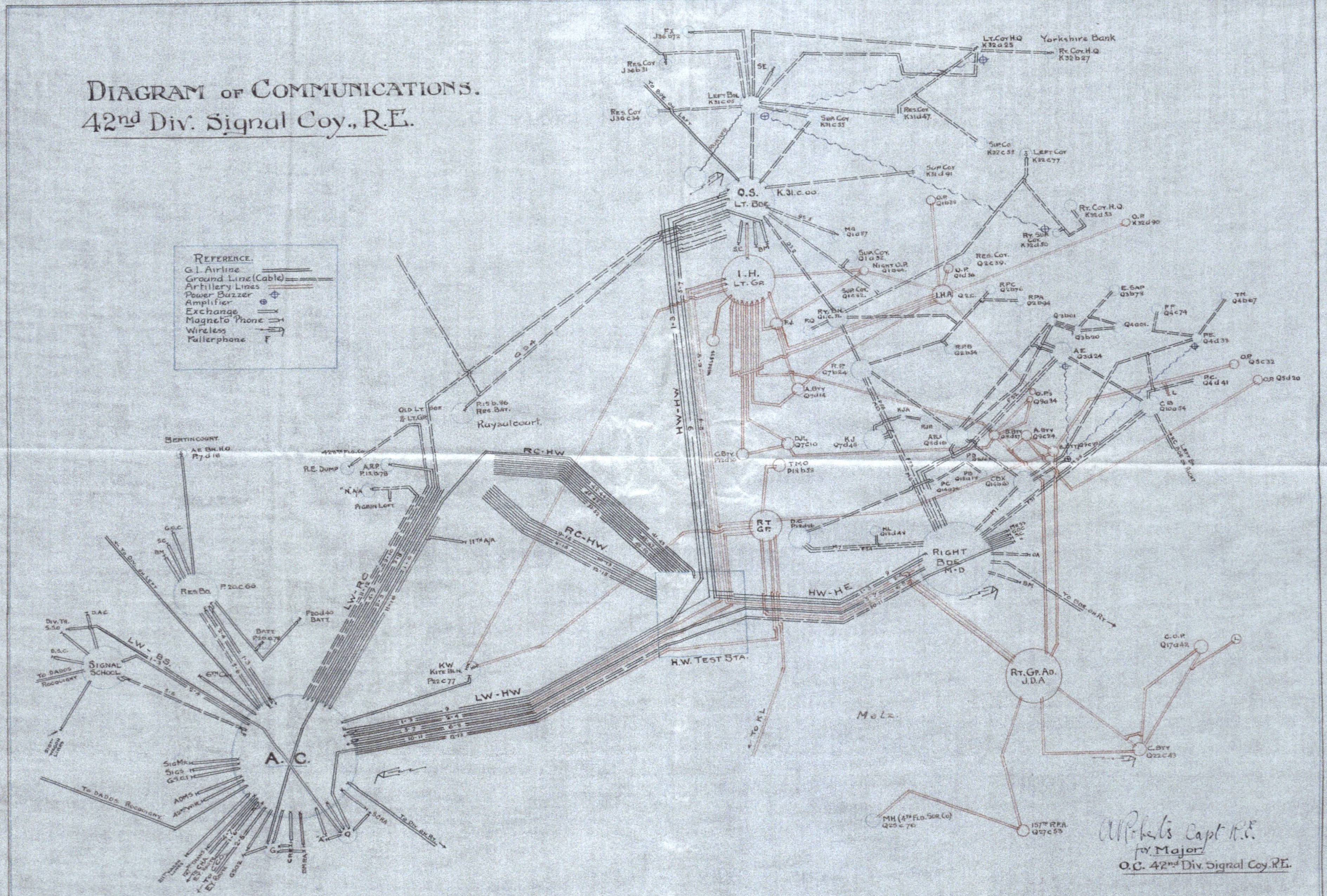

REFERENCE.
G.I. Airline
Ground Line (Cable)
Artillery Lines
Power Buzzer
Amplifier
Exchange
Magneto Phone
Wireless
Fullerphone
A.C.
Q.S. LT. BDE. K.31.c.00
I.H. LT. GR.
RIGHT BDE. M.D.
RT. GR. AD. J.D.A.
RT. GR.
SIGNAL SCHOOL
RES. BD.
H.W. TEST STA.
HW-HW
HW-HE
LW-HW
RC-HW
LW-RC
LW-BS
Yorkshire Bank
Ruyaulcourt.
Bertincourt
Metz.
WRoberts Capt R.E.
for Major
O.C. 42nd Div. Signal Coy. R.E.

Identification Trace for use with Artillery Maps.

APPENDIX B

DIAGRAM OF BURIED ROUTE.

NOTE.—(1). These traces are intended to facilitate the communication of information as to the position of targets, which have been located on a squared map.

(2). The squares on this trace are 500 yards in length on the 1/10,000 scale, 1,000 yards in length on the 1/20,000 scale, and 2,000 yards in length on the 1/40,000 scale.

(3). The squares on the trace are fitted to the squares of the map showing the targets, which are then drawn on the trace. Sufficient letters and numbers must also be added to enable the recipient to place the trace in the correct position on his own map. A little detail may also be traced, but this is not essential. The name and scale of the map to which the trace refers must be always given. The trace can be used for the 1/10,000, 1/20,000, or 1/40,000 scale.

G.S.G.S. 3023.

Tracing taken from Sheet 57C N.E.& S.E.

of the 1:20,000 *map of* FRANCE.

Signature .... *Date* ....

AR

APPENDIX. E.

MESSAGE GRAPH

42nd DIVISIONAL SIGNAL COMPANY.

JUNE 1917.

1 2 3 4 5 6 7 8 9 10 11 12 13 14 15 16 17 18 19 20 21 22 23 24 25 26 27 28 29 30

600
560
520
480
440
T
400
360 D.R.L.S.
320
280
240
200
160 B
R
C
120
80

Reference
D.R.L.S.
TOTAL
R
B
C

1 2 3 4 5 6 7 8 9 10 11 12 13 14 15 16 17 18 19 20 21 22 23 24 25 26 27 28 29 30

S. Gordon [illegible] Major.
42nd DIVISIONAL SIGNAL Co.

W A R   D I A R Y

APPENDIX "B" JUNE, 1917.

DESCRIPTION OF BURIED CABLE SCHEME.

The Buried system as commenced by the Division is as follows:-

The points L, M, U, etc are deep dug-outs, approximately 30 feet deep, into which the cables are led and at intervals of ¼ mile between each dug-out are test boxes through which the cables pass. These test boxes consist of small dug-outs in which the cables are jointed as it is issued in ¼ mile lengths, the joint serving as a suitable place to test without interfering with the armour or lead covering.

The cables were laid in trenches about 3'0" wide, 7'6" deep from 'L' to 'M' and 3'6" deep from 'M' to 'U', the digging of which was very difficult owing to the fact that the trenches ran through Havrincourt Wood, the undergrowth of which is very dense.

The cables laid in the LMU section consisted of 5 twin Iron I.R. heavy and 5 E & C.C. 14/10, making in all 40 pairs. The twin iron was issued in coils of ¼ mile length and the E & C.C. on drums of ¼ mile. These drums weighed about 3½ cwts and to facilitate laying a horse drawn sledge was issued, but owing to the difficult nature of the ground it was impossible to use this sledge in the manner designed, the only method being to leave it stationary and pull the cable out along the route. It was found that the best way to do this was to space an infantry working party along the trench at regular intervals of about 15 yards. Then the end of the cable was taken by a sapper and drawn out and as he passed the men standing at the edge of the trench, they caught hold of the cable and gently passed it through their hands, care being taken that no unnecessary slack was allowed to accumulate between any two men. To do this satisfactorily, it was found necessary to post a number of sappers at intervals to watch and correct any errors in this direction. This procedure worked quite well and after several cables had been run out and the men became accustomed to handling it, a drum could be loaded on to the sledge and the cable run out in 20 minutes.

WAR DIARY

APPENDIX "B" (CONT'D) JUNE, 1917.

Owing to the delicate nature of the lead covering of the E. & C.C., the twin iron was run first. This was laid in the trench and covered with about 6" of soft earth. Then the E. & C.C. were run out. These were not laid in the trench straight away but were placed on the opposite side of the trench to where the men were standing until all the five were run out. Then two sappers with gum boots on, commenced to lay the cable from the centre of the trench towards each end. When this was complete the order was given to fill in.

The method was quite satisfactory and reliable as proved by the fact that a portion of the length 'LM' had to be laid during the night, the trench being in full view of the enemy. This was done without any trouble whatever.

A Roberts Capt RE.
for Major.

4.7.17. O.C., 42nd Divisional Signal Coy., R.E.

WAR DIARY.

APPENDIX "C". JUNE 1917.

HONOURS AND AWARDS.

His Majesty, the King, has been graciously pleased to approve the following awards.

THE MILITARY CROSS.

to

Lieut, R.S. Newton, 1/6th Lancs. Fusiliers (T.F.) attached 42nd Divisional Signal Company, R.E. (T.F.)

2/lieut. A. Cameron, Lowland Divisional Signal Company, R.E. att'd 42nd Divisional Signal Company, R.E. (T.F.)

A N Roberts
Capt RE.
for Major.

4.7.17. O.C., 42nd Divisional Signal Coy. R.E.

WAR DIARY.

APPENDIX "D". JUNE 1917.

WEEKLY STRENGTHS, CASUALTIES, REINFORCEMENTS.

STrength,	Week ending June 2nd.	7 officers,	240 other ranks.
	" " " 9th.	7 "	237 " "
	" " " 16th.	8 "	246 " "
	" " " 23rd.	8 "	247 " "
	" " " 30th.	8 "	257 " "

Casualties.

Killed.	Nil.
Wounded.	Nil.
Sick.	12 O.R. to Hospital.
Total.	12 O.R.

Reinforcements.

From Hospital.	16 O.R.
From Depot.	1 officer, 16 O.R.
Total.	1 officer, 32 O.R.

C.W. Roberts Capt RE.
for Major.

4.7.17. O.C., 42nd Divisional Signal Coy R.E.

W A R   D I A R Y

APPENDIX "F".   JUNE 1917.

EFFECT OF THUNDER STORMS ON COMMUNICATIONS.

On the 12th of June a storm of extraordinary violence occurred during the early morning. It came on in three distinct periods, each of about one hours duration with half hour intervals.

Line protection is afforded by the army test panels, 12 line, on which are mounted fuses and "disc" lightning dischargers and every line, including locals, is led through these panels. Nearly fifty fuses were blown during the first and second periods of the storm so all lines were disconnected at the "U" links for the third period to prevent further damage to instruments and the consequence was a "sparking" display rarely seen.

In this office two "galvo" coils and one sounder coil were burnt out without affecting the transformers through which they worked and only blowing one fuse of six in the circuits concerned. In addition, to the line discharge and fuses, one is in circuit on each superimposed line and signs of a heavy discharge were noticeable on the lightning dischargers of three of the six superimposed lines which means that a discharge took place after passing through the transformers.

The transformers at headquarter office were toroidal repeaters and those at brigade headquarters office were seven terminal transformers. A brigade superimposed line was struck and each of the four coils of the transformer were burnt out in addition to the sounder. One fuse of the two in circuit was blown in this case and both dischargers acted.

A local line of 30 yards length was struck and a bell coil fused. Practically all dischargers shewed signs of having acted, and 20% of the indicators on the switchboards were affected.

Several airline faults occurred; in one case only a few small pieces of a 200 yard length of galvanised iron wire

W A R   D I A R Y

APPENDIX "F" (CONT'D) JUNE 1917.

remained, and several ebonite insulators had been split. A ten yard length of "D twin" wire was brought in "cracked" at fairly regular intervals of about 2 feet.

Several storms have occurred since but none so severe as the first. When a storm is imminent the Signalmaster has instructions to warn subscribers and to disconnect the lines going towards the storm area, disconnecting and joining up according to the direction and intensity of the storm, care being taken to disconnect lines for as short a period as possible.

A Roberts Capt R.E.
for Major.

4.7.17. O.C., 42nd Divisional Signal Company, R.E.

W A R D I A R Y

APPENDIX "G".   JUNE 1917.

SIGNALLING TO KITE BALLOONS.

Experiments were undertaken to prove the possibility of visual signalling with lamps from the front line to a kite balloon about 5,000 yards back from the line. Experiments were carried out on three occasions.

In the daytime, the results were poor. As a balloon swings from side to side when in the air, a concentrated beam of light cannot be used. Owing to the large ~~of~~ angle of dispersion necessary, the source of light (i.e. the glow lamp and battery) of the electric signalling lamp is insufficient for daylight signalling.

At night the signalling was successfully carried out, provided always that the lamp used had sufficient dispersion to allow the balloon to swing without leaving the beam of light. A "Lucas" electric lamp was used but probably more certain results would be obtained by a lamp having a slightly greater angle of dispersion. It is absolutely necessary if the signals from the front are to be accurately read, that the signaller in the balloon should be a fully trained and experienced man. The failure of the first experiments done was due to poor reading by an inexperienced man in the balloon.

A Roberts Capt RE
for Major.

4.7.17.   O.C., 42nd Divisional Signal Co R.E. (T.F.)

10 Vol 5 42

SECRET

WAR DIARY

42nd DIV SIG COY R.E. {T.F}

Chapter 9. July 1917.

Instructions regarding War Diaries and Intelligence Summaries are contained in F. S. Regs., Part II. and the Staff Manual respectively. Title Pages will be prepared in manuscript.

WAR DIARY
or
~~INTELLIGENCE SUMMARY~~
(Erase heading not required.)

Army Form C. 2118.

Place	Date	Hour	Summary of Events and Information	Remarks and references to Appendices
			42nd Divisional Signal Company, R.E. (T.F.) Page 1.	
			Reference Maps, FRANCE, 1/100,000 Lens. 11.	
YTRES.			CHAPTER 9. JULY, 1917.	
			During the early portion of this month we were warned that we should be relieved by the 58th Division, and the period up to the 9th of July was occupied in carrying on with the buried system, and handing over to the 58th Division.	
ACHIET-LE-PETIT.			On the 9th of July the Divisional Headquarters moved from YTRES and were established at ACHIET LE PETIT. The 127th Brigade also moved to ACHIET LE PETIT, the 125th Brigade to COMIECOURT, andthe 126th Brigade to BIHUCOURT.	
			On the following day however, the 126th Brigade was moved to COURCELLES.	
			The lines employed were all lent to us by the Sixth Corps and were carried on their permanent routes. The whole system employed and the local lines are shown on the diagram(Appendix "A").	APPENDIX "A"
			For the remainder of the month the units of the Division remained in the situation described and the period was occupied by training.	
			As far as The Signal Company was concerned a very considerable portion of the time	

Instructions regarding War Diaries and Intelligence Summaries are contained in F. S. Regs., Part II. and the Staff Manual respectively. Title Pages will be prepared in manuscript.

WAR DIARY
or
~~INTELLIGENCE SUMMARY~~
(Erase heading not required.)

Army Form C. 2118.

Place	Date	Hour	Summary of Events and Information	Remarks and references to Appendices
			Page 2.	
			was spent in training men as horsemen. The dismounted men were chiefly trained in wireless work.	
			Detachment training was carried out with the Cable Wagons and a very considerable improvement in the work was noticeable.	
			Special points in the training which were brought out are shown in the Appendices.	
			Appendix "B" describes the recreational training, and Appendix "C" gives a detailed description of a scheme of attack which was issued to the Brigade Sections for training purposes. The Signallers of the various Regiments of the Brigade also took part in this scheme.	APPENDIX "B" APPENDIX "C"
			During the month the Signal School had approximately 200 pupils who were put through a course. The report which was sent out to units at the termination of the course is attached as Appendix "D".	APPENDIX "D".
			APPENDICES TO THIS DIARY. (A) Circuit Diagram. (B) Recreational Training. (C) Training Scheme.	

2449 Wt. W14957/M90 750,000 1/16 J.B.C. & A. Forms/C.2118/12.

Instructions regarding War Diaries and Intelligence Summaries are contained in F. S. Regs., Part II. and the Staff Manual respectively. Title Pages will be prepared in manuscript.

WAR DIARY
or
INTELLIGENCE SUMMARY

(Erase heading not required.)

Army Form C. 2118.

Place	Date	Hour	Summary of Events and Information	Remarks and references to Appendices
			Page 3.	
			APPENDICES TO THIS DIARY, (CONT'D)	
			(D) Report on Signal School.	
			(E) Honours and Awards.	
			(F) Weekly Strengths, Casualties, and Reinforcements.	
			(G) Monthly Message Charts.	
			A Roberts Capt R.E. for Major,	
			6.3.17. O.C. 42nd Divisional Signal Co. R.E. (T).	

2449 Wt. W14957/M90 750,000 1/16 J.B.C. & A. Forms/C.2118/12.

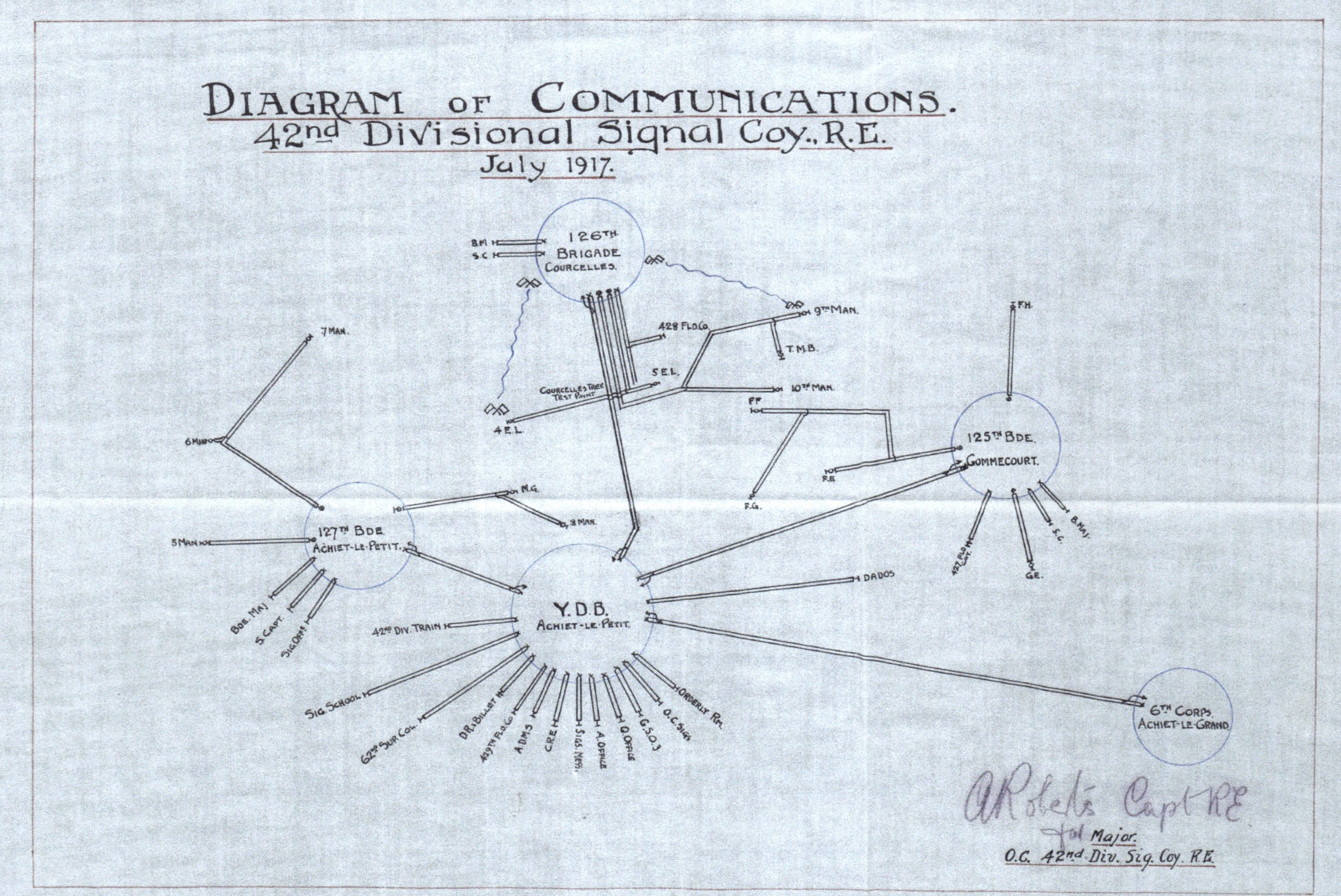

DIAGRAM OF COMMUNICATIONS.
42nd Divisional Signal Coy., R.E.
July 1917.
126TH BRIGADE COURCELLES.
B.M.
S.C.
428 FLD.CO.
9TH MAN.
T.M.B.
S.E.L.
10TH MAN.
COURCELLES TREE TEST POINT
4 E.L.
F.F.
F.H.
F.G.
R.E.
125TH BDE. GOMMECOURT.
B.MAJ.
S.C.
G.E.
7 MAN.
6 MAN.
127TH BDE. ACHIET-LE-PETIT.
5 MAN.
M.G.
8 MAN.
BDE. MAJ.
S. CAPT.
SIG.OFFR.
Y.D.B. ACHIET-LE-PETIT.
DADOS
42ND DIV. TRAIN
SIG. SCHOOL
62ND SUP. COL.
DR. BILLET
A.D.M.S.
C.R.E.
SIGS. MESS.
A. OFFICE
Q. OFFICE
G.S.O.3
O.C. SIGS.
ORDERLY RM.
6TH CORPS ACHIET-LE-GRAND
A Roberts Capt RE
for Major.
O.C. 42nd Div. Sig. Coy. R.E.

WAR DIARY

APPENDIX "D". JULY, 191[illegible]

Recreational Training.

During July, a considerable period every day was devoted to Riding, Driving and practical horse-management. Classes were organised to give preliminary instructions in riding to dismounted sappers and others unable to ride. Troop drill, riding school figures, and jumping were practised by all mounted men. During their spare time opportunity was given to the men to carry on independent riding, and to encourage this, tent pegging and lemon cutting were introduced. Great keenness was shewn by all the more experienced riders, several of whom soon acquired considerable skill.

Under the supervision of the Company Sergeant Major, the drivers underwent training in driving through gates and posts with excellent results.

Mounted sports were organised on July 25th, in which all had opportunities of competing. Prizes were awarded for the best turned out six horse team, pair, mounted and dismounted man, and motor cyclist. All available men and horsesentered, and a very keen competition took place.

One of the most successful events of the afternoon was the driving competition. This was preceded by the march past of the four competing teams, hooked into the cable wagons - first trotting in column of route and afterwards in line at the canter. An excellent line was kept during the latter, shewing a high standard of efficiency on the part of the drivers which was well maintained later by the individual teams when driving between the posts.

As will be seen from the attached programme, there were competitions for all ranks in tent pegging, lemon cutting and "heads and posts". There were numerous entries by the men for these events and also for the horse jumping. Most of the competitors did very creditably and a marked improvement in the general standard of horsemanship throughout the Company was noticeable.

A Roberts Capt RE
for Major.
O.C., 42nd Div'l Signal Coy. R.E.

No.	EVENT.	Time.	JUDGES.
1.	Best turned out six horse team.	11.0 a.m.	LT.Col. R.J.Slaughter, D.S.O., Lt.Col.A.N.Lawford
2.	Best turned out pair.	11.0 a.m.	" " " " " " "
3.	Best turned out Motor Cyclist.	11.0 a.m.	Lt.Col.D.S.MacInnes, C.M.G., D.S.O. Lt.Col. A.N.Lawford.
4.	Best turned out mounted man.	11.0 a.m.	Lt.Col. D.S.MacInnes, C.M.G., D.S.O. Lt.Col. A.N.Lawford.
5.	Best turned out dismounted man.	11.0 a.m.	Lt.Col. D.S.MacInnes, C.M.G., D.S.O. Lt.Col. A.N.Lawford.
6.	220 yards Flat Race. Open to dismounted men. (Handicap by age).	12 noon.	2/Lieut. C.H.Woodhall & 2/Lieut. H.A.Riley.
7.	P.H. Helmet Race. Open to pupils at Signal School.	12.15 p.m.	" " " " "
8.	Tent Pegging with swords. (W.O., N.C.O's and Men.)	2.30 p.m.	Capt. G.N.Robinson & Lieut. H.Horner.
9.	Wrestling on Horseback. Teams of six from Sections & H.Q.	2.45 p.m.	" " " " " "
10.	Horse Jumping. (W.O.; N.C.O's, and Men.)	3.0 p.m.	Brig. Gen. The Hon. A.M.Henley, D.S.O. Lt.COl. E.G.K. Cross.
11.	Heads & Posts, and lemon cutting. Open to all ranks in the Division.	3.20 p.m.	Lt.Col. B.J.Curling, D.S.O. Major The Hon. E.C. Pery.
12.	V.C. Race.	3.40 p.m.	Major The Hon. E.C. Pery, 2/Lieut. W.H. Hewitt-Dean, & 2/Lieut.V.H.Glendening.
13.	Officers' Tent Pegging. Open to Division.	3.50 p.m.	Lt.Col. B.J.Curling, D.S.O. Major The Hon. E.C.Pery.
14.	Motor Cycle Race.	4.15 p.m.	Capt. M.F. Hammond-Smith, M.C. Capt. C.R.Maude, M.C.
15.	Driving Competition.	4,30 p.m.	Lt.Col. D.S.MacInnes, C.M.G., D.S.O. Lt.Col. R.J.Slaughter, D.S.O.
16.	Horse Jumping, Officers. Open to Division.	5.0 p.m.	Lt.Col. R.J.Slaughter, D.S.O. Lt.Col. E.G.K. Cross.
17.	Musical Chairs.	5.30 p.m.	2/Lieut. A.J.Ellis & 2/Lieut. J.E.Crawshaw.
18.	Team Tent Pegging. Open to Division. Teams of three, at Least one to be an Officer.	5.45 p.m.	Lt.Col. B.J.Curling, D.S.O. Major The Hon. E.C.Pery.
19.	Band Race.	6.0 p.m.	2/Lieut. H.A.Riley & 2/Lieut. V.H.Glendening.

Major General B.R. Mitford, C.B., C.M.G., D.S.O., has kindly consented to present the prizes.

The above Officers have kindly consented to judge in the events stated against their names.

42ND S I G N A L   C O Y. R E.

M O U N T E D   S P O R T S.

Achiet-le-Petit.
July, 25th 1917.

W A R   D I A R Y

APPENDIX "C". JULY, 1917.

TRAINING SCHEME.

Ref:- France, 1/40,000, Sheet 57 C.

As noted in the War Diary itself, the 42nd Division was during July withdrawn from the front line at YTRES into reserve of the VI Corps. The Divisional Headquarters was established at ACHIET-LE-PETIT on July 9th, 1917, the Brigade Headquarters being opened at the same time at GOMMIECOURT (125th Inf. Bde.), COURCELLES (126th Inf. Bde.) and ACHIET-LE-PETIT, (127th Inf Bde.)

The information had already been received that the period to be spent in reserve was to be regarded as a training period. Thus some definite scheme had to be prepared for the training of the signallers of the Division.

The individual training of signallers was first discussed and as a result the attached (A) letter was circularised to the units of the Division in order that Regimental Signalling Officers might have something definite on which to base the sub-division of the time allotted to them for the training of their battalion signallers. This training, for which about six days were set aside, was preceded by a period of about 3 days, during which time the signallers were with their companies doing elementary infantry training.

It was desired at the end of the first ten days to commence signalling training for a possible attack. Each of the Brigade Signalling Officers was instructed that the Battalion Signalling Officers were to be thoroughly familiar with the principles of the pamphlet S.S.148, "Intercommunication in Battle", and that Battalion and Brigade Signallers were to be trained with a view to providing the signal organisation laid down therein. Each unit signal officer drew up and carried out small schemes based on the above pamphlet.

In order to practice the writing of signal orders and to show how the various methods of signalling would be coordinated in an actual attack, divisional signal orders, (See B attached) were got out and sent to the Brigade Signal Officers. As the Division had been holding a position just west of HAVRINCOURT, and had had orders, which were afterwards cancelled, to prepare the position for an attack upon HAVRINCOURT, the signal orders were issued in the form of orders for a possible attack on that place. The recipients of the orders, all of whom knew the ground mentioned, thus had a much more definite idea of the scheme than would have been the case if the orders had been based on a purely imaginery area of attack.

Upon receipt of the Divisional Orders, the Brigade Signalling Officers got out their signal orders for the same scheme and sent them to the Battalion Signal Officers.

Various points which arose in connection with the scheme, were discussed at a meeting of Signal Officers.

Each Brigade Signal Officer then prepared and carried out a signal scheme in accordance with the orders. Many small points were brought out and had to be settled as a result of these schemes. Furthermore all regimental signal officers were able to see clearly in what way or ways their signallers required training, in order to provide the signal personnel for an offensive action.

Other Brigade Signal Schemes were afterwards carried out, either as part of the general schemes carried out by each brigade or simply as schemes for signallers only. By the end of July each Brigade Signal Officer had carried out three or four such schemes.

A Roberts Capt R.E.
for Major.

6.8.17. O.C., 42nd Div'l Signal Coy., R.E.

Nth Divisional Signal Order No. 3059,
by Major "Y",
O.C. Signals, "N" Division.

Reference FRANCE 1/20,000, sheet 57c S.E.
" " 57c N.E.
" " 2nd Edition, RIBECOURT, Sheet 1.

1. The Division is to attack the HINDENBURG LINE from K.34.a.9.3. on the right to the CANAL DU NORD on the left.

2. The attack is divided into two phases. In the first phase, the "X" Brigade on the right will attack and capture the HINDENBURG LINE from K.34.a.9.3 to the western edge of HAVRINCOURT VILLAGE. The Yth Brigade on the left, the HINDENBURG LINE from the western edge of HAVRINCOURT to the CANAL DU NORD.

In the second phase the Division will capture and consolidate a line west of the FLESQUIERES RIDGE to form a defensive flank as far as the CANAL DU NORD, where the Hindenburg Line crosses the Canal.

3. Brigade forward stations will be established as follows:-

"X"th Brigade.	K.28.d.78.	
"Y"th Brigade.	K.27.c.38.	
"Z"th Brigade.	K.32.d.Central.	(As reserve)

4. ZERO HOUR will be notified later.

5. DIVISIONAL REPORT STATION WILL be at P.6.b.88.

6. A CENTRAL VISUAL STATION for the Divisional front will be established at K.31.d.73 and connected by cable to Divisional Report Station, P.6.b.88.

7. O.C., Signals, "Y"th Brigade will detail a Visual Signalling Station at K.32.b.58 to xxxxx act as transmitting station if necessary, from Brigade forward stations to Central Visual Station.

8. O.Cs., Signals, "X"th and "Y"th Brigades will arrange for two pairs of Cables to be laid to each Brigade Forward Station from Q.3.d.24 to "X"th Brigade Forward Station and from K.32.c.97 (head of buried cable system) to "Y"th Brigade forward station.

The Signal equipment of each Brigade forward station will consist of :-

Telephone (or fullerphone) station.
Power Buzzer Station.
Aeroplane Signalling Station.
Visual Station to work to Central Visual Station.
Pigeon Station.

A chain of runners will be arranged along the cable routes, relay posts to be not more than 300 yards apart.

One pair of cables will be used for communication from advanced brigade headquarters to brigade forward station. The other will be at the disposal of signals, R.A. for communication to F.O.Os.

9. Amplifier Stations will be at Q.3.d.24 for reception from Power Buzzer at "X"th Brigade forward station and at K.32.c.97 from Power Buzzer at "Y"th Brigade forward station.

10. A Wireless (Transmitting and receiving station) will be established at K.32.c.86 as soon as possible after the attacking infantry has left our first line trenches, for communication to the directing station at P.22 Central. This duplicates communication in case of a breakdown of the buried cable system.

11. The present head of the buried cable system is at K.32.c.97. A Signal Station manned by Signal Company headquarters personnel will be established at this point.

12. Contact patrol aeroplanes will fly over the attacking infantry at half hourly intervals, commencing fifteen minutes after zero hour. Communication will be carried out to the machines from the ground by means of flares and lamps.

13. Communication to the Signal Tank will be by Wireless and Visual The central visual station will be prepared to communicate with this tank at any time. The marking of the Signal Tank will be notified later. The wireless receiving station for communication to this tank, will be at P.6.b.88.

Signed. "C".
Lt. Colonel.
General Staff.
Nth Division.

30.2.21.

G.S.5/82

G.S.5/82.

In order to standardise the training of the Signallers and Runners throughout the Division, the following training programme is suggested for Battalion Signallers and Runners to be carried out under Battalion Signalling Officers.

Periods.	Signallers.
1.	Daylight Lamp, Reading and Sending.
1.	Canvas Shutter, Reading and Sending.
1.	Lecture, "Station Work", "Message Form and counting words", "Fullerphone", Signalling in the attack".
2.	Buzzer reading and sending in code groups.
2.	Cable Jointing and laddered cable laying.
	Runners.
1.	Cable Jointing.
1.	Lecture "Map Reading", Delivering messages", "Use of Ground".
3.	Walking and running exercise, combined with a scheme, "Carrying messages to different points across country".

Each period will consist of $\frac{3}{4}$ of an hour with 15 minutes interval between each.

The foregoing training will last for 4 days; on the following days where Signallers and Runners are not required by Battalions for Company, Battalion or Brigade Exercises, this training will be continued during the morning. In the afternoons, however, a Brigade Signal Scheme will be worked out under instructions to be issued by the O.C., Divnl. Signal Coy., in which the Brigade Signal Section and Battalion Signallers and Runners will take part.

In making out these Brigade Signal Schemes, the O.C., Divnl. Signal Coy., will collaborate with the Staffs of Brigades in order that the training in communications may be co-ordinated with tactical requirements, and it is further suggested that Brigade Majors who work out such schemes should use Adjutants of Battalions to assist them.

Bryan Curling

Lt. Colonel,
General Staff,
42nd Division.

12th July 1917.

WAR DIARY

APPENDIX "D" JULY, 1917.

REPORT ON SIGNAL SCHOOL.

The Fourth Course at the Divisional Signal School terminated yesterday, and the men have been returned to their respective units today.

The class consisted of the following:-

Infantry Officers.	5
Infantry N.C.Os.	4
Each Infantry Battalion, (8),	96
H.Q., 210th Artillery Brigade.	3
A, B, & C, Batterys, 210 Bde RFA.(3)	9
D. Battery, 210th Bde. R.F.A.	2
H.Q., 211th Artillery Brigade.	4
Each Battery, 211th Artillery Bde.(4)	16
125th Machine Gun Coy.	3
126th Machine Gun Coy.	3
127th Machine Gun Coy.	3
126th Light T.M. Battery.	2
127th Light T.M. Battery.	3
"V" T.M. Battery.	2
"X" T.M. Battery.	4
"Z" T.M. Battery.	3
R.F.A., attached D.A.C.	13
Total.	175

The following numbers did not finish the Course for the reasons stated :-

Returned to Unit, inefficient.	14
To Hospital.	18
To U.K. for Signal Course.	1
Compassionate Leave to U.K.	1
Total.	34

The results of the Final examination were :-

Number passed out as trained regimental signallers.	120
Number failed to pass test.	21
Total.	141

The test for passing out as a regimental signaller was eight words per minute on all instruments, reading and sending.

Of the 21 men who failed, 16 failed in one test only and, if it is so desired, will be re-tested at any time after four weeks. The remaining five men will never make satisfactory signallers.

The certificates for those who passed, are attached to the copy of this report sent to the units concerned.

The Officers and men in the class shewed the greatest keenness in their work.

The large majority, on joining the School, had practically no previous knowledge of signalling. Out of the 120 who passed out, there were 52 passed at rates of 14 words a minute and over, and of this last number 13 passed at 18 words a minute and over.

The results of this Course, as in previous courses, has shewn that the men who do the best are those who have a fairly good education, can write well and are young.

There were a large number of artillery men on the course and these men did remarkably well, only two failing to pass out, and a very large proportion of those who passed, passed out at high rates. Seven out of the 13 men on the Course who passed out at 18 words a minute and over, were artillery men.

S. G. Johnson. Major,
O.C., 42nd Div'l Signal Coy. R.E.

5.8.17.

WAR DIARY.

APPENDIX "E". JULY 1917.

HONOURS AND AWARDS.

The following Officers, W.O., N.C.O's. and Man have been mentioned in despatches by General Sir Archibald Murray G.C.M.G., K.C.B., C.V.O., D.S.O., for distinguished service in the Field:-

Major S.G. Johnson. M.C.

Capt. A. Roberts.

Lieut. R.S. Newton. M.C.

2/Lieut. A. Cameron. M.C.

444019 C.S.M. Nichols, G.R.

444104 Sgt. Ellwood, J.

444594 " Mallalieu, J.

444601 " Pinder, H.

94602 " Hackett, F.G.

444038 Cpl Moores, H.N.

444030 " Barlow, F.

444607 L/Cpl Bleasdale, E.

444361 Spr Hall, W.H.

A Roberts Capt RE

for Major,

6.8.17. O.C. 42nd Divisional Signal Co. R.E.

WAR DIARY.

APPENDIX "F". JULY 1917.

WEEKLY STRENGTHS, CASUALTIES, REINFORCEMENTS.

Strength.	Week ending July 7th.	8 Officers	258 Other ranks.
	" " " 14th	8 "	255 " "
	" " " 21st	8 "	254 " "
	" " " 28th	8 "	254 " "

Casualties.

Killed.	1 O.R.
Wounded.	Nil.
Sick.	1 Officer, 10 O.R. to Hospital.
Total.	1 officer, 11 Other ranks.

Reinforcements.

From Hospital.	6 O.R.
From Depot.	5 O.R. (not included in weekly strength of 28th July. Joined 29/7/17)
Total.	11 O.R.

A Roberts Capt RE
for Major.

6.8.17. O.C., 42nd Div'l Signal Coy. R.E.

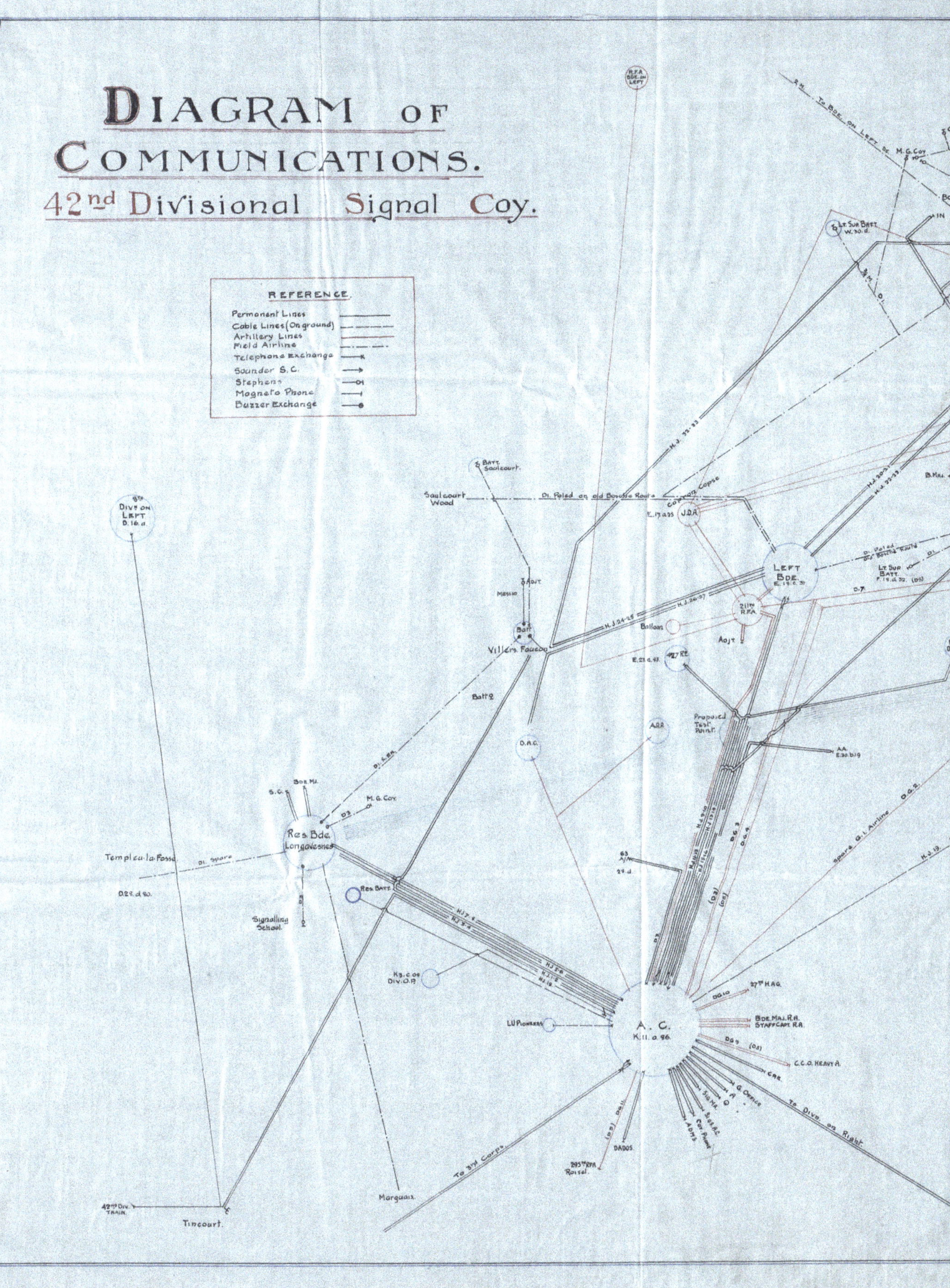

DIAGRAM OF
COMMUNICATIONS.
42nd Divisional Signal Coy.
REFERENCE.
Permanent Lines
Cable Lines (On ground)
Artillery Lines
Field Airline
Telephone Exchange
Sounder S.C.
Stephens
Magneto Phone
Buzzer Exchange
Saulcourt Wood
Villers Faucon
Res Bde. Longavesnes
Templeux-la-Fosse
Signalling School
LEFT Bde.
A. C.
K.11.a.96.
Tincourt.
Marquaix.
To 3rd Corps
To Divn on Right
C.C.O. HEAVY A.
Bde. Maj. R.A.
Staff Capt. R.A.
Proposed Test Point.
Res Batt.
LU Pioneers

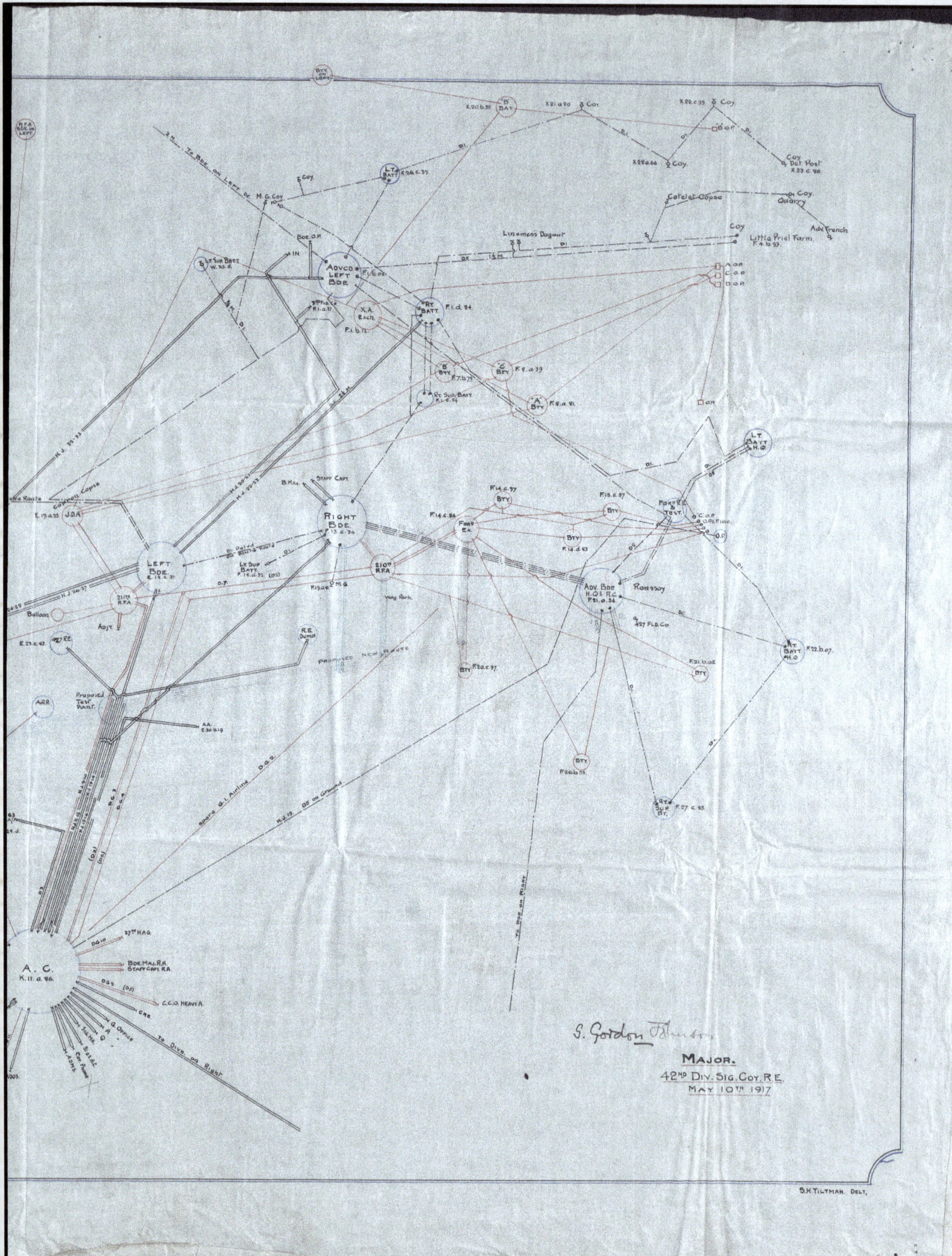

Coy.
Cotelet Copse
Coy. Quarry
Adv. Trench
Linesmen's Dugout
Little Priel Farm.
ADVCD LEFT BDE
RT. BATT. F.1.d.84
LT. BATT. H.Q.
RIGHT BDE. F.13.c.34
LEFT BDE. E.19.c.31
FORD. R.C. & TEST.
ADV. BDE H.Q.S. R.C. F.21.a.84
Ronssoy
427 FLD. Co.
210TH R.F.A.
Balloon
Proposed Test Point.
PROPOSED NEW ROUTE
R.E. DUMP
Spare G.1 Airline
To BDE on Right
A. C. K.11.a.96
27TH H.A.G.
BDE MAJ. R.A.
STAFF CAPT. R.A.
C.C.O. HEAVY A.
To Divn on Right
S. Gordon
MAJOR.
42ND DIV. SIG. COY. R.E.
MAY 10TH 1917
S.H. TILTMAN. DELT.

Circuit Diagram of Communicatio

42nd Divisional Signal Coy. R.E.

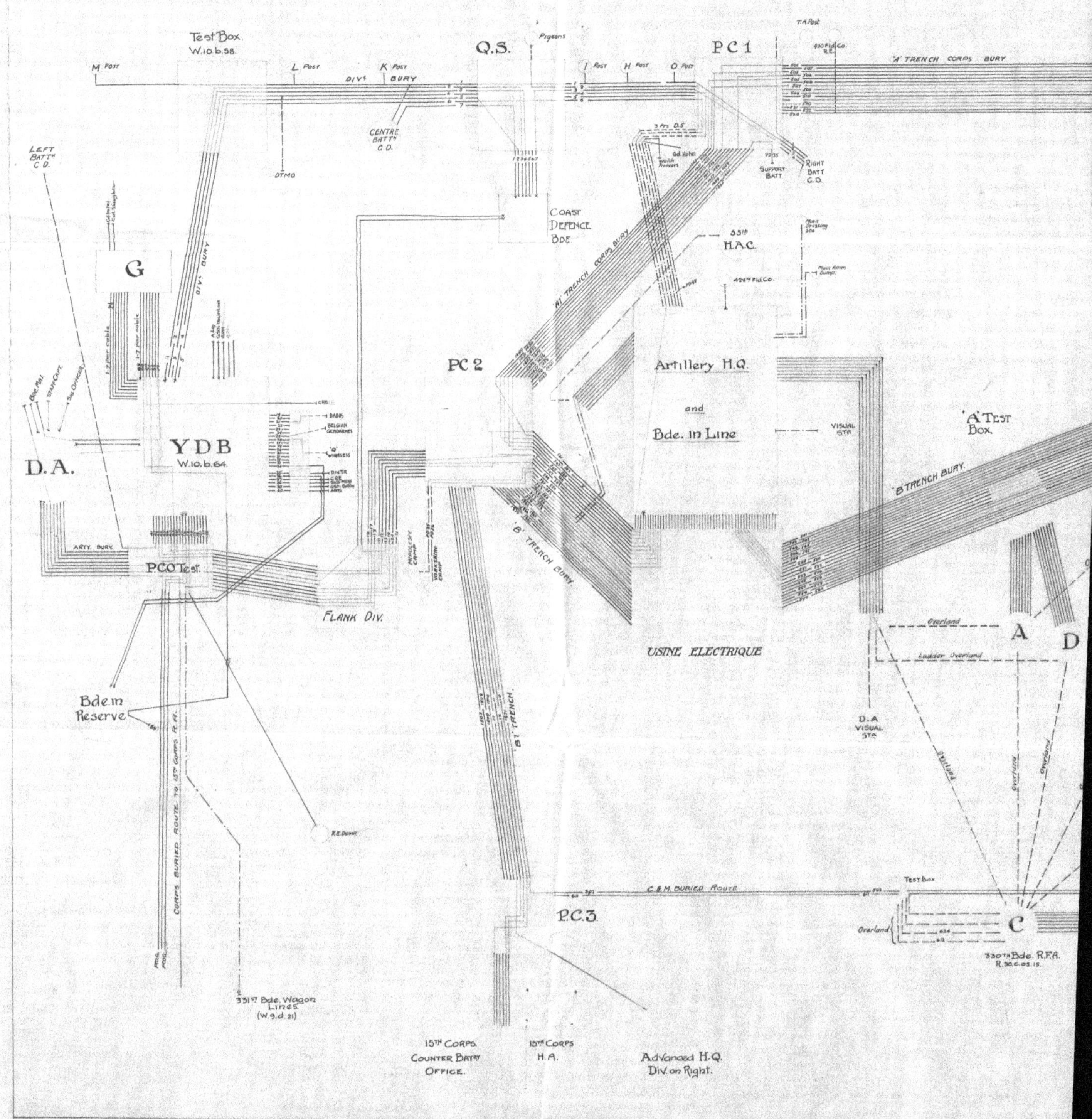

APPENDIX 'C'

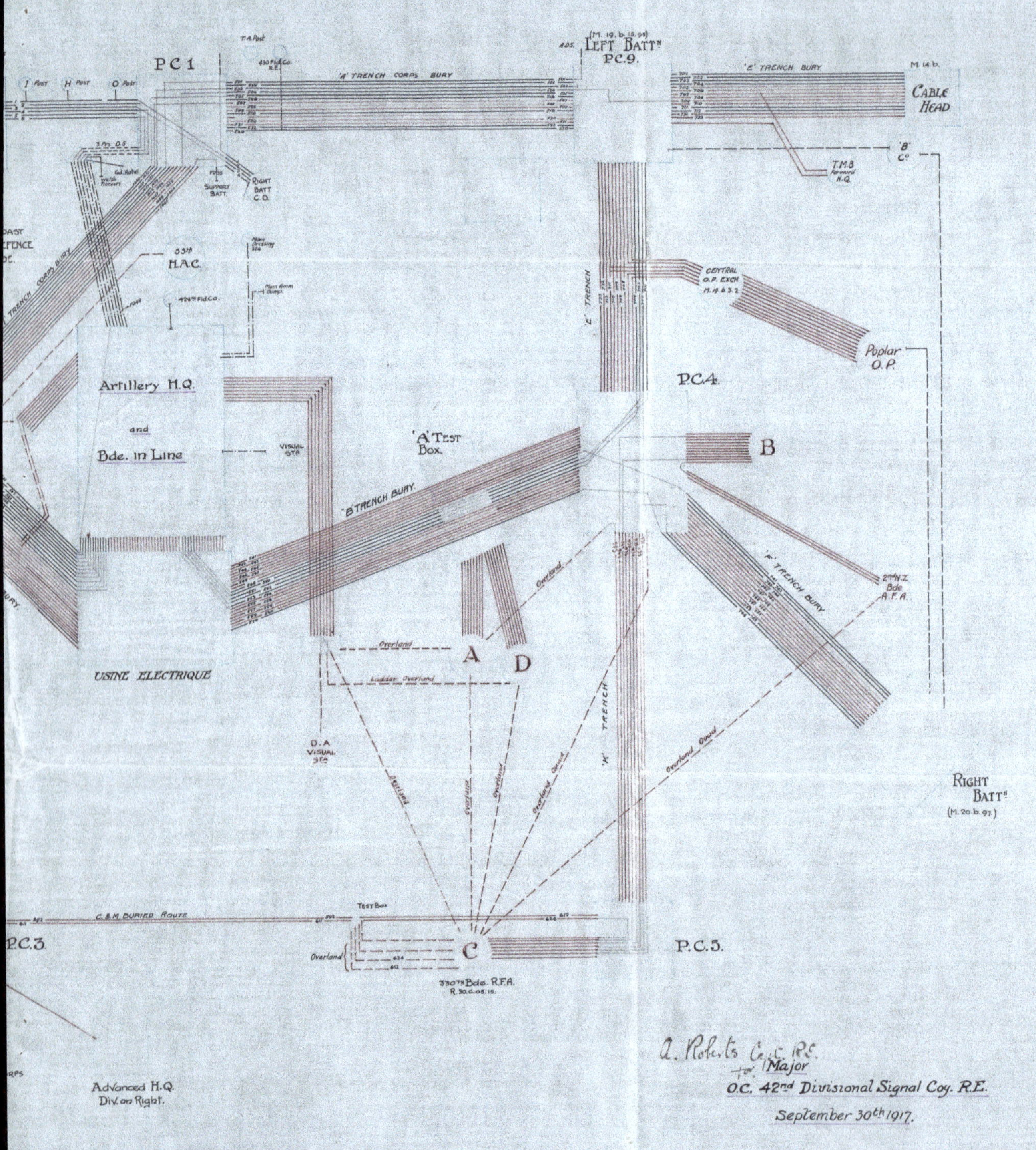

A. Roberts Capt. R.E.
for Major
O.C. 42nd Divisional Signal Coy. R.E.
September 30th 1917.

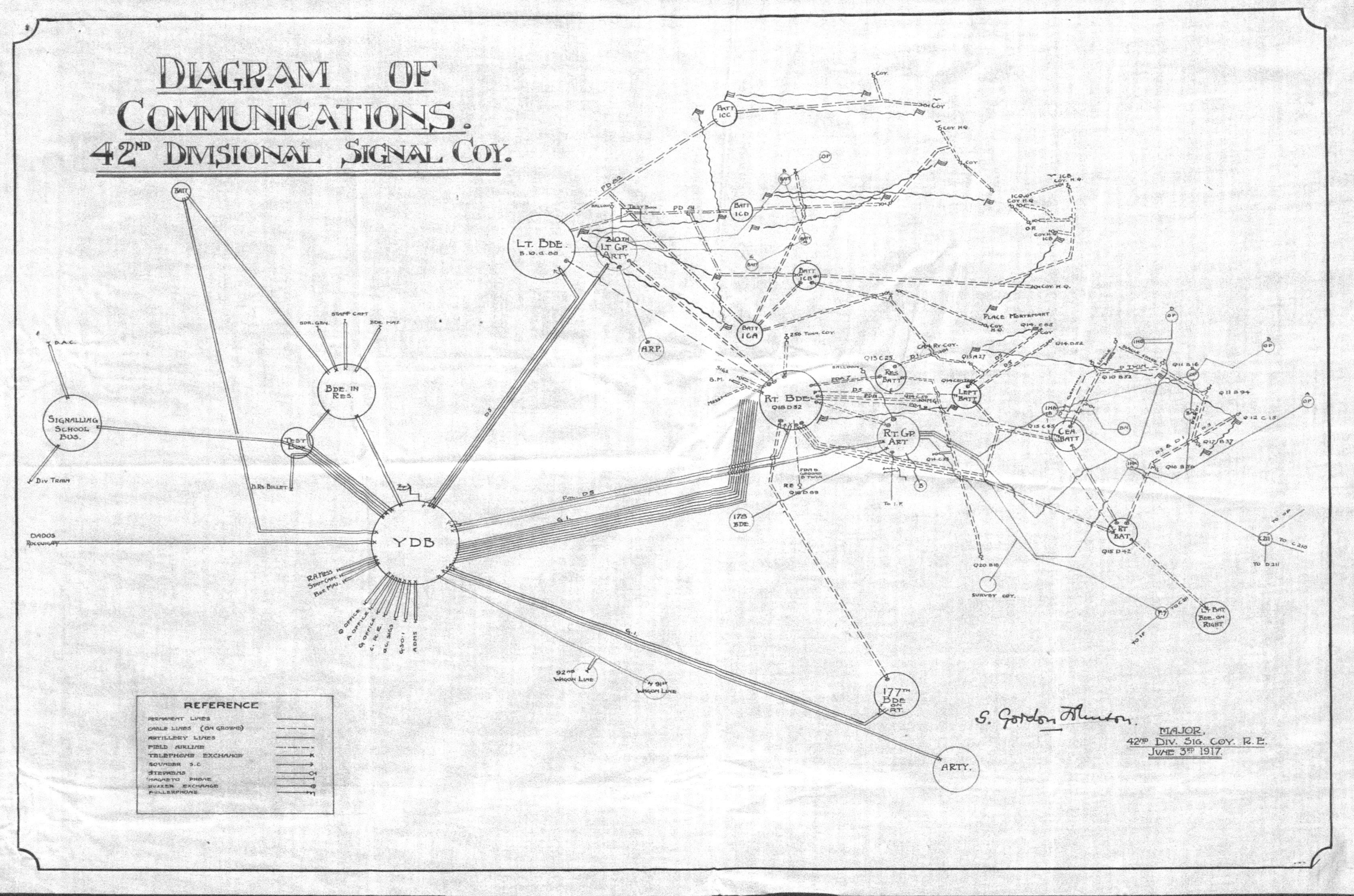

DIAGRAM OF COMMUNICATIONS.
42ND DIVISIONAL SIGNAL COY.
YDB
LT. BDE. B.10.d.88
210TH LT GP ARTY
RT. BDE. Q18 D32
RT. GP ART
BDE. IN RES.
TEST BOX
SIGNALLING SCHOOL BDS.
BATT ICC
BATT ICD
BATT ICB
BATT ICA
RES BATT
LEFT BATT
CEN. BATT
RT BAT. Q15 D42
178 BDE
177TH BDE ON RT.
ARTY.
A.R.P.
PLACE MORTEMART
SURVEY COY.
LT BATT BDE ON RIGHT
92ND WAGON LINE
91ST WAGON LINE
D.A.C.
DIV TRAIN
DADOS ROCQUIGNY
D.R.s BILLET
BDE MAJ.
STAFF CAPT
BDR. GEN.
G OFFICE
A OFFICE
Q OFFICE
C.R.E.
D.C. SIGS
G.30.1
ADMS
R.A. MESS
STAFF CAPT.
BDE MAJ.
REFERENCE
PERMANENT LINES
CABLE LINES (ON GROUND)
ARTILLERY LINES
FIELD AIRLINE
TELEPHONE EXCHANGE
SOUNDER S.C.
STEPHENS
MAGNETO PHONE
BUZZER EXCHANGE
FULLERPHONE
S. Gordon Thurston
MAJOR.
42ND DIV. SIG. COY. R.E.
JUNE 3RD 1917.

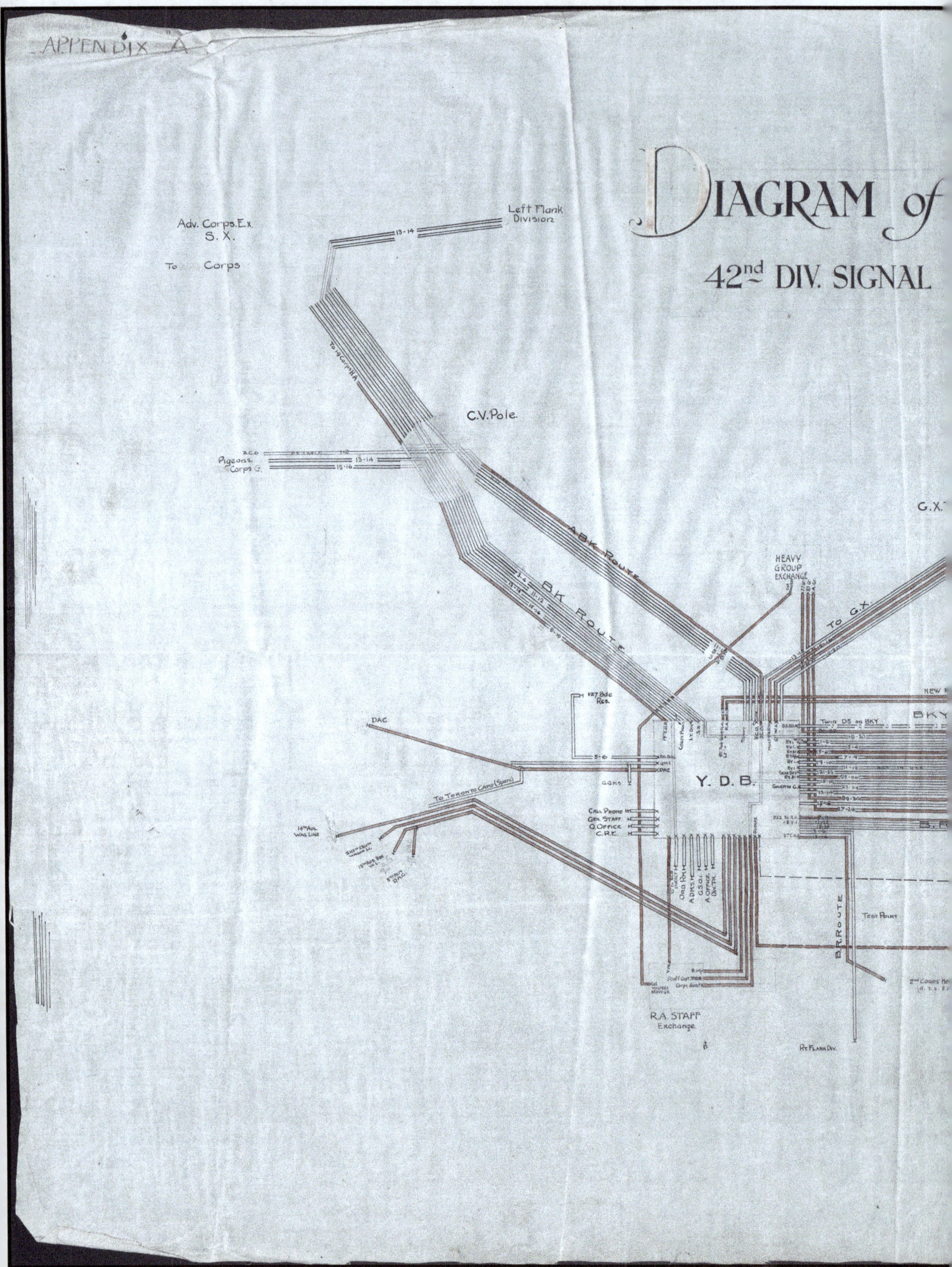

APPENDIX "A"
DIAGRAM of
42nd DIV. SIGNAL
Left Flank Division
Adv. Corps.Ex.
S.X.
Corps
C.V. Pole.
Pigeons.
Corps G.
ABK Route
BK Route
HEAVY GROUP EXCHANGE
TO G.X.
Y. D. B.
DAC
127 Bde Res.
Twin DS on BKY
CALL PHONE
GEN. STAFF
Q. OFFICE
C.R.E.
R.A. STAFF
Exchange
B.R. ROUTE
TEST POINT
Rt Flank Div.

M *of* COMMUNICATIONS

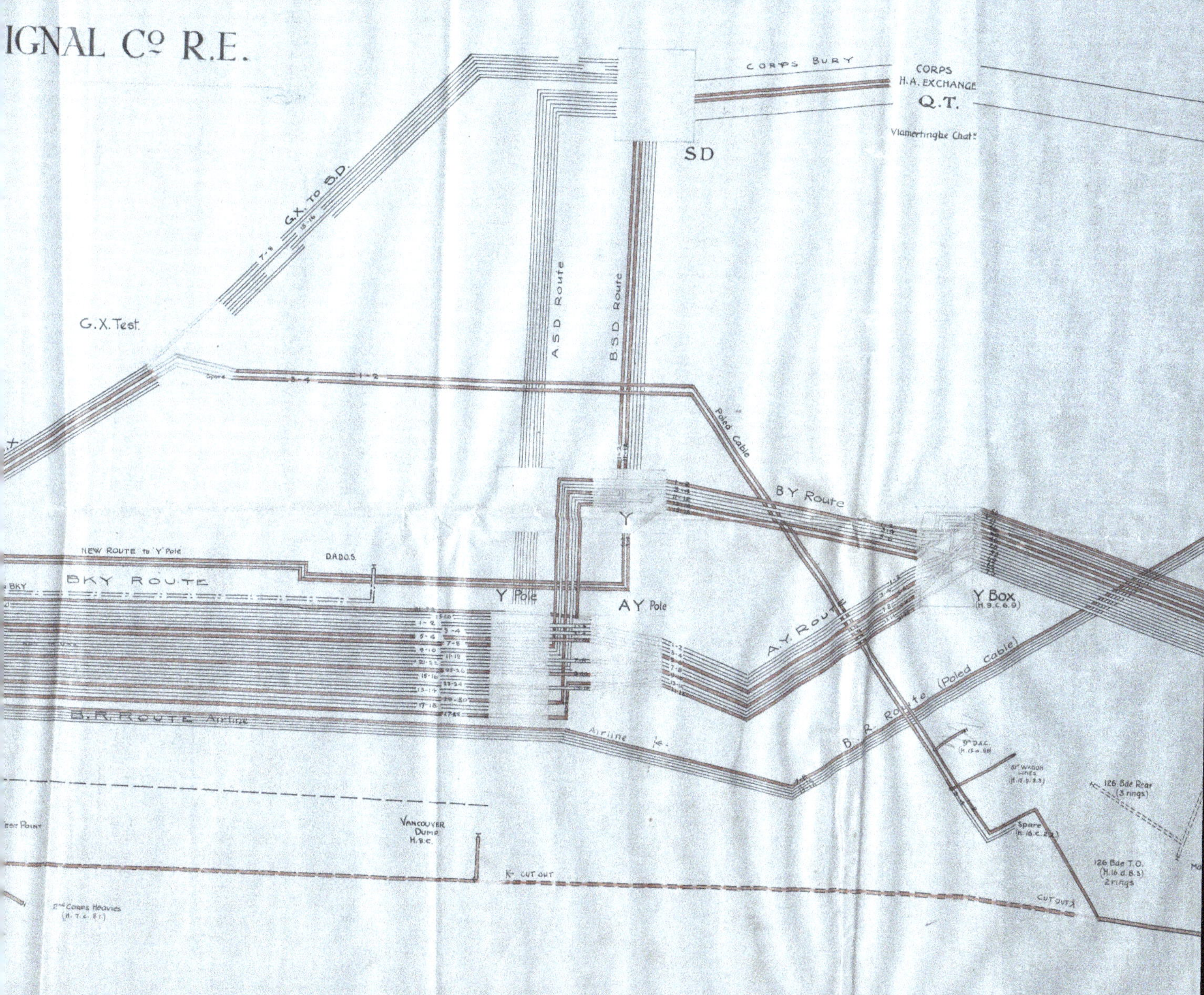

DIAGRAM 'B'

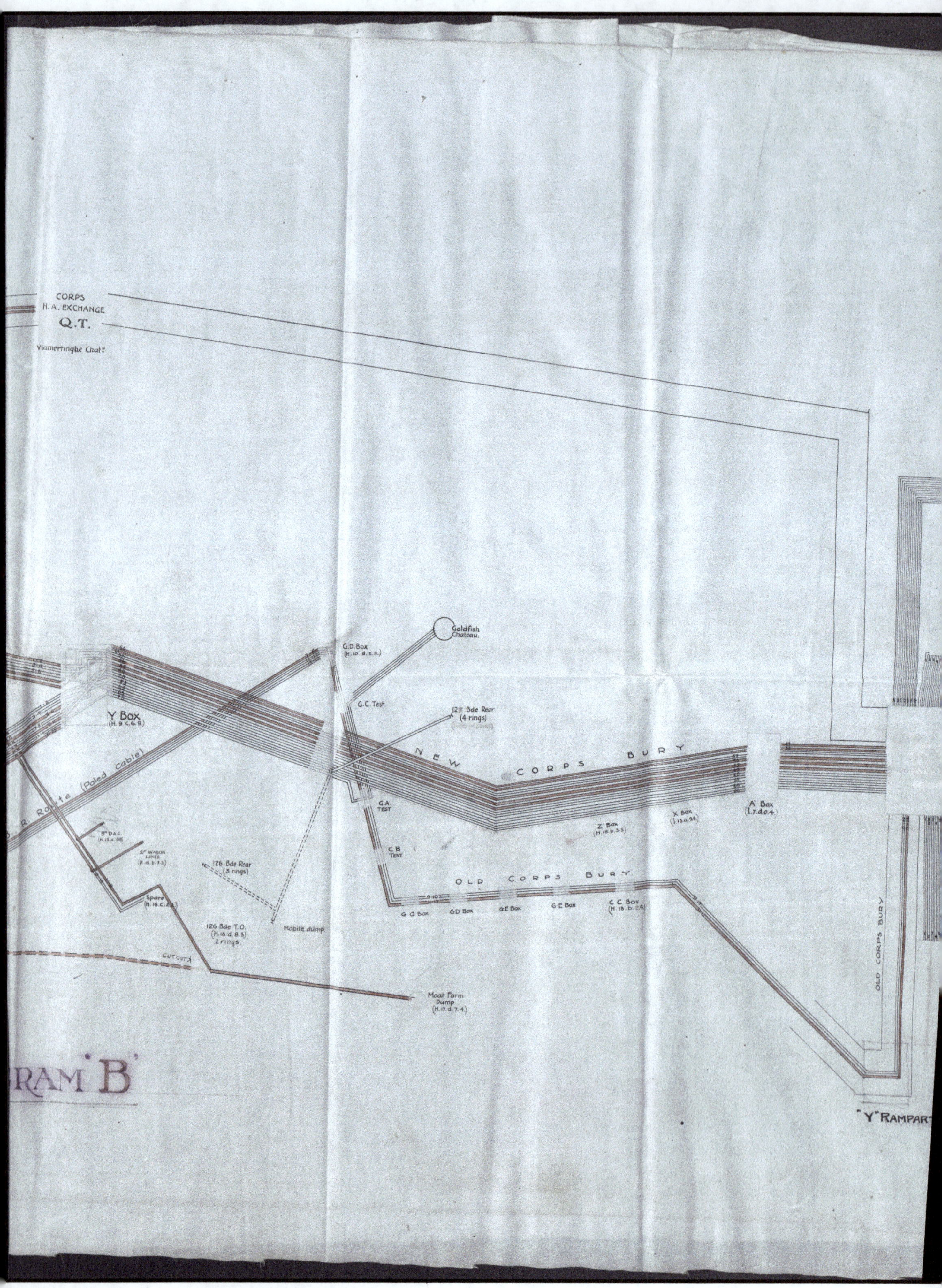

CORPS
H.A. EXCHANGE
Q.T.
Vlamertinghe Chat?
Goldfish Chateau
G.D. Box
G.C. Test
Y Box
NEW CORPS BURY
A Box
Z Box
X Box
G.A. TEST
C.B. TEST
OLD CORPS BURY
G.G. Box
G.D. Box
G.E. Box
C.C. Box
126 Bde Rear (3 rings)
126 Bde T.O. 2 rings
Mobile dump
Spare
Cut out
Moat Farm Dump
OLD CORPS BURY
"Y" RAMPART
RAM "B"

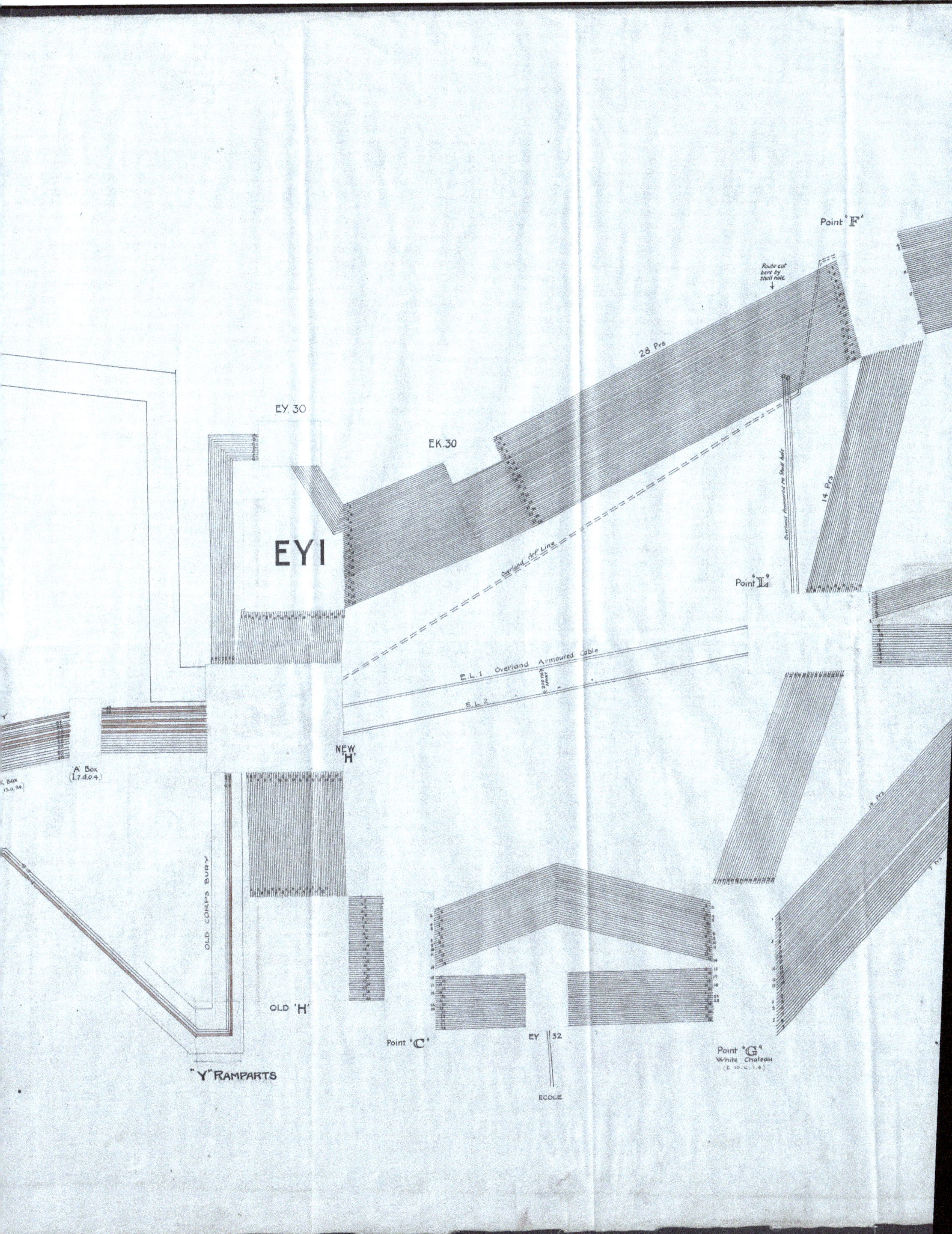

Point "F"
Route cut here by Shell hole
28 Prs
EY. 30
EK.30
EYI
Overland Arty Line
14 Prs
Point "L"
E.L.1 Overland Armoured Cable
E.L.2
NEW 'H'
A Box (I.7.d.0.4.)
OLD CORPS BURY
OLD 'H'
Point 'C'
EY 32
ECOLE
Point "G" White Chateau
"Y" RAMPARTS

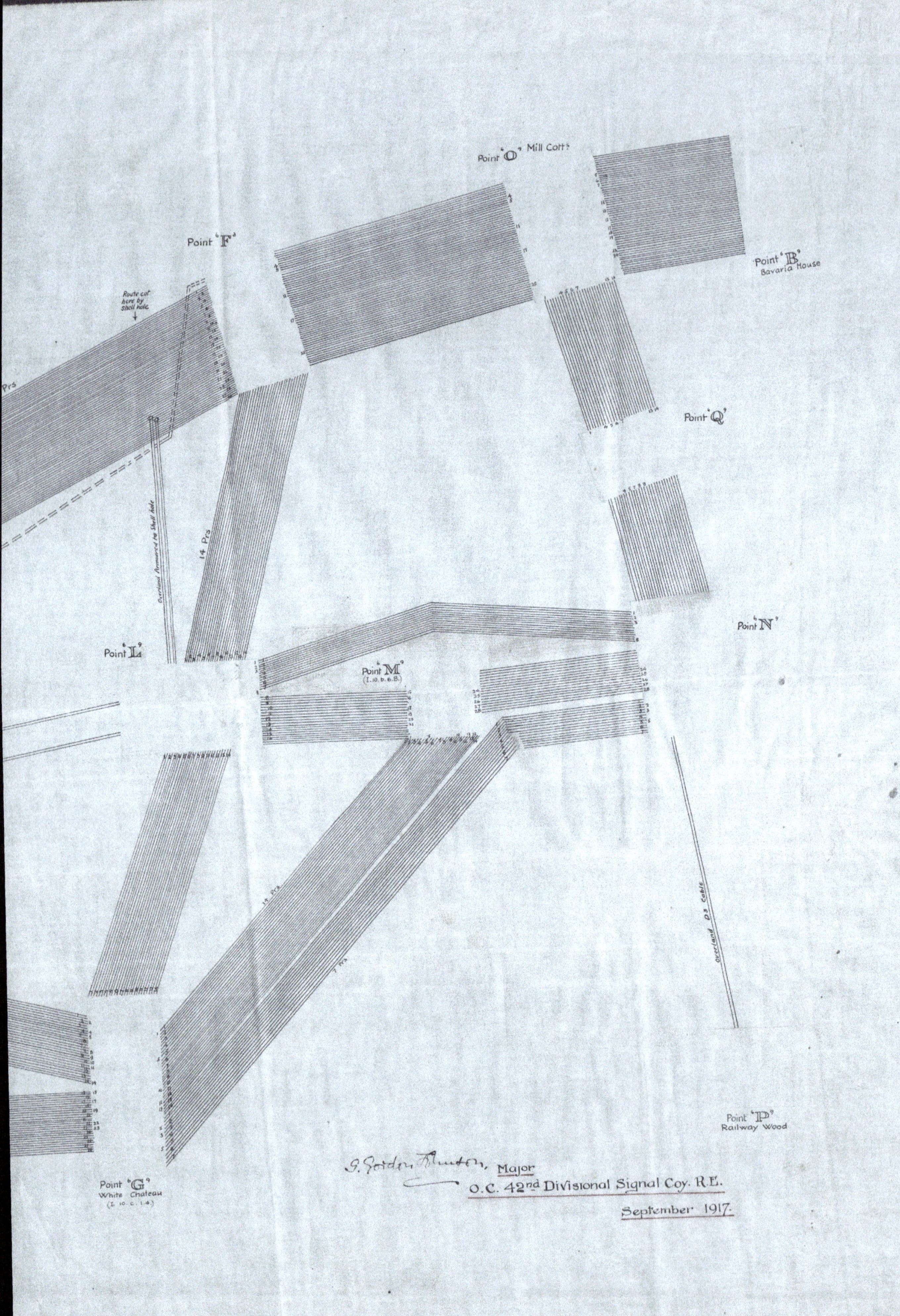
Point 'O' Mill Cott^s
Point 'F'
Point 'B' Bavaria House
Route cut here by shell hole
Prs
Point 'Q'
Overland Drummond by Shell hole
14 Prs
Point 'N'
Point 'L'
Point 'M' (I. 10. b. 6. 8.)
Overland D3 Cable
Point 'P' Railway Wood
Point 'G' White Chateau (I. 10. c. 1. 4)
G. Gordon Munton, Major
O.C. 42nd Divisional Signal Coy. R.E.
September 1917.

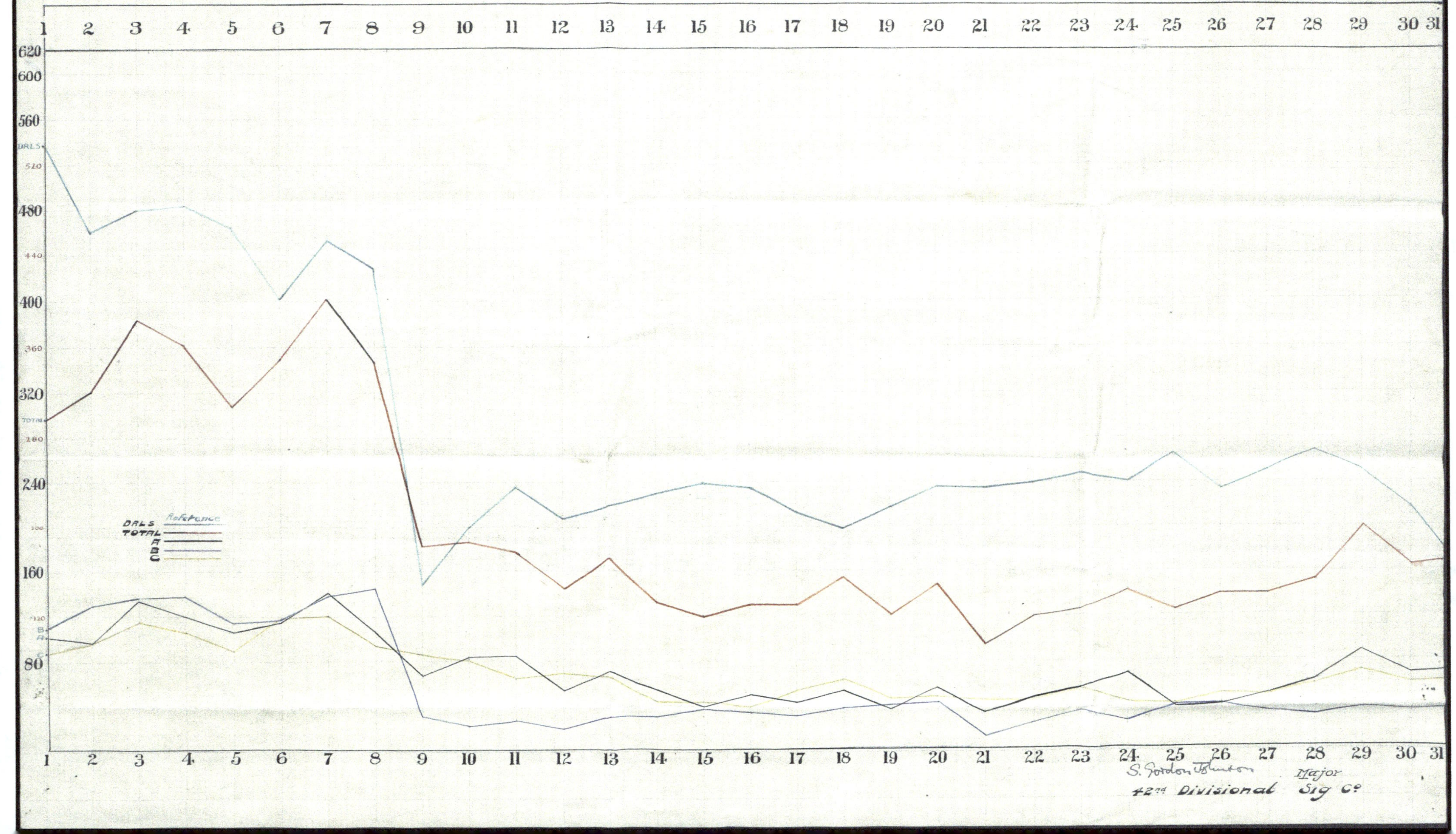
MESSAGE GRAPH.
42nd DIVISIONAL
JULY 1917.
SIGNAL COMPANY.
1 2 3 4 5 6 7 8 9 10 11 12 13 14 15 16 17 18 19 20 21 22 23 24 25 26 27 28 29 30 31
620
600
560
DRLS
520
480
440
400
360
320
TOTAL
280
240
200
160
120
B
A
C
80
Reference
DRLS
TOTAL
A
B
C
S. Gordon Blunton Major
42nd Divisional Sig Co

Secret

1-9

42

Vol 6

42nd Divisional Signal Co. {R.E.}

WAR DIARY.

Chapter 10.

August · 1917.

Instructions regarding War Diaries and Intelligence Summaries are contained in F. S. Regs., Part II. and the Staff Manual respectively. Title Pages will be prepared in manuscript.

WAR DIARY
or
~~INTELLIGENCE SUMMARY~~
(Erase heading not required.)

Army Form C. 2118.

Place	Date	Hour	Summary of Events and Information	Remarks and references to Appendices
			42nd (East Lancs) Divisional Signal Company R.E. (T.F.) Page1.	
			Reference Maps, FRANCE 1/100,000. LENS 11, BELGIUM AND FRANCE, Sheet 28, Edition 3.	
			CHAPTER 10. AUGUST 1917.	
ACHIET-le-PETIT.			From the 1st to the 19th of the month the Company, together with the Division, remained in "rest". Communication remained unchanged. The training described in Chapter 9 was continued.	
			A refresher Course was held at the School from the 10.8.17 to the 19.8.17 and a copy of the report sent to the units concerned is attached. (APPENDIX "A")	APPENDIX "A"
	20th		Orders received to move on the following day by march route, to ACHEUX and for an advance party of one officer and 10 other Ranks to entrain at ACHIET-LE-GRAND at 3.30 pm for WATOU, detraining at HOPOUTRE.	
BEAUCOURT	21st		Moved by march route to BEAUCOURT and bivouaced for two nights.	
	22nd		Additional advance party of one officer and 40 men by rail to PROVEN. Advance party arrived at WATOU and communication established to 19th Corps on existing line through Fifth Army Exchange at WATOU.	
			From this date until the 31st, the Company remained at WATOU, communication by	

2449 Wt. W14957/M90 750,000 1/16 J.B.C. & A. Forms/C.2118/12.

Instructions regarding War Diaries and Intelligence Summaries are contained in F. S. Regs., Part II. and the Staff Manual respectively. Title Pages will be prepared in manuscript.

WAR DIARY
or
~~INTELLIGENCE SUMMARY~~

(Erase heading not required.)

Army Form C. 2118.

Place	Date	Hour	Summary of Events and Information	Remarks and references to Appendices
			Page 2	
			telephone and telegraph (superimposed) being maintained by existing lines to Corps and all Brigades.	
WATOU	23rd		Remainder of Company by rail entrained at BEAUCOURT to PROVEN and thence by march route to WATOU.	
	27th		Orders received that the Division would relieve 15th Division and take over the right Sector of the 19th Corps front, East of YPRES.	
			An advance party of linemen were immediately sent to be attached to the 15th Divisional Signal Company in order to become thoroughly acquainted with the routes, test boxes etc. From this date until the relief was effected on the 31st inst every effort was made ~~made~~ to gain knowledge of the communication in the area mentioned.	
	31st		The Company moved by march route from WATOU to BRANDHOEK, moving into billets occupied by the 15th Divisional Signal Company. The relief was effected at 10 a.m.	
			S. Gordon [signature] Major 9.9.17. O.C. 42nd Divisional Signal Co. R.E.	

2449 Wt. W14957/M90 750,000 1/16 J.B.C. & A. Forms/C.2118/12.

Army Form C. 2118.

Instructions regarding War Diaries and Intelligence Summaries are contained in F. S. Regs., Part II. and the Staff Manual respectively. Title pages will be prepared in manuscript.

WAR DIARY
or
~~INTELLIGENCE SUMMARY.~~

(*Erase heading not required.*)

Place	Date	Hour	Summary of Events and Information	Remarks and references to Appendices

Page 3.

APPENDICES TO THIS DIARY.

(A). Report of Refresher Course at Signal School.

(B). Honours and Awards.

(C). Weekly Strengths, Casualties, and Reinforcements.

(D). Monthly Message Chart.

S. Gordon Johnston
Major.
O.C. 42nd Divisional Signal Co. R.E.

9.9.17.

1577 Wt. W10791/1773 500,000 1/15 D. D. & L. A.D.S.S./Forms/C. 2118.

WAR DIARY.

APPENDIX "A" AUGUST 1917.

O.C.

Herewith Signalling certificates for the men of your unit who attended the 5th (Refresher) Course at the Divisional Signal School.

I wish to bring the following observations to your notice in connection with this course at the Signal School.

1. The Morse key sending (either buzzer, sounder, or lamp) both as regards style and spred, varies very greatly among men who reach approximately the same standard of morse reading. This can only be accounted for by ignorance on the part of Battalion Signalling Officers of the importance of careful sending.

2. The shutter sending on the whole was good, very few men seemed to have any difficulty in manipulating it at eight words per minute and in sending well at that speed.

3. Although the men who came to the School could nearly all read accurately, a short visual message, they could not keep this speed up unless the sending shutter or lamp was very near. There was considerable improvement in this direction towards the end of the course. I do not think it is generally realised that it is the Signallers' eyesight which gets "out of practice" under the conditions of trench warfare. I am given to understand that several Battalions practice their signallers with short visual messages. Although most messages now usually sent while operations are in progress are short, this practising with short messages is unsound.

4. Many of the men were keen and attentive listeners to the lectures. Battalion signalling officers should encourage their more intelligent men to take an interest in the technical working of their instruments.

5. The standard of handwriting varied from excellent to atrocious. The block capitals made by some men were nearly as illegible as their handwriting. Neatness and care in writing the message and completing the message form should be insisted upon by all signal officers, and men should practice in handwriting and be taught to write a good, clear, round, hand.

6. Signal Officers should keep careful not of any changes which are from time to time made in signalling procedure. Many of the men were ignorant of the latest alterations.

7. Most of the men were careless of instruments. The importance of careful handling of signalling apparatus deserves more attention. This should be constantly impressed upon the men.

S. Gordon Elmston

Major.

9.9.17. O.C. 42nd Divisional Signal Co. R.E.

SIGNALLING CERTIFICATE.
42nd Divisional School of Signalling.

No.........Rank............Name.........................

Regiment.....................attended the Fifth Course (Refresher)

at the Divisional School from 10.8.17.to 19.8.17. and has a.......

......................knowledge of:-

Theory of Signalling.
Connecting of Instruments.
Fullerphone, D.3 Telephone, Magneto phone.
Power buzzer and buzzer unit.
Cable laying, jointing and labelling.
Office wiring and organisation.
The Message form.
Daylight Lamp and Signalling Shutter.

He has passed a reading and sending test as under:-

Sending on	Receiving on
Buzzer........words per minute.	Buzzer.........words per minute.
Lamp.........words per minute.	Lamp...........words per minute.
Shutter.......words per minute.	Shutter........words per minute.

S. Gordon Thurston
Major.

9.9.17. O.C. 42nd Divisional Signal Co. R.E.

B

WAR DIARY.

APPENDIX. "B". AUGUST 1917.

HONOURS AND AWARDS.

NIL.

S. Gordon Johnston
Major.
O.C. 42nd Divisional Signal Co. R.E.

9.9.17.

WAR DIARY.

APPENDIX. "C". AUGUST 1917.

WEEKLY STRENGTHS, CASUALTIES, REINFORCEMENTS.

Strength.	Week ending August 4th.	7 Officers	258 Other Ranks.
	" " " 11th	7 "	258 " "
	" " " 18th	7 "	282 " "
	" " " 25th	8 "	280 " "

Casualties.

Killed.	Nil.
Wounded.	Nil.
Sick.	5 O.R. to hospital.
England for Commission.	1 O.R.
Total.	6 O.R.

Reinforcements.

From hospital	6 O. R.
From Depot.	Nil.
" East Lancs. R.F.A.	1 Officer.
" 35th Division.	1 " 1 O.R.
Total.	2 Officers, 7 Other Ranks.

S. Gordon Johnston

Major.

9.9.17. O.C. 42nd Divisional Signal Co. R.E.

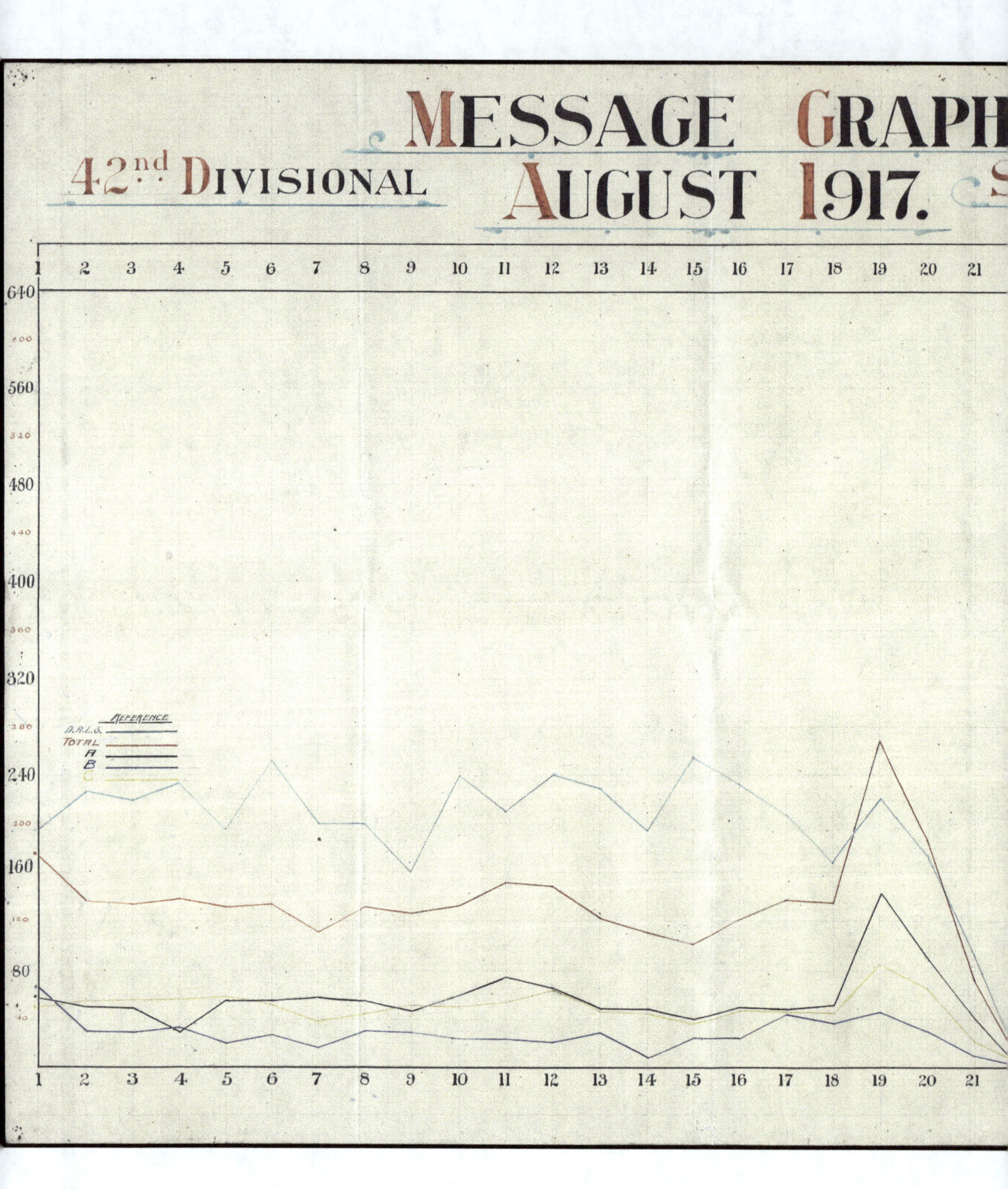
MESSAGE GRAPH
42nd DIVISIONAL
AUGUST 1917.
1 2 3 4 5 6 7 8 9 10 11 12 13 14 15 16 17 18 19 20 21
640
600
560
520
480
440
400
360
320
280
240
200
160
120
80
40
REFERENCE
D.R.L.S.
TOTAL
A
B
C

MESSAGE GRAPH.

AUGUST 1917. SIGNAL COMPANY.

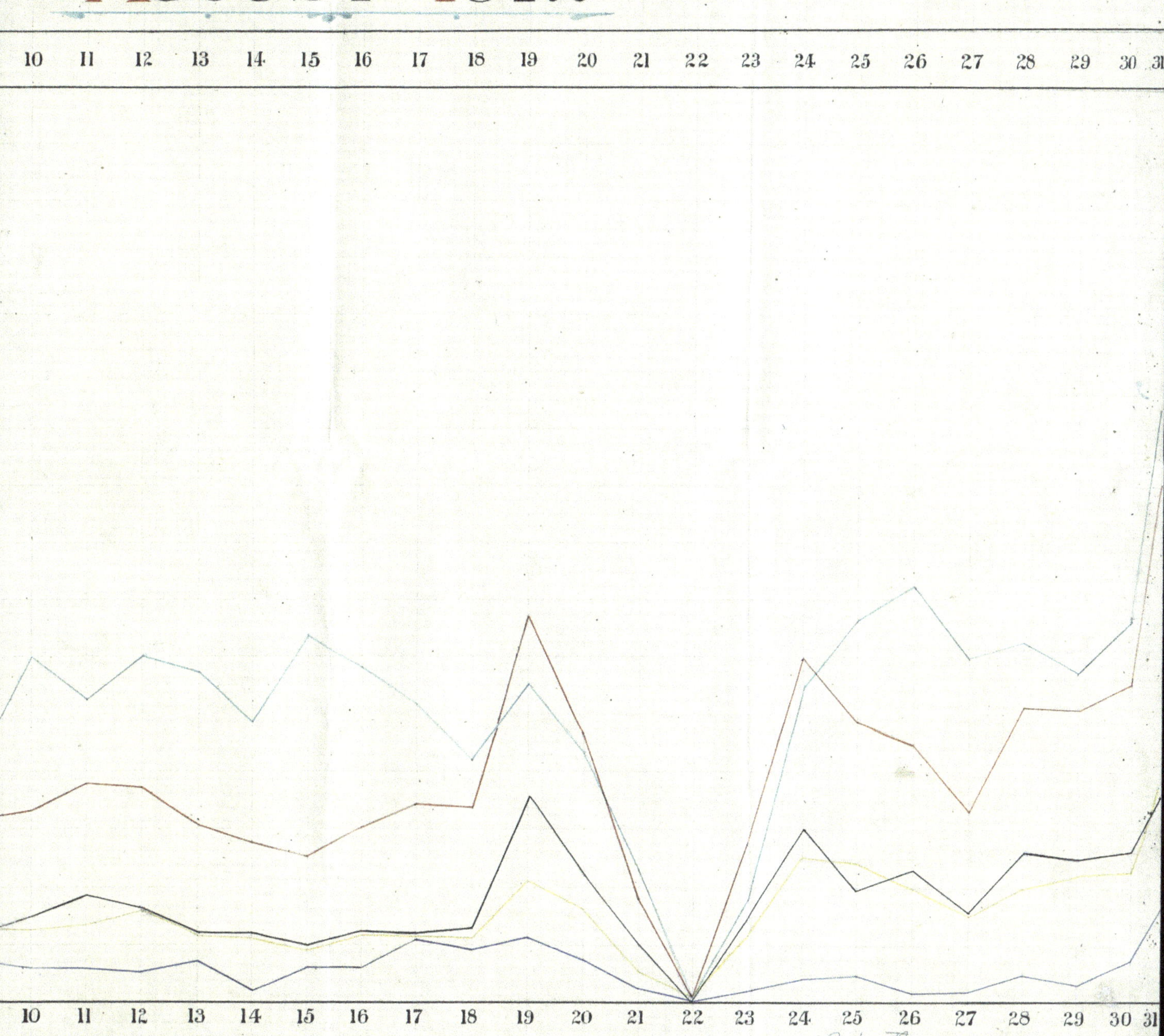

WAR DIARY.

APPENDIX "D"

AUGUST 1917.

MONTHLY MESSAGE CHART.

3

Vol 7

~~Secret~~ Confidential

42nd Divisional Signal Coy

WAR DIARY.

Chapter XI

September 1917.

Instructions regarding War Diaries and Intelligence Summaries are contained in F. S. Regs., Part II. and the Staff Manual respectively. Title Pages will be prepared in manuscript.

WAR DIARY
or
~~INTELLIGENCE SUMMARY~~
(Erase heading not required.)

Army Form C. 2118.

Place	Date	Hour	Summary of Events and Information	Remarks and references to Appendices
			42nd (East Lancs.) Divisional Signal Company R.E. (T.F.) Page 1.	
			Reference Maps BELGIUM and FRANCE Sheets 27 & 28 BELGIUM Sheet 11.	
			CHAPTER XI. SEPTEMBER 1917.	
Brandhoek.	1.9.17 to 18.9.17.		The Division held the line East of YPRES, with rear Headquarters at BRANDHOEK (H.7c 7.8, Sheet 28) and battle Headquarters at the RAMPARTS, YPRES (I.8.d.0.8). Communicat-ions during this period were as per diagram attached. (APPENDIX "A"). Notes on communications attached (APPENDIX"B")	APPENDIX "A" APPENDIX "B"
	13th		Warning Orders received that the 9th Division would shortly relieve the 42nd.	
Poperinghe	18th		Relieved at 10.0 a.m. by the 9th Divisional Signal Company. Moved by march route to POPERINGHE (G.1.d.6.4, sheet 28). Communications established to Corps and Brigades on existing Corps and Army Lines. Move in accordance with Order No. 4 attached.	
Poperinghe.	21st		Cable detachments and all horse transport moved to WINNEZEELE (J.17a central, sheet 27) and thence under orders of G.O.C. 126th Infantry Brigade to WORMHOUDT (C 16b central sheet 27) and bivouacked for the night.	
Poperinghe.	"		Orders received that the Division would leave the Fifth Army area for the Fourth Army area.	

2449 Wt. W14957/M90 750,000 1/16 J.B.C. & A. Forms/C.2118/12.

Instructions regarding War Diaries and Intelligence Summaries are contained in F. S. Regs., Part II. and the Staff Manual respectively. Title Pages will be prepared in manuscript.

WAR DIARY
or
~~INTELLIGENCE SUMMARY~~
(Erase heading not required.)

Army Form C. 2118.

Place	Date	Hour	Summary of Events and Information	Remarks and references to Appendices
WORMHOUDT	22nd		Transport moved from WORMHOUDT to LA PANNE BAINS, arriving at 10.15 p.m.	
POPERINGHE.	"		Signal Office closed at 7 a.m. and opened at LA PANNE BAINS (W.15.a.7.9 sheet 11) at 1 p.m. Company moved by bus and lorry. Lines to Corps and Brigades on existing Corps and Army lines. Move in accordance with Order No. 5 attached.	
LA PANNE BAINS.	23rd.		Orders received that the 42nd Division would shortly relieve the 66th Division in the NIEUPORT BAINS sector and COXYDE BAINS Coast Defence sector.	
"	24th		Advance party of linemen sent to 66th Divisional Signal Company to learn all the lines and test points.	
" ST IDESBALDE.	25th		Advance Signal Office staff left by lorry at 7.0 a.m. Office closed at LA PANNE at 10 a.m. and opened at ST. IDESBALDE at the same hour. Move in accordance with Order No. 6 attached.	
			Communications were as per diagram attached (APPENDIX"C")	APPENDIX "C"
			APPENDICES TO THIS DIARY. (A) Diagram of Communications. (B) Notes on communications. (C) Diagram of communications.	

2449 Wt. W14957/M90 750,000 1/16 J.B.C. & A. Forms/C.2118/12.

Army Form C. 2118.

Instructions regarding War Diaries and Intelligence Summaries are contained in F. S. Regs., Part II. and the Staff Manual respectively. Title pages will be prepared in manuscript.

WAR DIARY
or
~~INTELLIGENCE SUMMARY~~.
(Erase heading not required.)

Hour, Date, Place	Summary of Events and Information	Remarks and references to Appendices
	Page 3. APPENDICES TO THIS DIARY (CONTD) (D) Honours and Awards. (E) Weekly strengths, Casualties and Reinforcements. (F) Monthly Message Chart. ARoberts Capt RE for Major. O.C. 42nd Divisional Signal Co. R.E.	

(73989) W4141—463. 400,000. 9/14. H.&J.Ltd. Forms/C. 2118/10.

SECRET. Copy No. .

42nd DIVISIONAL SIGNAL COMPANY. R.E.

ORDER No.6.

Reference sheet Dunkerque I.A.

1. The 42nd Division will relieve the 66th Division on the 25th of September.

2. The Signal Office at LA PANNE will close at 10 a.m. and open at ST. IDESBALDE at the same hour.

3. The Company will take over the office and billets vacated by the 66th Divisional Signal Company. Sgt. Harrison will act as billeting N.C.O.

4. An advance Signal Office staff under Sgt. Ellwood will leave for the new Headquarters by lorry at 7 a.m. The second lorry will leave at the same time. Lorries will all be loaded over-night under the supervision of the C.Q.M.S.

5. Cable detachments and all horse transport will leave at 8 a.m.

6. N.C.O's and men riding bicycles will leave at 8 a.m. under 2/Cpl Campbell.

7. D.R's will leave under arrangements to be made by Sgt. Harrison.

8. The lorries will return and leave again at 9 a.m. One lorry will take the Orderly Room stores and staff, Officers' valises and mess stores. Officers' batmen and Cook will travel by this lorry.

9. The School will proceed by march route at 8 a.m.

A J Ellis

2/Lieut. R.E.

24.9.17. for O.C. 42nd Divisional Signal Co. R.E.

Issued by orderly at p.m. 24.9.17.

Copy No.1. T.O.
2. A.O.
3. C.S.M. & C.Q.M.S.
4. Signalmaster.
5. Sgt. Harrison.
6. File.
7. Wardiary.

AR.

SECRET. Copy No.

42nd DIVISIONAL SIGNAL COMPANY. R.E.

ORDER No.5.

Ref. Sheets. N.W. Europe, Sheet 1 and part of 4.
Dunkerque. 1.a.

1. The 42nd Division will relieve the 66th Division. Relief in front line XV Corps to be completed by 10 a.m. 26th September.

2. The Signal Office at Poperinghe will close at 7 a.m. 22nd September and open at LA PANNE at 1 p.m. 22nd September.

3. An advance Signal Office staff under Sgt. Ellwood will leave for the new Headquarters by lorry 12 noon 21st September. The second lorry will be loaded and leave at the same time. Sgt Harrison will detail two D.R's to proceed to the new Headquarters leaving at 12 noon 21st September.

4. P.E.L. set, Orderly Room stores and staff, Officers' valises and mess stores will be loaded on the P.E.L. lorry and leave at 7 a.m. on the 22nd inst. Officers batmen and cook will travel on this lorry.

5. All remaining stores will be loaded on the Company lorry and one lorry from the D.S.C. at 6 a.m. Both lorries will leave at 7 a.m.

6. 70 N.C.O's and men, including the School, under Sgt Grunwell will leave by lorries assembling outside D.H.Q. at 6.30 a.m.

7. N.C.O's and men riding bicycles will leave at 7 a.m. under Cpl Meakins.

8. D.R's by road under Sgt. Harrison.

[signature]

2/Lieut. R.E.

21.9.17. for O.C. 42nd Divisional Signal Co. R.E.

Issued by orderly at p.m. 21.9.17.

Distribution as follows:-

Copy No. 1. T.O.
2. A.O.
3. C.S.M. & C.Q.M.S.
4. Signalmaster.
5. Sgt. Harrison.
6. File.
7. War diary.

[initials]

SECRET. Copy No. 6.

42nd DIVISIONAL SIGNAL COMPANY. R.E.

ORDER No. 4.

Ref. Sheet. 28.

1. The 42nd Division will be relieved by the 9th Division on the 18th September and move to the POPERINGHE area.

2. The Company will take over the office and billets vacated by the 9th Divisional Signal Company at POPERINGHE at 10 a.m. 18th September.

3. An advance Signal Office Staff under L/Cpl Strathdee will leave for the new H.Q. by lorry at 6 p.m. 17th September.

4. Sgt. Harrison will detail two D.R's to proceed at 8 a.m. 18th September.

5. Both Company lorries will be loaded and proceed at 7 a.m. 18th September. They will return loaded with 9th Divisional Signal Company Stores. One will then go to the Ramparts to fetch the stores and staff and proceed to the new H.Q.

At 10.15 a.m. the other lorry will take the P.E.L. set, Office valises and Signal Office staff to POPERINGHE.

6. All remaining stores will be loaded on the 9th Divisional Signal Company lorry arriving 9 a.m.

7. The cable Sections and horse transport will move off at 8.30 a.m. 18th September.

8. The Signal Office relief with the 9th Divisional Signal Company at BRANDHOEK, RAMPARTS and POPERINGHE will be effected at 10 a.m. 18th September.

9. The School will move with the Company.

A.Ellis

2/Lieut. R.E.

16.9.17. for O.C. 42nd Divisional Signal Co. R.E.

Issued by orderly at p.m. on 16.9.17.

Distribution as follows:-

Copy No. 1. T.O.
2. A.O.
3. C.S.M.
4. Signalmaster.
5. Sgt. Harrison.
6. File.
7. War diary.

A.R.

Appendix. A
Diagram A

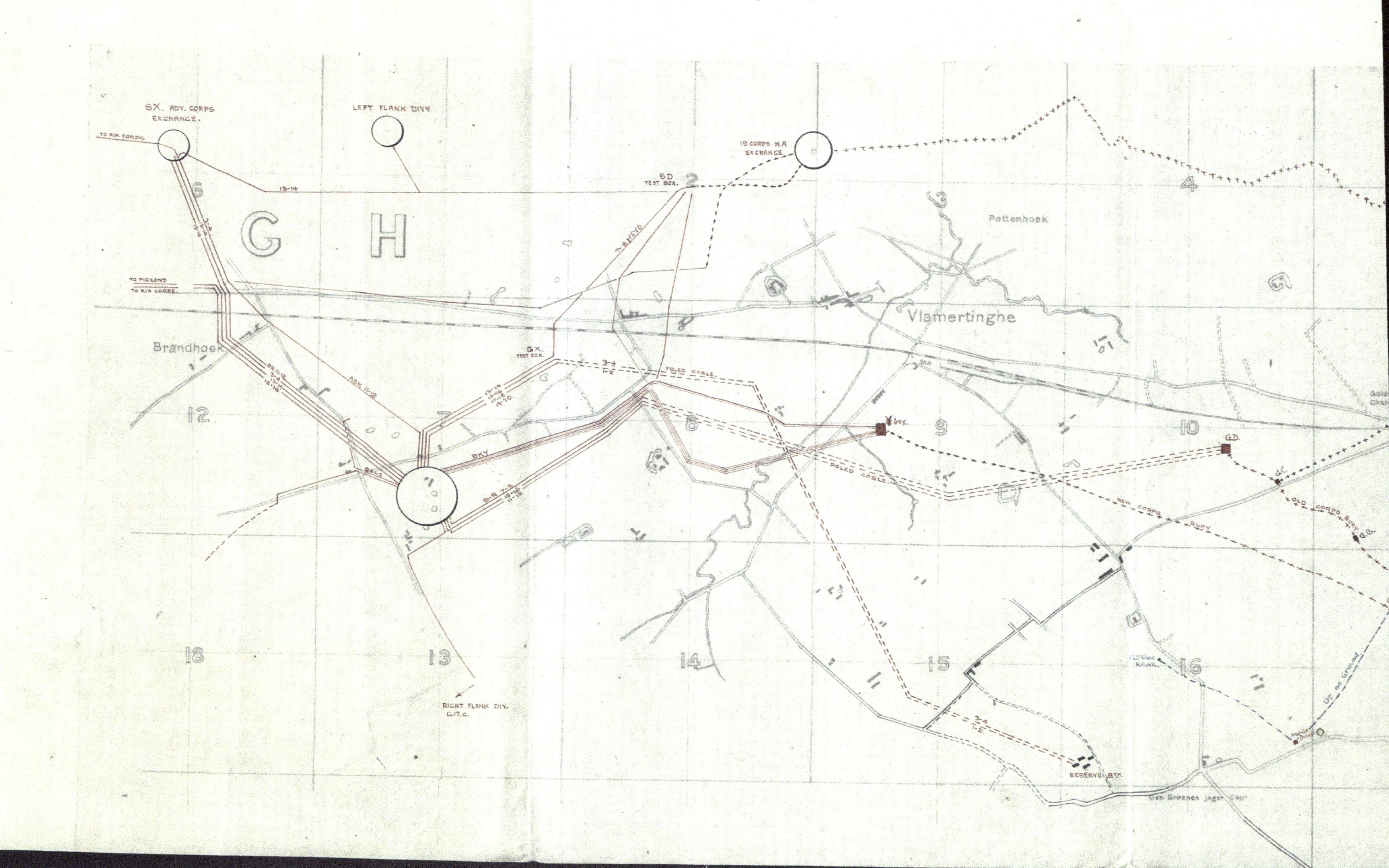

SX. ADV. CORPS EXCHANGE.
TO XIX CORPS
LEFT FLANK DIVN
18 CORPS H.A EXCHANGE
5D TEST BOX.
13-14
G
H
TO PIGEONS
TO XIX CORPS
Brandhoek
G.X. TEST BOX.
POLED CABLE.
Vlamertinghe
Pottenhoek
ABK 11-12
BKY
RIGHT FLANK DIV. G.17.c.
NEW CORPS BURY
OLD CORPS BURY
RESERVE BTN.
Den Groenen Jager Cabt
12
13
14
15
16
18
8
9
10
3
4
6

DIAGRAM 'A'
Menin Gate
Cloth Hall
Ecole
Goldfish Chateau
Belgian Battery Corner
Belgian Chau
Zillebeke
Vijverbeek
Old Corps Bury

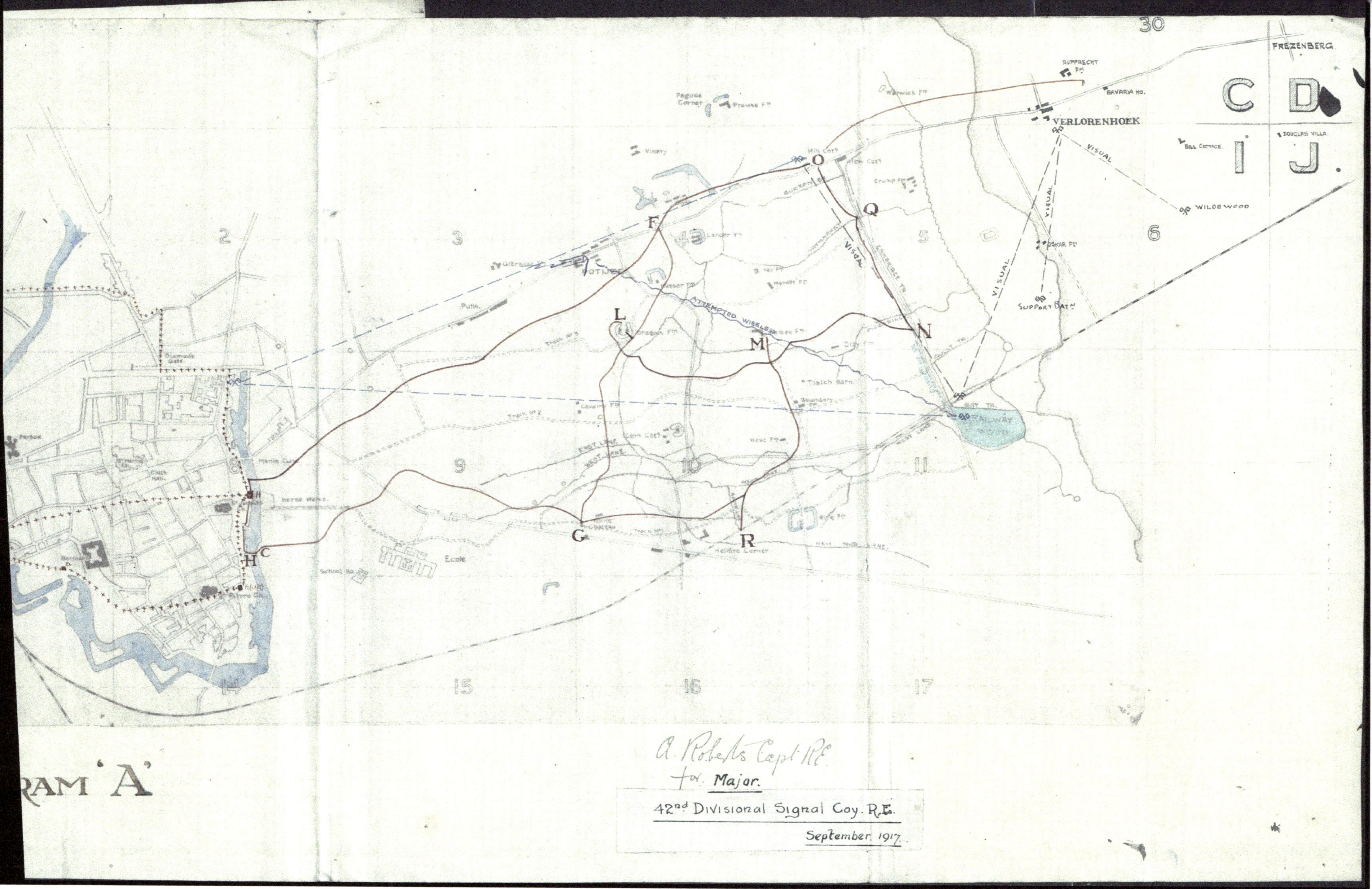

RAM 'A'
FREZENBERG
C
D
I
J
30
VERLORENHOEK
BAVARIA HO.
RUPPRECHT Fm
DOUGLAS VILLA
BILL COTTAGE
WILDEWOOD
VISUAL
SUPPORT BATN
OSKAR Fm
RAILWAY WOOD
ATTEMPTED WIRELESS
POTIJZE
Pagoda Corner
Prowse Fm
Vinery
Menin Gate
Herne Works
School Ho.
Ecole
Prison
Cloth Hall
Helfire Corner
Thatch Barn
Boundary Fm
Digy Fm
Crump Fm
Lancer Fm
Dragon Fm
Cork Cott
East Lane
West Lane
New Mud Lane
Putts
Gibraltar
Track No. 3
Track No. 2
Track No. 1
O
Q
N
F
L
M
G
R
H
C
2
3
5
6
9
10
11
14
15
16
17
A. Roberts Capt RE
for. Major.
42nd Divisional Signal Coy. R.E.
September 1917.

Diagram A.

Signal Co. R.E.

Capt.

Signal Co. R.E.

Signal Co. R.E.

Appendix "B".

NOTES ON COMMUNICATIONS IN THE YPRES SECTOR.

When this Division relieved the 15th Division in the Sector immediately East of YPRES the communications in the forward area were found to be in a very poor condition.

A. The buried cable system was totally inadequate, as regards the number of buried circuits, to provide communication for the units and Headquarters in the area, and to provide alternative routes for us use in case of breakdown. The cable was buried chiefly to a very small depth. Tha vaerage depth was about 3 ft. 6 ins. and was nowhere more than 5 ft. The area was very heavily shelled and interruptions were frequent with the result that the many joints in the cables rendered them leaky. The poor insulation resistance of all the lines was further accentuated by the very wet nature of the ground. Only in a very few places was it possible to dif a trench more than 3 ft. deep without raching a waterlogged sub-soil. In many places the buried cable consisted of D.5 cable hurriedly put down and buried to join up the ends of a route which had been broken by shell fire. Although probably the routes were well planned when first made the continual movement of batteries from one position to another often involved the fact that a battery took up a position on top of a buried cable route. The heavy local shelling which followed almost invariably broke down the route. It was also found that in those cases where a heavy battery took up a position near a route the repeated concussion due to the firing of the guns was sufficient to strain the cable and cause insulation trouble.

Diagram A attached.

The Divisional communications on the buried cable system can be considered in two parts.

1. The communication from rear Divisional Headquarters at BRANDHOEK to advanced Divisional H.Q. in the YPRES RAMPARTS.

There were two main routes, (A) The Old Corps Bury which, starting at BRANDHOEK as airline went underground at G.D. test box and was buried to Y (RAMPARTS) box and thence by bury to H test point in the RAMPARTS. (B) The new Corps Bury from BRANDHOEK on the B.K.Y. and A.Y. airline routes was buried from Y box to the H test point in the RAMPARTS. From H test box a sufficient number of pairs were led into the advanced Divisional H.Q. (a distance of 40 yards through a tunnel) to extend the lines into the Signal Office.

Both of these were good buries which were seldom interrupted and which gave practically no trouble. Speech and magneto ringing were good through all the pairs, and superimposed sounder working gave no trouble if the circuit was not used continuously. For continuous working arrangements were made to change over from one of two superimposed circuits to the other about every half hour to avoid "fatigue". If this was not done the Morse Signals were "split" and poor operation resulted.

2. In front of the RAMPARTS the cable system was not so good. There were two sections of the buried scheme. The routes G-H, G-L, L-M, M-N,

See Diagram A attached.

and Q-O were maintained by the Division in the sector. These with the exception of M-N and N-Q-O has been buried for some considerable time (in the case of H-G and G-L nearly 18 months) and were in poor condition. They were not, however, subject to interruption and were kept "through" without great difficulty. Magneto ringing however was not possible through any of them and speech was poor. A sounder was successfully worked through a circuit running from H through G and L to M except in wet weather when the leakage became too great. This was the communication with the Brigade at M (James Farm) and was fairly satisfactory.

2. When the Right Brigade moved to RAILWAY WOOD on 3rd September 1917

France 1/40,000 sheet 28 11.b. central

the circuits from the advanced Divisional H.Q. to this Brigade had to be extended from M through M N route and from N by about 500 yards of ground cable to the new Brigade H.Q. Sounder working and magneto ringing then became impossible while speech was very poor. The Brigade H.Q. itself was usually heavily shelled and the over-ground circuits into it often cut. The arrangement described below of a Fullerphone working with a powerful sending battery provided satisfactory telegraphic communication with this Brigade as long as the circuit was not totally interrupted. The other Section of the

See Diagram A attached.

buried cable system consisted of the routes H-F, F-O, O-B, and B-D and the branch route F-L. These were newer routes and were in much better condition than the older ones. They were maintained by the Corps in that sector of the line. The route H-F ran however through an area to the South of the YPRES-POTIJE road in which there were many battery positions. As a result, the route was badly damaged shortly after its completion and could not be repaired. The portion F-Owas however a good route and it was possible to maintain circuits via H-G, G-L, L-F, and F-O from the advanced Divisional H.Q. to the Left Brigade at O. (MILL COT) over which ringing and speaking and superimposed sounder working were normally fairly satisfactory. Lateral communication between the Brigades was provided by a pair from O (MILL COT) through O-Q and Q-N routes and from N by a pair of overland cables to RAILWAY WOOD. The number of pairs used for communication from Divisional H.Q. to advanced Divisional H.Q. and from advanced Divisional H.Q. to the Brigades and for Artillery communications are shown on the Diagram.

See Diagram B attached.

The necessity for some more sensitive telegraph instrument than the ordinary S.C. set was felt as soon as the poor quality of the insulation of the lines became evident. An ordinary S.C set therefore was connected to the line through the ordinary transformer and a battery of about 30 cells used for sending. The leads on the set to t the sounder were disconnected underneath the instrument and in its place a Fullerphone was connected as the receiving instrument. This arrangement, by which a battery of 30 cells was used for sending to a Fullerphone, would work satisfactorily through a line which was so leaky that even Buzzer Signals were very faint.

The forward portions of the Corps buried route (i.e O-B, & B-D) were not buried more than 4 ft. deep and consequently were very liabl to interruption. Most of the lines in these "buries" were in use by artillery and Infantry Brigades and kept through for a great portion of the time.

The Artillery Divisional and Brigade telephone communications depended on the same buried cable scheme as the Infantry Divisional and Brigade communications. A forward battery exchange was established at a point known as E K 30(I.3.d.7.3) from which lines ran the various batteries many of which were in the immediate neighbourhood POTIJE.

The Artillery Brigades themselves were in the RAMPARTS, there being in all 7 Brigades R.F.A. under the control of the Divisional Artillery. The batteries of two Brigades were connected to E K 30 exchange from where lines on the buried cable routes were provided backwards to the RAMPARTS and forwards to F.O.O's and liaison officers. Another Brigade had similar forward exchange at point N from which lines to the batteries overland and lines to the RAMPARTS on the buried system from N were provided. Each of the other Brigades had a similar arrangement..As however the battery positions were continuously being changed no diagram of communications is given here.

B. Wireless, in the front area was not possible owing to the impossibility of maintaining aerials. Various arrangements of ground antennae with Trench W/T sets and also a special ground antennae set were tried but without success.

C. Power Buzzers and Amplifiers, worked extremely well in the forward areas over distances up to 1500 yards . A Diagram(C) is attached showing the stations established.

See Diagram C Attached.

D. The visual scheme was poor and efforts were made to improve it. It was found after several tries that it was possible to establish a central visual station on the Northern end of the RAMPARTS from which communication with both MILL COT and RAILWAY WOOD was possible. A station was accordingly arranged at that point (I.8.b.1.7) and lamp positions with properly aligned tubes and head cover for operators built. This station was a complete success and did excellent work.

Reference France 1/40,000 sheet 28

Each of the Brigades in the front line used visual signalling with success. It was however often impossible to maintain stations owing to the heavy shell fire. One Battalion Signalling officer was unfortunately killed while attempting to operate a visual station at SQUARE FARM.

Visual signalling was also used by the Artillery as an emergency means of communication from F.O.O's. A station at GREY RUIN communicating wiyh another at MILL COT was used for this purpose.

E. Pigeons were extremely useful particularly when an attack was taking place. They provided often the only means of communication with the forward Infantry posts.

F. Runners routes and relay posts were established from Brigade H.Q. forwards to Battalions and Companies. The casualties to runners were less than could have been expected.

From advanced Divisional H.Q. to Brigade H.Q. Motor Cyclists were used in the day time and runners at night time. Four Despatch Rider Letter Services were sent forward daily in addition to many "Special" runs.

The following points raised in the above notes deserve attention in connection with any scheme of communication.

A. The Buried Cable System. When planning any system a sufficient number of pairs should be buried to provide for any future operations which may take place in the sector. Usually when offensive operations are decided upon there is not time to make a proper system with the result that routes are hurriedly buried, probably only to a very shallow depth. The faults and breaks which develop as soon as operations begin cause much confusion and congestion.

The siting of the routes should be very carefully done.

It is not usually possible to avoid battery positions but care can be taken to take the routes through ground where it seems unlikely that batteries will take up positions. It is always inadvisable to take the route along or close to and parallel with a road. Any road is certain to be shelled more or less heavily.

The route should be taken at least 150 yards and if possible 250 yards from the road. The strain on a route due to its passing close to a battery and being subject to concussion should be remembered in connection with the choice of cable to be buried.

Lead covered cable is quite useless where there is much firing unless it is deeply buried or is in very stiff ground.

B. Wireless cannot be pushed very far forward owing to the impossibility of maintaining an aerial in heavily shelled localities

Any system of forward wireless which is to operate under these conditions must be able to work with a shorter and lower aerial than that of the ordinary 50 Watt "trench" set.

C. Amplifiers and Power Buzzers. The success of any system of Amplifiers depends to a very great extent on the regularity of a supply of fresh accumulators. If this is not assured and the care of the batteries is not in charge of technical personnel the service given by the system will not be satisfactory. A Battalion signaller put in charge of a Power Buzzer station is very apt to regard discharged accumulators as he would exhausted dry cells and, unless he is carefully supervised, will fail ti return discharged batteries to the rear for re-charging.

D. Visual Signalling system is always worth establishing. In many cases when it seems impossible to get communication between two points owing to intervening obstacles a line will be found from one station to the other if the attempt is persevered in. The stations having been fixed it is worth while spending a considerable amount of labour on the proper construction of the stations with properly aligned sighting tubes and with head cover for the signaller, more particularly the rear stations, owing to their having in an emergency to signal forward.

E. Pigeons. Many more pigeon messages are lost owing to ill-treatment of the birds than from any other cause. Too much insistence therefore cannot be laid on the necessity for training Battalion signallers to handle pigeons.

F. Runners. The success of any runner system depends on the proper organisation of the posts and relay points.

AWR.

Appendix "C"

DIAGRAM 'C'
Power Buzzers A Amplifiers
FRONT LINE 21st AUG 1917
Frezenberg
Frost House
Low Fm
Grey Ruin
Rupprecht Fm
Bavaria Ho
Outpost Buildings
Oder Ho
Verlorenhoek
Eitel Fritz Fm
The Stables
Oskar Fm
Bill Cottage
Douglas Villa
North Station Buildings
South Station Buildings
Rabbit Villa
Halt
Railway Dump
Wilde Wood
Sexton Ho
The Chapel
The Rectory
Kit & Kat
Red Lodge
Zieth Ho
Lake Fm
Bellewaarde Fm
Railway Wood
Wee Co
Y Wood
Gully Fm
Chump Fm
New Cott
Mill Cott
Warwick Fm
Cambridge Road
Crump Trench
Fleet Street
Ibex
Iberia
Idea Row
Identity
Idiot
Iguana
Cameron
Ice Lane
Avenue
Crescent
5th Field Survey Co R.E. (1449). 6.7.17.
Yards 500 400 300 200 100 0 500
Scale 1:10,
42nd Signal Co
Date
Ref. No.
Royal Engineers

WAR DIARY.

APPENDIX. D. SEPTEMBER 1917.

HONOURS AND AWARDS.

Under Authority delegated by the Field Marshal Commanding-in-Chief, the Corps Commander has awarded:-

THE MILITARY MEDAL

to

No. 444566 Cpl Fielding, J.

No. 444030 A/Cpl Barlow, F.

No. 444162 MC/Cpl Rawling. A.

No. 444270 Spr Porter, F.

No. 444434 " Whelan, M.

No. 443937 Pnr Mills, I.

Under Authority delegated by His Majesty the King, the Corps Commander has been pleased to award the

THE MILITARY MEDAL

to

No. 444309 Pnr Sinclair, J.

No. 444351 " Rawlin, E.

No. 251332 Pte G.V. Parkinson. (attached 42nd Divisional Signal Co. R.E.)

No. 300288 " J.B. Poke. (" " " ")

A Roberts. Capt R.E.

for Major.

3.10.17. O.C. 42nd Divisional Signal Co. R.E.

WAR DIARY.

APPENDIX. E. SEPTEMBER 1917.

WEEKLY STRENGTHS, CASUALTIES, REINFORCEMENTS.

Strength.

Week ending September 1st	8 officers	277 Other ranks.	
" " " 8th	9 "	259 " "	
" " " 15th	8 "	263 " "	
" " " 22nd	8 "	252 " "	
" " " 29th	8 "	254 " "	

Casualties.

	O.	O.R.
Killed.	Nil.	Nil.
Wounded or gassed	3 ø	43 X
Sick to hospital.	-	9
Injured to "	-	1
Total.	3	53

ø 2 Officers attached)
X 1 O.R. attached.)

Reinforcements.

	O.	O.R.
From Depot	-	19
From hospital.	-	4
" 5th Army.	1	-
Total.	1	23

A Roberts Capt R.E.
for Major.

3.10.17. O.C. 42nd Divisional Signal Co. R.E.

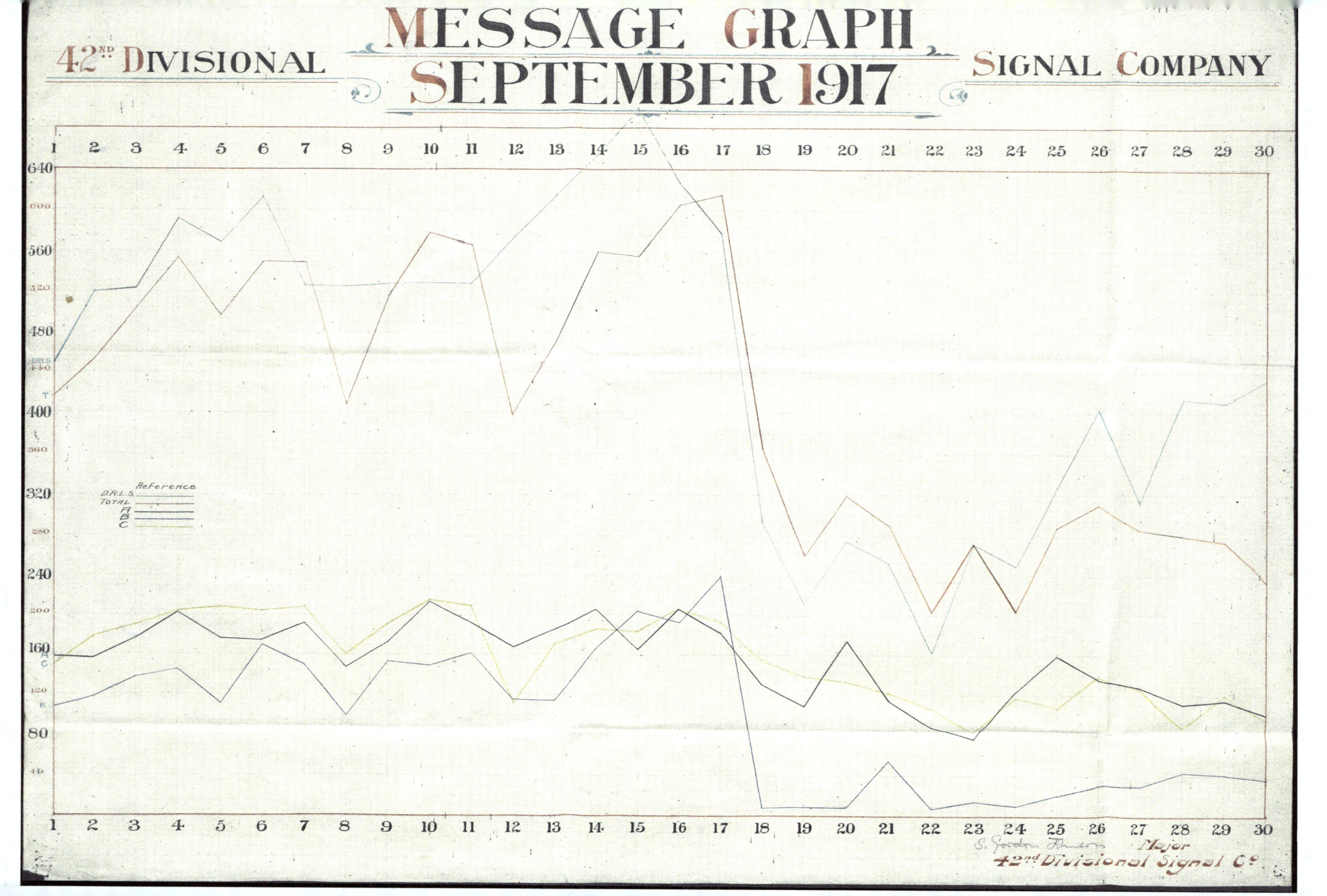

42ND DIVISIONAL
MESSAGE GRAPH
SEPTEMBER 1917
SIGNAL COMPANY
1 2 3 4 5 6 7 8 9 10 11 12 13 14 15 16 17 18 19 20 21 22 23 24 25 26 27 28 29 30
640
600
560
520
480
D.R.L.S. 440
T
400
360
320
280
240
200
160
A
C
120
B
80
40
Reference
D.R.L.S.
TOTAL
A
B
C
Major
42nd Divisional Signal Co.

Appendix "F

Secret. 17

Vol 8

War Diary.

42nd Div. Signal Coy. R.E.

October, 1917.

S. Gordon Blunson.

Major

O.C. 42nd Div. Signal Coy. R.E.

Chapter 12.

Instructions regarding War Diaries and Intelligence Summaries are contained in F. S. Regs., Part II. and the Staff Manual respectively. Title Pages will be prepared in manuscript.

WAR DIARY
or
~~INTELLIGENCE SUMMARY~~

(Erase heading not required.)

Army Form C. 2118.

Place	Date	Hour	Summary of Events and Information	Remarks and references to Appendices
			42nd (East Lancs.) Divisional Signal Company. R.E. (T.F).	
			CHAPTER XII. OCTOBER 1917. Reference maps BELGIUM. Oost-Dunkerke Sheet 11. " Sheet 12.	
ST. IDESBALDE	1.10.17 to 7.10.17.		The Division remained in the NIEUPORT BAINS SECTOR until relieved by the 41st Division on the 7.10.17 and on the same day relieved the 32nd Division in the NIEUPORT sector. Move in accordance with attached Order No. 7.	
COXYDE BAINS.	7.10.17.		Move completed.	
" "	7.10.17. to 31.10.17.		The Division held the NIEUPORT sector. Communications as per diagram attached. (APPENDIX A). For notes on communications see APPENDIX B.	APPENDIX A. APPENDIX B
			APPENDICES to this Diary.	
			(A) Diagram of communications. (B) Notes on communications. (C) Monthly message Chart. (D) Honours and Awards. (E) Weekly strengths, casualties and reinforcements.	

S. Gordon Johnston
Major.
O.C. 42nd Divisional Signal Co. R.E.

2449 Wt. W14957/M90 750,000 1/16 J.B.C. & A. Forms/C.2118/12.

SECRET.

42nd DIVISIONAL SIGNAL COMPANY. R.E.

ORDER No. 7.

Reference sheet, Coast Administrative Map 1/100,000.
Special maps Nos. 4 & 5 1/100,000.

1. The 42nd Division will be relieved by the 41st Division on the 7th October and will relieve the 32nd Division on the same day.

2. The Signal Office at ST. IDESBALDE will close at 10 a.m. and reopen at COXYDE BAINS at 11.0 a.m. 7th October.

3. The Company will take over the Office and billets vacated by the 32nd Divisional Signal Company. Sgt. Harrison will act as billeting N.C.O.

4. An advance Signal Office staff under L/Cpl Strathdee will leave for the new Headquarters at 2 p.m. on the 6th October.

5. Cable detachments and all horse transport will leave at 9a.m on the 7th October under 2/Lieut. Reid.

6. N.C.O's and men riding bicycles will leave at 9.30 a.m.

7. D.R's will leave under arrangements to be made by Sgt. Harrison.

8. Lorries will be loaded under the supervision of the C.Q.M.S. and make as many journeys as may be necessary. One lorry will collect Officers' valises and mess stores at 9.30 a.m. at the Officers' mess. The cook and batmen will travel by this lorry.

2/Lieut. R.E.

6.10.17. for O.C. 42nd Divisional Signal Co. R.E.

Issued by orderly at 2 p.m. 6.10.17.

Copy No.1 T.O.
2 A.O.
3 C.S.M.
4 C.Q.M.S.
5 Signalmaster.
6 Sgt. Harrison.
7 File.

COMMUNICATIONS.

A. TELEPHONE COMMUNICATIONS IN DIVISIONAL SECTOR. (DIAGRAM A.)

THE DIVISIONAL COMMUNICATIONS.

From Divisional Headquarters to No.1 Infantry Brigade Headquarters thereare 2 lines; to the No. 2 Infantry Brigade Headquarters, 4 lines by alternative routes.

To each Artillery Group (6 in all) there is one direct line.

In addition, there are 2 forward telephone exchanges, "PELICAN" (S.4.a.3.3) and "AMIRAL" (X.6.a.4.8). The former is connected by 3 lines, andthe latter by 4 lines on different routes to Divisional Headquarters. These two exchanges are connected together by 3 lines.

"PELICAN". There is 1 line from "PELICAN" exchange to the No.1 Infantry Brigade Headquarters, and 1 to the No. 1 Infantry Brigade Report Centre (R.C.) (H.34.d.6.4) and 2 lines to the No. 2 Infantry Brigade.

"AMIRAL". Has 1 line to No. 1 Infantry Brigade, and 1 to No 2 Infantry Brigade. In addition, there is a second small telephone exchange in the "AMIRAL" dugout to which are connected 3 lines to No. 1 Infantry Brigade Headquarters, and 3 lines to No. 1 Infantry Brigade Headquarters, and 3 line to No. 1 Infantry Brigade Report Centre.

Artillery Groups. In addition to the 1 direct line from Divisional Headquarters to each of the Artillery Groups, the following are provided for alternative communication:-

A. Group is connected by 2 lines to "PELICAN" exchange.

B,C,D, and E. Groups are connected to "AMIRAL" exchange.

B. Group by 2 lines.

C. Group by 1 line.

D. Growup by 2 lines.

E. Group by 1 line..

As far as possible these lines are on different routes from those of the direct lines to the Division.

The two forward exchanges "AMIRAL" and "PELICAN" thus provide alternative means of communication from Divisional Headquarters to Artillery Groups and Infantry Brigade Headquarters. They also provide lateral communication and alternative liaison lines from between Artillery Groups and Infantry Brigades.

<u>No. 1 Brigade Communications.</u> The lines from Brigade to Battalions are very long owing to the position of the Brigade Headquarters. A forward Brigade Report Centre, therefore, is established in the Belgian Railway Embankment at M.34.d.6.4. From this point, 3 lines are run to Right and 3 to the Left Battalion. The 3 lines in each case are not close together so that one shell cannot cut all three.

Communications with the Machine Gun Company is provided by a triple spur off the lines from the Report Centre to the Left Battalion.

There are two lines connecting the Brigade Report Centre to Brigade Headquarters by different routes. There are 3 lines from Report Centre to "AMIRAL" exchange, and 1 to "PELICAN". This Brigade has 3 lines to "AMIRAL", and 1 to "PELICAN".

<u>No. 2 Brigade Communications.</u> In this sector the chief difficulty is to maintain communication across the canal. The telephone cables have been taken away from the bridges and are now suspended over the canal at several different points. At four of the crossings, a length of rope is slung permenently across the canal from drums or coils at either end, so that a new cable can be quickly pulled over should one be broken by shell fire. The rope is similarly renewed by pulling a fresh length over by means of the cable. (The combination of rope and cable is used in place of two cables, because the rope is much less liable to breakage by concussion.)

From the Brigade Headquarters there are one line each to the Left, Right, and Support Battalions, and to the Artillery Liaison Officer on the Northern bank of the canal, one to the reserve

Battalion and Wireless Station at the LOCKS, and one to the Brigade O.P. in NIEUPORT.

The lines from the Brigade Headquarters across the canal are so arranged that 3 lines to the RUBBER HOUSE, and 3 lines to the OUTER REDAN cross the canal all at different places so as to diminish the possibility of a total interruption of communication with those points. The 3 lines to the OUTER REDAN are, however, joined together as one line before reaching the Battalion Headquarters, as the line there is less vulnerable and more easy to repair than at the canal crossing.

There are direct liaison lines from the Brigade exchange to B. and D. Artillery Groups.

Divisional Observation Post. There is a line from PELICAN exchange to the Divisional Observation Post near the FIVE BRIDGES.

This provides communication from the Observation Post to either Infantry Brigade or via "AMIRAL" exchange to any of the Artillery Groups.

S. Gordon Johnson
Maj.

B. VISUAL COMMUNICATIONS IN DIVISIONAL SECTOR.
(DIAGRAM B.)

The attached diagram shows the stations which have been established. The full lines indicate that the visual communication between two stations is in use, i.e. signalling lamps are kept permanently on the stations and signals exchanged at fixed intervals even if messages are not being sent by visual.

Dotted lines indicate communications which are not normally in use, but which have been tried and found satisfactory, and which are put into use for an hour or two for practice purposes at intervals of ten or fourteen days.

S. Gordon Johnson
Major.

C. WIRELESS COMMUNICATIONS.
(DIAGRAM C).

No. 1 Infantry Brigade Sector.

There are Wireless Stations at the following points:-

VACHE CREVEE (Right Battalion H.Q.).
C. Artillery Group.
VILLA JULIETTE (No. 1 Inf. Brigade H.Q.)

In addition, there is a station at the Divisional O.P. (FIVE BRIDGES).

Allthese stations work on the same system (continuous wave), and can communicate with one another. They provide communication from the Battalion in the line to the Brigade and the supporting Artillery.

No. 2 Infantry Brigade Sector.

In this Sector, the most forward wireless communication is by Power Buzzer and Amplifier.

The following stations are established:-

Forward station (Right Coy. Right Battalion).
OUTER REDAN (Right Battalion).
REDAN (Left Battalion)
LOCKS Signal Station (M.27.b.8.1).
B Artillery Group.

Each of these stations is equipped with a Power Buzzer and Amplifier, so that transmission forwards, as well as backwards, is provided. The "chain" is thus complete from front Company to supporting Artillery, each station communicating with the next one on either side of it.

There are spark wireless stations at:-

REDAN (Left Battalion).
LOCKS Signal Station (M.27.b.8.1).
B Artillery Group.
WULPEN ("Directing" Station)

These Stations all work on the "Spark" system, and on the same wave length, each being able to communicate with any other of them

The WULPEN Directing Station is in direct telephonic communication with Divisional Headquarters. Should this line be broken a station at "Q" Wireless Station, ST. IDESBALDE, can be manned; from the 'Q' Section Station, an Orderly has a short bicycle ride to Divisional Headquarters if the 'Q' Section direct buried telephone line is also broken.

The Station at the LOCKS is connected by telephone and Orderly with Headquarters No. 2 Infantry Brigade.

This system provides communication from Battalion to Brigade, and from Battalion or Brigade to Artillery as well as directly from each to Divisional Headquarters.

The Amplifier and Power Buzzer and spark wireless system "overlap" as regards the "REDAN" LOCKS, and B. Group Stations in order to provide for the possibility of breakdown of either system under heavy fire which may cut the earth leads of the former, or knock down the aerial of the latter system.

The Station at the REDAN is particularly liable to have its aerial broken.

S. Gordon Johnson
Major.

D. DESPATCH RIDERS AND RUNNERS.

Motor cyclists are used from Divisional Headquarters to No. 1 Infantry Brigade Headquarters and to all Groups of Artillery. Despatches to No. 2 Infantry Brigade Headquarters are carried to PELICAN by motor cyclist and thence to Brigade Headquarters by foot orderly.

For use in case of emergency, a motor-cyclist is stationed at No. 1 Infantry Brigade Headquarters, and a motor-cyclist and two runners at PELICAN for No. 2 Infantry Brigade Headquarters. No. 1 Infantry Brigade. uses its report centre (Belgian Railway Embankment, M.34.d.6.3) as a runner relay post. From Brigade Headquarters despatches are carried by cyclist to the Report Centre and thence by runner to the Headquarters of the Battalions in the line. Two cyclist and about 4 runners are stationed at the Report Centre. There is a runner relay post at M.35.b.8.3., which can be manned if necessary. No. 2 Infantry Brigade. uses runners from Brigade Headquarters direct to the Battalion Headquarters without relay posts as the distances between the headquarters are small. As far as possible, men who are swimmers are chosen for these runs so that they can cross the canal by swimming if the bridges are broken.

S. Gordon Johnson

Major.

E. PIGEONS.

Eight pigeons to No. 1 Infantry Brigade, and eight to No. 2 Infantry Brigade are sent up daily from the Corps Lofts.

There are 3 lofts, two in OOST DUNKERQUE, connected by telephone with No 1. Brigade Headquarters, and one in COXYDE BAINS, connected by Cyclist Orderly with Divisional Headquarters.

The lofts "relieve" one another in rotation, the number of pigeons sent up from each varying according to health and fitness of the birds.

The pigeons are sent up from the lofts in the morning or early afternoon for release during, or just before, sunset the next day.

In No. 1 Brigade, four birds each are sent to the Headquarters of the Battalions in the line for release there or for distribution to forward posts accordiggto the situation.

In No. 2 Brigade, two birds are usually kept at the left Battalion Headquarters for use in case of emergency, the remainder being sent to the two battalions in the line for distribution according to the situation.

If it is desirable for tactical reasons to increase the number of birds in the line at any time, a number up to three times the normal supply can be sent up ; Application to O. i/c Pigeons, Corps being made for them. The regular use of more than the 16 usually sent up might result in exhaustion of the lofts.

S. Gordon Johnson

Major.

F. ROCKETS.

Message carrying Rockets are kept at the RUBBER HOUSE (Headquarters Left Battalion, No. 2 Brigade) for use in case of emergency for messages to NIEUPORT.

They are to be fired from an improvised stand.

Owing to the erratic course they take they will not be used except when all other means fail.

Arrangements are being made to use rockets for pulling a light telephone cable across the canal if all other lines are broken. Experiments have shown this is quite feasible.

S. Gordon Johnston

Major.

WAR DIARY.

APPENDIX "D". OCTOBER 1917.

HONOURS AND AWARDS.

Under Authority delegated by the Field Marshal Commanding-in-Chief, the Corps Commander has awarded:-

THE MILITARY MEDAL

to

No. 443952 Pnr Bellamy, H.

No. 443928 " Hodgin, J.

No. 155187 Gnr Wilkinson, E.(210th Brigade R.F.A. attached 42nd Divisional Signal Co.R.E.)

S. Gordon Johnson
Major.
4.11.17. for O.C. 42nd Divisional Signal Co. R.E.

WAR DIARY.

APPENDIX "E". OCTOBER 1917.

WEEKLY STRENGTHS, CASUALTIES, REINFORCEMENTS.

STRENGTH.

	Officers.	O.R.
Week ending October 6th	10	259
" " " 13th	10	267
" " " 20th	10	265
" " " 27th	10	270.

CASUALTIES.

	Officers.	O.R.
Killed.	-	-
Wounded or gassed.	-	4
Sick to hospital	-	7
Total.	-	11

REINFORCEMENTS.

	Officers.	O.R.
From Depot.	-	13
" Hospital.	ø 1	11
" Fourth Army.	ø 1	-
Transferred to R.E.	-	8
Total.	2	32.

ø Attached supernumerary.

4.11.17.

S. Gordon Johnston Major.
O.C. 42nd Divisional Signal Co. R.E.

Appendix "A".

Diagram of Communications

42nd Div. Signal Coy. R.E.

October 12th 1917.

S. Gordon Johnson Maj.

O.C. 42nd Divisional Signal Coy. R.E.

Y.D.B.

P.C.1 (R.26.d.93)

P.C.2.

Corps Test Hut.

C.B.-S.S. Route

C.B.-L.L. Route Airline

C.B.-Z.P. Airline

R.33.b.07 Usine Electrique

Adv. 42nd R.A.

Sykes Gp.

Y.D.B.R.

Z.L.F.

R.34.c.32

Amiral Exchange X.6.a.27

Armoured & D8 Cable

Armoured Cable

FR-AM

G.L.

P.C.AL

Amiral Test

H.A.

Coxyde Cable

Coxyde Test X.7.d.02

Coxyde Exchange

Counter Battery

"E" Group

"C" Group

"A" Group

P.C.7.

P.C.6. X.31.a.31.

B. Group M.31.b.70

D. Group M.31.d.21

B Post

P.C. Lock M.26.d.99

YU17.

North Test Box

Bde. Maj.

Reach R.C.

Div. O.P.

G.R.-YZ7. S.3.d.32. Pelican Bridge

South Test

Wulpen Test

Wireless Directing St.

Canada Camp

72nd A.F.A. Wag. Lines

D.A.C.

FR-AM Route

WP-GR

Spare & Bad

Poled Cable & Overground

Belgian Div.

ZLG

La Panne

G.

R.A.

Rear 126th Bde.

CRE

A.P.M.

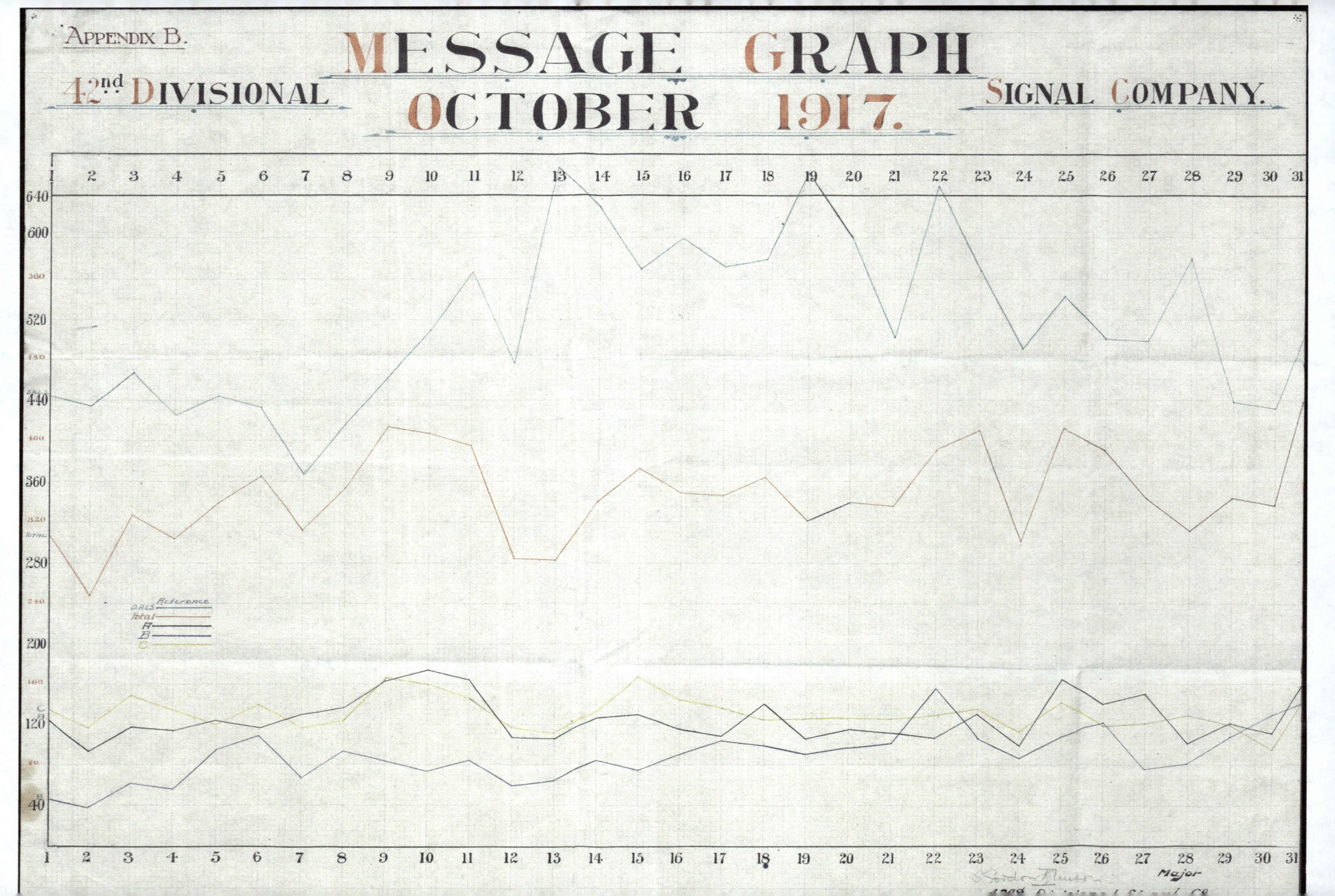

Appendix B.
MESSAGE GRAPH
42nd DIVISIONAL
OCTOBER 1917.
SIGNAL COMPANY.
1 2 3 4 5 6 7 8 9 10 11 12 13 14 15 16 17 18 19 20 21 22 23 24 25 26 27 28 29 30 31
640
600
520
440
360
280
200
120
40
Reference
D.R.L.S.
Total
A
B
C
Major

Diagram "C."

Wireless and Power Buzzer Communications.

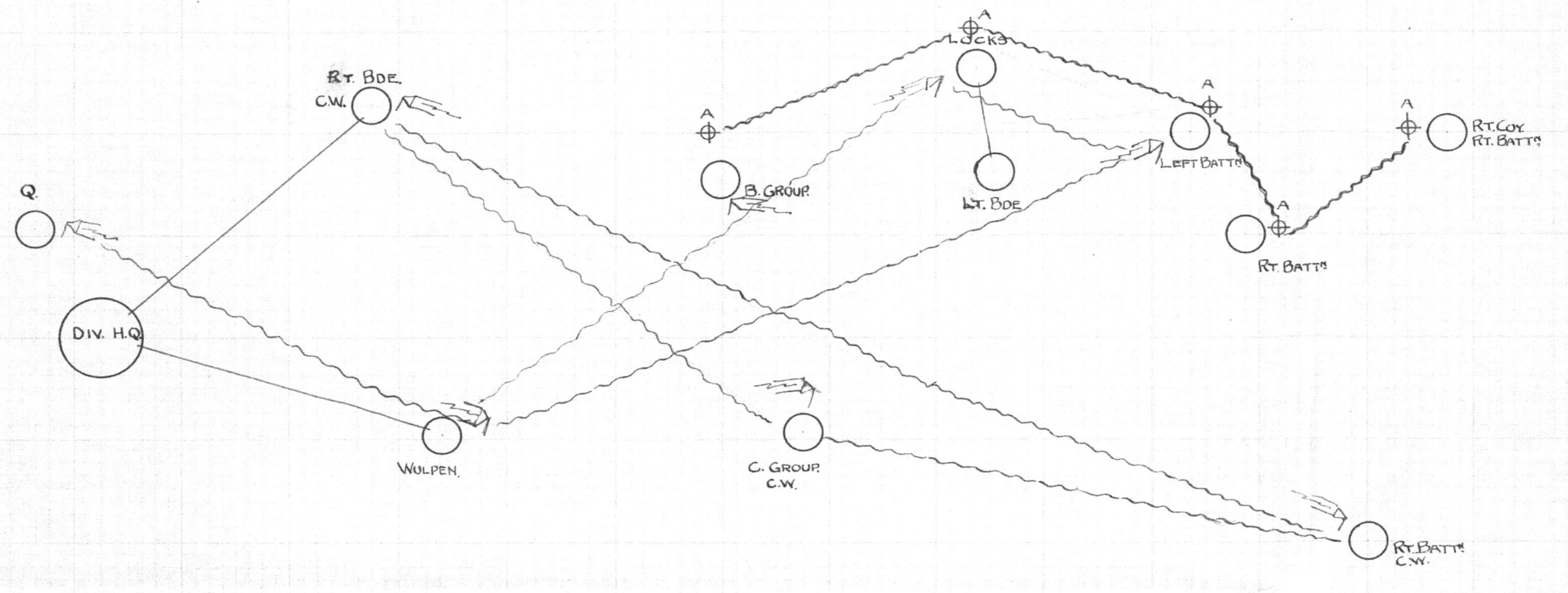

A Roberts

Capt.

for O.C. 42nd Divisional Signal Coy R.E.

October 28th 1917.

DIAGRAM "B."

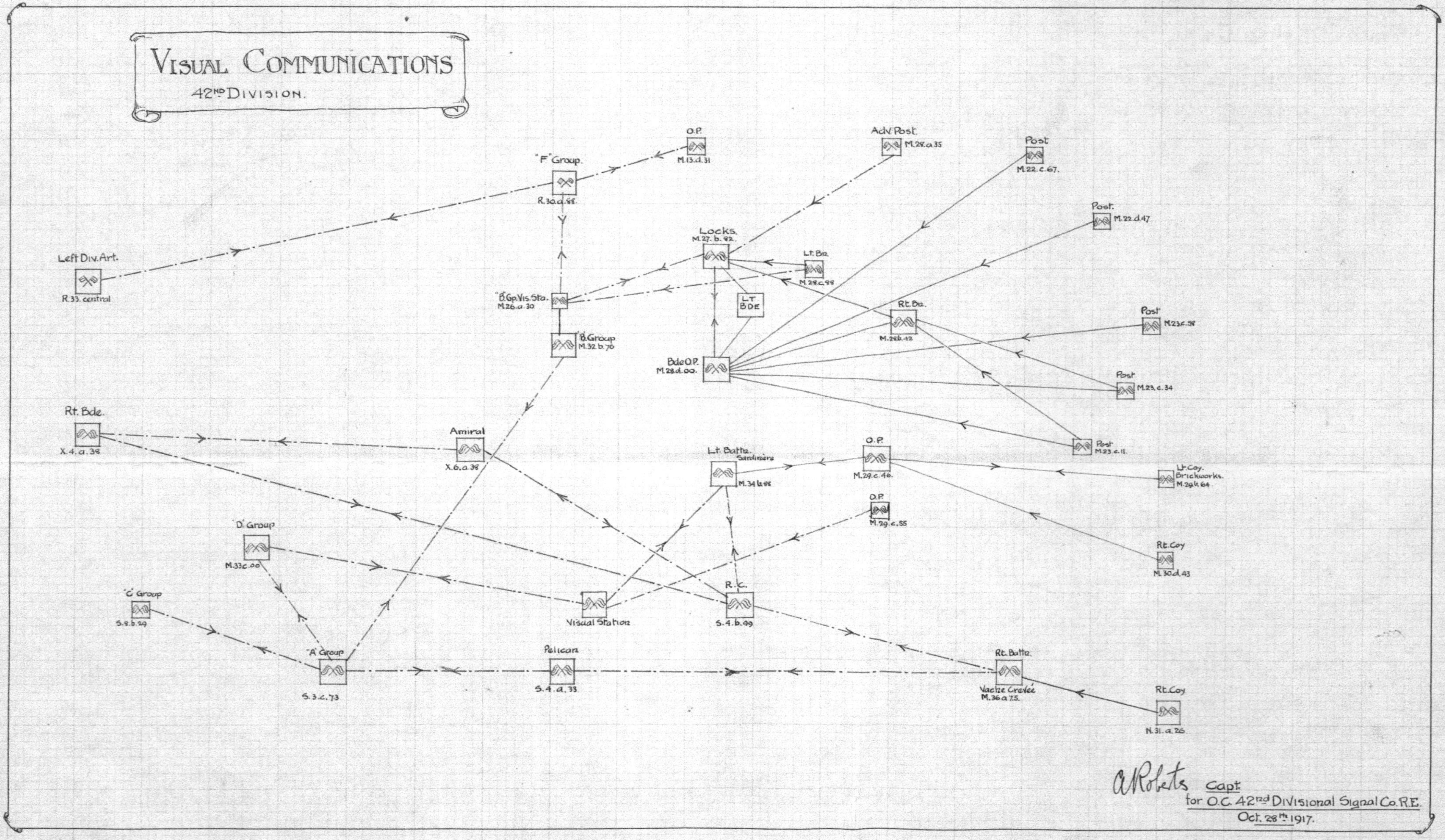
VISUAL COMMUNICATIONS
42ND DIVISION.
O.P.
M.13.d.31
"F" Group.
R.30.a.88.
Adv. Post
M.28.a.35
Post
M.22.c.67.
Post.
M.22.d.47
Left Div. Art.
R.33. central
Locks.
M.27.b.92.
Lt. Bn.
M.28.c.98
"B" Gp. Vis. Sta.
M.26.a.30
LT BDE
Rt. Bn.
M.28.b.12
Post
M.23.c.58
"B" Group
M.32.b.70
Bde O.P.
M.28.d.00.
Post
M.23.c.34
Rt. Bde.
X.4.a.38
Amiral
X.6.a.38
Post
M.23.c.11.
Lt. Battn.
Sandinière
M.34.b.88
O.P.
M.29.c.46.
Lt. Coy.
Brickworks.
M.29.d.64.
O.P.
M.29.c.55
"D" Group
M.33.c.00
Rt. Coy
M.30.d.43
"C" Group
S.9.b.29
Visual Station
R.C.
S.4.b.99
"A" Group
S.3.c.73
Pelican
S.4.a.33
Rt. Battn.
Vache Crevée
M.36.a.75.
Rt. Coy
N.31.a.26.
A Roberts Capt.
for O.C. 42nd Divisional Signal Co. R.E.
Oct. 28th 1917.

Secret

Vol 9

WAR DIARY.

for

November 1917.

42nd Div. Signal Coy. R.E.

Chapter XIII

S. Gordon Johnston

Major

O.C. 42nd Divisional Signal Coy.
R.E.

Army Form C. 2118.

Instructions regarding War Diaries and Intelligence Summaries are contained in F. S. Regs., Part II. and the Staff Manual respectively. Title pages will be prepared in manuscript.

WAR DIARY
or
~~INTELLIGENCE SUMMARY.~~
(Erase heading not required.)

Place	Date	Hour	Summary of Events and Information	Remarks and references to Appendices
			42nd (East Lancs.) Divisional Signal Company.R.E.,T.F. Reference Maps BELGIUM Oost Dunkerque. Sheet 11. " Sheet 12. BETHUNE. CHAPTER XIII. NOVEMBER 1917.	
COXYDE BAINS.	1.11.17.		The Division held the NIEUPORT Sector until relieved by the 133rd French Division on the 19th November. The communications in the Divisional Sector remained unaltered and were as described in the last Chapter with the exception that the advanced Divisional Telephone Exchange at PELICAN BRIDGE was moved to S.4.b.9.8. This was done to avoid the continual interruption of communication caused by the shelling of PELICAN BRIDGE which was on the main traffic route to the front. A new buried cable route was dug from P.C.7 test point (S.8.b.2.5) to this point to connect the new Exchange to the general buried cable system. All the overground cable lines were extended and diverted to the new Exchange so that the diagram of communications is identical with that given in the last Chapter. A local route chart is given herewith showing the chhnges which have to be made to the previous route chart.	APPENDIX"A"
COXYDE BAINS.	18.11.17.		The Signal Class dispersed temporarily and will reassemble after completion of move.	
COXYDE BAINS.	19.11.17.		Move in accordance with attached Order No.8.	
AIRE.	19.11.17.		The communications from Division to Infantry Brigades during the move and while the D.H.Q. remained at AIRE were established by the use of existing Army and Corps Lines and the Despatch Rider Letter Service.	

Instructions regarding War Diaries and Intelligence Summaries are contained in F. S. Regs., Part II. and the Staff Manual respectively. Title pages will be prepared in manuscript.

WAR DIARY
or
~~INTELLIGENCE SUMMARY.~~
(Erase heading not required.)

Army Form C. 2118.

Place	Date	Hour	Summary of Events and Information	Remarks and references to Appendices
			- 2. -	
AIRE.	29.11.17.		The Division relieved the 25th Division at noon. Move in accordance with attached Order No. 9. The communications will be described in the next Chapter.	
			APPENDICES TO THIS DIARY. (A). Local Route Chart. (B). Monthly message Graph. (C). Honours and Awards. (D). Weekly Strengths, Casualties, Reinforcements.	
			4.12.17. S. Gordon Thurston [signature] Major. O.C. 42nd Divisional Signal Co. R.E.	

A7092). Wt. W12839/M1291 750,000. 1/17. D. D & L., Ltd. Forms/C2118/14.

Copy.No. 8

SECRET.

42nd DIVISIONAL SIGNAL COMPANY. R.E.
ORDER No. 8

Reference Sheets DUNKERQUE 1a.
HAZEBROUCK 5a.

---

1. The 42nd Division will be relieved by the 133rd French Division on the 19th November. Divisional Headquarters will close at COXYDE BAINS at 10.0 a.m. and reopen at AIRE at 12 noon same day.

2. An advance Signal Office party under 2/Cpl Jones will leave by lorry at 8.30 a.m. 18.11.17.

3. Sgt. Harrison and half of the Despatch Riders will leave at 7 a.m. 19.11.17. Sgt. Harrison will act as Billeting N.C.O. at AIRE.

4. Two Despatch Riders will report to Lieut. Fletcher at 10 a.m. 19.11.17. and remain behind with the Artillery.

5. The remaining Despatch Riders (with the exception of two) will leave for AIRE under the Senior N.C.O. at 10 a.m. 19.11.17.

6. The Electric Light Lorry with Officers' valises and mess stores will leave at 9 a.m. 19.11.17. Officers' Cook and two batmen will travel on this lorry.

7. All horse transport and the Company lorry under 2/Lieut. Ellis will move to WORMHOUDT "A" area, leaving at 9 a.m. 19.11.17. Two Motor Cyclists, men riding bicycles and dismounted men will leave at the same time.

8. One lorry from the Divisional Supply Column will leave at 11 a.m. for AIRE. This lorry will take technical and Orderly Room stores. Orderly Room staff will travel by this lorry.

9. On the 20th November the horse transport etc, will proceed from WORMHOUDT "A" area to WORMHOUDT "B" area. On the 21st to WALLON CAPPEL and on the 22nd inst to AIRE.

10. N.C.O's and men in the forward area will assemble at D.H.Q. at 11.0 a.m. and proceed by lorry to AIRE.

11. Instructors and Cooks at the Signal School will rejoin the Company tomorrow 18.11.17.

[signature]

2/Lieut. R.E.

18.11.17. for O.C. 42nd Divisional Signal Co. R.E.

Issued by Orderly at 3.30 p.m. 17.11.17.

Copy No.1 "T.O."
2 "A.O"
3. C.S.M.
4. C.Q.M.S.
5. Signalmaster.
6. Sgt. Harrison.
7. File.
8. War Diary.

SECRET. 42nd DIVISIONAL SIGNAL COMPANY. R.E. Copy No. 8

ORDER No. 9.

---

1. The 42nd Division relieves the 25th Division in the line at noon 29th inst.

2. The 42nd Divisional Signal Company takes over charge of the Divisional communications from the 25th Divisional Signal Co. with Headquarters at LOCON at noon 29th inst.

3. The No. 1 Section (less those men already gone to new area) and the mounted men and transport of H.Q. Section will parade at 8.45 a.m. 29th to move to LOCON i/c Sgt. Wood. Route AIRE- ST HILIARE-LILLERS-CHOQUE-BETHUNE-LOCON. Before moving off Sgt. Wood will satisfy himself that the horse lines and mens' accomodation etc, have been properly cleaned up. Each man will carry a haversack ration.
The party will halt at mid-day for ¾ hour, when the horses will be watered, a small feed will be given and the mens' haversack ration eaten.

4. Two Motor lorries from 42nd Divisional Train have been instructed to report to Signal Company at CHATEAU at 8 a.m. The remaining Q.M. Stores and technical stores will be loaded on these lorries.
Sgt. Wood will detail the personnel which is to travel in the lorries, which will move to LOCON in charge of Cpl Richardson at 9 a.m. Route as above.

5. The electric light lorry will pick up all Officers' kit and mess stores and move to LOCON at 9.30 a.m. i/c Sgt. Grunwell. Officers' servants will travel on this lorry. Route as above.

6. The Signal Company Lorry will be loaded with technical and Orderly Room Stores and will leave at 7 a.m. for LOCON, where it will be immediately unloaded and return to AIRE. It will then be loaded with all Signal Office furniture and instruments remaining when the present Signal Office closes at 12 noon. The Signal Office relief last on duty and any remaining men will travel on this lorry on its second journey.
A party detailed by Sgt. Wood of 1 junior N.C.O. and 4 men which will remain to clean the barracks and other accomodation now used by the Signal Company will also travel by it. It will leave at 2.30 p.m. for LOCON and will call on its way at the Signal Office LILLERS to pick up the three telegraphists of this Company there. Route as above.

(Signed) (A Roberts)
Captain.R.E.

28.11.17. for O.C. 42nd Divisional Signal Co. R.E.

Issued at 10 p.m. by Orderly 28.11.17.

Copy No.1 "T" Officer.
2 "A" Officer.
3 C.S.M. & C.Q.M.S.
4. Sgt. Harrison.
5. Signalmaster.
6. File.
7. Horse Lines.
8. War Diary.

WAR DIARY.

APPENDIX "C". NOVEMBER 1917.

HONOURS AND AWARDS.

Under Authority delegated by His Majesty the King, the Corps Commander has been pleased to award the following decoration to the undermentioned man:- Military Medal.

No. 444287 Pioneer J. BUTTLE. 42nd Divisional Signal Co. R.E.

S. Gordon Johnson.

Major.

4.12.17. O.C. 42nd Divisional Signal Co. R.E.

WAR DIARY.

APPENDIX "D". NOVEMBER 1917.

WEEKLY STRENGTHS, CASUALTIES, REINFORCEMENTS.

		Officers.	O.R.
STRENGTH.	Week ending Nov. 3rd.	10	274
	" " " 10th	9	278
	" " " 17th	9	277
	" " " 24th	9	282
CASUALTIES.	Killed.	-	-
	Wounded or Gassed.	∅ 1	1
	Sick to Hospital.	-	9
	Struck off Strength.	1	-
		2	10
REINFORCEMENTS.			
	From Depot.	-	6
	" Hospital.	-	5
	Transferred to R.E.	-	6
		-	17

∅ Attached Supernumerary.

S. Gordon Blunson

Major.

4.12.17. O.C. 42nd Divisional Signal Co. R.E.

LOCAL ROUTE CHART.
Appendix "A"

Reference Sheets Nos. 4 & 5 (NIEUPORT SECTOR)
1/10000.

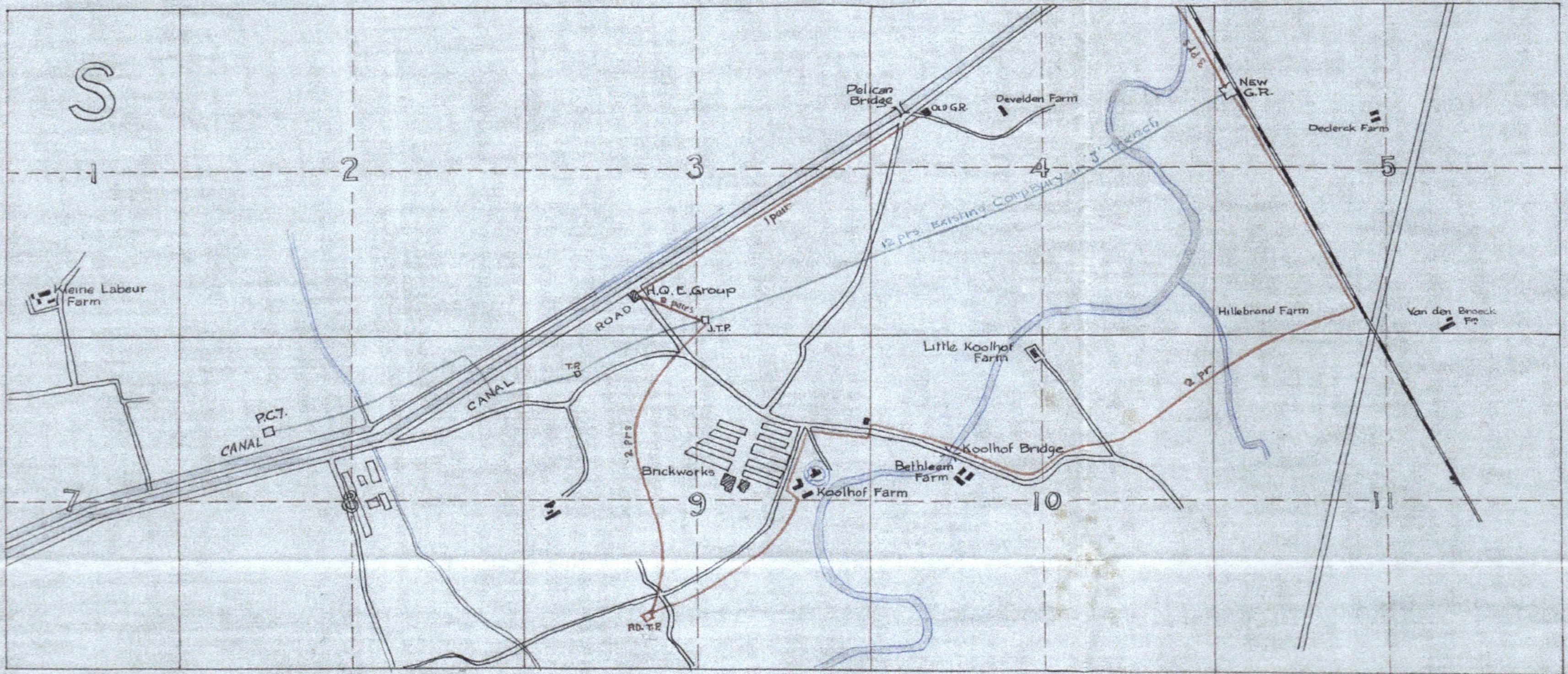
S
1
2
3
4
5
7
8
9
10
11
Kleine Labeur Farm
P.C.T.
CANAL
CANAL
ROAD
H.Q. E. Group
J.T.P.
T.P.
Pelican Bridge
Develden Farm
New G.R.
Dederck Farm
Hillebrand Farm
Van den Broeck Fm
Little Koolhof Farm
Koolhof Bridge
Bethleem Farm
Koolhof Farm
Brickworks
RD. T.P.
1 pair
2 prs
2 pr
3 prs
12 prs. Existing Company in "J" Trench

S. Gordon Fellowes, Major
O.C. 42nd Div. Signal Coy. R.E.
Nov. 1917.

APPENDIX "B".

MESSAGE GRAPH

42nd DIVISIONAL

NOVEMBER 1917.

1 2 3 4 5 6 7 8 9 10 11 12 13 14 15 16 17 18 19 20 21

600
560
480
400
320
240
160
80

Reference.
D.R.L.S.
TOTAL
A
B
C

1 2 3 4 5 6 7 8 9 10 11 12 13 14 15 16 17 18 19 20

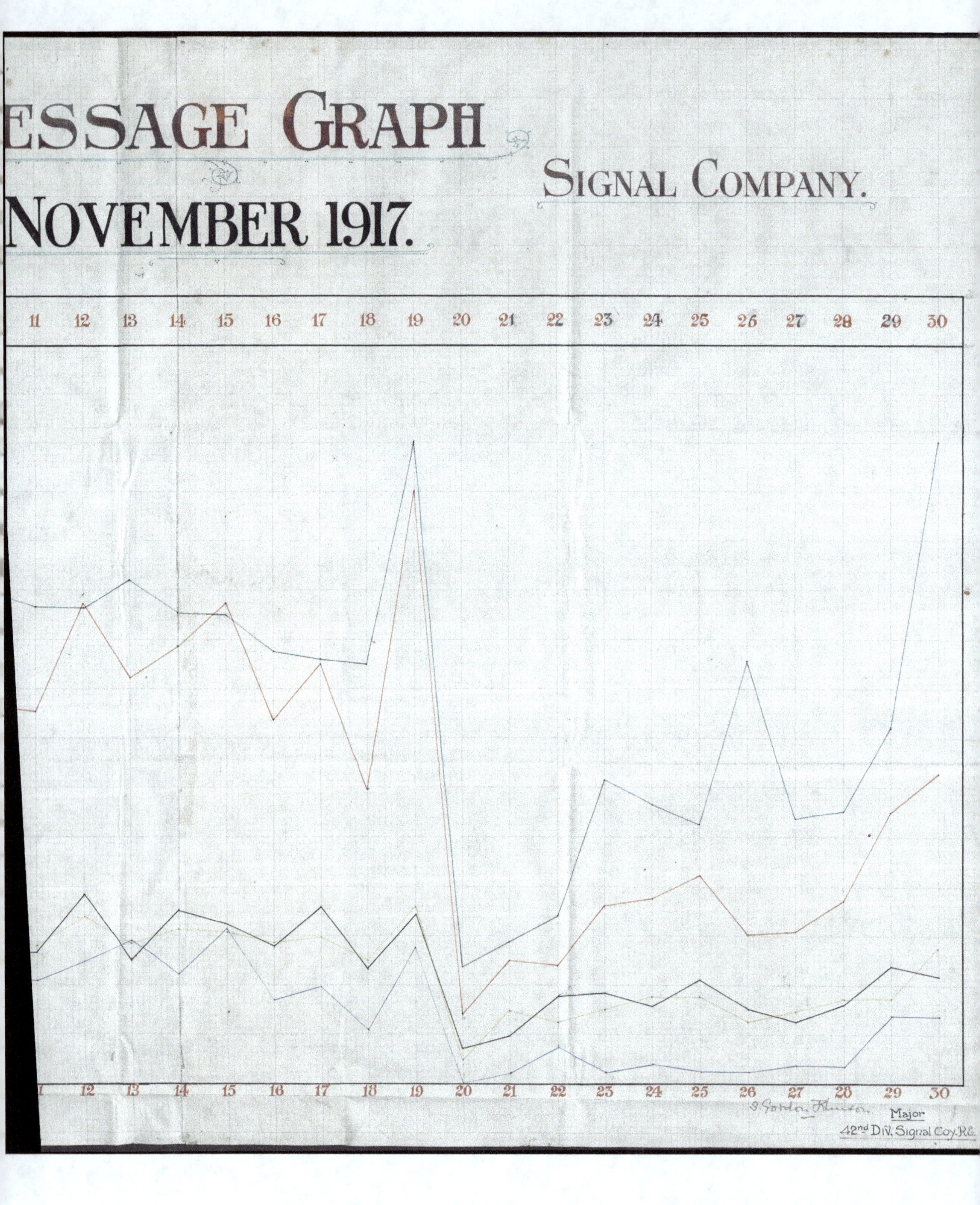
ESSAGE GRAPH
SIGNAL COMPANY.
NOVEMBER 1917.
11 12 13 14 15 16 17 18 19 20 21 22 23 24 25 26 27 28 29 30
11 12 13 14 15 16 17 18 19 20 21 22 23 24 25 26 27 28 29 30
Major
42nd DIV. Signal Coy. R.E.

14 Vol 10

SECRET.

WAR DIARY

42nd Div., Signal Co., R.E.

CHAPTER XIV.
December 1917.

S. Gordon Johnston, Major,
O.C. 42 Div., Signal Co., R.E.

Instructions regarding War Diaries and Intelligence Summaries are contained in F. S. Regs., Part II. and the Staff Manual respectively. Title pages will be prepared in manuscript.

WAR DIARY
or
~~INTELLIGENCE SUMMARY.~~
(Erase heading not required.)

Army Form C. 2118.

Place	Date	Hour	Summary of Events and Information	Remarks and references to Appendices
			42nd (East Lancs) Divisional Signal Coy., R.E.(T.F.)	
			Ref. Map. FRANCE, BETHUNE, (1/40,000) Combined sheet.	
			CHAPTER XIV, DECEMBER, 1917.	
LOCON.	1.12.1917.		During the month of December, 1917, the 42nd Division held the GIVENCHY SECTOR with headquarters at LOCON (X.7.c.7.8). For particulars and diagrams of communications see Appendices "A" and "B".	APPENDICES "A" & "B".
Near BETHUNE.	9.12.17.		The Signal Class (Strength 196) reassembled at W.28.d.9.4. In addition to the usual instruction, a Wireless Class was formed. The results will be furnished next month when the Class disperses.	

Appendices to this Diary.

"A" Notes on Communications.
"B" Diagrams of Communications.
"C" Monthly Message Chart.
"D" Honours and Awards.
"E" Weekly strengths, casualties, reinforcements.

4.1.18.

S. Gordon Johnson
Major.
O.C., 42nd Divisional Signal Coy., R.E.

1577 Wt. W10791/1773 500,000 1/15 D. D. & L. A.D.S.S./Forms/C. 2118.

PART 1.

METHODS OF COMMUNICATION.

In arranging the communications of this Sector, in view of a defensive battle, every possible means have been arranged for ; that is to say :-

A. Telegraph and Telephone.
   (i) Airline.
   (ii) Ground Cable.
   (iii) Buried Cable.

B. Wireless.

C. Despatch Riders and Runners.

D. Pigeons.

E. Visual Signalling.

F. Message Rockets.

G. War Dogs.

Each of the above means is described under the headings given.

In this Sector, the following points have to be taken into consideration :-

(a) The left half of the Sector is marshy and buries cannot be constructed.

(b) The possibility of the enemy overhearing buzzer and telephone conversations is very considerable owing to the conductivity of the subsoil.

Owing to (a), it is necessary to have alternative ground cable routes from the Brigade to the Battalions and a complete Wireless System from the front line, back, and owing to (b), it is essential that stringent orders are issued for restricting conversations and the sending of messages on important matters, in front of the Brigade.

Instructions for action to be taken by Signals in the case of a Gas Attack, are given in Part 3.

PART 2.

"A" - TELEGRAPH AND TELEPHONE.

The communications in the Divisional Area are, to a great extent airline. Alternative ground cable routes are provided, so that, in case of breakdown of the airline, owing to shellfire or other causes, the main communication shall not be interrupted. In the Brigade Areas there are buried cable and ground cable routes. The "buries" are entirely in the right front sector, south of GIVENCHY, where, owing to the nature of the ground, it is possible to bury cable to a depth of seven or eight feet.

In the left front sector (i.e. North of GIVENCHY), the forward line communications depend entirely upon cable, either laid on the ground or poled where sufficiently hidden from view.

All lines are shewn in Diagram "A", the actual routes of all lines are shewn on map "B".

As far as possible, when there are more than one line between two headquarters, they are taken by different routes.

i. DIVISIONAL COMMUNICATIONS.

(a) AIRLINE ROUTES. From Divisional Headquarters to the RIGHT INFANTRY BRIGADE HEADQUARTERS there are two telephone and one telegraph lines ; to the LEFT INFANTRY BRIGADE HEADQUARTERS there are three telephone and one telegraph lines.

To the Divisional Artillery Headquarters there are three telephone lines.

From Divisional Artillery Headquarters, there is one telephone line and one telegraph line to each Artillery Brigade. Artillery Brigades can be communicated with alternatively via the Infantry Brigades who have each two lines to them.

There is an Advanced Divisional Telephone Exchange at LE QUESNOY. From LE QUESNOY Exchange there is one line to each of the Right and Left Artillery and Right and Left Infantry Brigades. LE QUESNOY Exchange is connected with the Divisional Headquarters exchange by two telephone lines.

(b) GROUND CABLE ROUTES. There is a ground cable route of 12 circuits, running forwards from Divisional Headquarters to Left Infantry and Artillery Brigade Headquarters, thence to Right Artillery and Infantry Brigade Headquarters. This provides three telephone lines from Divisional Headquarters to each Infantry Brigade Headquarters, and two lines to each Artillery Brigade Headquarters, leaving two lines spare. Further, it provides two laterals between Infantry Brigades and one between the Artillery.

ii. ARTILLERY GROUP COMMUNICATIONS.

(a) EACH GROUP is connected by a telephone line with the Group on either side of it and also with the Heavy Artillery O.P. Exchange at X.28.d.8.1. All these lines are above ground.

There is a direct telephone line from each Group Headquarters to each of the Batteries which it controls. In addition, there are lateral lines between the batteries of the brigades, so that in case of breakdown of the direct line to a battery, the Group can get communication with that Battery via one of the other Batteries. Each Group is connected by two lines to the Infantry Brigade which it supports.

(b) O.P. EXCHANGES. There is an O.P. Exchange in each Sector.
Right Sector at FANSHAWE CASTLE (A.14.a.5.5)
Left Sector at BREWERY (S.20.c.8.2)

Each Artillery Group has two lines to the O.P. Exchange in its sector and there are two lines connecting the Exchanges together. Each Battery is connected to one of the two exchanges and each Battalion in the line has one line to the nearest of

(b) O.P. EXCHANGES (Cont'd)

them. All the O.P's in the Area are connected through the O.P. Exchanges so that any O.P. can be connected to any Battery.

The CAMBRIN O.P. Exchange (A.26.a.3.2) is connected to the FANSHAWE CASTLE O.P. Exchange so that the Right Group Batteries can be controlled, if necessary, from this O.P. which is in the Sector of the Division on the Right. Three Batteries of the Right Group have direct lines to CAMBRIN O.P. Exchange.

(c) T.M.B. COMMUNICATIONS The Advanced T.M.B. Headquarters is at PONT FIXE, (A.14.d.3.7), from which there are direct lines to all T.M. Batteries and also to the O.P's at KINGSCLERE, and SAPPER HOUSE. Each T.M.B. has also a direct line to its own O.P.

iii. RIGHT INFANTRY BRIGADE COMMUNICATIONS. Practically the whole of the lines in this Brigade Area are buried. There is an Advanced Brigade Exchange and Test Station at FANSHAWE CASTLE (A.14.a.5.5)

From Brigade Headquarters there are two direct lines to each Battalion in the line. In addition there are two lines from Brigade Headquarters to FANSHAWE CASTLE EXCHANGE and a line from FANSHAWE CASTLE Exchange to each Battalion in the line and to the Support Battalion.

The Reserve Battalion is connected to Brigade Headquarters by a short line.

This Brigade has also alternative communicationto its Battalions in the line by four circuits of ground cable running South from Brigade Headquarters to the Test Cellar at F.29.a.9.8, near ANNEQUIN, from which point a bury runs forward and provides two buried telephone lines by this route to each of the Left and Right Battalioms.

iv. LEFT INFANTRY BRIGADE COMMUNICATIONS. In the Left Brigade Area, the ground is wet and low lying, so that it is not possible to bury cable. All the lines, therefore, from the Brigade Headquarters are overground, either airline or cable.

All the lines forward from Brigade Headquarters, with the exception of one direct to the Left Battalion and two to the Right Battalion on the "bury" (described below), pass through a Test Point at F.6.c.9.1, whence they branch off in various directions. From Brigade Headquarters through this Test Point there are two lines to each of the Right, Left, and Support Battalions and a common line to the Machine Gun Company and Trench Mortar Battery affiliated to the Brigade. There is also a line to the Visual Station at F.11.d.7.2.

Two circuits, of the 12 pair overground cable route from the Brigade Headquarters to Right Brigade Headquarters at CANAL HOUSE, are connected on to the bury at the latter point so as to provide buried circuits for communication to the Battalion in GIVENCHY.

v. SMALL UNITS. The Small units (e.g. Field Coys. R.E., Field Ambulances etc.) in the Divisional Area are connected to the nearest exchange. The Exchange to which they are connected is given in the attached list (List "A") of telephone connections to all exchanges in the Area.

"B" - WIRELESS COMMUNICATIONS. (DIAGRAM "C").

i. DIVISIONAL COMMUNICATIONS. There is a Spark Wireless Station at Divisional Headquarters for communication to either Infantry Brigade in the line or to Corps Headquarters. There are "Spark" Wireless Stations at both Left and Right Infantry Brigades, which, beside providing communication with the Divisional Headquarters, communicate with each other and so complete the chain of Wireless communication from the front line to Left Brigade Headquarters as described below.

ii. RIGHT INFANTRY BRIGADE. There are Power Buzzer Stations at the Right Company, Right Battalion and Centre Company, Left Battalion, both of which stations transmit to the Amplifier Station at the Left Battalion Headquarters. This latter station transmits to and receives from the Power Buzzer and Amplifier Station at the Headquarters of the Right Battalion Left Brigade at A.8.d.7.3.

iii. LEFT INFANTRY BRIGADE. There are Power Buzzers at Right and Left Companies of Right Battalion which transmit to the Amplifier Station at Battalion Headquarters at A.8.d.7.3. There are Power Buzzers at the Right and Left Companies of the Left Battalion which transmit to the Amplifier Station at the Battalion Headquarters at S.26.d.4.9. The Power Buzzer and Amplifier Station at the Right Battalion transmits to and receives from the Station at the Left Battalion, Right Brigade and to and from the Station at the Left Brigade Test Point at A.1.d.0.2.

The Station at the Left Battalion Headquarters also transmits to and receives from the Station at the Test Point.

The Station at the Test Point is similarly in "both way" communication with the Power Buzzer and Amplifier Station at the Right Brigade Headquarters.

The Spark Wireless Station at the Right Brigade Headquarters is in communication with the similar station at the Left Brigade Headquarters.

There is, thus, a complete chain of Wireless communication from each of the Power Buzzer Stations in the front line to Divisional Headquarters.

iv. POWER BUZZERS AND AMPLIFIERS work well in this Area owing to the nature of the ground. They can be relied on to transmit and receive loud signals over a range of 2,000 yards with "bases" of normal length (100 to 150 yards).

"C" - DESPATCH RIDERS AND RUNNERS.

i. FROM DIVISIONAL HEADQUARTERS motor Cyclists are used to both Infantry Brigade Headquarters.
For use in case of emergency, a motor cyclist is stationed at each Infantry Brigade Headquarters,

ii. THE RIGHT INFANTRY BRIGADE uses Cyclists along the CANAL as far as HARLEY STREET, from where the despatches are carried by Runners to the Battalion Headquarters.

iii. THE LEFT INFANTRY BRIGADE uses Cyclists from Brigade Headquarters as far forward as WINDY CORNER and the entrance to FESTUBERT Village, from which points the despatch carrier has to run to the Right and Left Battalions in the line, respectively.

iv. RUNNERS are stationed at Company and Battalion Headquarters for use as required for communication between them in both Brigades.

"D" - PIGEONS. (DIAGRAM "D").

Four Pigeons are sent up daily to each Infantry Brigade in the line from the BETHUNE Lofts. There are three lofts connected by telephone with Advanced Divisional Headquarters Exchange in LE QUESNOY.

Messages carried back by birds are telephoned directly to Brigades and Division.

From the Brigade Headquarters, the birds are sent up to Company Headquarters in the line as required, where they are kept for release in case of emergency.

Birds are sent from the lofts in the morning or early afternoon each day for release during the following day. During the winter months the birds are not released unless to carry an urgent message in an emergency, but are sent back in their baskets on the evening of their day in the front line.

"E" - VISUAL COMMUNICATIONS IN THE DIVISIONAL SECTOR. (DIAGRAM "D").

The Attached Diagram ("D") shews the Stations which are established in the Divisional Sector. The Station at F.11.d.7.2 can be regarded as the Central Visual Station for both Right and Left Infantry Brigades.

Only a limited amount of Visual Signalling is possible owing to the number of trees in the area and the configuration of the country.

To connect by "visual" those headquarters where "visual" does not already exist would involve the placing of so many transmitting stations as to make the system impracticable.

"F" - ROCKETS.

Rockets are kept at Company Headquarters in the front line for use in case of breakdown of other communications. They are fired to Battalion Headquarters. A watch is kept for them at these Headquarters when communication from the advanced stations, by other methods breaks down. All Company Headquarters should have two stakes driven firmly into the ground giving the direction of Battalion Headquarters.

"G" - WAR DOGS (DIAGRAM "D")

Kennels are established at Left Battalion, Left Brigade and Left Battalion, Right Brigade.

The Dogs at the Left Battalion, Left Brigade work from any point on that Battalion front, taking the messages to the Battalion Headquarters.

Those in the Right Brigade carry messages from any point on the Brigade front to the Left Battalion at KINGSCLERE.

PART 3.

SIGNALLING INSTRUCTIONS FOR GAS CLOUD ATTACK.

i. FORM OF MESSAGE. The warning message will take the following form :-

GAS. (Map Reference) , (time).

for example :- GAS, Q.4.c., TEN TWENTY.

This message will only be sent by an officer, or in case one is not present, by an N.C.O. who has actually seen the gas cloud. There will be no "address from" or preamble other than the word "gas" in the message.

ii. MESSAGES KEPT READY. Messages addressed to all units with the word "Gas" in the text will be kept ready at each Signal Office. The Map Reference of the Company Headquarters will also be put in after the word "Gas" in the case of the Companies in the front line ; the time being added when the message has actually to be sent.

iii. MAP REFERENCE AND TIMES. In giving the map reference, only the letters and figures giving squares will be stated, not the actual point. The time will be spelt out in letters and will be to the nearest ten minutes.

iv. MESSAGE FROM ANOTHER DIVISION. A Signal Office receiving a gas warning message from a unit of another Division will add "XXX" to the text before transmitting the message, thus :-

XXX GAS Q.4.c. TEN THIRTY.

v. A unit receiving a message starting XXX will not pass it on to a unit in another Divisional Area, except in the case of the Divisional Headquarters Office, which will do so only when specially instructed by the General Staff.

vi. AT COMPANY. When a gas attack is notified to Company Headquarters the warning message will be sent to the Companies on the Left and Right and back to Battalion Headquarters. The Company is also responsible for warning any other troops that may be in its area.

vii. AT BATTALION. The Battalion Headquarters, on receiving the message, will pass it on to the Battalion on their left and right, all their companies, brigade headquarters and supporting Battery, if connected to the latter by wire, and any other troops that may be in their area.

viii. AT BRIGADE. When the Brigade receives the message, it will send it to all Battalions, Field Companies, Machine Gun Company, Trench Mortar Battery, and Artillery Brigade supporting and any other troops that are in its area. The Message will also be sent to the Brigades on their flanks and to the Division.

ix. STROMBOS HORN. On a message coming through to a Headquarters where there is a Strombos Horn, an orderly will be sent immediately to the sentry on duty giving him the warning,

x. LIST OF UNITS. A list of units to be warned by a Company, Battalion, Brigade and Divisional Headquarters will be kept in a prominent position in each Signal Office at all times

xi. ORDERLIES. Units not connected by wire will be warned by an orderly, mounted when possible.

xii. REPEATED MESSAGE. An office receiving a message will not send it on if it has already sent the same timed message.

xiii. SHELL GAS. In the case of a Gas Shell bombardment of any description, the text of the message will be.

SHELL GAS, X.4.c. SIX TWENTY.

xiv. DIAGRAM "X", attached, shews the lines on which the warning is circulated.

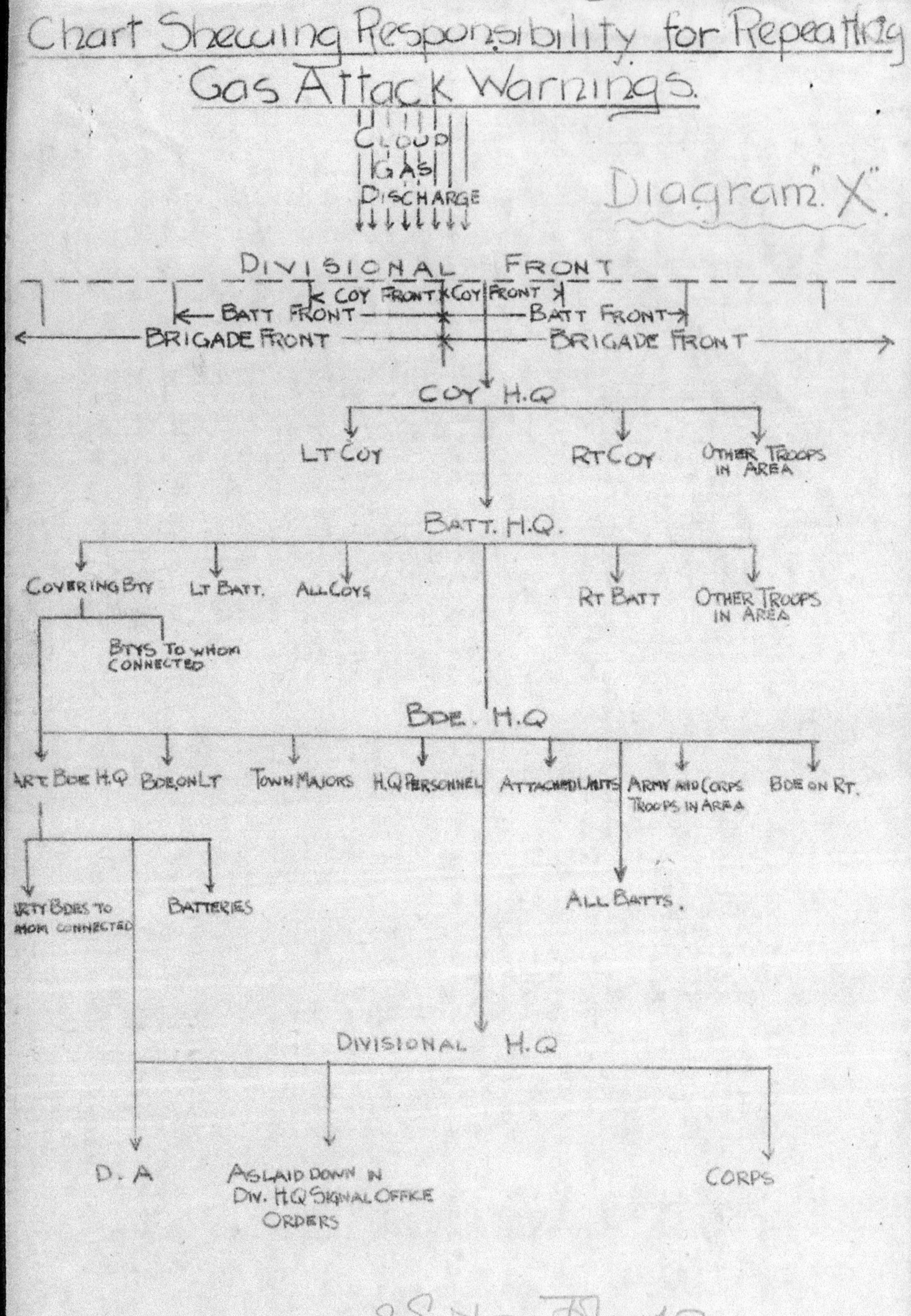
Chart Shewing Responsibility for Repeating Gas Attack Warnings.
CLOUD GAS DISCHARGE
Diagram "X"
DIVISIONAL FRONT
COY FRONT
COY FRONT
BATT FRONT
BATT FRONT
BRIGADE FRONT
BRIGADE FRONT
COY H.Q
LT COY
RT COY
OTHER TROOPS IN AREA
BATT. H.Q.
COVERING BTY
LT BATT.
ALL COYS
RT BATT
OTHER TROOPS IN AREA
BTYS TO WHOM CONNECTED
BDE. H.Q
ART. BDE H.Q
BDE ON LT
TOWN MAJORS
H.Q PERSONNEL
ATTACHED UNITS
ARMY AND CORPS TROOPS IN AREA
BDE ON RT.
ARTY BDES TO WHOM CONNECTED
BATTERIES
ALL BATTS.
DIVISIONAL H.Q
D. A
AS LAID DOWN IN DIV. H.Q SIGNAL OFFICE ORDERS
CORPS
S. Gordon Johnston
Major
O.C. 42nd DIV. Signal Coy RE

LIST "A".

42nd DIVISIONAL EXCHANGES.

D.H.Q. Exchange.

1. G.O.C.
2. G.S.O.1.
3. G. Office,
4. Q. Office.
5. Left Brigade.
6. Right Brigade.
7. O.C. XV Corps Troops.
8. XV Corps.
9. XV Corps.
10. Le Quesnoy. (Advanced D.H.Q.)
11. Signals, Lines Officer.
12. Spare.
13. LE Quesnoy. (Advanced D.H.Q.)
14. Spare.
15. D.A.D.O.S. Stores.
16. Artillery Exchange.
17. C.R.E.
18. Divisional Train.
19. Left Brigade.
20. O.C., Signals.
21. A. Office.
22. G.S.O.1 Bedroom and A. Mess.
23. Reserve Brigade.
24. Artillery Exchange.
25. Corps Claims Officer.
26. Spare.
27. D.A.D.O.S.
28. A.D.M.S.
29. Intelligence Officer,
30. Signalmaster.
31. 3rd Field Ambulance.
32. Portuguese Division.
33. Signals Mess.
34. Left Group Waggon Lines.
35. A.P.M.
36. C.Q.M.S
37. Instrument Stores.

G.S.O.1. Exchange.

1. G.O.C.
2. Bde. Major, R.A.
3. C.R.E.
4. 42nd Div. Exchange.
5. XV Corps "G".
6. Bde. Major, Left Brigade.
7. Bde. Major, Right Brigade.
8.
9.
10.

ADVANCED D.H.Q. (Le Quesnoy) EXCHANGE.

1. 42nd Division
ø 2. Buzzer Unit.
3. Right Brigade.
4. Left Brigade.
5.
6. Divisional Canteen.
7. S.A.A.
8. No. 2 R.E. Park.
9. No. 4 Special Coy and "D" Special Coy. R.E.
10. 46th Division.
11.
12. Pigeons, Bethune.
13. 428th Field Coy. R.E.
14. Divisional Wing.
15.
16. Left Group.
17. Right Group.
18. 42nd Division.
19.
20. D. & B. Right Group, Wagon Lines.

ø 5 - line Buzzer Unit.

1. D/210 Wagon Lines.
2. B/210 Wagon Lines.

RIGHT INFANTRY BRIGADE EXCHANGE.

1. 42nd Division.
2. Le Quesnoy Exchange.
3. Left Brigade.
4. Staff Captain.
X 5. Buzzer Unit.
6. Adjutant Left Battalion.
7. Adjutant Right Battalion.
8. Brigade Major (Night).
9. 427th Field Coy. R.E.
10. 138th Bde.
11. Right Group.
12. Bde. Major.
13. Mess.

X 2 - 5 Line Buzzer Units.

1. Right Battalion.
2. Left Battalion.
3. Reserve Battalion
4. Support Battalion
5. Right Bde. M.G.Company.
6. Right Bde. T.M. Battery.
7. Transport Officer, Right Bde.

LEFT INFANTRY BRIGADE EXCHANGE

1. 42nd Division.
ø 2. Transfer to Buzzer Unit.
3. Left Group R.A.
4. Bde. Major.
5. Advanced D.H.Q. (Le Quesnoy)
6. Bde. on Right.
7. Staff Captain.
8. 429th Field Coy. R.E.

ø **2 - 5 line Buzzer Units.**

1. One Battalion.
2. One Battalion
3. One Battalion.
4. One Battalion.
5. Left Bde. M.G.Coy.
6. Left Bde. T.M.Battery.

RESERVE INFANTRY BRIGADE EXCHANGE.

1. 42nd Division.
2.
3. Mess.
4. Staff Captain.
5. Bde. Major.
6.
7.
X 8. Buzzer Unit.
9. Signalmaster.

X **5 - line Buzzer Unit.**

1. One Battalion.
2. One Battalion.
3. One Battalion.

42nd R.A. HEADQUARTERS EXCHANGE.

1. Bde. Major.
2. Staff Captain.
3. 42nd Division.
4. Right Group.
5. Left Group.
6. R.A. Mess.
7. G.O.C., R.A.
8. Signal Officer.
9. Bde. Major. (Bedroom)
10. 46th Div. Arty.
11. Sound Ranging Section (Heather)
12. A.R.P.
13.
14. "X" Group. (AZALIA)
15.
16. 42nd Division.

RIGHT GROUP R.F.A. EXCHANGE.

1. Cambrin Exchange.
2. D/210.
3. C/210.
4. B/210.
5. A/210.
6. Right Bde.
7. D.T.M.O.
8. Adjt, 210th Bde.
9. 42nd Div. Arty.
10. Left Group.
11. Left Group.
12. Advanced D.H.Q. (Le Quesnoy).
13. T.M.B and Left Group.
14. Fanshawe Castle O.P. Exchange.
15. Heavy Artillery.
16. Mess.

LEFT GROUP R.F.A. EXCHANGE.

1. 42nd Div. Arty.
2. Right Inf. Bde.
3. Orderly Room.
4. H. Arty Exchange.
5. Brewery O.P. Exchange.
6. Portuguese Right Group.
7. B/211.
8. C/211.
9. D/211.
10. C/210.
11. T.M.B. and Right Group.
12. Right Group.
13. Right Battalion.
14. Divisional Forward Exchange. (Le Quesnoy)
15. Adjutant.
16. Signal Officer.

APPENDIX "D". WAR DIARY. DECEMBER, 1917.

HONOURS AND AWARDS.

Mentioned in Field Marshal Sir Douglas Haig's Despatch, November 7th, 1917, Authority, Supplements to London Gazettes, December, 1917.

Major S. G. Johnson, M.C.,

2/Lieut. A. J. Ellis.

No. 444349, 2/Cpl. Folwell, A.T.

No. 444058, L/Cpl. Duffy. J.

S. Gordon Johnson
Major.

4.1.18. O.C., 42nd Div'l Signal Coy., R.E.

WAR DIARY.

APPENDIX "E". DECEMBER, 1917.

WEEKLY STRENGTHS, CASUALTIES, REINFORCEMENTS.

		O.	O.R.
STRENGTH.	Week ending Dec 1st.	9	281.
	" " Dec 8th.	9	280.
	" " Dec 15th.	10	275.
	" " Dec 22nd.	10	275.
	" " Dec 29th.	10	275.
CASUALTIES.	Killed.	-	-
	Wounded .	-	-
	Sick to Hospital.	-	4
	Returned to Depot.	-	3
	To R.E . Cadet Unit.	-	1
		-	8
REINFORCEMENTS.			
	From 2nd Army Signals.	1	1
	From 1st Army Signals. ∅	1	-
		2	-

∅ Attached supernumerary.

S. Gordon Johnston Major.

4.1.18. O.C., 42nd Div'l Signal Coy. R.E.

Wireless. Power Buzzer, & Amplifier Communications in 42nd Division Area.

Reference Bethune Combined. 1/40.000

Wireless Directing Sta W 9.d.

Divisional Wireless Sta X.7.b.02.

X S F A

Directing Sta

Wireless Sta Trench Set. X.28 a 48

To Directing Sta.

Wireless Sta Trench Set

P.B & Amp

Test Point

P.B & Amp

A.1.d.02.

Festubert

P.B. & Amp

Lt. Bn.

P.B. Lt. Coy S.21 d.80

Rt. Coy P.B. A 3.a.48

P.B A 3.c.15 Lt Coy Rt. Bn.

P.B & Amp. A.8.d.73 Rt. Bn.

P.B Rt. Coy. A.9.c.63

Givenchy

Cen. Coy Lt. Bn.

A.15.b.23.

P.B & Amp A.15.c.45

Lt. Bn.

Cuinchy

P.B Rt. Coy Rt. Bn. A 27.b.28

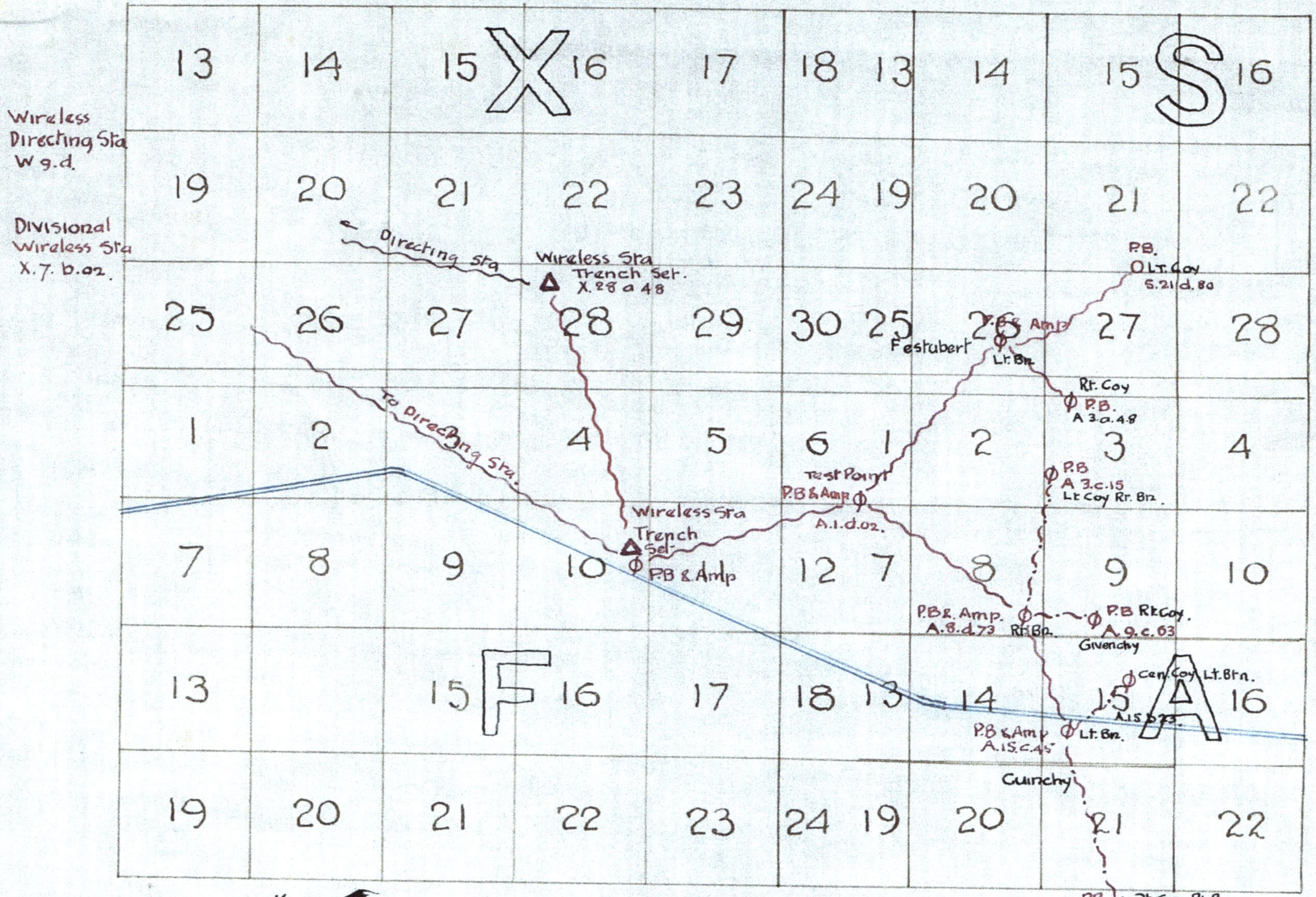

Map "C".

Major
O.C. 42nd Div. Signal Coy. RE.

Visual Communications in 42nd Divisional Area.

Reference Bethune (Combined Sheet) 1/40.000

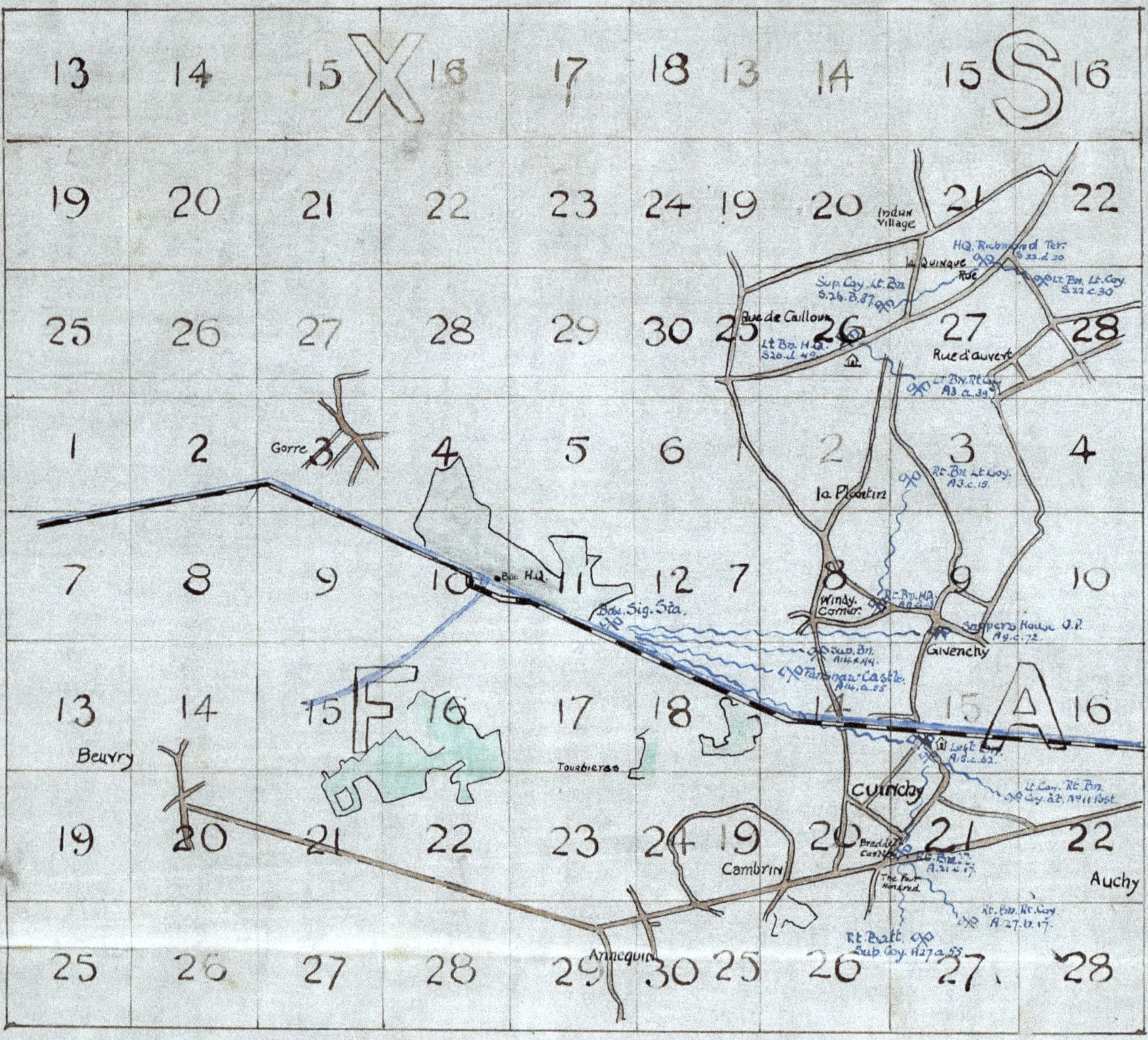

X S F A

Indian Village
HQ. Richmond Ter. S.22.d.20
la Quinque Rue
Sup. Coy. Lt. Bn. S.26.b.87.
Lt. Bn. Lt. Coy. S.22.c.30
Rue de Cailloux
Lt. Bn. H.Q. S20.d.49.
Rue d'auvert
Lt. Bn. Rt. Coy. A3.a.39.
Gorre
Rt. Bn. Lt. Coy. A3.c.15.
Bde. H.Q.
Bde. Sig. Sta.
Windy Corner.
Rt. Bn. HQ.
Sappers House O.P. A9.c.72.
Givenchy
Sup. Bn. A14.a.44.
Fanshaw Castle. A14.a.55
Beuvry
Tourbieres
Left Bn. A15.c.62.
Cuinchy
Lt. Coy. Rt. Bn.
Coy. at No 11 Post.
Braddell Castle
Rt. Bn.
A.21.c.17.
The Fort Hundred
Cambrin
Auchy
Rt. Bn. Rt. Coy. A.27.b.17.
Rt. Batt. Sub. Coy. A27.a.55
Annequin

War Dog Kennels

Map "D."

Major
O.C. 42nd Div. Signal Coy. R.E.

Map "B".

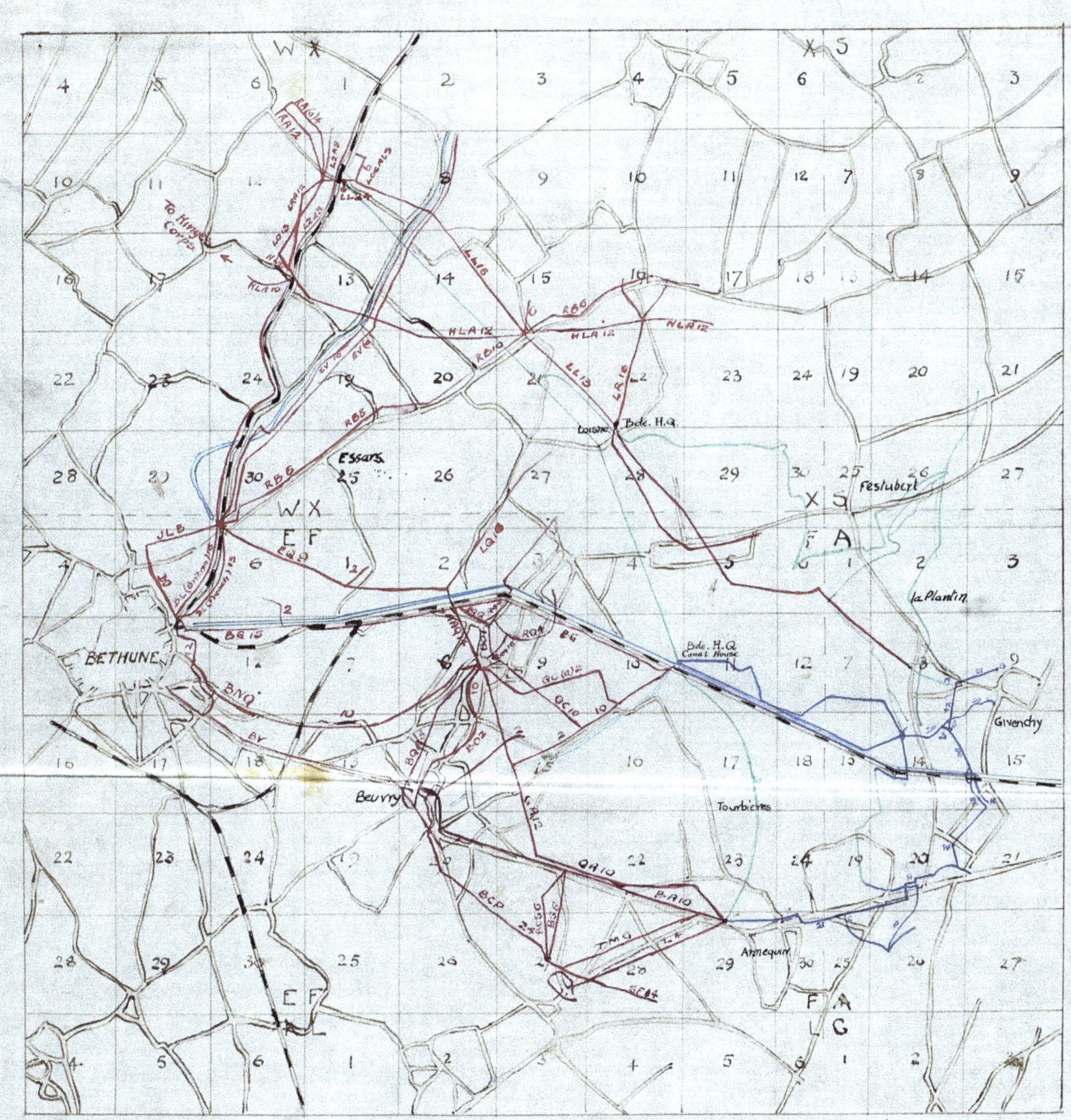

Route Chart of Communications in 42nd Divisional Area.

Airline	10	Figures denote	No. of wires.
Buried Routes	10	" "	No of circuits.
Overground		" "	No of "

Major
O.C. 42nd Div. Signal Coy R.E.

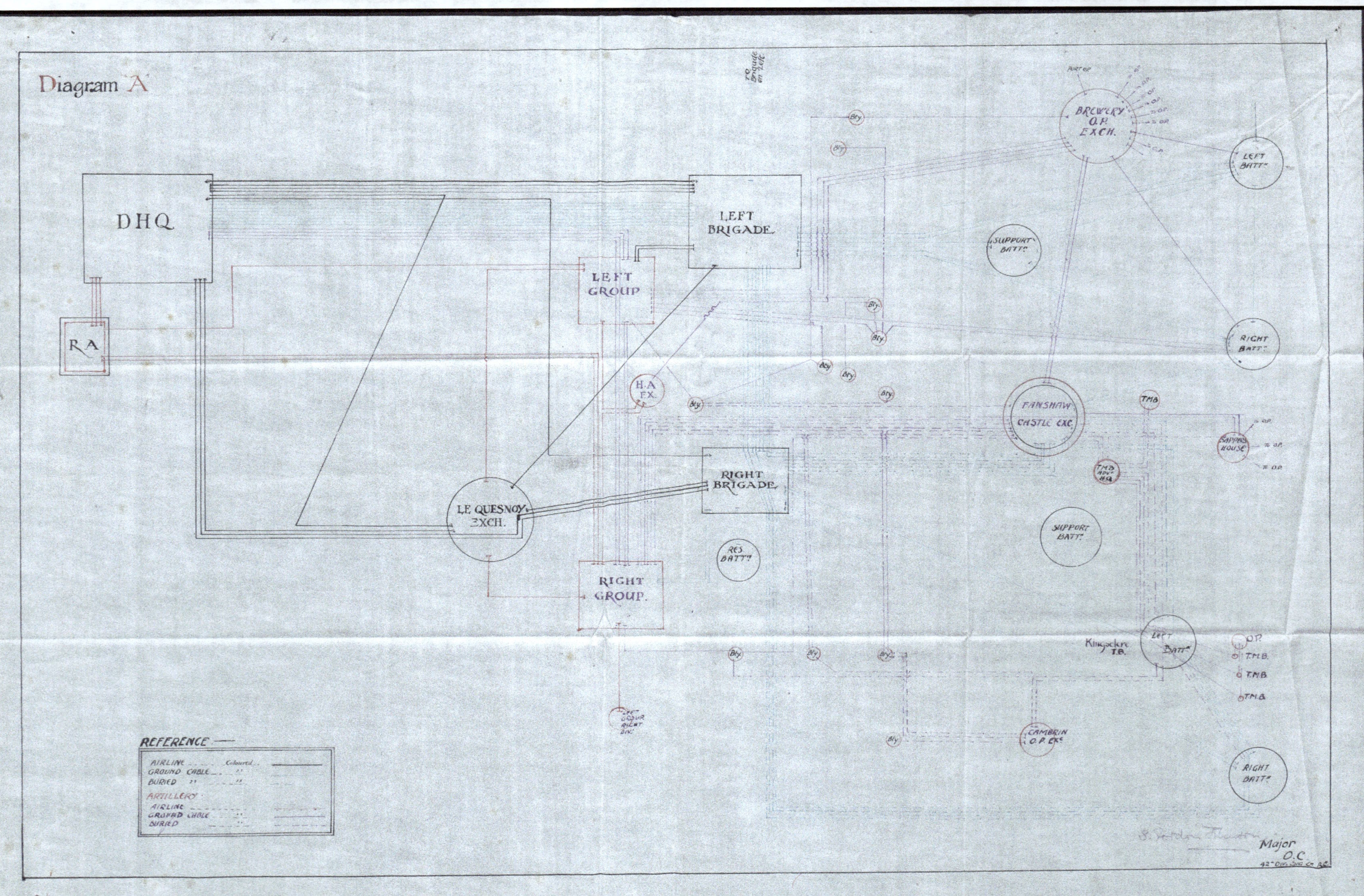

Diagram A
DHQ
RA
LEFT BRIGADE
LEFT GROUP
RIGHT BRIGADE
RIGHT GROUP
LE QUESNOY EXCH.
H.A. EX.
RES. BATT^Y
BREWERY O.P. EXCH.
LEFT BATT^Y
RIGHT BATT^Y
SUPPORT BATT^Y
FANSHAW CASTLE EXC.
SAPPERS HOUSE
TMB ADV HQ
TMB
SUPPORT BATT^Y
Kingsclere T.B.
LEFT BATT^Y
O.P.
T.M.B.
T.M.B
T.M.B
CAMBRIN O.P. EX^C
RIGHT BATT^Y
Bty
REFERENCE
AIRLINE
GROUND CABLE
BURIED
ARTILLERY
AIRLINE
GROUND CABLE
BURIED
Major
O.C.

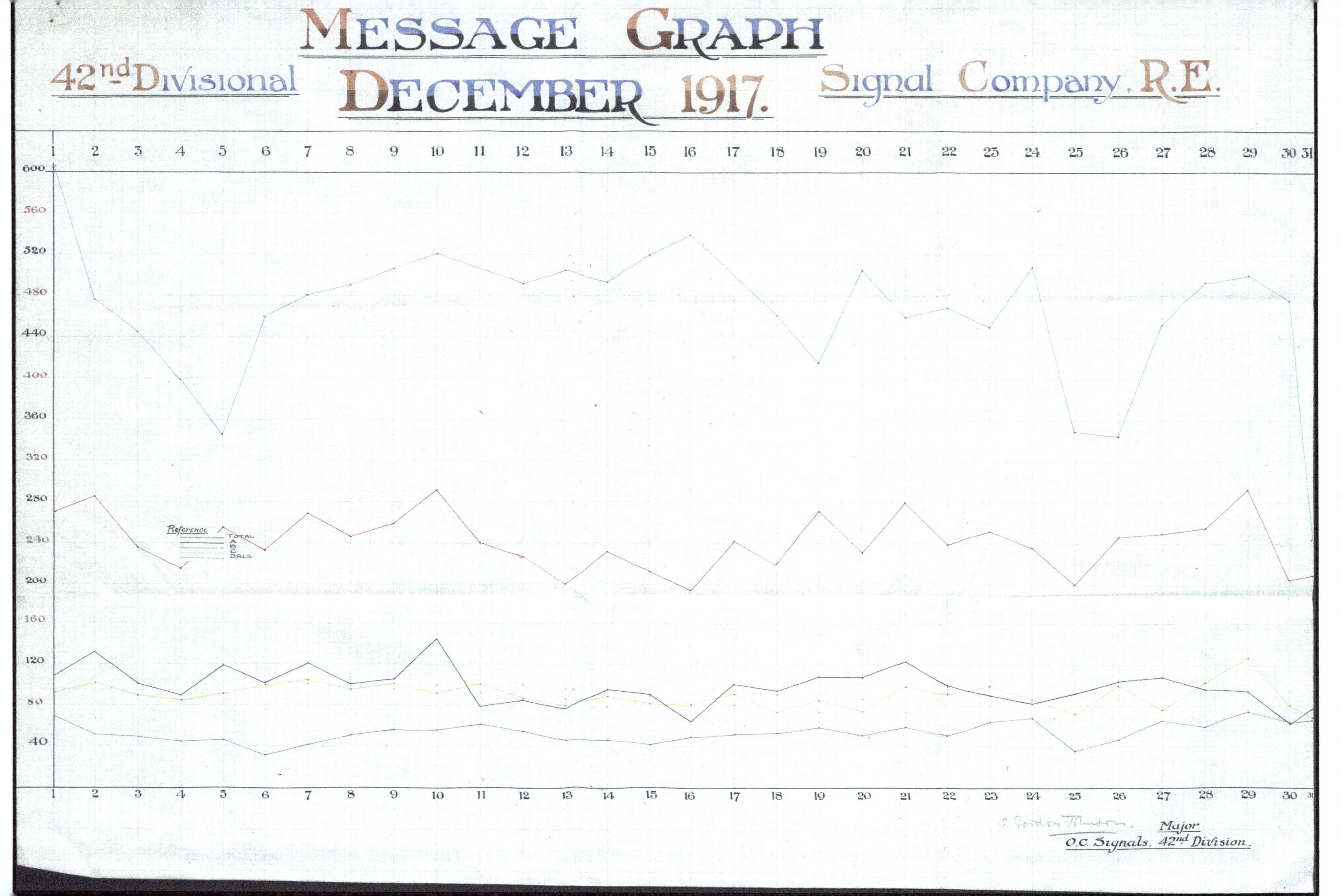

MESSAGE GRAPH
42nd Divisional
DECEMBER 1917.
Signal Company, R.E.
1 2 3 4 5 6 7 8 9 10 11 12 13 14 15 16 17 18 19 20 21 22 23 24 25 26 27 28 29 30 31
600
560
520
480
440
400
360
320
280
240
200
160
120
80
40
Reference
TOTAL
A
B
C
D.R.L.S.
Major
O.C. Signals. 42nd Division.

Vol 11

Secret.

WAR DIARY.

42ND DIV., SIGNAL CO., R.E.

Chapter XV.

S. Gordon Blunton: Major. O.C. Signals,
42 Division.

Army Form C. 2118.

Instructions regarding War Diaries and Intelligence Summaries are contained in F. S. Regs., Part II. and the Staff Manual respectively. Title pages will be prepared in manuscript.

WAR DIARY
or
~~INTELLIGENCE SUMMARY.~~

(Erase heading not required.)

Place	Date	Hour	Summary of Events and Information	Remarks and references to Appendices
			42nd (East Lancs) Divisional Signal Company.R.E. (T.F.). Reference Map FRANCE,BETHUNE, (1/40,000) combined sheet	
			CHAPTER XV January 1918.	
LOCON. (X.7.c.8.8.)	1.1.18.		The Division continued to hold the GIVENCHY and LA BASSEE CANAL Sectors with one Brigade in each. Communications were slightly altered and Appendix A gives the amended Scheme. The changes were due to the additions of the following routes to the Corps buried system:- (1). 20 pair rope laid in the inner flange of the railway running from point F.11.c.4.6. to ANNEQUIN. At the Northern end these were buried into a test point under the Western end of the Bridge over the BEUVRY CANAL at F.10.d.7.8. (2). 40 pairs buried from F.10.6.6.1. to Left Brigade Office at LOISNES. This route was taken through the Breastworks running past the Western end of the Tuning Fork where another route of 30 pairs was commenced towards FESTUBERT. The Southern end of the LOISNES bury was also carried through the Canal into the test point at F.10.d.7.8. The following were also commenced by the Corps:- 30 pairs from Test point at F.10.d.7.8 in the LA BASSEE CANAL to C.R. Test point at F.15.c.0.75. 30 pairs from test point at F.10.d.7.8. in the LA BASSEE CANAL back towards GORRE. 30 pairs from test point at F.10.d.7.8. in the BEUVRY CANAL towards BEUVRY. Maintainence work was carried on on all open wires routes and general overhauls were undertaken. (For Diagram of communications see APPENDIX "B")	APPENDIX "A". APPENDIX "B"
NR BETHUNE. (W.28.d.8.8)	6.1.18.		The Seventh Course at the Divisional Signal Class dispersed. For particulars and results see Appendix D.	APPENDIX "D".
" "	6.1.18.		The Third Wireless and Power Buzzer- Amplifier Course for selected Infantry Signallers assembled 6.1.18. The Course lasts two weeks.	
" "	7.1.18.		84th Army Brigade R.F.A. arrived in back areas preparatory to moving into action to	

A7092). Wt. W12839/M1297 750,000. 1/17. D. D & L., Ltd. Forms/C2118/14.

Instructions regarding War Diaries and Intelligence Summaries are contained in F. S. Regs., Part II. and the Staff Manual respectively. Title pages will be prepared in manuscript.

WAR DIARY

or

~~INTELLIGENCE SUMMARY.~~

(*Erase heading not required.*)

Army Form C. 2118.

Place	Date	Hour	Summary of Events and Information	Remarks and references to Appendices
			reinforce the Divisional Artillery.	
	10.1.18.		Left Infantry Brigade Headquarters was shelled with 10.5 C.M. and direct hit scored on Signal Office. Office destroyed and all personnel wounded or killed. Total Signal Company casualties 2 killed, one wounded. Communications were restored in the cellar within half an hour by means of 7 pair lead cables previously run by the Brigade to the various routes coming in on the LOISNES CAGE. During the interval traffic for the Infantry Brigade was circulated via the Left Group R.A.	
	15.1.18.		84th Brigade. R.F.A. Headquarters moved to LOCON and connected up to Divisional Exchange	
	17.1.18.		The 8th Course at the Divisional Signal Class assembled 17.1.18. The course will be divided into two classes. (1). A Refresher Class for trained Signallers lasting four weeks. (2). For untrained men, lasting eight weeks. The proportion of men for each class being decided by the units concerned in accordance with their requirements.	
	20.1.18.		A Report on the Third Wireless and Power Buzzer- Amplifier Course which terminated 20.1.18 is shown in Appendix E.	APPENDIX "E"
	23.1.18.		B and C Batteries 84th Brigade R.F.A. moved into action at X.22.d.6.6. and F.10.d.9.4 respectively. Communication had previously been laid for these Batteries by the Left Group R.A.	
	26.1.18.		Headquarters 84th Brigade. R.F.A. relieved 211th Brigade at LOISNES . 211th Brigade Headquarters moved into LOCON.	
	" "	"	In accordance with Defence Scheme in case of a successful/hostile attack on the Northern flank, it was decided that Divisional Headquarters would move to W.30.a.8.8. on the BETHUNE - LA GORGUE Road (present Divisional Train Headquarters). Lines on pole on main route on this road were terminated on a 7 pair cable run onto a terminal board in the cellar , for use when required.	

A7092). Wt. W12839/M1297 750,000. 1/17. D. D & L., Ltd. Forms/C2118/14.

Instructions regarding War Diaries and Intelligence Summaries are contained in F. S. Regs., Part II. and the Staff Manual respectively. Title pages will be prepared in manuscript.

WAR DIARY
or
~~INTELLIGENCE-SUMMARY.~~
(Erase heading not required.)

Army Form C. 2118.

Place	Date	Hour	Summary of Events and Information	Remarks and references to Appendices
	31.1.18.		A Battery 84th Brigade moved into action at X.23.a.9.1. under Left Group. Communications were laid previously.	
	" "	"	Divisional Signal Office moved into cellar under "G" Office.	

APPENDICES TO THIS DIARY.

("A") Notes on communications.
("B") Diagram of communications.
("C") Monthly Message Chart.
("D") Report on Divisional Signal Class.
("E") Report on Third Wireless & Power Buzzer- Amplifier Course.
("F") Honours and Awards.
("G") Weekly strengths, casualties, reinforcements.

S. Gordon Johnston
Major.
O.C. 42nd Divisional Signal Co. R.E.

A7092). Wt. W12839/M1293 750,000. 1/17. D. D & L., Ltd. Forms/C2118/14.

APPENDIX "A". WAR DIARY. JANUARY 1918.

PART 1.

METHODS OF COMMUNICATIONS.

In arranging the communications of this Sector, in view of a defensive battle, every possible means have been arranged for; that is to say :-

A. Telegraph and Telephone
(i) Airline.
(ii) Ground Cable.
(iii) Buried Cable.

B. Wireless.

C. Despatch Riders and Runners.

D. Pigeons.

E. Visual Signalling.

F. Message Rockets.

G. War Dogs.

Each of the above means is described under the headings given.

In this Sector, the following points have to be taken into

(a) The left half of the Sector is marshy and buries can only be constructed in certain drier parts of it.

(b) The possibility of the enemy overhearing buzzer and telephone conversations is very considerable owing to the conductivity of the subsoil.

Owing to (a), it is necessary to have alternative ground cable route from the brigade to the battalions and a complete wireless system from the front line back, and owing to (b) it is essential that stringent orders are issued for restricting conversations and sending messages on important matters in front of the Brigade.

~~Instructions for action to be taken by Signals in the case of a Gas attack are given in part 3.~~

PART 2.

"A" TELEGRAPH AND TELEPHONE.

The communications in the Divisional area are, to a great extent airline. The airlines are terminated short of Brigade Headquarters and the circuits taken into the Headquarters Office by buried cable circuits.

In the Brigade areas there are buried cable and ground cable routes.

All the lines are shown in Diagram"J", the actual routes of all lines are shown on map "J,1"

As far as possible, when there are more than one line between two Headquarters, they are taken by different routes.

i. DIVISIONAL COMMUNICATIONS.

From Divisional Headquarters to the Right Infantry Brigade Headquarters there are two telephone and one telegraph lines; to the Left Infantry Brigade Headquarters there are three telephone and one telegraph lines.

To the Divisional Artillery Headquarters, there are three telephone lines.

From Divisional Artillery Headquarters there is one telephone line and one telegraph line to each Artillery Brigade. Artillery Brigades can be communicated with alternatively via the Infantry Brigades.

There is an advanced Divisional telephone exchange at LE QUESNOY. From LE QUESNOY exchange there is one line to each of the Right and Left Artillery and ~~Left~~ Right and Left Infantry Brigades. LE QUESNOY exchange is connected with the Divisional Headquarters exchange by two telephone lines.

ii. ARTILLERY GROUP COMMUNICATIONS.

(a) Each GROUP is connected by a telephone line with the Group on either side of it and also with the Heavy Artillery O.P. Exchange at X.28.d.9.1.

There is a direct telephone line from each Group Headquarters to each of the Batteries which it controls. In addition, there are lateral lines between the Batteries of the Brigades, so that in case of breakdown of the direct line to a battery, the Group can get communication with that battery via one of the other batteries.

Each Group is connected to the Infantry Brigade which it supports.

(b) O.P.EXCHANGES. There is an O.P. Exchange in each Sector
Right Sector at FANSHAWE CASTLE (A.14.a.5.5)
Left Sector at BREWERY (S. 20.c.8.2)

Each Artillery Group has two lines to the O.P. Exchange in its Sector and there is a line connecting the Exchanges together.

Each Battery is connected to one of the two exchanges and each Battalion in the line has one line to the nearest of them.

All the O.P's in the area are connected (in addition to the direct line from each to a Battery) to the O.P. exchanges so that any O.P. can be connected to any Battery.

The CAMBRIN O.P. exchange (A.26.a.3.2.) is connected to the FANSHAWE CASTLE O.P. exchange so that the Right Group Batteries can be controlled, if necessary, from this O.P. exchange which is in the Sector of the Division on the Right. One Battery of the Right Group has a direct line to CAMBRIN O.P. exchange.

(c) T.M.B. COMMUNICATIONS. Headquarters of V,X, and Z, T.M.Batteries are situated at PONT FIXE. An exchange has been installed there and is connected to all guns and O.P's, Left Battalion Right Brigade, FANSHAWE CASTLE O.P. exchange, and to Y T.M. Battery H.Q. at A.9.c.10.75. Y Battery in addition to its line to PONT FIXE is connected to Left Group R.F.A. and Right Battalion Left Bde.

The D.T.M.O. is stationed at Right Group Headquarters and is connected to the exchange there.

iii. RIGHT INFANTRY BRIGADE COMMUNICATIONS. Practically the whole of the lines in this Brigade area are buried. There is an advanced Brigade exchange and test Station at FANSHAWE CASTLE (A.14.a.5.5.) From Brigade Headquarters there are two direct lines to each Battalion in the line. In addition there are two lines from Brigade Headquarters to FANSHAWE CASTLE exchange and a line from FANSHAWE CASTLE exchange to each Battalion in the line and to the Support Battalion.

The reserve Battalion is connected to Brigade Headquarters by a short line.

This Brigade has also alternative communication to its Battalions in the line by four circuits of cable in the flanges of the Railway track running South, from Brigade Headquarters to the test cellar at F.29.a.9.8, near ANNEQUIN, from which point a bury runs forward and provides two buried telephone lines by this route to each of the Left and Right Battalions.

iv. LEFT INFANTRY BRIGADE COMMUNICATIONS. Telephone communication in the Left Brigade Sector is provided for both by buried and over-ground cable routes.

All the ground lines forward from Brigade Headquarters pass through a test point at F.6.c.9.1. whence they branch off in various directions. From Brigade Headquarters through this Test point there are two lines to each of the Right, Left, and support Battalions and a common line to the Machine Gun Coy and Trench Mortar Battery affiliated to the Brigade. There is also a line to the visual station at F.11.d.7.2.

Buried cable routes run Southwards from the Brigade Headquarters to the Right Brigade Headquarters, and Eastwards to FESTUBERT. This system provides two buried circuits to each of the Right and Left Battalions and one each to the support Battalion and Machine Gun Coy.

v. SMALL UNITS. The small units (e.g. Field Companies R.E., Field Ambulances etc.) in the Divisional area are connected to the nearest exchange. ~~The exchange to which they are connected is given in the attached list (List"A") of telephone connections to all exchanges in the area.~~

"B" WIRELESS COMMUNICATIONS. (DIAGRAM "J2).

i. DIVISIONAL COMMUNICATIONS. There is a Spark Wireless Station at Divisional Headquarters for communication to either Infantry Brigade in the line or to Corps Headquarters. There are Spark Wireless Stations at both Left and Right Infantry Brigades, which beside providing communication with the Divisional Headquarters, communicate with each other and so complete the chain of Wireless communication from the front line to ~~the Left~~ both Brigade Headquarters as described below.

ii. RIGHT INFANTRY BRIGADE. There is a Power Buzzer Station at the Right Company, Right Battalion, which transmits to the Amplifier Station at the Left Battalion Headquarters. This latter Station transmits to and receives from H.Q. Right Brigade at F.10.d.99, and alsoto and from the Right Battalion Headquarters Left Brigade at A.8.d.85.45.

iii. LEFT INFANTRY BRIGADE. The Power Buzzer and Amplifier communication is tested hourly. There are Power Buzzers at ~~Right~~ Left and Centre Companies of Right Battalion which transmit to the Amplifier Station at Battalion Headquarters at A.8.d.85.45. There is a Power Buzzer at the Left Company of the Left Battalion which transmits to the Amplifier Station at the Battalion Headquarters at S.26.d.4.9. The Power Buzzer and Amplifier Station at the Right Battalion transmits to and receives from the Battalions on Right and Left, and to and from the Left Brigade Headquarters at X.28.a.45 75. The Station at the Left Battalion Headquarters also transmits to and receives from Left Brigade Headquarters.

It has been found possible to arrange a very long secure base in the tunnel at GIVENCHY on which the Centre Company Right Battalion can transmit messages direct to Left Brigade Headquarters. This is tested once every night and is used for S.O.S. only.

The Spark Wireless Station at the Right Brigade Headquarters is in communication with the similar station at the Left Brigade Headquarters.

There is thus a complete chain of Wireless communication from each of the Power Buzzer Stations in the front line to Divisional Headquarters.

iv. POWER BUZZERS AND AMPLIFIERS. work well in this area owing to the nature of the ground. They can be relied on to transmit and receive loud signals over a range of 2000 yards with "bases" of normal length (100 to 150 yards) and between Battalion and Brigade Headquarters work well as a rule at a range of from 3500 to 4500 yards.

"C" - DESPATCH RIDERS AND RUNNERS.

(1) From Divisional H.Q. Motor cyclists are used to both Inf. Brigade H.Q.
For use in case of emergency, a motor cyclist is stationed at each Inf. Brigade H.Q.

(ii) The Right Inf. Brigade uses cyclists along the canal and as far as HARLEY STREET from where the despatches are carried by runners to the Battalion H.Q.

(iii) The Left Inf. Brigade uses cyclists from Brigade H.Q. as far forward WINDY CORNER and the entrance to FESTUBERT Village, from which points the despatch carrier has to run to the Right and Left Battalions in the line respectively.

(iv) Runners are stationed at Company & Battalion H.Q. for use as required for communication between them, in both Brigades.

"D"- PIGEONS. (DIAGRAM J.3)

Four pigeons are sent up daily to each Inf. Brigade in the line from the BETHUNE Lofts. There are three lofts connected by telephone with Adv. Divisional H.Q. Exchange LE QUESNOY. Messages carried back by birds are telephoned directly to Brigades and Division. From the Brigade H.Q. the birds are sent up to Company H.Q. in the line as required where they are kept for release in case of emergency. Birds are sent from the lofts in the morning or early afternoon each day for release during the following day. During the winter months the birds are not released unless to carry an urgent message in an emergency, but are sent back in their baskets on the evening of their day in the front line.

"E" VISUAL COMMUNICATIONS IN THE DIVISIONAL SECTOR.
(DIAGRAM "J3.")

The attached diagram ("J3") shows the Stations which are established in the Divisional Sector. The Stations at F.5.a.12.25 acts as a central visual station for both Artillery and Infantry Brigades in the left Sector, and the Station at F.10.d.25 serves the same purpose in the right Sector.

Only a limited amount of visual signalling is possible owing to the number of trees in the area and the configuration of the country.

To connect by "visual" those Headquarters where "visual" does not already exist would involve the placing of so many transmitting stations as to make the system impracticable.

"F"- ROCKETS.

Rockets are kept at Company Headquarters in the front line for use in case of breakdown of other communications. They are fired to Battalion Headquarters. A watch is kept for them at these Headquarters when communication from the advanced stations by other methods breaks down. All Company Headquarters should have two stakes driven firmly into the ground giving the direction of Battalion Headquarters.

"G" WAR DOGS (DIAGRAM "J3")

Kenneld are established at Left Battalion, Left Brigade and Left Battalion, Right Brigade.

The dogs at the Left Battalion, Left Brigade work from any point on that Battalion front, taking the messages to the Battalion Headquarters.

Those in the Right Brigade carry messages from any point on the Brigade front to the Left Battalion at KINGSCLERE.

S. Gordon Blunton
Major.

APPENDIX "D". WAR DIARY. JANUARY 1918.

42nd Division.

Herewith report and results of the Seventh Course at the Divisional Signal School:-

Course assembled. 3.10.17.
Course disbanded 15 to 18.11.17.
Course re-assembled. 9 & 10.12.17.
Course dispersed. 6.1.18.

	O	N.C.O's.	Men.
Number who finished course.	5	2	132
Number to hospital.	-	-	26
No. returned to unit inefficient.	-	-	27
No. failed to re-assemble.	-	-	26
No. to Army & Corps Schools.	4	2	-
Total.	9	4	211

The following were the results of the final test:-

	O.	N.C.O's.	Men
Passed 1st Class (8 words(or above) on all instruments).	4	2	108
Passed 2nd Class (6 words(or above) on all instruments)	1	-	21
Failed.	-	-	3
Total.	5	2	132.

The results of the course are good and the men showed considerable keenness, but of the original numbers sent there were a large number of men ~~of~~ who were of the type that are never likely to make really first-rate signallers. That is to say, they were lacking in intelligence, insufficiently educated or too old. It is important that men sent for training as signallers are able to write well, have good eyesight and good hearing, and also are not over 25 in the case of those who have not any previous knowledge of signalling.

It is essential that at least one Battalion Signalling Officer be sent to the School to assist in the training and general administration of the School. At present there is no Battalion Signalling Officer at the School. Lieut. Maule, 1/6th Manchester Regiment, being required with his Battalion, has been sent back.

(Signed) S. Gordon Johnson

Major.

11.1.18. O.C. 42nd Divisional Signal Co. R.E.

Copy

SIGNALLING CERTIFICATE.

42nd Divisional School of Signalling.

No...........Rank............Name...

Regiment........................attended the Seventh Course at the

Divisional School from...........to.................and has been

instructed in :-

Theory of Signalling.
Connecting of Instruments.
Fullerphone, D.3 telephone, Magneto phone.
Power Buzzer and Buzzer Unit.
Cable laying, jointing and labelling.
Office wiring and organisation.
The message form.
Daylight Lamp and Signalling Shutter.

He has passed a reading and sending test as under:-

Sending on.	Receiving on.
Buzzer.........Words per minute.	Buzzer......Words per minute.
Lamp...........Words per minute.	Lamp........Words per minute.
Shutter........Words per minute.	Shutter......Words per minute.

and is considered a..............Signaller.

10.1.18.

Major.

O.C. 42nd Divisional Signal Co. R.E.

42nd Division.

Herewith results of the Third Wireless and Power Buzzer-Amplifier Course held at the Divisional Signal Class. With the exception of the three last named on the list, all are qualified Wireless and Power Buzzer- Amplifier operators and have been included in the Brigade Wireless Sections. The three men referred to have been returned to their respective units.

I also attach a nominal roll of the men at present employed on Wireless, Power Buzzer-Amplifier duties in the Division and included in the Brigade Wireless Sections. In order to bring these Sections up to strength, i.e. 24 per Brigade, it is proposed to commence the Fourth Wireless Course on 24.1.18. Pupils should assemble on the 23.1.18 rationed up to 23.1.18. They will be rationed by the School on and from 24th January 1918.

The following are the men who are suitable for training as Wireless operators in the Division. It is suggested that 12 of these men be sent on the next course:-

No.	203478	Pte	Needham, J.	1/5th	Lancs.	Fusrs.
No.	203457	"	Cottham, E.	"	"	"
No.	204205	"	Astbury.	1/6th	"	"
No.	240233	"	Smethurst, H.	"	"	"
No.	305725	"	Minor, J.	1/8th	"	"
No.	20159	"	Hostwaite, W.	1/4th	East	Lancs.
No.	241667	"	Rose, A.	1/5th	"	"
No.	352225	"	Moss, F.	1/9th	Manchester	Regt.
No.	350444	"	Walker, R.	"	"	"
No.	54213	"	Coppins, F.	1/10th	"	"
No.	54212	"	Budden, A.	"	"	"
No.	376110	"	Chaplin, L.	"	"	"
No.	375253	L/Cpl	Hesketh, H.	"	"	"
No.	200264	Pte	Daniels, S.	1/5th	"	"
No.	352637	"	Wood, G.	"	"	"
No.	201828	"	Newton, R.	"	"	"
No.	250275	"	Bancroft, H.	1/6th	"	"
No.	251218	"	Jones, C.F.	"	"	"
No.	250489	"	Piper, T.	"	"	"
No.	275914	"	Longland, E.	1/7th	"	"
No.	275780	"	Matthews, A.	"	"	"
No.	275633	"	Wilkes, F.W.	"	"	"
No.	301481	"	Butters, A.	1/8th	"	"

At present there are no N.C.O's with the Brigade Wireless Sections (with the exception of three L/Corporals).

It is suggested that each Section consist of 1 Sergeant, 1 Corporal, 2 L/Corporals and 20 O.R. making the authorised total of 24 O.R.

(Signed) S. Gordon Johnson

Major.

21.1.18. O.C. 42nd Divisional Signal Co. R.E.

42nd DIVISIONAL SIGNAL CLASS.

RESULTS OF THIRD WIRELESS COURSE.

No.	Rank.	Name.	Regiment.	W/T Practical	W/T Theory.	P.B. & Cipher.	Total Marks.	Marks Obtd.	Remarks.
251292	Pte	Tongue.E.	1/6th Manchesters.	40	25	35	100	100	Very Good
250942	"	Shawcross,E.	" "	40	25	34	100	99	" "
275840	"	Denholme,J.	1/7th "	39	25	35	100	99	" "
201357	"	Forshaw.R.	1/5th "	40	25	34	100	99	" "
306176	"	Fenton,J.	1/8th L.Fusrs.	40	25	33	100	98	" "
27609	"	Rigby.S.	1/7th Mchrs.	40	25	33	100	98	" "
201290	"	Moore,W.	1/5th "	37	25	35	100	97	" "
301205	"	Atherley,W.	1/8th "	38	25	34	100	97	" "
241128	"	Pilling,	1/6th Lancs.Fus.	40	21	33	100	94	" "
200131	"	Hatch.E.	1/5th " "	39	25	29	100	93	" "
301246	"	Stennett,F.	1/8th Manchrs.	38	22	31	100	91	" "
280084	"	Jones,H.	1/7th Lancs.Fus.	34	22	31	100	87	Good.
281657	"	Nottingham,A.	" " "	37	19	28	100	84	Good
200356	"	Brierly,F.	1/5th " "	33	23	27	100	83	Fair.
305290	"	Maycox, A.	1/8th " "	28	23	31	100	82	Fair.
240416	"	Banks,J.	1/6th " "	25	23	24	100	72	Poor.

NOMINAL ROLL OF SIGNALLERS TRAINED IN WIRELESS POWER BUZZER AND AMPLIFIER WORK.

125th Brigade.

No. 200185	Pte	Withington.	1/5th Lancs. Fusrs.	
No. 20131	"	Hatch.E.	" " "	
No. 241128	"	Pilling,H.	1/6th " "	
No. 240289	"	Horrocks.	" " "	
No. 280044	"	Jones,H.	1/7th " "	
No. 281657	"	Nottingham,A.	" " "	
No. 281628	"	Bennett.	" " "	
No. 300061	"	Abraham.	" " "	
No. 280245	"	Hornby.	" " "	
No. 306176	"	Fenton,J.	1/8th " "	
No. 306199	L/Cpl	Rutland.	" " "	
No. 306054	Pte	Webb.	" " "	
			Total	12

126th Brigade.

No. 200159	Pte	Houstwaite.	1/4th East Lancs.	
No. 200199	"	Wilding.	" " "	
No. 200368	"	Thompason.A.	" " "	
No. 241085	L/Cpl	Driver.W.H.	1/5th " "	
No. 240790	Pte	Tillottson,	" " "	
No. 240414	"	Hough,D.A.	" " "	
No. 305603	L/Cpl	Bates.T.	1/9th Manchesters.	
No. 351414	Pte	Naish,H.	" "	
No. 350745	"	Crane,W.	" "	
No. 376401	"	Mellor,J.	1/10th "	
No. 376258	"	Sandiford,W.	" "	
No. 39712	"	Valet.T.	126th Machine Gun Co.	
			Total	12

127th Brigade.

No. 201357	Pte	Forshaw.R.	1/5th Manchesters.	
No. 201290	"	Moore.W.	" "	
No. 250845	"	Wyatt,J.	1/6th "	
No. 251292	"	Tongue,H.	" "	
No. 250942	"	Shawcross,E.	" "	
No. 275840	"	Denholme,J.	1/7th "	
No. 276137	"	Day,F.	" "	
No. 27609	"	Rigby.S.	" "	
No. 301205	"	Atherley.W.	1/8th "	
No. 301246	"	Stennett,F.	" "	
			Total	10.

Grand total. 34

APPENDIX "F". WAR DIARY. JANUARY. 1918.

HONOURS AND AWARDS.

Military Cross.

Captain A. ROBERTS. Authority Supplement to London Gazette 1.1.18.

Distinguished Conduct Medal.

No. 444601 Sgt. Pinder, H. Authority London Gazette dated 1.1.18.

3.2.18.

S. Gordon Johnson.
Major.
O.C. 42nd Divisional Signal Co. R.E.

APPENDIX "G". WAR DIARY. JANUARY, 1918.

WEEKLY STRENGTHS, CASUALTIES, REINFORCEMENTS.

		O.	O.R.
Strength.	Week ending January 5th	9.	279
	" " " 12th	9	272
	" " " 19th	9	273
	" " " 26th	9	274
Casualties.	Killed.	-	2
	Died of wounds.	-	1
	Wounded.	-	1
	Sick to hospital.	-	7
		-	11.
Reinforcements.	From hospital.	-	2
	" Base Signal Depot.	-	2
	" First Army Signals. ø	1	-
		1	4

ø Attached supernumerary.

S. Gordon Johnston.

3.2.18. O.C. 42nd Divisional Signal Co. R.E. Major.

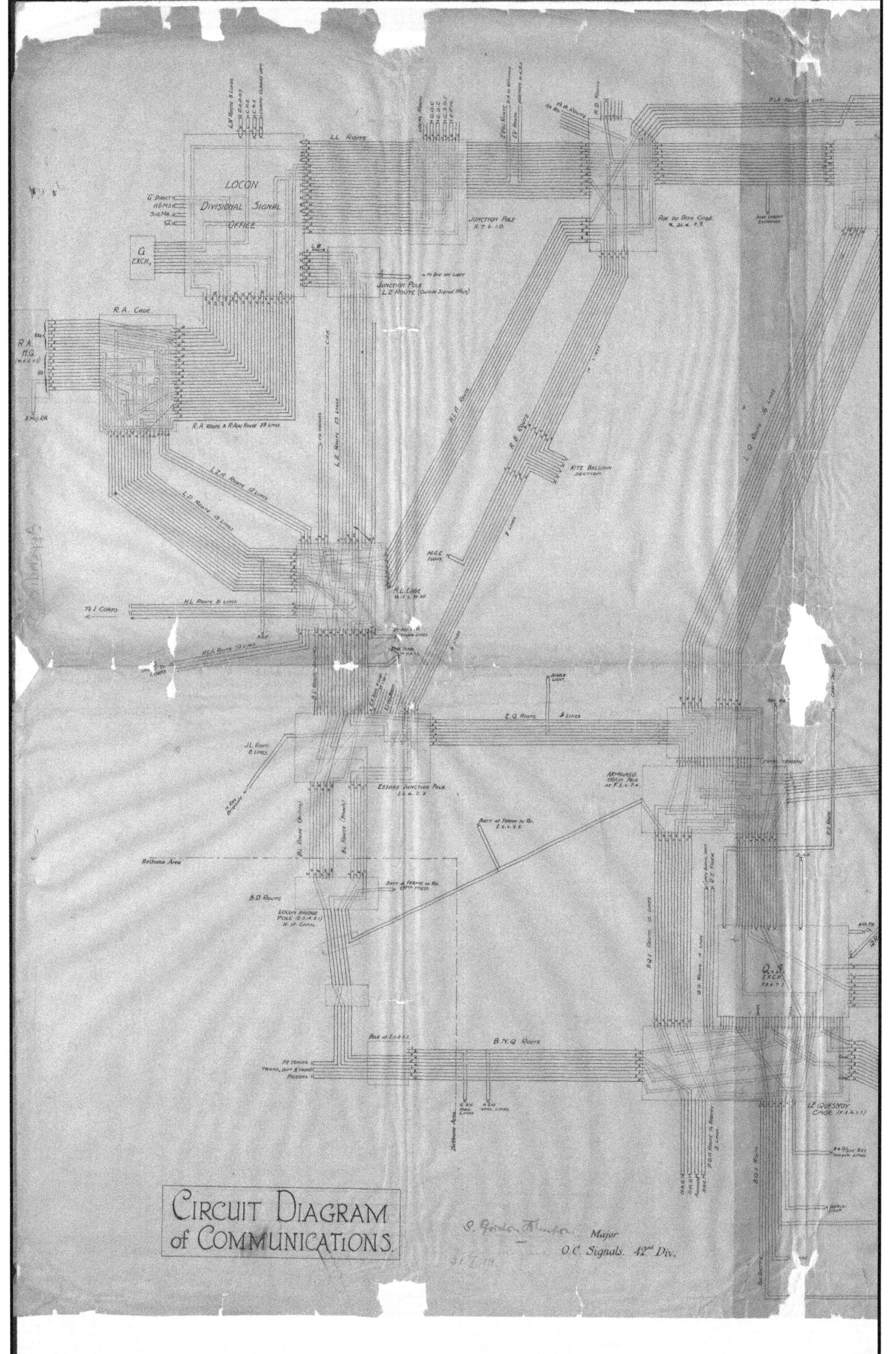

LL Route
LOCON
Divisional Signal
Office
G EXCH.
Junction Pole
Rue du Bois Cage
Junction Pole
L.Z. Route (Outside Signal Office)
R.A. Cage.
R.A. H.Q.
R.A. Route & R.A(B) Route 28 Lines
L.Z.A. Route 12 Lines
L.D. Route 13 Lines
L.E. Route 23 Lines
H.L.A. Route
R.B. Route
Kite Balloon Section
H.L. Cage
H.L. Route 21 Lines
To I Corps
H.L.A. Route 12 Lines
E.Q. Route 9 Lines
J.L. Route 8 Lines
Essars Junction Pole
Armoured Train Pole
Bethune Area
B.D. Route
Locon Bridge Pole
B.L. Route
B.N.Q Route
L.Q. Route 16 Lines
S.Q.1 Route 12 Lines
Q.S. EXCH.
Le Quesnoy Cage
Circuit Diagram of Communications.
Major
O.C. Signals. 42nd Div.

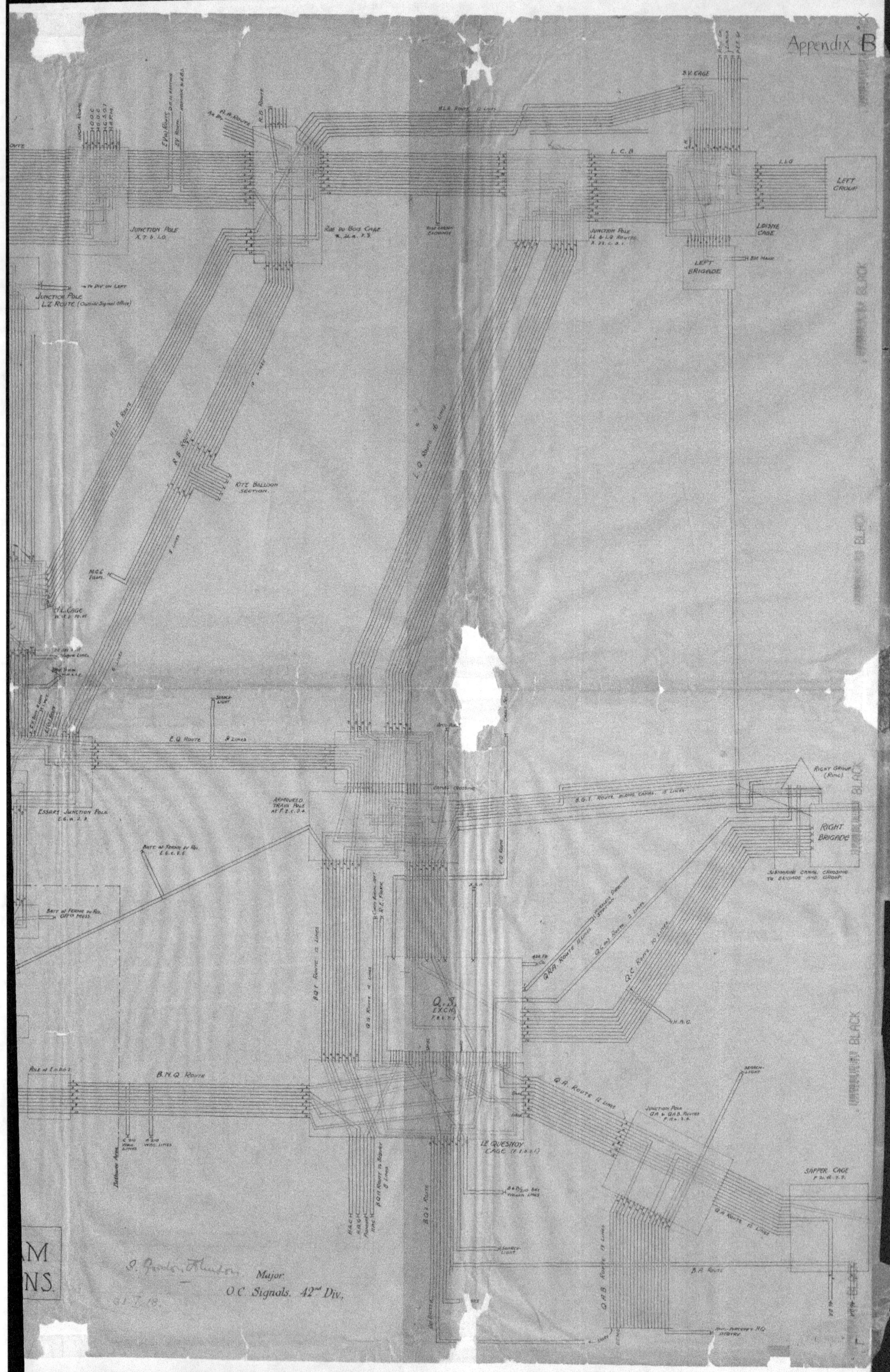

Appendix B
LEFT GROUP
LEFT BRIGADE
RIGHT BRIGADE
RIGHT GROUP (Ring)
JUNCTION POLE X.7.b.1.0.
RUE DU BOIS CAGE
JUNCTION POLE LZ ROUTE (Outside Signal Office)
L.C.B
L.L.G
L.Q. ROUTE 16 LINES
R.B. ROUTE
H.L.B. ROUTE
KITE BALLOON SECTION.
H.L. CAGE
E.Q. ROUTE 9 LINES
ESSARS JUNCTION POLE
ARMOURED TRAIN POLE
CANAL CROSSING
B.G.T. ROUTE ALONG CANAL 13 LINES
SUBMARINE CANAL CROSSING TO BRIGADE AND GROUP
Q.S. EXCH.
B.Q.1 ROUTE 12 LINES
Q.C. ROUTE 10 LINES
B.N.Q. ROUTE
LE QUESNOY CAGE
Q.A. ROUTE 12 LINES
JUNCTION POLE Q.A. & Q.A.B. ROUTES
SAPPER CAGE
Q.A. ROUTE 12 LINES
B.Q.2 ROUTE
Q.A.B. ROUTE 13 LINES
B.A. ROUTE
AM
NS.
Major.
O.C. Signals. 42nd Div.

Secret.

Vol 12

WAR DIARY.

42nd Divisional Signal Coy., R.E.

February 1918.

Chapter XVI

S. Gordon Johnston.

MAJOR.

O.C. 42nd Divisional Signal Coy. R.E.

Instructions regarding War Diaries and Intelligence Summaries are contained in F. S. Regs., Part II. and the Staff Manual respectively. Title pages will be prepared in manuscript.

WAR DIARY
or
~~INTELLIGENCE SUMMARY.~~

(*Erase heading not required.*)

Army Form C. 2118.

Place	Date	Hour	Summary of Events and Information	Remarks and references to Appendices
			42nd(East Lancs)Divisional Signal Company.R.E.(T.F). Reference Maps:- FRANCE, BETHUNE (1/40,000) combined Sheet.	
			CHAPTER XVI. FEBRUARY 1918.	
LOCON. (X.7.c.8.8)	1.2.18.		From the beginning of the month until the 15th when the Division was relieved by the 55th Division the maintenance party overhauled all open wire routes, repaired stays regulated and labelled wires and soldered joints. The work on the buried routes was continued and cables laid from LOISNE to FESTUBERT. Communications remained as already described in the previous Chapter.	
LOCON.	12.2.18.		A forecast diagram of communications in the reserve area together with instructions for the forthcoming relief were issued to all concerned. Copies attached.	
LOCON-LENGLET. CHOCQUES. HINGES.	15.2.18.		Relief took place at 10 a.m. and the Signal Company moved to the reserve billeting area in accordance with Order No. 10. In order to assemble and train the whole of the Company during the period the Division would be out of the line, the Signal Office at D.H.Q. at HINGES was staffed by Battalion Signallers. For the Programme of training as carried out until the end of the month see APPENDIX "A".	APPENDIX "A".
Nr. BETHUNE. (W.28.d.88)	16.2.18.		The Fourth Wireless and Power Buzzer-Amplifier Course at the Divisional Signal School terminated after three weeks training which consisted of Theoretical and Practical training in the use of the Trench and Loop Wireless Sets, Power Buzzer and Amplifier. Instruction was given in the design and connections of the various instruments, in Procedure and Station work, and in Intercommunication by means of outdoor Schemes. Eighteen men attended this Course, of whom fifteen passed the final tests.	
" "	17.2.18.		The Eighth (Refresher) Course at the Divisional Signal School dispersed. For a Report on the training and results attained see APPENDIX "B".	APPENDIX "B".

Contd/

Instructions regarding War Diaries and Intelligence Summaries are contained in F. S. Regs., Part II. and the Staff Manual respectively. Title pages will be prepared in manuscript.

WAR DIARY
or
~~INTELLIGENCE SUMMARY~~.

(Erase heading not required.)

Army Form C. 2118.

Place	Date	Hour	Summary of Events and Information	Remarks and references to Appendices
Nr. BETHUNE (W.28.d.8.8)	17.2.18.		The Tenth (Refresher) Course at the Divisional Signal School assembled for a Course of training lasting four weeks.	

APPENDICES TOTHIS DIARY.

A - PROGRAMME OF TRAINING.

B - REPORT ON EIGHTH (REFRESHER) COURSE AT DIVISIONAL SCHOOL.

C - HONOURS & AWARDS.

D - CASUALTIES; WEEKLY STRENGTHS, REINFORCEMENTS.

E - MONTHLY MESSAGE CHART.

4.3.18.

S. Gordon Thurston. Major.

O.C., 42nd Divisional Signal Coy., R.E.

A7092). Wt. W12839/M1293 750,000. 1/17. D. D & L., Ltd. Forms/C2118/14.

SECRET.   Copy No. 12

CORRIGENDUM
to
42nd Divisional Signal Company. R.E. Order No.10.

Para. 3 is hereby cancelled and the following distribution substituted:-

HINGES. Signal Office personnel as detailed.
Despatch Riders.
P.E.L. Set.

CHOCQUES. Transport.
Horses(Less mounted Linemens'Riders).
Drivers.
Infantry Brigade Sections Stores.) One man from each
Artillery Brigade Section Stores.) Section or Sub-section to be in charge of Stores.

LENGLET. Company Headquarters.
Remainder of Company.
Brigade Wireless Sections.

Nos. 2 and 3 Sections will be billetted at CHOCQUES for the night of the 14th February only.

210th Brigade Sub-section will join the Company on the 16th and not on the 15th as previously stated.

[signature]

2/Lieut.R.E.
13.2.18.   for O.C. 42nd Divisional Signal Co. R.E.

Issued by D.R.L.S. at   p.m.

Copy No.		Copy No.	
1	O.C.	7	No. 4 Section.
2	"A" & File.	8	210th R.F.A. Sub-section.
3	"T"	9	211th R.F.A. Sub-section.
4	H.Q. R.A. Section.	10	C.S.M. & C.Q.M.S.
5	No. 2 Section.	11	Signalmaster.
6	No. 3 Section.	12	War Diary. ✓

Acknowledge.

SECRET.   Copy. No. 12

42nd Divisional Signal Company R.E.
Order No. 10.

Map Reference Sheets 36A & 36B.

(1). The 42nd Division will be relieved by the 55th Division on the 15th February 1918. Divisional Headquarters and R.A. Headquarters will close at LOCON at 10 a.m. and reopen at HINGES at the same hour.

(2). The Brigades will move to the undermentioned places on the dates shown. Communication will be as shown in attached diagram. D.R.L.S. as per Time tables.

14.2.18.	125th Brigade.	-	FOUQUIERES.	Direct Line Fullerphone superimposed.
14.2.18.	126th Brigade.	-	BUSNES.	Direct Line.
12.2.18.	127th Brigade.	-	BURBURE.	via ACO and L.R.S. (LILLERS)
15.2.18.	210th Brigade.	-	FOUQUIERES.	via 125th Brigade.
16.2.18.	211th Brigade.	-	ANNEQUIN.	Direct Line.

(3) The 42nd Divisional Signal Company (including Infantry Brigade Sections and Artillery Sub-sections) will move to HINGES, CHOCQUES, and LENGLET. The distribution of the Company will be as follows:-

HINGES. Signal Office personnel as detailed.
Despatch Riders.
Instrument Repairers.
Technical Stores.

CHOCQUES. Company Headquarters.
C.Q.M.S. Stores.
Horses & Transport.
Drivers.
Linemen.
Inf. Brigade Sections.) Less Signalmen A & B.
Art. Brigade Sub-sections.)

LENGLET. Headquarters Wireless Section.
Telegraph Operators B.
Signalmen A & B.
Brigade Wireless Sections.

(4). The Signal Class will remain at BETHUNE (W.28.d.8.8).

(5). Brigade Sections and Sub-sections will join the Coy. as below:-

Section.	Date.	Place.
No.4	12.2.18.	LOCON.
No.3	14.2.18.	CHOCQUES.
No.2	14.2.18.	CHOCQUES.
210th Bde. Sub-sec.	15.2.18.	LOCON.
211th "	15.2.18.	LOCON.

(6). Each Section will bring two days rations and three dixies.

(7). All horse transport will move to CHOCQUES at 8.30 a.m. 15.2.18.

(8). The Company lorry to CHOCQUES, and a lorry to HINGES, from the D.S.C. will be loaded under the supervision of the C.Q.M.S. at 7 a.m. 15.2.18. Double journeys will be made if necessary.

(9). The electric light lorry will leave for HINGES at 9 a.m. 15.2.18.

12.2.18.

[signature] 2/Lieut.R.E.
for O.C. 42nd Divisional Signal Co. R.E.

Issued by orderly at p.m.

Copy No.1 O.C.
2 "A" & File.
3. "Q"
4. H.Q. R.A. Sect.

Copy No.5 No.2 Sect.
6.No.3 "
7 No.4 "
8 210th R.F.A.Sub-sec.

No.9 211th R.F.A. Sub-sec.
10 C.S.M. & C.Q.M.S.
No 11 Signalmaster.
No.12 War Diary.

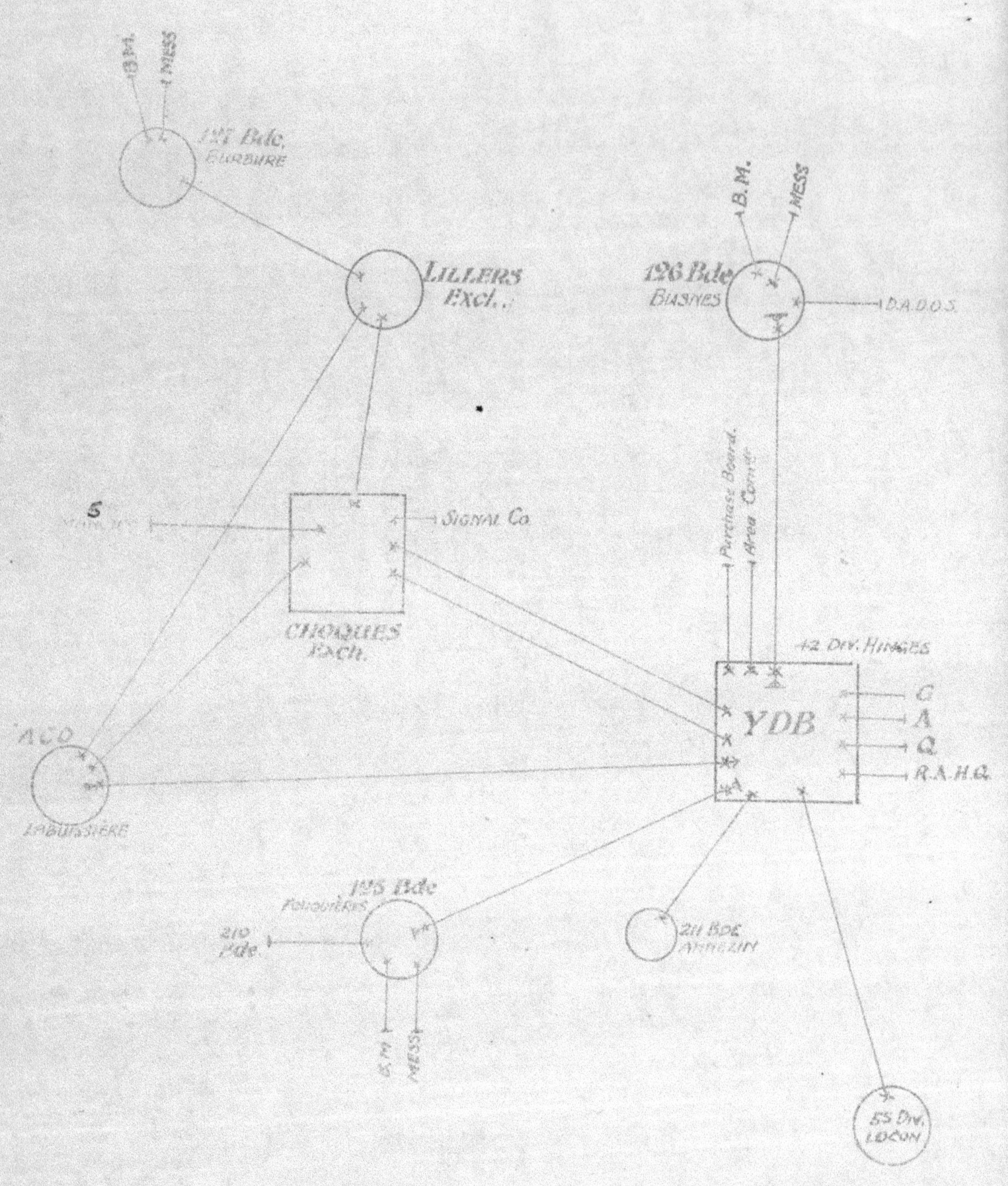

Forecast Diagram of Communications
of 42nd. DIV., at 10-0 am. on
15. 2. 18

APPENDIX A.

LENGLET.

TRAINING DAYS. (Monday, Wednesday, Thursday & Saturday).

6.30 a.m.	Reveille.
7.0 a.m. to 7.30 a.m.	Roll Call. Company Orders for day.
[illegible]	Fatigues, cleaning billets.
9.0 a.m.	O.C's Parade.
9.0 to 9.45 a.m.	Foot, rifle, gas or Flag drill.
10.0 to 11.0 a.m.) 11.15 to 12.30 p.m.)	Signal training according to Trade. ∅
2.0 to 3.0 p.m.) 3.15 to 4.15 p.m.)	Ditto.
5.30 to 6.30 p.m.	Special training for backward men.

RECREATION DAYS. (Tuesday & Friday).

6.30 a.m.	Reveille.
7.0 to 7.30 a.m.	Roll Call, Compang Orders for day, Fatigues, and cleaning billets.
9.0 a.m.	O.C's Parade.
9.0 to 9.45 a.m.	Recreational Training.
10.0 to 11.0 a.m.) 11.15 to 12.30 p.m.)	Signal Training according to Trade. ∅

SUNDAYS.

6.30 a.m.	Reveille.
7.0 to 7.30 a.m.	Roll Call, Company Orders for day, Fatigues and cleaning billets.
9.0 to 9.15 a.m.	Inseatlon of billets.
9.30 a.m.	Church Parade.
11.0 a.m.	Running.
2.0 p.m.	Football Match.

∅ (1). Telegraph Operators B and Brigade Wireless Section Operators.

(2). Signalmen A and B.

(3). Mounted and dismounted Linemen.

WIRELESS TRAINING. 42nd Divisional Signal Co. R.E.

FIRST WEEK.

CLASS "A" H.Q. Telegraphists. CLASSES "B" & "C" Brigade Wireless Sections. — As per attached Programme.

SECOND WEEK.

Continuation of the same. The exact programme will depend entirely on progress made.
During the third and fourth weeks other subjects of a more general nature will be introduced such as "Communication in the Attack" etc.
There will be foot drill or rifle drill every morning from 9.0 to 9.45 a.m. Lectures will be on the following subjects:-

Cypher.Procedure.
General principles of Wireless,
Waves.
Induction Coils & Spark Gap.
Condenser.
Capacity & Inductance.
Self Inductance.
Coupling.
Closed and open circuits.
Reception & Transmission.
Crystals.
Station work & discipline.
Accumulators.
Theory of the Valve.
Trench Set.
Loop Set.
Wilson Set.
Power Buzzer & Amlifier
Press reception.

PRACTICAL WORK.

Power Buzzer & Amplifier.
Trench Set.
Loop Set.
Press.
Erection of Aerials.

	A	B	C		A	B	C
Mon. 10 - 11	Cypher.	Cypher.	Cypher.	Thurs. 10 -11.	Lecture P.B.&A	Lecture P.B.&A	Trench Set.
11.15 - 12.30	Procedure.	Procedure.	Procedure.	11.15 12.30	P.B.&A.	W/T Lecture.	Trench Set.
2.0- 3.0	W/T Lecture.	Trench Set.	Loop Set.	2.0- 3.0	W/T Lecture.	P.B. & A.	W/T Lecture.
3.0 - 4.30	Aerial erection.	Trench Set.	Loop Set.	3.0- 4.30	W/T Lecture.	P.B.& A	Aerial erection.
Tues. 10-11.	Loop Set.	W.T. Lecture	P.B.& A.	Fri. 10-11	W/T Lecture.	Loop Set.	W/T Lecture.
11.15 12.30	Loop Set.	Procedure prac.	P.B. & A.	11.15 12.30	W/T Lecture.	Loop Set.	Lecture P.B& A.
Wed. 10-11.	Cypher.	Loop Set	W/T Lecture.	Sat. 10-11.	Loop Set.	W/T Lecture.	P.B. & A.
11.15 12.30	Procedure prac.	Loop Set.	Procedure prac.	11.15 12.30	Loop Set.	W/T Lecture.	P.B.& A.
2-3	W/T Lecture	Aerial erection.	Loop Set.	2-3	W/T Lecture.	P.B.& A	W/T Lect.
3-4,30	Procedure prac.	W/T Lecture.	Loop Set.	3-4.30	W/T Lecture.	P.B.& A	W/T Lecture.

(2). SIGNALMEN "A" and "B".

"A" 28
"B" 36

Total 64.

TRAINING DAYS. (Monday, Wednesday, Thursday, & Saturday).

TIME TABLE.

Class.	10.0 to 11.0	11.15 to 12.30	2.0 to 3.0	3.15 to 4.15	5.30 to 6.30
A	B	V	L	C	As necessary.
B	V	L	B	C	" "
C	L	B	V	C	" "

RECREATION DAYS. (Tuesday & Friday).

TIME TABLE.

Class.	10.0 to 11.0 a.m.	11.15 to 12.30 p.m.
A	T.S. or V.S.	T.S. or V.S.
B	" " "	" " "
C	" " "	" " "

Key:- B- Buzzer reading & sending.
V- Visual- Lamp & Shutter.
L- Lecture- See List.
T.S. or V.S.- Traffic or Visual Schemes.
C- Cable Instruction, Testing, locating and repairing faults.

LECTURES.

First Week.

Elementary electricity.
Elementary magnetism.
Theory of telephone.
Communication in the attack.

Second Week.

Signal Work in the Field and Station discipline.
D3 Telephone.
Office routine, registers and diagrams.
Linemens' duties.

Third Week.

Electricity & Magnetism
D3 Telephone.
D.R.L.S. & Runners.
Fullerphone.

Fourth Week.

Power Buzzer.
Wireless.
Communications- General review.
Wireless.

TRAINING - MOUNTED AND DISMOUNTED LINEMEN.

Mounted Linemen - H.Q. 16.
Dismounted " - Nol Sec 8.

Permanent Linemen.- H.Q. 4

R.A. Sub-sec. 6.
R.A. H.Q. 3
Brigade Sects. 15.
H.Q. R.A. 4
No 1 Section 2

Dismounted Linemen.

6.30 to 7.30 a.m.	Stables.
9.0 to 9.45 a.m.	Foot Drill.
10.0 to 11.0 a.m. or 10.0 to 11.40 a.m	Airlaine drill or Cable drill.
12.0 to 12.30 a.m.	Morse.
2.0 to 3.0 p.m.	Jointing (all classes of wire and cables)
3.15 to 4.15 p.m.	Lecture.
4.15 to 5.0 p.m.	Stables.

Mounted Linemen.

6.30 to 7.30 a.m.	Stables.
9.0 to 9.45 a.m.	Foot drill (or riding drill until 11
10.0 to 11.0 a.m.	Cable drill.
11.15 to 11.45 a.m.	Harness cleaning.
11.45 to 12.30 p.m.	Stables.
2.0 to 3.0 p.m.	Jointing all classes of wire & cables.
3.15 to 4.15 p.m.	Lecture.
4.30 to 5.0 p.m.	Stables.

TIME TABLE - FIRST WEEK.

	Morning.		2.0 to 3.0		3.15 to 4.15.		
	Mounted	Dismounted.	Mtd.	Dismtd.	Mtd	Dismtd.	
Monday.	C E	A	Lecture	Lecture	Instruments.		
Tuesday.	E C	A	Recreational Training.				
Wednesday.	C E	A	A J	C J	Instruments.		
Thursday.	E C	A	A J	Overhauling cable	Ditto.		
Friday.	P E	A	Recreational training.				
Saturday.	E P	A	Overhauling cable.	C J	Instruments.		

Key:- A - Airline.
C - Cable drill.
E - Exercise.
P - Poled cable.
J - Jointing.

LECTURES.

Theory of Airline (Field and Permanent) Construction.
Instruments.
Linemen's duties.
Testing.
Line Faults.- Locating and repairing.
Horse Management.

CHOCQUES.

O.i/c Lieut. Brown.
Assistants:-
Sgt. Turner.
F/Sgt. Powell.

DRIVERS.

TRAINING DAYS.

6.0 a.m. Reveille.
6.30 to 7.30 a.m. Morning stables.
9.0 to 11.0 a.m. Troop drill & riding.
11.15 to 12.30 p.m. Stables.
2.0 to 3.0 p.m. Foot, rifle, gas drill or lecture.
3.0 to 4.15 p.m. Cleaning Harness & Wagons.
4.30 to 5.0 p.m. Evening Stables.
6.0 p.m. Picquet Mounting.

RECREATION DAYS. (Tuesday & Friday)

6.0 a.m. Reveille.
6.30 to 7.30 a.m. Morning Stables.
9.0 to 10.30 a.m. Exercising Horses.
10.45 to 12.30 p.m. Grooming, cleaning Harness, Mid-day stables.
4.30 to 5.0 p.m. Evening Stables.
6.0 p.m. Picquet Mounting.

SUNDAYS.

6.0 a.m. Reveille.
6.30 to 7.30 a.m. Morning Stables.
9.0 a.m. Church Parade.
11.30 to 12.30 p.m. Mid-day Stables.
4.30 to 5.0 p.m. Evening Stables.
6.0 p.m. Picquet Mounting.

LECTURES.

6 Lectures on Horse Management. Capt. Stokes.
6 Lectures on Linemens' duties, cable laying, locating faults etc. Signal Officers (Days to be arranged).

HINGES.

Officer i/c Lieut............
Assistant. Sgt. Harrison.

DESPATCH RIDERS.

TRAINING DAYS (Monday, Wednesday, Thursday & Friday)

6.30 a.m.	Reveille.
7.0 to 7.30 a.m.	Roll Call, Company Orders for day, Fatigues & cleaning billets.
9.0 to 9.45 a.m.	Foot or gas drill.
10.0 to 11.0 a.m.	Lecture.
11.15 to 12.30 p.m.	Cleaning machines.
2.0 to 3.0 p.m.	Map reading & Field sketching.
3.15 to 4.30 p.m.	Visual Signalling.

RECREATION DAYS. (Tuesday & Friday).

6.30 a.m.	Reveille.
7.0 to 7.30 a.m.	Roll Call, Company Orders for day, Fatigues & cleaning billets.
9.0 to 9.45 a.m.	Recreational training.
10.0 to 11.0 a.m.	Lecture.
11.15 to 12.30 p.m.	Cleaning machines.

SUNDAYS.

6.30 a.m.	Reveille.
7.0 to 7.30 a.m.	Roll Call, Company Orders for day, Fatigues & cleaning billets.
9.0 to 9.15 a.m.	Inspection of billets.
9.30 a.m.	Church parade.
11.0 a.m.	Running.
2.0 p.m.	Football Match.

LECTURES.

The action of the Petrol Engine.
Tactical Use of D.R's.
Map Reading.
Field sketching.
D.R.L.S. Registers & Dockets.
Elementary Electro-Magnetism.
The Magneto.
Visual Signalling.

APPENDIX "B"

REPORT OF TRAINING AND RESULTS of the EIGHTH (REFRESHER) COURSE 42nd Divisional Signal School.

This Course consisted of Partially Trained Signallers from units of the Division, and reinforcements Signallers from England who reported at the School on various dates from the Divisional Wing.

The following is a Distribution List, according to units, of men who attended the whole or a portion of the course:-

	Reported. From Unit.	Reported. From Div.Wing.
5th Lancs. Fusrs.	4	3
6th " "	5	0
7th " "	4	0
8th " "	0	0
4th East Lancs. Regt.	5	1
5th " " "	0	5
9th Manchester Regt.	0	0
10th " "	2	0
126th M.G.Coy.	0	1
5th Manchester Regt.	2	1
6th " "	4	6
7th " "	2	0
8th " "	3	13
210th Bde. R.F.A.	5	0
211th Bde. R.F.A.	6	0
42nd D.A.C.	0	10
	42	40

The Course assembled on ....Jan. 16th 1918.
Training commenced .... " 17th "
Training completed ....Feb. 16th "
The Course dispersed on .... " 17th "
Duration of Training .... Four Weeks.

The men sent to this Course by units showed considerable keenness in their work, and their standard of intelligence was, on the whole, good.

The reinforcement signallers on arrival were generally inefficient and their style of sending was bad; many of them having done no signalling for six months; after a week or two's training these men showed considerable improvement.

TRAINING. Full instruction has been given in the following subjects:-

Flag drill.
Sending and reading on:-
D3 Telephone & Vibrator.
Fullerphone.
Daylight Lamp.
Folding shutter.
Message Form.
Buzzer Unit.
Signal Office Routine.
Intercommunication by D3 telephone & Fullerphone.
Intercommunication in the Field by Lamp & Shutter.
Station Calls and Code Names.
D.R.L.S. and Runners.
Cable jointing and Linemen's duties.

Partial Instruction, in the following subjects:-
Map reading.
Elementary Magnetism & Electricity.
Theory and connections of Instruments.

Partial Instruction (Contd).

Circuit diagrams.
Pigeon Service.
Forward communications in battle.
Earth Induction Sets.

Signal Office Work. Each man completing this Course has spent several whole days on a Traffic Scheme consisting of six small Signal Offices equipped with D 3 telephones or Fullerphones and Buzzer Units representing a Brigade or Battalion communication system.

Signalmaster's duties have been performed by each man.

The results of this training have been exceedingly good.

Visual Station Work. Several extensive Schemes of Visual communication in open country have been held, and each man has been practised in the establishment of Visual Stat ions and in the various duties at a Terminal or Transmitting Station.

The work on these Schemes has been very satisfactory.

TESTS AND EXAMINATION. At the end of the Course a Sending and Reading Test on the various Instruments was held in which each man to pass as First Class had to obtain 98% accuracy in the following:-

Send a Classification message on the Buzzer at 10 words per minute.
Read " " " " " Buzzer at 10 words " "
Read " " " " " Lamp at 8 words " "
Read " " " " " Shutter at 6 words " "

In addition a Test Examination Paper of questions on Message work, Visual Station work, Map reading, Linemen's duties, Signal Office Routine, and D 3 telephone was held.

The following Table shows the numbers of men per unit who attended or left the Course and who qualified or failed:-

Unit.	No. attendg Course	To other Schools	To Hospital	Retd to Unit	Failed	Qualified
5th Lancs. Fusrs.	7	-	2	2	1	2
6th " "	5	-	-	5	-	-
7th " "	4	-	1	-	2	1
4th East Lancs.	6	-	-	6	-	-
5th " "	5	-	-	-	1	4
10th Manchester Regt.	2	-	-	-	-	2
126th M.G.Coy.	1	-	-	-	-	1
5th Manchester Regt.	3	-	1	-	1	1
6th " "	10	-	-	-	-	10
7th " "	2	-	1	-	-	1
8th " "	16	-	2	-	-	14
210th Bde. R.F.A.	5	1 ø	-	-	-	4
211th Bde. R.F.A.	6	-	1	-	-	5
42nd D.A.C.	10.	-	-	-	1	9
	82	1	8	13	6	54

ø One Officer (the only one of course) to First Army Signal School.

Of the number of men completing the Course- 90% Qualified
10% Failed.

Average rate of Buzzer reading- On entering School 8½ words per minute
On leaving school 11 words " "

S. Gordon Johnston

Major.

24.2.18. O.C. 42nd Divisional Signal Co. R.E.

APPENDIX "C" WAR DIARY. FEBRUARY 1918.

HONOURS AND AWARDS.

His Majesty the King of the Belgians has been pleased to award the Belgian CROIX DE GUERRE to the undermentioned N.C.O's and man in recognition of their services whilst the Division was employed in Belgium:-

No. 444050 Sgt. Harrison.R.

No. 444045 Sgt. Wood,J.

No. 444007 Sgt. Watters,W.

No. 444776 Spr Redfern. G.

S. Gordon Thurston
Major.
O.C. 42nd Divisional Signal Co. R.E.

3.3.18.

APPENDIX "D" FEBRUARY 1918.

WAR DIARY.

WEEKLY STRENGTHS, CASUALTIES, REINFORCEMENTS.

WEEKLY STRENGTHS.

	O.	O.R.
Week ending 2nd February 1918.	9	273
" " 9th " "	9	271
" " 16th " "	9	274
" " 23rd " "	9	274

CASUALTIES.

	O.	O.R.
Killed.	-	-
Wounded.	-	-
Sick.	-	18
Returned to Depot.	-	2
	-	20

REINFORCEMENTS.

	O.	O.R.
From Depot.	-	3
" Hospital.	-	8
Transferred to R.E.	-	10
	-	21.

[initials]

3.3.18.

S. Gordon Johnson
Major.
O.C. 42nd Divisional Signal Co. R.E.

APPENDIX "E"

42nd Divisional MESSAGE GRAPH.

✣ FEBRUARY ✣ 1918 ✣

MESSAGE GRAPH.

FEBRUARY 1918

Signal Co., R·E

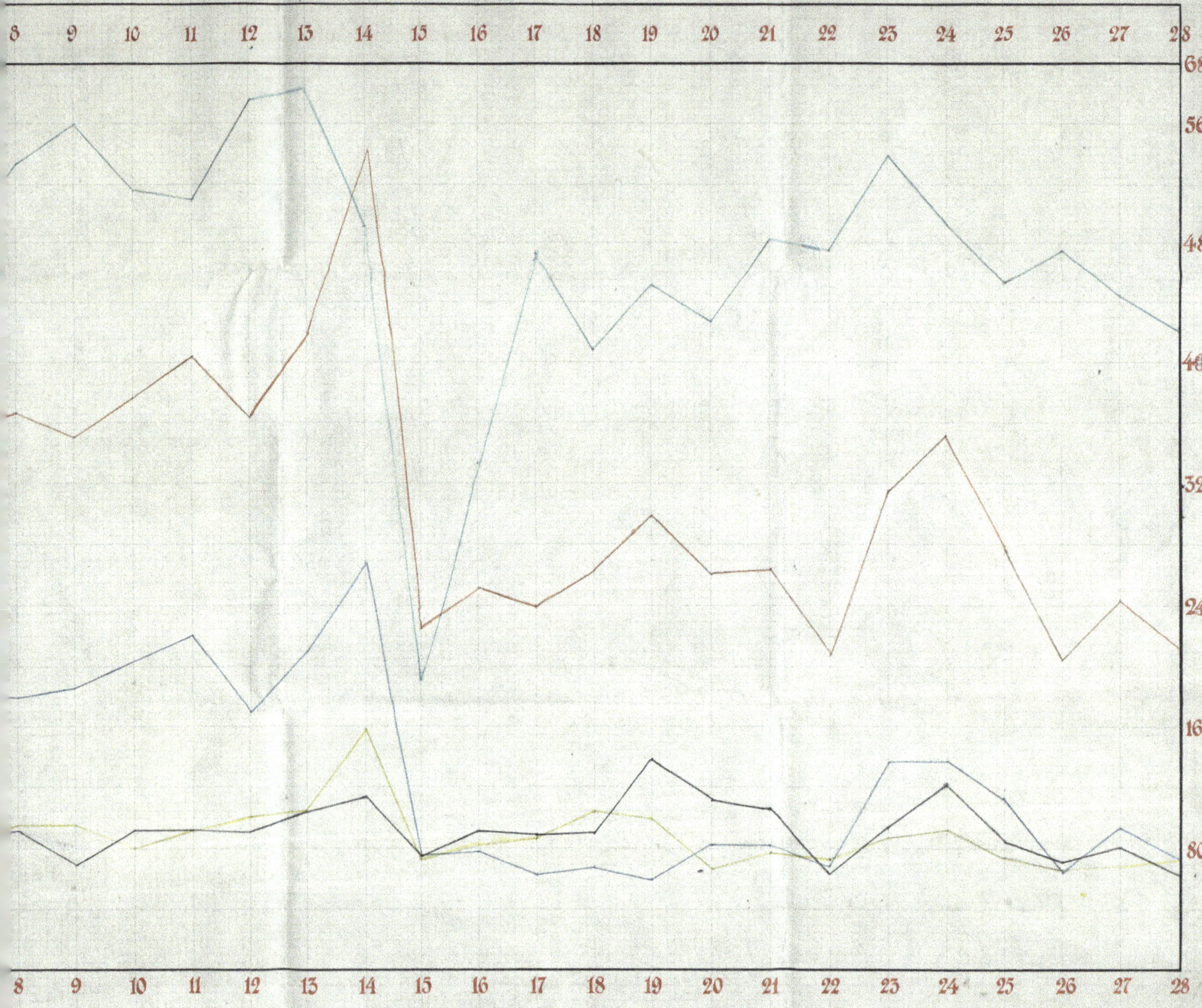

8 9 10 11 12 13 14 15 16 17 18 19 20 21 22 23 24 25 26 27 28

680
560
480
400
320
240
160
80

8 9 10 11 12 13 14 15 16 17 18 19 20 21 22 23 24 25 26 27 28

S. Gordon [illegible] Major. O.C. Signals.
42nd Division.

42nd Divisional Engineers

42nd DIVISIONAL SIGNAL COMPANY R. E.

MARCH 1 9 1 8

Attached:-

Appendices A. B. C & D.

O.O. No. 11.

Diagrams of
Communications.

Instructions regarding War Diaries and Intelligence Summaries are contained in F. S. Regs., Part II. and the Staff Manual respectively. Title pages will be prepared in manuscript.

WAR DIARY
or
INTELLIGENCE-SUMMARY.
(Erase heading not required.)

Army Form C. 2118.

42 D Signals
Vol 13

Place	Date	Hour	Summary of Events and Information	Remarks and references to Appendices
			42nd (East Lancs) Divisional Signal Co.R.E.(T.F.) Reference Map FRANCE BETHUNE (1/40,000) combined sheet. " " Sheets 51c & 57d (1/40,000).	
			CHAPTER XVII. MARCH 1918.	
HINGES LENGLET CHOCQUES	1.3.18.		The distribution of the Company until the 5th remained as described in the previous Chapter, when D.H.Q. moved from HINGES to LABEUVRIERE. Communications were obtained by utilising existing Corps and Army Lines. Diagram "A" shows the circuits in use before and after the move. Move in accordance with attached Order No.11. Training continued and those men who had reached the necessary standard were tested for re-mustering.	
NR BETHUNE. (W.28.d.8.8).	17.3.18.		The Ninth (Beginners) and Tenth (Refresher) Courses at the Divisional Signal Class dispersed. For reports and results of training see Appendix"A".	APPENDIX "A".
LENGLET.	23.3.18.		The dismounted men of the Company and the Staff and details of the Divisional Signal Class embussed near HESDIGNEUL and proceeded by road to Third Army Area debussing near DOUCHY, and bivouacing with Divisional Headquarters at ADINFER (X.21.d,sheet 51.c)	
ADINFER.	24.3.18.		The Company moved with Divisional Headquarters to MONCHY-LE-BOIS, where the transport which had proceeded by road from LENGLET, joined it in the evening. Communications from this date to March 31st are described in Appendix "B".	APPENDIX "B".
MONCHY-LE-BOIS.	25.3.18.		Divisional Headquarters proceeded to BUCQUOY with the Company and transport, the Signal Class and details proceeding to SOUASTRE , 42nd Division taking over a Sector of the front line..	
BUCQUOY.	26.3.18.		Divisional Headquarters with the Company moved back to FONQUEVILLERS and the Signal Class, details and transport proceeded to ST. AMAND.	
FONQUEVILLERS ST. AMAND.	27.3.18. 28.3.18.		The Division remained at FONQUEVILLERS until the 28th when it moved to ST AMAND, the Company having its Headquarters there and remaining there until the 31st. On the night of March 29/30th The Division was relieved in the line by the 41st Division, the	

Instructions regarding War Diaries and Intelligence Summaries are contained in F. S. Regs., Part II. and the Staff Manual respectively. Title pages will be prepared in manuscript.

WAR DIARY
or
~~INTELLIGENCE SUMMARY.~~
(Erase heading not required.)

Army Form C. 2118.

Place	Date	Hour	Summary of Events and Information	Remarks and references to Appendices

arrangements for communication being detailed in attached Company Order No.9.

APPENDICES TO THIS DIARY.

(A). Reports on Ninth (Beginners) and Tenth (Refresher) Courses at the Divisional Signal Class.

(B). Communications.

(C). Honours and Awards.

(D). Casualties, Weekly Strengths, Reinforcements.

~~(E). Monthly Message Chart.~~

S. Gordon Johnson

Major.

4.4.18. O.C. 42nd Divisional Signal Coy.R.E.

A7092). Wt. W12839/M1293 750,000. 1/17. D. D & L., Ltd. Forms/C2118/14.

APPENDIX "A" (War Diary)

REPORT ON TRAINING and RESULTS
of the
NINTH (BEGINNERS) COURSE,
42nd Divisional Signal Class.

This Course consisted of untrained men from the undermentioned units of the Division, and a small party from the 84th Brigade R.F.A.

The following numbers attended the Course:-

Officers............5
O.R................89

The Course assembled on...... Jan. 17th 1918.
Training commenced....... " 18th "
Training completed....... Mch. 16th "
The Course dispersed......... " 17th & 18th 1918.
Duration of Training..... Eight Weeks.

The Officers, N.C.O's and men attending this Course showed exceptional keenness and interest in their training.

Commencing with practically no knowledge of signalling and therefore with no wrong ideas they quickly learnt and adopted correct methods and style.

TESTS AND EXAMINATION. The final tests were as follows:-

The Buzzer test being a 5 minute test at the rate given. Qualification required an accuracy of 98%.

Send a classification message on the Buzzer at 10 words per minute.
Read " " " " " Buzzer at 10 " " "
Read " " " " " Lamp at 8 " " "
Read " " " " " Shutter at 6 " " "
obtain 45% of marks in a test examination paper of questions on Message Procedure, Visual Station Work, Cable and Line Work, D.III Telephone, Circuit Diagrams, Map Reading, Fullerphone, Signal Office Routine, and Forward Communications in Battle.

The following Table shows the numbers of personnel per unit who attended or left the Course, and who qualified or failed:-

Unit.	No. attendg Course.	Retd to Unit.	Retd to unit ineffic.	To Hosp.	To other Schools	Failed	Qualified.
5th Lancs.Fusrs.	6	-	1	2	-	1	2
6th " "	6	6	-	-	-	-	-
7th " "	1	-	-	-	-	-	1
8th " "	7	-	-	1	-	2	4
125th T.M.B.	1	-	-	-	-	-	1
4th East Lancs.Rgt.	6	6	-	-	-	-	-
5th " " "	10	-	1	1	-	4	4
8th Manchesters.	2	-	-	-	1	-	1
9th "	10	10	-	-	-	-	-
10th "	8	-	3	2	-	1	2
5th "	12	-	-	1	-	1	-
7th "	10	-	-	-	-	-	10
42nd M.G. Bn. (125 Co)	3	-	-	2 ø	-	1	-
42nd Trench Mortar Bty	1	-	-	-	-	-	1
210th Brigade.R.F.A.	4	-	-	2	-	-	2
211th " R.F.A.	2	-	-	-	-	1	1
42nd D.A.C.	6	-	-	-	-	2	4
84th Brigade.R.F.A.	4	-	-	2	-	-	2
I Corps Cyc. Bn.	5	-	-	-	-	2	3
	94	22	5	13	1	15	38

ø One man killed by bomb.

of the number of personnel completing the Course, 72% qualified.

Average rate of Buzzer reading :-
On entering School......... 0½ words per minute.
On leaving school..........10½ words per minute.

~~The detailed results by units are given on the attached sheets.~~

It should be noted that five men qualified in reading and sending tests but failed on the test paper, and also that the Officer and 4 men of the Corps Cyclists had only about five weeks training.

TRAINING. Full instruction had been given in the following subjects:-

Flag drill.
Sending & Reading on
D.3 Telephone & Vibrator.
Fullerphone.
Daylight Lamp.
Folding Shutter.
Message Form.
Buzzer Units.
Signal Office Routine.
Intercommunication by D.3 Telephone & Fullerphone.
Intercommunication in the Field by Lamp & Shutter.
Station Calls & Code Names.
Artillery Abbreviations (Artillery Signallers only)
D.R.L.S. & Runners.
Cable jointing, labels, & linemens duties.

Partial instruction in the following subjects:-

Map Reading.
Elementary Magnetism & Electricity.
Theory, connections and care of instruments.
Circuit Diagrams.
Pigeon Service.
Forward Communications in Battle.
Power Buzzer.

Signal Office Work. Though a few men were hardly far enough advanced, each Officer and man completing the Course has spent several days on a Traffic Scheme consisting of six small Signal Offices equipped with D.3 Telephones or Fullerphones, & Buzzer Exchanges, representing a Brigade or Battalion or Brigade system of Communications. Signal Masters' duties have been performed by each Officer and man.

The results of this training have been exceedingly good.

Visual Station Work. Several extensive schemes of visual communication in open country have been held, and each officer and man has been practised in the establishment of visual stations, and in the various duties at a Terminal or Transmitting Station.

The work on these stations has been carried out with much interest and intelligence.

Linemens' Duties. A few selected men have received additional training in Cable and Linemens' work.

AR

(Signed) A Roberts

Captain.R.E.

21.3.18. for O.C. 42nd Divisional Signal Co.R.E.

APPENDIX "A"

REPORT ON TRAINING AND RESULTS OF THE TENTH (REFRESHER) COURSE.

42nd Divisional Signal Class.

This course consisted of trained and partially trained signallers from the units of the Division, and also a number of Reinforcement Signallers from England who reported at the School on various dates from the Divisional Wing.

The following numbers attended the course: -

Officers 3
O.R. 155

The Course assembled on .... February 17, 1918.
Training Commenced ....February 18, 1918.
Training Completed .... March 16th, 1918.
The Course dispersed on .... March 17 & 18, 1918.
Duration of Training.............. Four weeks.

The Officers, N.C.O's and men attending this Course were, on arrival, very "rusty", and the initial Test failed to obtain a single "Pass out" on all three instruments. In every case Visual was the weak point.

At the end of one week's training, 37% reached the qualifying standard and this progress was maintained.

The Flag Drill was at first bad, particularly in respect to the Reinforcements who had developed unorthodox methods, but quickly improved.

The knowledge of Message Procedure and Signal Office work was frequently found to be poor and out of date; special instruction was given to correct this.

The Course generally took much interest in the instruction imparted and worked well.

The innovation of requiring a minimum number of marks awarded in the Test Paper for Qualification has proved itself of great value.

<u>TESTS AND EXAMINATION.</u> The Final Tests and Written Examination were as detailed in the Report on the Ninth Course, this being now the Standard Qualification for FIRST CLASS at this School.

The Test Paper was on the whole well and intelligently answered.

The following table shews the numbers of personnel per unit who attended or left the Course, and who qualified or failed :-

UNIT.	No. Attendg Course.	Retd to Unit.	Retd to Unit ineffic.	To Hosp.	To other Schools	Failed	Qualified.
5th Lancs Fus.	15	-	-	3	-	1	11
7th Lancs Fus.	11	-	-	1	-	-	10
8th Lancs Fus.	12	-	-	1	-	2	9
5th East Lancs.	8	-	-	-	-	1	7
8th Manchesters.	9	-	-	1	-	-	8
10th Manchesters.	9	-	-	-	-	2	7
5th Manchesters.	9	-	-	-	-	1	8
6th Manchesters.	8	-	-	1	-	-	7
7th Manchesters.	9	-	-	-	-	-	9
42nd M.G. Battalion.	24	1	-	-	-	-	23
42nd T.M.B.	2	-	-	-	-	-	2
210 Bde. R.F.A.	13	-	-	-	-	1	12
211 Bde. R.F.A.	22	-	-	4	-	1	17
42nd D.A.C.	5	-	-	-	-	-	5
42nd Div.Sig.Co.RE.	2	-	-	-	-	1	1
	158	1	-	11	-	10	136

of the number of Personnel completing the Course, 93% qualified.

<u>Average Rate of Buzzer Reading.</u>

On entering the School..... $7\frac{1}{2}$ words per minute.
On leaving the School ..... 14 words per minute.

The detailed results by units are given on the attached sheets.

TRAINING. Full instruction has been given in the following subjects:-

Flag Drill.

Sending & Reading on

D.3 Telephone and Vibrator.

Fullerphone.

Daylight Lamp.

Folding Shutter.

Message Form.

Buzzer Unit.

Signal Office Routine.

Intercommunication by D.3 Telephone and Fullerphone.

Intercommunication in the Field by Lamp and Shutter.

Station Calls and Code Names.

Artillery abbreviations (Artillery signallers only)

D.R.L.S. and Runners.

Cable jointing, labels and Linemens duties.

Writing.

Partial Instruction in the following subjects :-

Map Reading.

Elementary Magnetism & Electricity.

Theory, connections and care of instruments.

Circuit diagrams.

Forward communications in Battle.

Power Buzzer.

Signal Office Work. Each Officer, N.C.O. and man completing the Course has spent several days on a Traffic Scheme consisting of six small Signal Offices equipped with D.3. telephones or Fullerphones, and Buzzer exchanges, representing a Brigade or Battalion system of communications. Signalmasters duties have been performed by each individual.

This training has proved itself most necessary and useful.

Visual Station Work. - Each Officer, N.C.O. and man has taken part in several extensive Visual Schemes of communication in open country practising in turn the various duties at different stations.

These schemes have proved of much benefit and brought forth good results.

(Sd) S Gordon Johnson

Major.

2.4.18. O.C., 42nd Div'l Signal Coy., R.E.

APPENDIX B. WAR DIARY. MARCH 1918.

COMMUNICATIONS. Reference 1/40,000. Sheets 51 c and 57 c & D.

23.3.18. Divisional Headquarters moved from LA BEUVRIERE to BASSEUX. Communication with 6th Corps was established at BASSEUX at noon. At 3.30 p.m. Orders were received that Divisional Headquarters would immediately move to ADINFER. Communication with 6th Corps from the latter place was established through the advanced Corps Exchange at that place.

Meanwhile 125th, 126th, and 127th Infantry Brigades were moving down by bus from First Army Area, communication with them being maintained by Motor Cycle D.R. The Divisional Artillery, Headquarters, and 210th and 211th Brigades R.A. were marching from the same Area, and communication with them was similarly maintained.

24.3.18. By early morning 24.3.18. the three Infantry Brigades had established Headquarters as follows:-
125th and 126th Infantry Brigades in ADINFER WOOD in close proximity to Divisional Headquarters, communication with them being by runner. 127th Infantry Brigade at AYETTE, then the Headquarters of the 31st Division through whom communication with 127th Brigade Headquarters was established.

It was at this time impossible to establish communication by telephone with Brigades as no cable was available. The Cable Sections of the Company were still on the march from 1st Army to 3rd Army Area.

Divisional Headquarters moved to MONCHY-LE-BOIS in the morning of 24.3.18.

Telephone communication with VI Corps Headquarters was established from that place at 11.0 a.m.

A Forward Divisional Office was left at ADINFER to which place messages for the 125th and 126th Infantry Brigades were sent, being delivered thence by runner. Communication with 127th Infantry Brigade at AYETTE was still via VI Corps and 31st Division.

On arrival at MONCHY and after communication via VI Corps with ADINFER (for 125th & 126th Bdes) and AYETTE (for 127th Bde) had been established, direct communication between MONCHY and ADINFER was established by using one pair of a seven pair cable already existing between these two places. The telephone lines in use on the night of 24.3.18 are shewn in Diagram 1.

25.3.18. Orders were received on 24.3.18 that 42nd Division was to relieve 40th Division next day in the GOMMIECOURT Sector of the line with Divisional Headquarters at BUCQUOY. Reliefs of Signal personnel proceeded to BUCQUOY at 6.0 a.m. on 25.3.18. Great difficulty in the relieving of the Signal personnel was experienced owing to the pressure of Signal traffic and the consequent reluctance of O.C., Signals, 40th Division to allow personnel of this Company to take over the working of the system.

The communication between Divisional Headquarters and the Infantry Brigades in this Sector in the early morning of 25.3.18. were as shown in diagram 2.

An attack accompanied by heavy shelling developed in the morning of 25.3.18 with the result that communication became very difficult to maintain.

Command of the Divisional Sector passed to G.O.C. 42nd Division at 10.30 a.m. Relief of Signal personnel was immediately undertaken the communication being completely taken over at noon. At that time there was one D.5 single cable line still "through" to GOMMIECOURT. The aerial of the wireless station at GOMMIECOURT had been blown down by shell fire earlier in the morning and shortly afterwards the station itself was destroyed by a direct hit.

At about 12.30 p.m. the visual station R Y (on diagram 2) was hit and the chain of visual stations between Divisional Headquarters and the Brigades thus interrupted.

At 1.30 p.m. the remaining telephone communication with

GOMIECOURT was interrupted by the cutting by shell fire of the remaining cable between BUCQUOY and that place. Every endeavour was made to get these lines through again, but the heavy shelling made this impossible and motor cycle D.R's were the only means of communication which was available.

A party consisting of an officer and eight linemen and operators with the necessary instruments had been sent at 8.0 a.m. on the morning of 25.3.18 to relieve the personnel of the 40th Divisional Signal Coy at the Advanced Divisional Office at GOMIECOURT. This party could not reach GOMIECOURT owing to the shelling, but established communication from a point on the eastern edge of LOGEAST WOOD with Divisional Headquarters at 2.0 p.m. The Officer in charge of this party (CAPTAIN R. T. HARMER) was seriously wounded shortly afterwards.

Early in the afternoon the position of the various infantry brigades was not known definitely and great difficulty was experienced by Despatch Riders in finding them.

At 4.30 p.m. a cable detachment was sent forward in charge of an officer. This detachment re-established communication as far forward as COURCELLES LE COMTE (Sheet 57.c, A.15 Central). At 6.30 p.m. orders were received that Divisional Headquarters would move to FONQUEVILLERS. Accordingly a cable pair (D.8 Cable) was laid from BUCQUOY Via ESSARTS to FONQUEVILLERS. An Advanced Divisional Signal Office was left at BUCQUOY through which communication with IV Corps and the Infantry Brigades was maintained.

At midnight a Divisional Report Centre was established at ABLAINZEVELLE (Sheet 57D., F.23.d.8.2) This communication was maintained until 6.0 a.m., 26.3.18, when orders were received to close down the Report Centre and Advanced Divisional Signal Office and re-open a Divisional Report Centre at ESSARTS. A temporary Signal Office was immediately opened behind BUCQUOY (Sheet 57D., F.26.d.6.2) and touch was kept with Divisional Headquarters and Brigades during the withdrawal. At 8.30 a.m. a Divisional Report Centre was established at ESSARTS, the D.8 Cable previously laid being utilised back to Divisional Headquarters and forward to BUCQUOY. The forward office was kept open until all Brigades opened their Headquarters at ESSARTS. Another line back to Division was then laid and this communication was maintained.

Communication with Corps. The communications of 40th Division with VI Corps consisted of two telephone lines. When the command of the Divisional Sector passed to G.O.C., 42nd Division command of the Sector also passed to G.O.C. Fourth Corps. Considerable difficulty was experienced in maintaining communication with Sixth Corps and when command of the Sector passed it was not possible to get direct communication with Fourth Corps. The direct communication was established at 1.30 p.m. by extending one existing Sixth Corps line to Fourth Corps, the change being made by Fourth Corps Signals. This line was fairly satisfactory. When 42nd Divisional Headquarters moved back to FONQUEVILLERS the two lines to Fourth and Sixth Corps remained through to BUCQUOY and the communication between the Division and the Corps was via the Advanced Divisional Office at BUCQUOY.

The communications at about mid-night 25th/26th - 3.18 were as shown in Diagram 3.

26.3.18. During the night 25th/26th - 3.18. orders were received that the 42nd Division was to take up a line running in front of BUCQUOY. The three Infantry and two Artillery Brigades established Headquarters in ESSARTS. Accordingly a Divisional Report Centre was established at that place for communication with the Divisional Units. Meanwhile an Advanced Fourth Corps Exchange was established in FONQUEVILLERS and communication with IV Corps established through it.

The communications at 9.0 a.m., 26.3.18 were as shewn in diagram 4. Owing to the false alarm the advanced IV Corps Exchange was destroyed by the personnel of that exchange at 10.30 a.m., so that from that time the Division was out of touch by telephone with Corps Headquarters. Communication was not restored until 9.45 p.m. in the evening, when a cable pair laid by IV Corps from POMMIER exchange was brought in to the Divisional Office at FONQUEVILLERS.

In the afternoon information was received that the Divisional Headquarters would move next day to POMMIER. This was later altered, however, to ST. AMAND. Accordingly a single D.5 cable was laid from FONQUEVILLERS via BIENVILLERS and POMMIER to ST. AMAND and a rear Signal Office established there. The cable was laid and working between FONQUEVILLERS and ST. AMAND at 9.30 p.m.

There had been during the day occasional shelling of FONQUEVILLERS and the Divisional Signal Office there was in a very exposed place. During the night 27-28/3/18, it was moved to a cellar at E.21.c.3.4.

The communications at midnight 26-27/3/18 were as shewn in diagram 5.

27.3.18. The communications remained as on 26.3.18. Divisional Headquarters did not move back to ST. AMAND. There was little shelling and the cable lines were easily maintained.

28.3.18. At 8.30 a.m. on 28.3.18, Divisional Headquarters arrived at ST. AMAND. Two single D.5 cables were laid from ESSARTS Via HANNESCAMP, BIENVILLERS and POMMIER to ST. AMAND. A linemen's and D.R's relay post was established at HANNESCAMPS and a linemen's post at POMMIER.

It was intended to close the office at FONQUEVILLERS as soon as the two cable lines described above were complete and then connect through the existing lines from FONQUEVILLERS to ESSARTS and to ST. AMAND so as to provide three lines between the latter two places. Owing to the heavy shelling the lines at HANNESCAMP cross roads could not be maintained and the FONQUEVILLERS office was kept open until 3.0 p.m. when all lines from it were cut including the line to POMMIER Exchange. Meanwhile a pair of cables was laid by IV Corps from POMMIER to ST. AMAND and communication from the Division to IV Corps via POMMIER Exchange established at 10.40 a.m.

Communication with ESSARTS was re-established at about 4.30 p.m., but was repeatedly interrupted up to midnight.

Communications at midnight 28-29/3/18 was as shewn in diagram 6.

29.3.18. During the night 28-29/3/18 another cable line was laid from ST. AMAND to HANNESCAMP, which avoided the roads and ran in trenches and in the open 200 to 500 yards south of the POMMIER - HANNESCAMP road. This line was never interrupted. Considerable difficulty was experienced all day in maintaining lines forward of HANNESCAMP but communication by at least one line remained uninterrupted during the day.

Information was received on this day that Brigades of the 42nd Division in the line would be relieved by the Infantry Brigades of the 41st Division during the night of the 29/30th and that command of the Sector would pass to G.O.C., 41st Division early on the 30th.

The 126th Infantry Brigade, however, would remain at ESSARTS under the command of the 41st Division. The 125th and 127th Infantry Brigades were to move to Headquarters in the immediate vicinity of GOMMECOURT.

It was decided to re-open the old advanced Divisional Headquarters at FONQUEVILLERS and to communicate with the Brigades in GOMMECOURT through that office.

For communication between Divisional Headquarters at ST. AMAND and Advanced Division at FONQUEVILLERS one twin D.8 Cable was laid cross country, avoiding cross roads and shelled areas and the single cable laid on the night 28-29th from ST. AMAND to HANNESCAMP was diverted to FONQUEVILLERS. In addition, the existing pair from POMMIER Exchange to FONQUEVILLERS was picked up. Forwards from FONQUEVILLERS there were already two single cable lines - one to each Brigade Headquarters. There was also a lateral line joining two brigades and, in addition, a single cable line was laid from 125th Brigade Headquarters to the Report Centre of the Division in the line at ESSARTS.

30.3.18. Communications on the morning of the 30th after the move of Brigades had taken place, were as shewn in Diagram 7.

The 210th and 211th Bdes R.A. remained in action under the command of the 41st Division, communication with them being via that Division.

31.3.18. Communications remained the same as on the previous day.

WIRELESS COMMUNICATION :- Communication between the trench set at ESSARTS and a Wilson Set at Divisional Headquarters was maintained during the period 27-30th.3.18.

On relief of the Division the trench set was moved to GOMMECOURT and communication there maintained with Divisional Headquarters up to the end of the month.

No difficulty was experienced with this communication as long as the aerial of the forward station could be maintained except that the jamming by enemy stations was very severe.

VISUAL SIGNALLING:- During the period 27-31.3.18 no real use was made of Visual Signalling behind Infantry Brigade Headquarters. This was chiefly due to conditions of weather and ground which precluded the possibility of any but shortest distances being covered by Visual signalling without a large number of transmitting stations.

S. Gordon Johnston
Major.

APPENDIX "C". WAR DIARY. MARCH 1918.

HONOURS AND AWARDS.

NIL.

S. Gordon Johnston

Major.

4.4.18. O.C. 42nd Divisional Signal Co. R.E.

APPENDIX "D". MARCH 1918.

WAR DIARY.

WEEKLY STRENGTHS, CASUALTIES, REINFORCEMENTS.

WEEKLY STRENGTHS.

	O.	O.R.
Week ending 2nd March 1918.	9	267
" " 9th " "	10	268
" " 16th " "	10	272
" " 23rd " "	10	279
" " 30th " "	10	270

CASUALTIES.

		O.	O.R.
Killed		-	2
Wounded.	∅	1	7
Sick.		-	4
		1	13

REINFORCEMENTS.

		O.	O.R.
From Depot.			13
" Hospital.			6
" Cavalry Corps Signals.			1
" First Army Signal Co.		1.	-
" Third Army Signal Co.	∅	1	-
		2	20

∅ Attached Supernumerary.

S. Gordon Johnston

4.4.18. Major.

O.C. 42nd Divisional Signal Co.R.E.

Order No. 11.

Diagrams of Communications.

SECRET. Copy No....6...

42nd DIVISIONAL SIGNAL COMPANY.R.E.
ORDER No. 11.

Map reference sheet 36, BETHUNE
(Combined sheet).

1. 42nd D.H.Q. will close at HINGES at 12 noon 5.3.18. and will reopen at LABEUVRIERE at the same hour.

2. An advance Signal Office party under Sgt. Wood,E. will leave HINGES by lorry at 7 a.m. 5.3.18.
(Except that of No 4 Section)

3. The Horse Transport/at CHOCQUES under 2/Lieut. Collinson will move to CENSEE LA VALLEE , leaving CHOCQUES at 9 a.m. 5.3.18. No. 4 Section's transport will move to BUSNES via LENGLET at the same hour.

4. The lorry proceeding from HINGES at 7 a.m. to LABEUVRIERE will afterwards report to O.C. Transport CHOCQUES at 8.30 a.m. and take blankets, stores etc to CENSEE LA VALLEE

5. The lorry will report to Lieut. Crawshaw at HINGES at 12 noon and take the remaining Signal Office Stores and Personnel to LABEUVRIERE.

6. No. 4 Section under Lieut. Horner will rejoin the 127th Brigade at BUSNES leaving LENGLET at 10 a.m.

[signature]

2/Lieut. R.E.

4.3.18. for O.C. 42nd Divisional Signal Co. R.E.

Copy No. 1 "A" and File.
2 O.C. Transport CHOCQUES.
3 O.C. No. 4 Section.
4 C.S.M. & C.Q.M.S.
5 O.C. Signals, HINGES.
6 War Diary. ✓

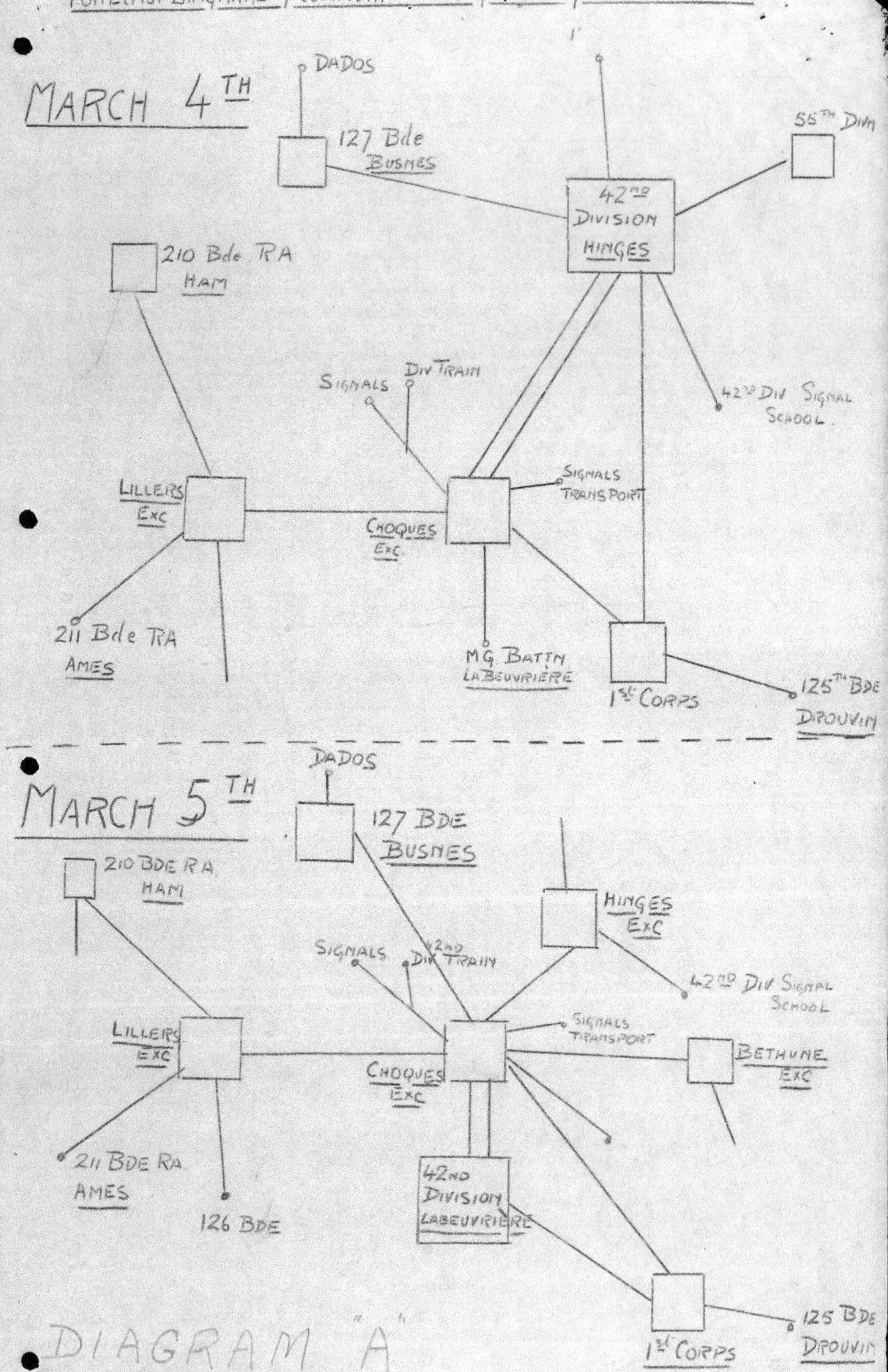
FORECAST DIAGRAMS of COMMUNICATIONS of UNITS of 42ND DIVISION.
MARCH 4TH
DADOS
127 Bde
BUSNES
55TH DIVN
42ND
DIVISION
HINGES
210 Bde RA
HAM
SIGNALS
DIV TRAIN
42ND DIV SIGNAL
SCHOOL
LILLERS
EXC
CHOQUES
EXC
SIGNALS
TRANSPORT
211 Bde RA
AMES
M.G. BATTN
LA BEUVRIÈRE
1ST CORPS
125TH BDE
DIROUVIN
MARCH 5TH
DADOS
127 BDE
BUSNES
210 BDE RA
HAM
HINGES
EXC
SIGNALS
42ND
DIV TRAIN
42ND DIV SIGNAL
SCHOOL
LILLERS
EXC
SIGNALS
TRANSPORT
BETHUNE
EXC
CHOQUES
EXC
211 BDE RA
AMES
126 BDE
42ND
DIVISION
LABEUVRIÈRE
1ST CORPS
125 BDE
DIROUVIN
DIAGRAM "A"

DIAGRAM 1

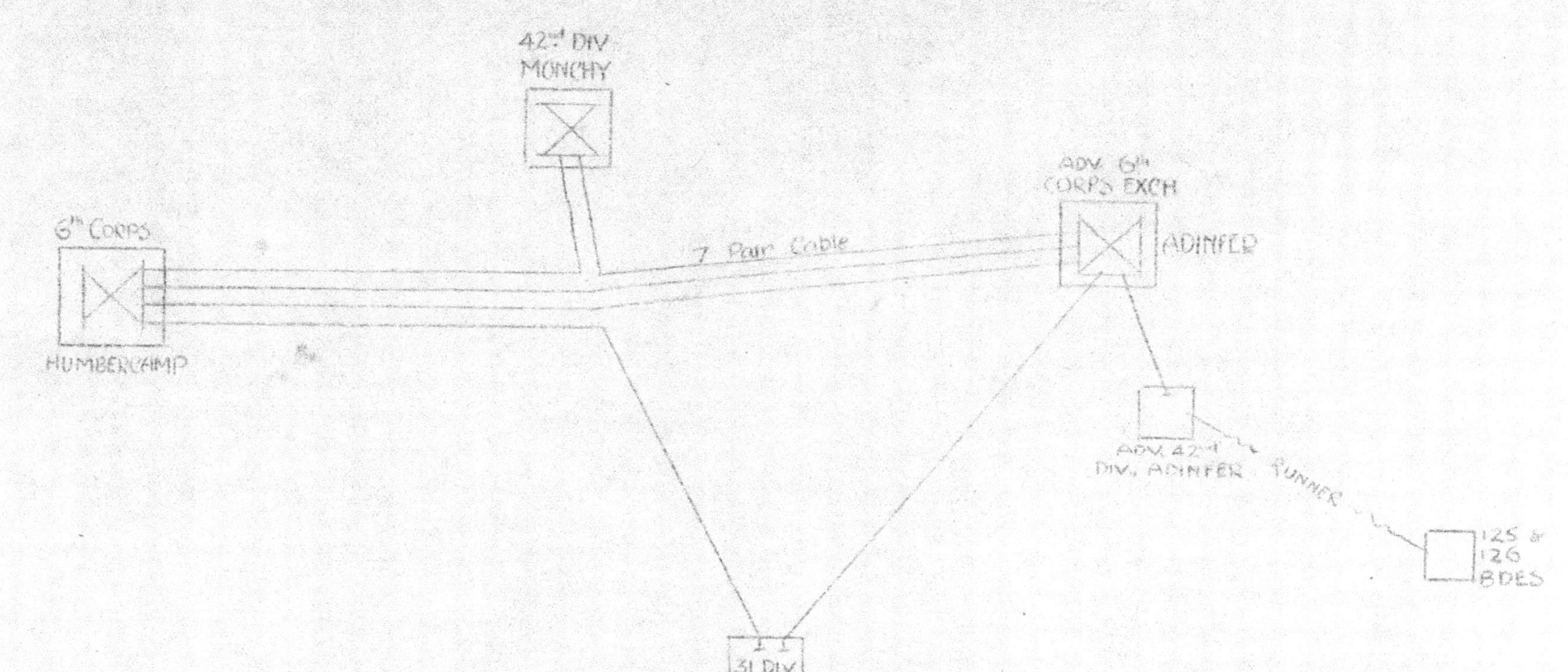

6th CORPS
HUMBERCAMP
42nd DIV
MONCHY
7 Pair Cable
ADV. 6th
CORPS EXCH
ADINFER
ADV. 42nd
DIV. ADINFER
RUNNER
125 &
126
BDES
31 DIV
AYETTE
RUNNER
127 BDE

DIAGRAM 2

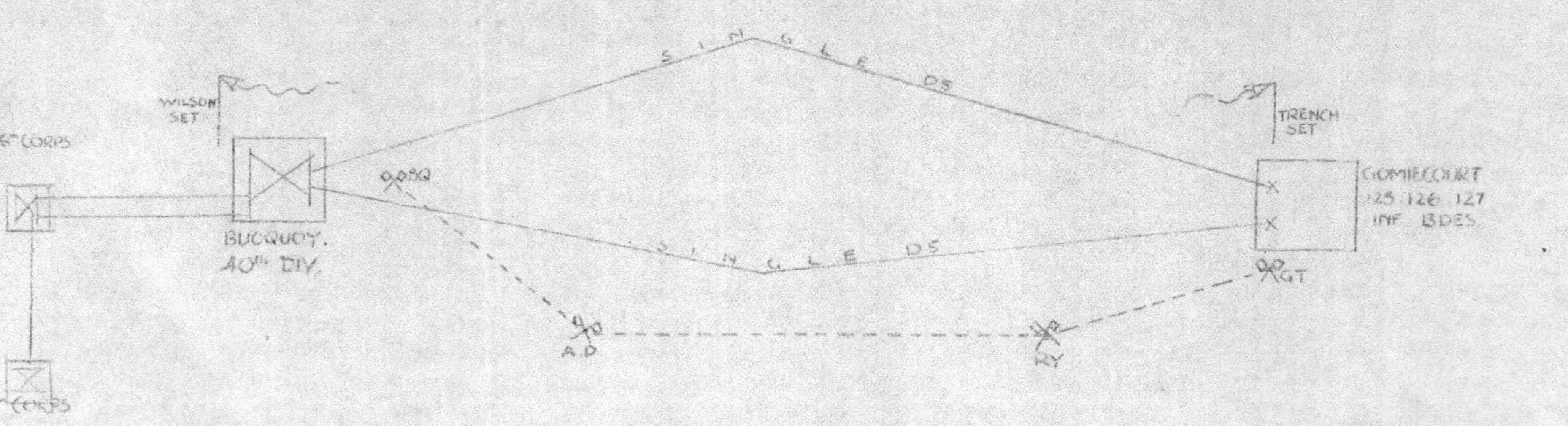

6th CORPS
4th CORPS
WILSON SET
BUCQUOY.
40th DIV.
SINGLE DS
SINGLE DS
TRENCH SET
GOMIECOURT
125 126 127
INF BDES.
A.D
RY
GT

DIAGRAM 3

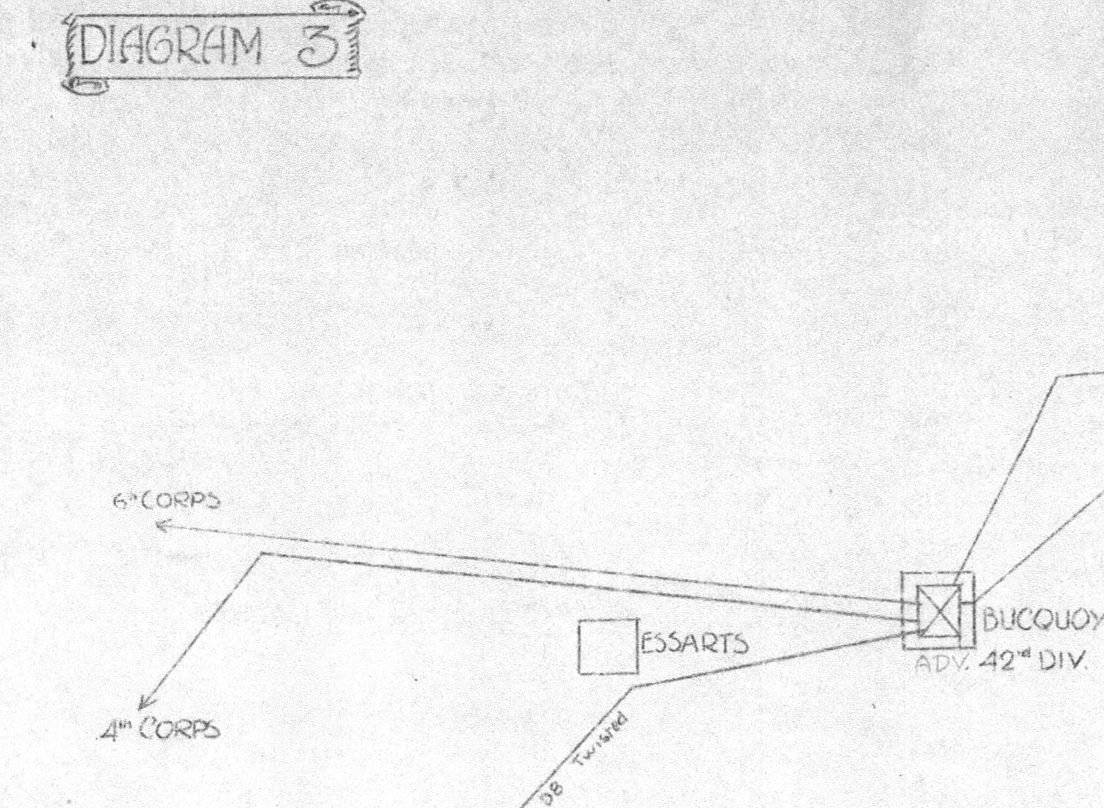

Div' Report Centre
F.25.d.8.2.
D5 Single
A.15.C.2.1.
6th CORPS
4th CORPS
ESSARTS
BUCQUOY
ADV. 42nd DIV.
D5 & D8 Twisted
FONQUEVILLERS

DIAGRAM 4

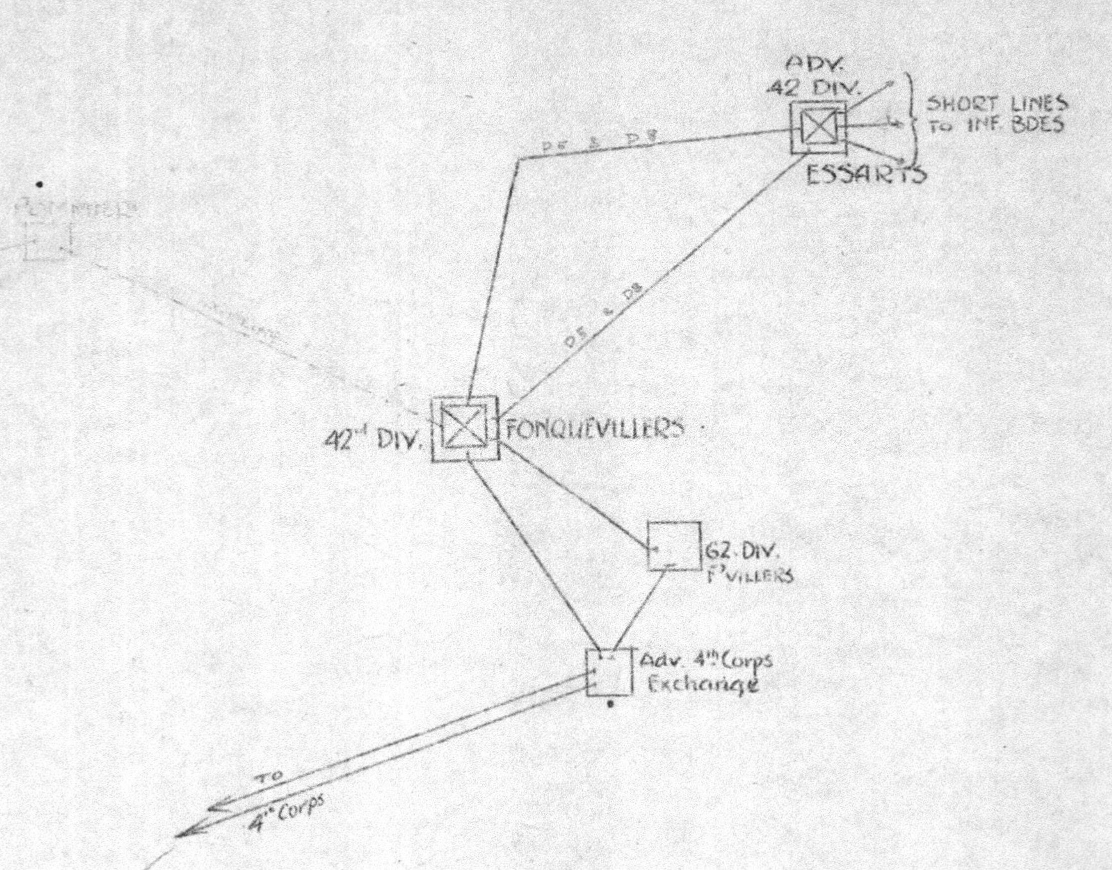

ADV.
42 DIV.
SHORT LINES
TO INF. BDES
ESSARTS
DE & DB
DE & DB
42nd DIV.
FONQUEVILLERS
62. DIV.
F'VILLERS
Adv. 4th Corps
Exchange
TO
4th Corps

DIAGRAM 5

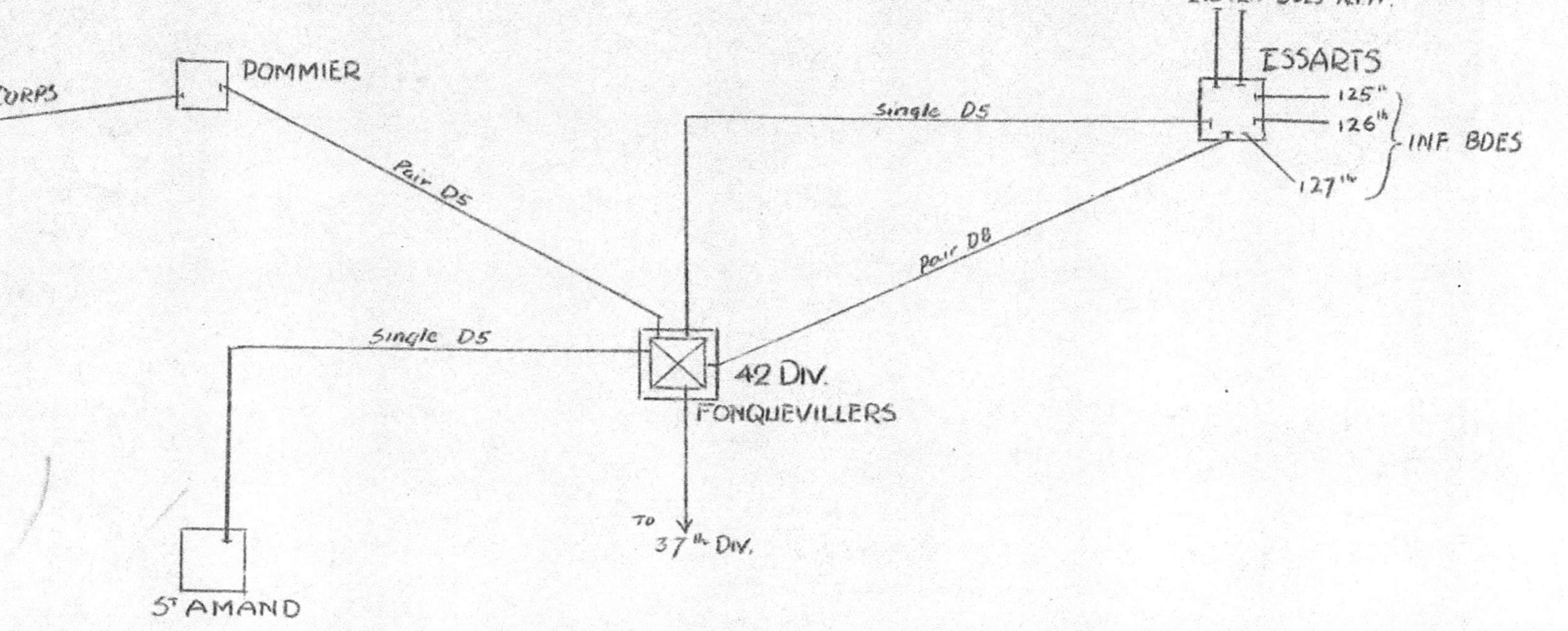

210. 211 BDES R.F.A.
ESSARTS
125th
126th
127th
INF BDES
POMMIER
TO 4th CORPS
Pair D5
Single D5
Pair D8
Single D5
42 DIV.
FONQUEVILLERS
TO 37th DIV.
St AMAND

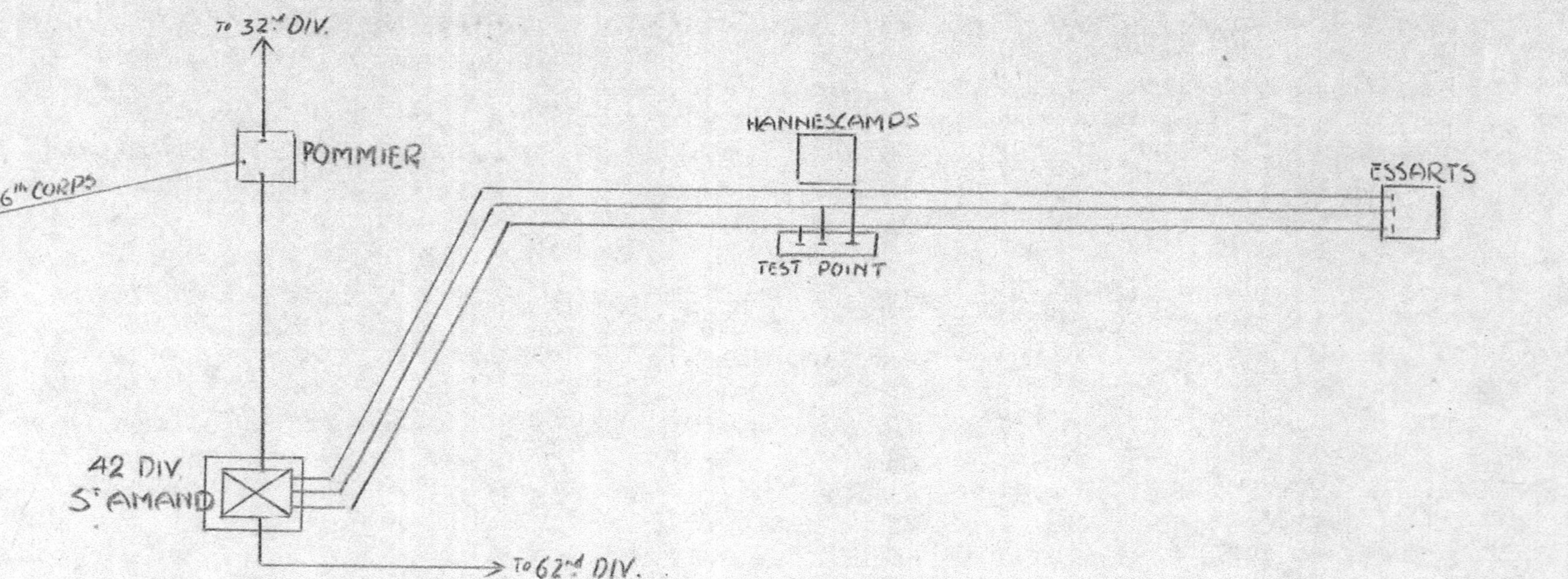

TO 32nd DIV.
POMMIER
TO 6th CORPS
HANNESCAMPS
ESSARTS
TEST POINT
42 DIV.
St AMAND
TO 62nd DIV.

DIAGRAM 6

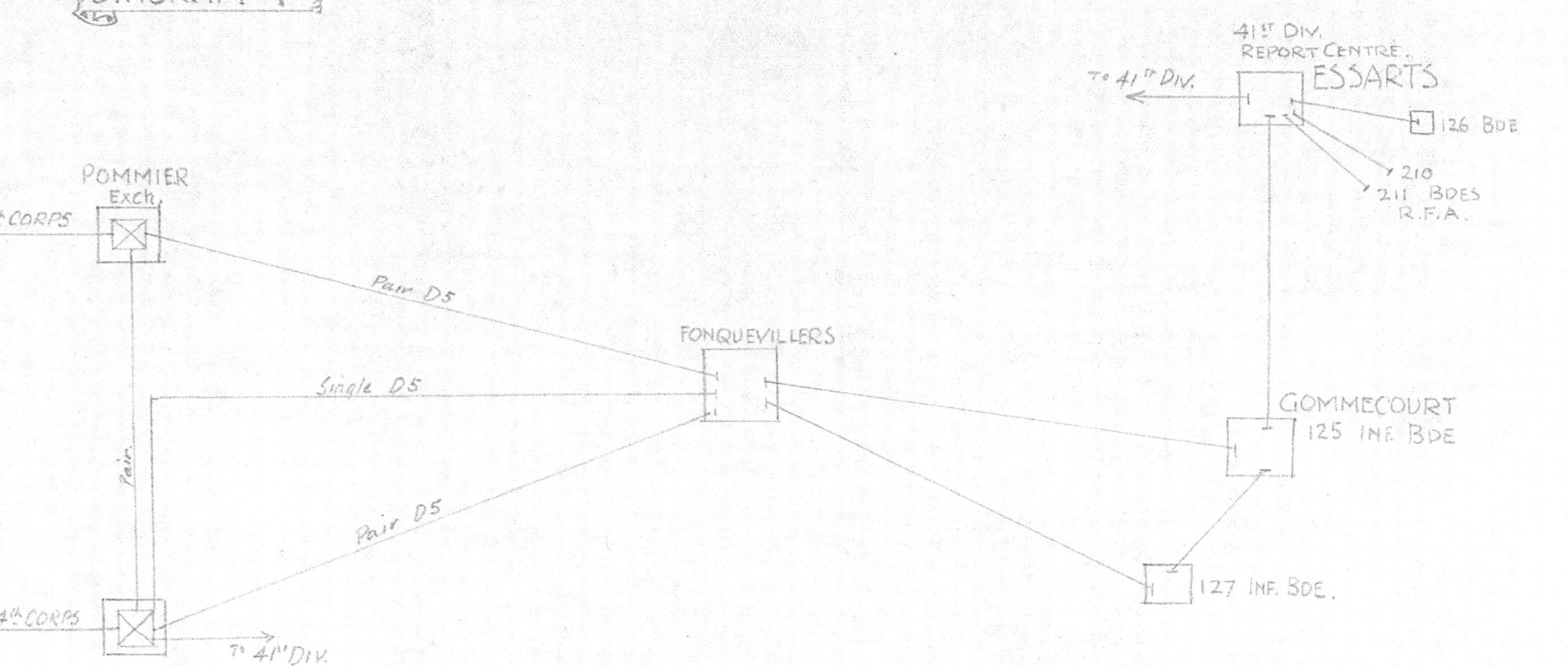

DIAGRAM 7
POMMIER Exch.
To 4th CORPS
To 4th CORPS
To 41st DIV.
Pair D5
Single D5
Pair D5
Pair.
FONQUEVILLERS
41st DIV. REPORT CENTRE.
ESSARTS
To 41st DIV.
126 BDE
210
211 BDES R.F.A.
GOMMECOURT
125 INF. BDE
127 INF. BDE.

IV.Corps.
Third Army.

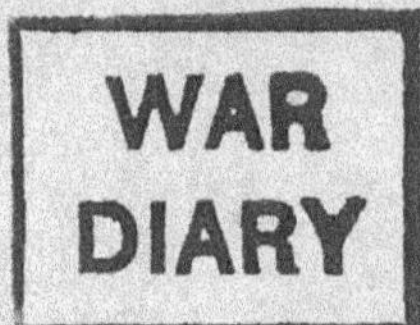

42nd DIVISIONAL SIGNAL COMPANY, R.E.

A P R I L

1 9 1 8

Attached:

Appendices "A", "B", "C" & "D".

Secret.

Vol 14

WAR DIARY.

42nd DIVISIONAL SIGNAL Co. R.E.

Chapter XVIII.

S. Gordon Johnston

Major,
O.C., Signals 42nd Div.,

Army Form C. 2118.

WAR DIARY
or
~~INTELLIGENCE SUMMARY.~~
(Erase heading not required.)

Instructions regarding War Diaries and Intelligence Summaries are contained in F. S. Regs., Part II. and the Staff Manual respectively. Title pages will be prepared in manuscript.

Place	Date	Hour	Summary of Events and Information	Remarks and references to Appendices
			CHAPTER XVIII. APRIL 1918. 42nd (East Lancs) Divisional Signal Coy. R.E.(TF).	
			Reference Map. FRANCE, 1/40,000.BUCQUOY.Combined sheet.	
ST. AMAND.	1.4.18.		Company Headquarters remained at ST. AMAND until the 3rd. The Division being in support until the 2nd inst when it took over a Section of the Front line from the 41st Division, for communications see Appendix "A".	APPENDIX "A".
HENU.	3.4.18.		Company Headquarters moved with Divisional Headquarters by road to HENU, opening at HENU at 10 a.m.	
PAS.	7.4.18.		As the Division was being relieved in the line by the 62nd Division, Divisional Headquarters and the Company moved to PAS and took over reserve area and billets in PAS Chateau Grounds from that Division. The relief was completed by 2 a.m. on the 8th inst. Orders for handing over communications being contained in Appendix "A". The Company remained at PAS resting and reorganising personnel and equipment until the 16th.	
COUIN.	16.4.18.		Divisional Headquarters and the Signal Company moved by road to COUIN relieving the 37th Division in the Centre Sector of the 4th Corps front. The relief being completed at 1 a.m. on the 17th inst. Communications whilst holding this Sector as per Appendix "A".	
	21.4.18.		A system of training signallers, trained and untrained, of the battle surplus of the Infantry of the Division was commenced at the Divisional Rest Camp at MARIEUX.	
	30.4.18.		The Division remained in this Sector until the 30th, Divisional Headquarters and Signal Company remaining at COUIN.	

A7092). Wt. W12839/M1293 750,000. 1/17. D. D & L., Ltd. Forms/C2118/14.

Army Form C. 2118.

WAR DIARY
or
~~INTELLIGENCE SUMMARY~~.

(Erase heading not required.)

Instructions regarding War Diaries and Intelligence Summaries are contained in F. S. Regs., Part II. and the Staff Manual respectively. Title pages will be prepared in manuscript.

Place	Date	Hour	Summary of Events and Information	Remarks and references to Appendices

APPENDICES TO THIS DIARY.

(A). Communications.
Sub-Appendices:-
(A.1). Communications in the event of Division holding the Red Line
(A.2). Communications in the GOMMECOURT Sector.

(B). Honours and Awards.

(C). Casualties, Weekly Strengths & Reinforcements.

(D). Weekly Message Chart.

G. Gordon Johnson, Major.

5.5.18. O.C. 42nd Divisional Signal Co. R.E.

A7092). Wt. W12839/M1293. 750,000. 1/17. D. D & L., Ltd. Forms/C2118/14.

A P P E N D I C E S

"A", "B", "C" & "D" .

APPENDIX "A". WAR DIARY. APRIL 1918.

COMMUNICATIONS.

Reference France 1/40,000.
BUCQUOY. Combined sheet.

1.4.18. Line communications at midnight 31st March/1st April were as
Diagram 1. shown on Diagram 1.
During the night 1st/2nd April the Infantry of the 42nd Division relieved the 41st Division in the front line.

2.4.18. At 2 a.m. on 2.4.18. the G.O.C. 42nd Division took over command of the Left Sector of the 4th Corps Front.
The line communications established with ESSARTS, at which place all three Brigade Headquarters were located, and were as shown in
Diagram2 Diagram 2. These communications were a combination of the 42nd Divisional existing communication to FONQUEVILLERS and GOMMECOURT (see Diagram 1) and those taken over from the 41st Division.
Wireless Stations at ESSARTS and FONQUEVILLERS were installed for communication with Divisional Headquarters Station.
The 4th Corps Advanced Exchange at POMMIER was closed and alternative cable routes constructed for communication with 4th Corps.
Between 5.45 p.m. and 6.15 p.m. there was heavy shelling in the forward area and as a consequence only one line could be kept through from FONQUEVILLERS to ESSARTS.
All forward lines were restored by 8 p.m.

.4.18. At 10 a.m. 3.4.18. Divisional Headquarters moved to HENU. An Exchange was left at ST.AMAND and three circuits laid from it to HENU. Communication between Divisional Headquarters and Advanced Divisional Headquarters at FONQUEVILLERS were then as shown in
Diagram 3. Diagram 3. There was no change in front of FONQUEVILLERS.
Divisional Wireless Directing Station remained at ST. AMAND and was in communication with the Exchange there by telephone.

4.4.18. Communications remained as on 3.4.18. until 6.4.18. when
5.4.18. another pair of D5 cable was laid direct from HENU to FONQUEVILLERS.
6.4.18. Visual communication was established between FONQUEVILLERS and ESSARTS but owing to weather conditions was of little value.
ST. AMAND Exchange was closed and the lines put straight through from HENU to FONQUEVILLERS.

.4.18. Communications on the night 6th/7th 4.18. were as shown in
iagram 4. Diagram 4.

.4.18. During the nights 7th/8th.4.18. and 8th/9th.4.18. the Infantry
.4.18. of the 42nd Division was relieved by the 62nd Division and command of the Divisional Sector passed to G.O.C. 62nd Division in the early morning of 9.4.18.

.4.18. Divisional Headquarters moved to PAS during the night and Brigade Headquarters were established as follows:-

125th Infantry Brigade ST. LEGER.
126th " " PAS.
127th " " LOUVENCOURT.

Communication with them and with 4th Corps was provided by permanent routes already existing.
iagram 8. Diagram 8 shows the lines in use for communication from PAS.
During the time that the Division remained at PAS communications were unaltered. No visual or Wireless communication was in use.
efence The 42nd Division while at PAS was held in readiness to garrison
cheme. a line of defence known as the RED LINE. Signal communications in the event of the occupation of this line were reconnoitred.
The scheme to be adopted was circulated to all concerned. Copy of orders issued is attached hereto (Sub Appendix A.1)

17.4.18. At 1 a.m. 17.4.18. the 42nd Division relieved the 37th Division in the Centre (HEBUTERNE) Sector of the 4th Corps front with Divisional Headquarters at COUIN. The existing communications were taken over from the 37th Divisional Signal Coy. The three Infantry Brigades of the Division (125th, 126th & 127th) were in the line and the 4th Australian Brigade with Headquarters at SAILLY AU BOIS was also under the command of the Division. The Headquarters of the Left and Left Centre Infantry Brigades were at E.29.a.0.3. (in GOMMECOURT WOOD), the Right Centre Infantry Brigade at E.27.b.3.9. (FONQUEVILLERS- and the Right (Australian) Infantry Brigade at SAILLY AU BOIS.

Diagram 9. Diagram 9 shows the scheme of line communications taken over from the 37th Division. There were Divisional Exchanges at SOUASTRE and FONQUEVILLERS, the latter being the Advanced Divisional Signal Office. Telegrams were tramsnitted by FONQUEVILLERS office for forward units. It was found possible to work a D.C. Sounder circuit from COUIN to FONQUEVILLERS, messages being sent forward from there by Fullerphone. Despatch riders were stationed at FONQUEVILLERS for runs back to COUIN and Runners for runs forward to Infantry Brigade Headquarters, Despatch Riders were used between COUIN and SAILLY AU BOIS.

Diagram 11. Wireless communication was as shown in Diagram 11.

Visual signalling was not used for any Divisional communication.

During the period 18.4.18. to 25.4.18. work was done on the exploitation of old buried cable routes in the area. The routes which were ultimately brought into use are shown in detail on the Route Map. (Map 2). A great deal of difficulty was experienced owing to the haphazard manner in which the cable had been buried and the lack of reliable information regarding the routes.

Map 2.

Overground and poled cable routes were made from COUIN to connect onto the buries at SR test point. When taken into use most of the buries proved to be quite workable with magneto calling in spite of the length of time which the cables had been buried. In many cases these cables were D5 field cable.

In order to obtain visual communication Divisional visual Stations were established at J.5.d central and D.23.d.central on 19th and 20th April. A Station was also established at FONQUEVILLERS. The visual communication via these Stations is shown in Diagram 12.

Diagram 12.

Wireless communication remained unchanged except that occasionally an extra Trench W/T Station was erected for special reasons at the Divisional Visual Station at J.5.d central.

Sub-Appendix A 2. A copy of the Appendix on communications to the Divisional Defence Scheme is attached as Sub Appendix A 2.

21.4.18. On 21st April the Right Centre Brigade moved Headquarters to SAILLY AU BOIS and lines to it were picked up on the SR SA Bury.

25.4.18. On 24th/25th April the New Zealand Division relieved the Right (Australian) and Right Centre (127th) Infantry Brigades and the Divisional Sector was reduced to the front of the Left and Left Centre Infantry Brigades.

Communications remained as before, the lines existing to SAILLY AU BOIS being spare.

30.4.18. At the end of April communications were as shown in Diagram B.

Diagram ~~A~~. 13 The routes taken by all circuits were as shown in Map 2.

Map 2.

Wireless and Visual communications were as shown in the Diagrams attached to the Divisional Defence Scheme (Sub-Appendix A2) as Diagrams B and C respectively.

S. Gordon Johnston

Major.

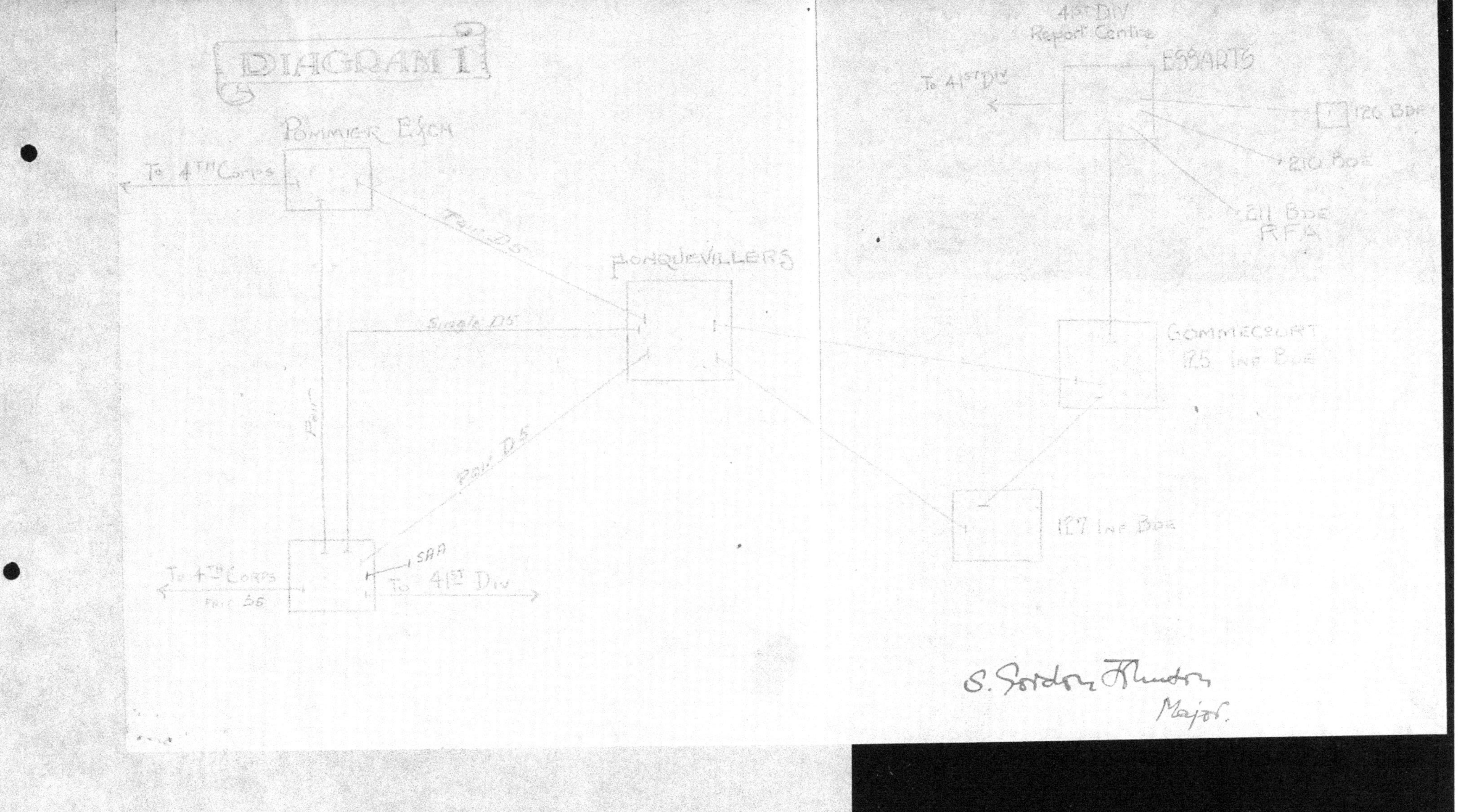
DIAGRAM I
POMMIER E'ch
To 4TH Corps
Pair DS
Single DS
Pair
Pair DS
FONQUEVILLERS
To 4TH Corps
Pair DS
SAA
To 41ST Div
41ST DIV
Report Centre
ESSARTS
To 41ST Div
126 Bde
210 Bde
211 Bde
RFA
GOMMECOURT
125 Inf Bde
127 Inf Bde
S. Gordon Thurston
Major.

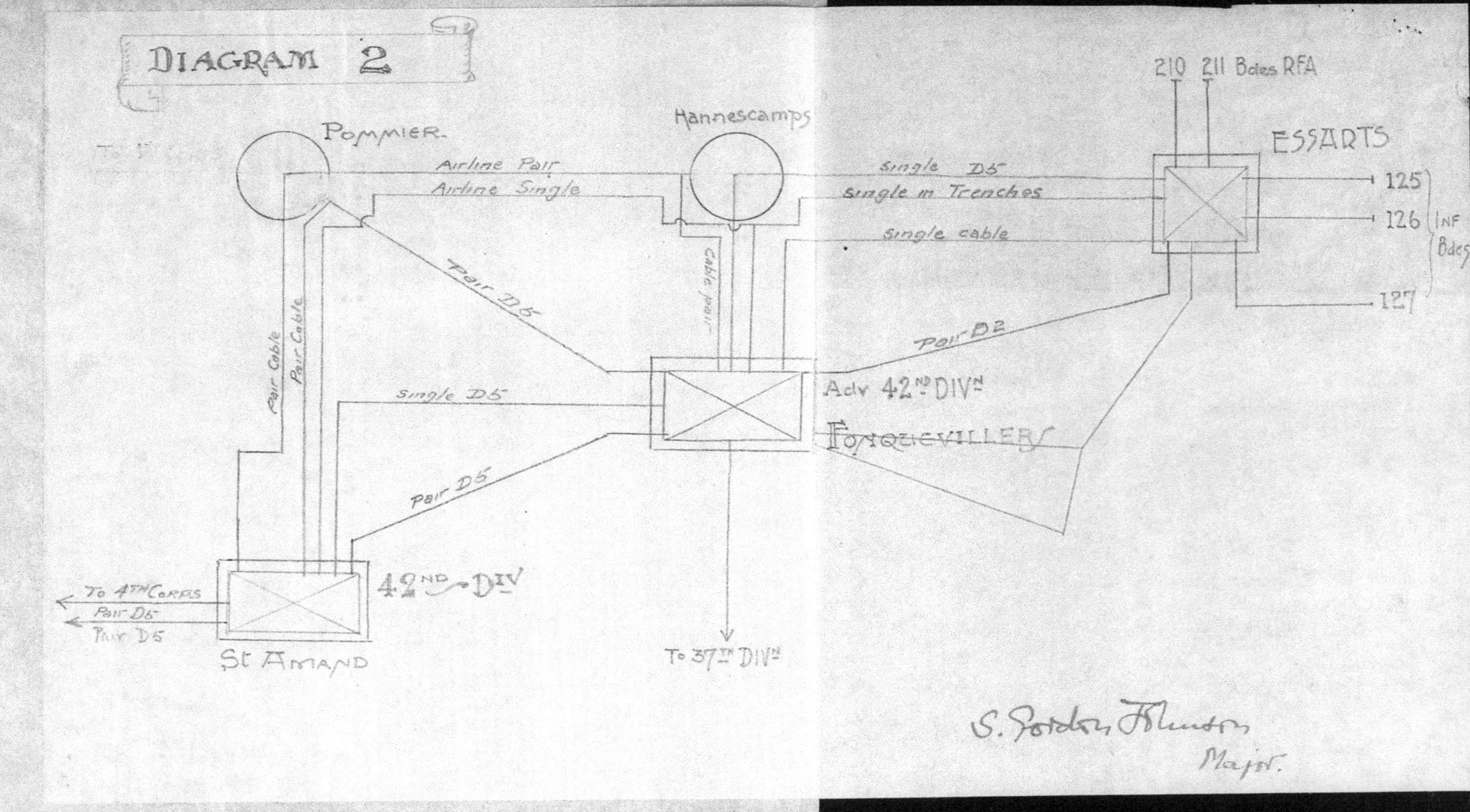
DIAGRAM 2
Pommier.
Hannescamps
ESSARTS
210 211 Bdes RFA
125
126
127
INF Bdes
Airline Pair
Airline Single
single D5
single in Trenches
single cable
Cable pair
Pair D5
Pair D5
Pair Cable
Pair Cable
single D5
Pair D2
Adv 42ND DIVN
FONQUEVILLERS
To 37TH DIVN
42ND DIV
To 4TH CORPS
Pair D5
Pair D5
St AMAND
S. Gordon Johnston
Major.

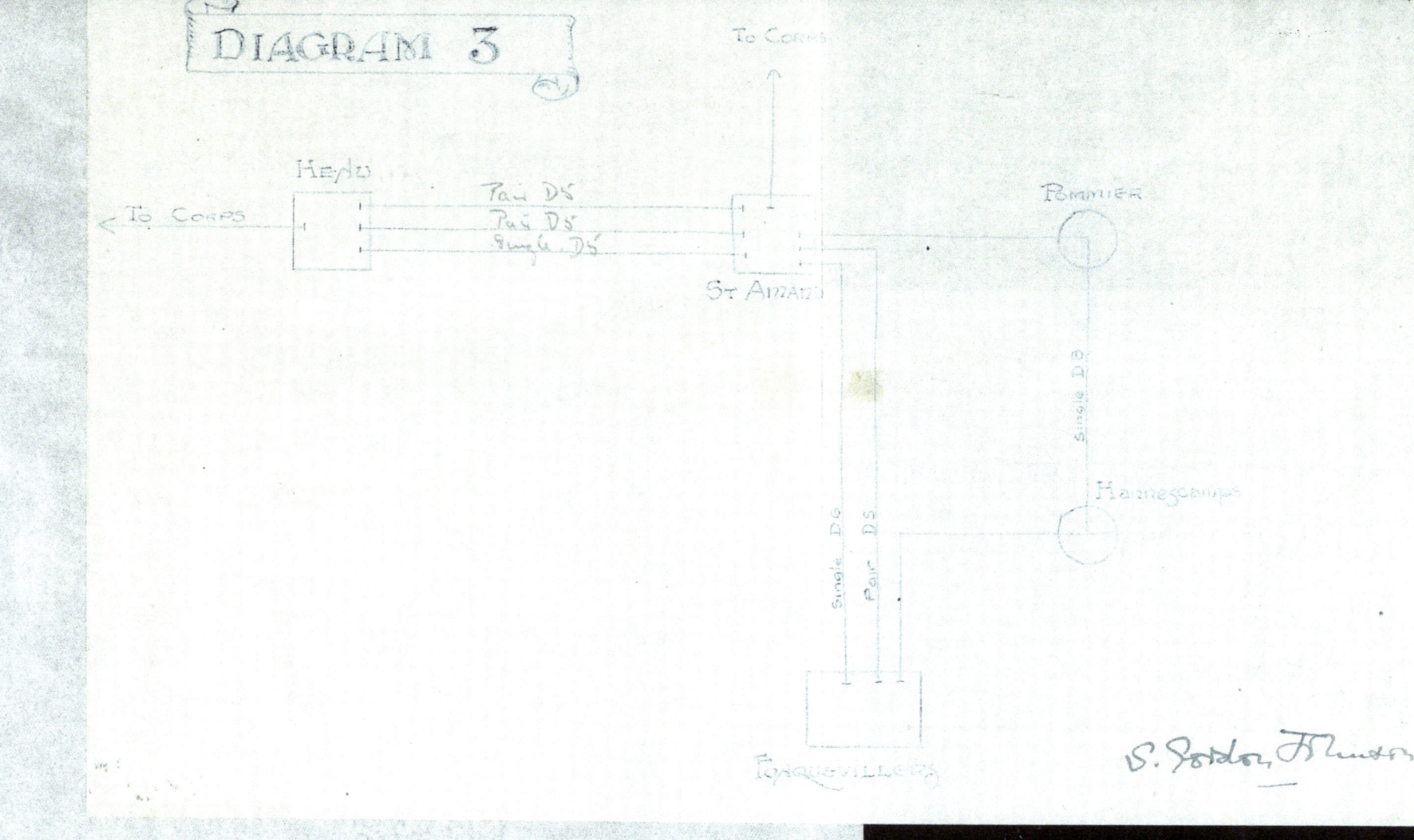
DIAGRAM 3
To Corps
Heads
Pair D5
Pair D5
Single D5
To Corps
St Amand
Pommier
Single D8
Hannescamps
Single D6
Pair D5
Fonquevillers
S. Gordon Johnston.

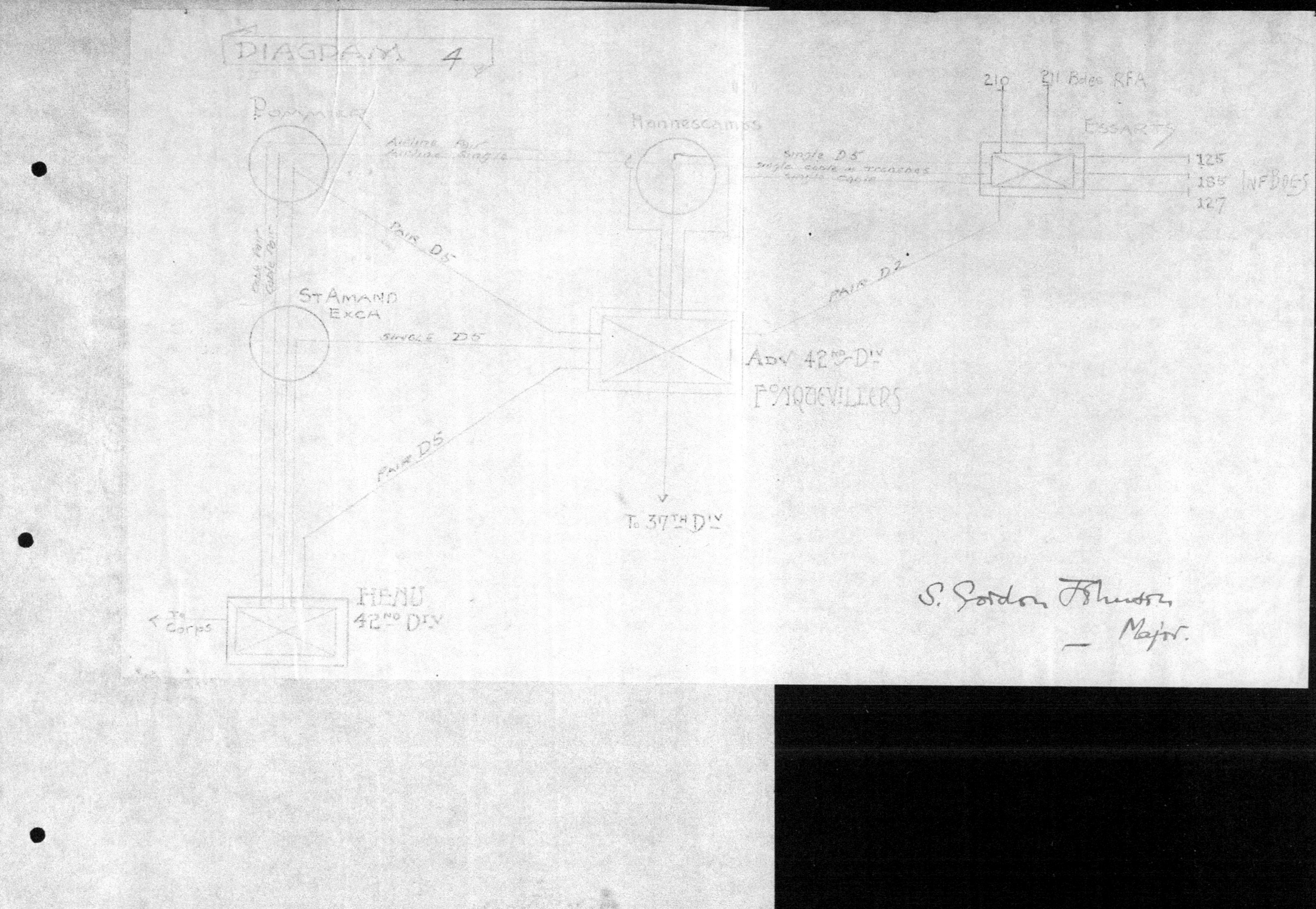

DIAGRAM 4
Pommier
Hannescamps
210
211 Bdes RFA
Essarts
125
185
127
INF Bdes
Single D5
Pair D5
St Amand Exch
Single D5
Pair D2
Adv 42nd Div
Fonquevillers
Pair D5
To 37th Div
Henu 42nd Div
To Corps
S. Gordon Johnston
Major.

No 8 DIAGRAM of COMMUNICATIONS 42nd DIVISION

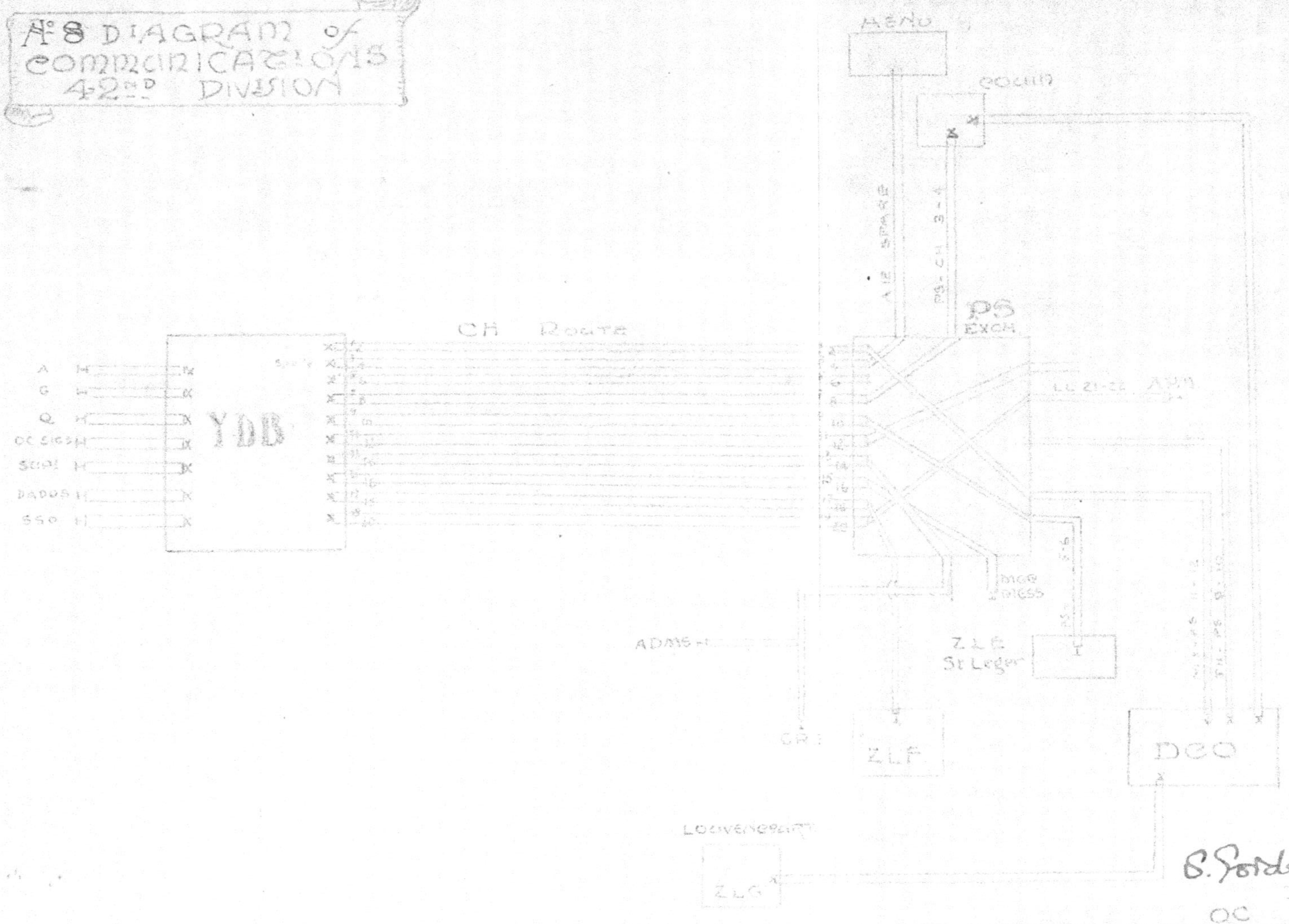

MENU

A 12 SPARE

PS-CH 3-4

PS EXCH

CH Route

YDB

A

G

Q

OC SIGS

DADOS

SSO

LL 21-22 ARM

MGE PRESS

Z L E St Leger

ZLF

DCO

ADAMS

CR

LOUVENCOURT

ZLG

B. Gordon [signature] MAJOR

OC SIGNALS 42nd DIV.

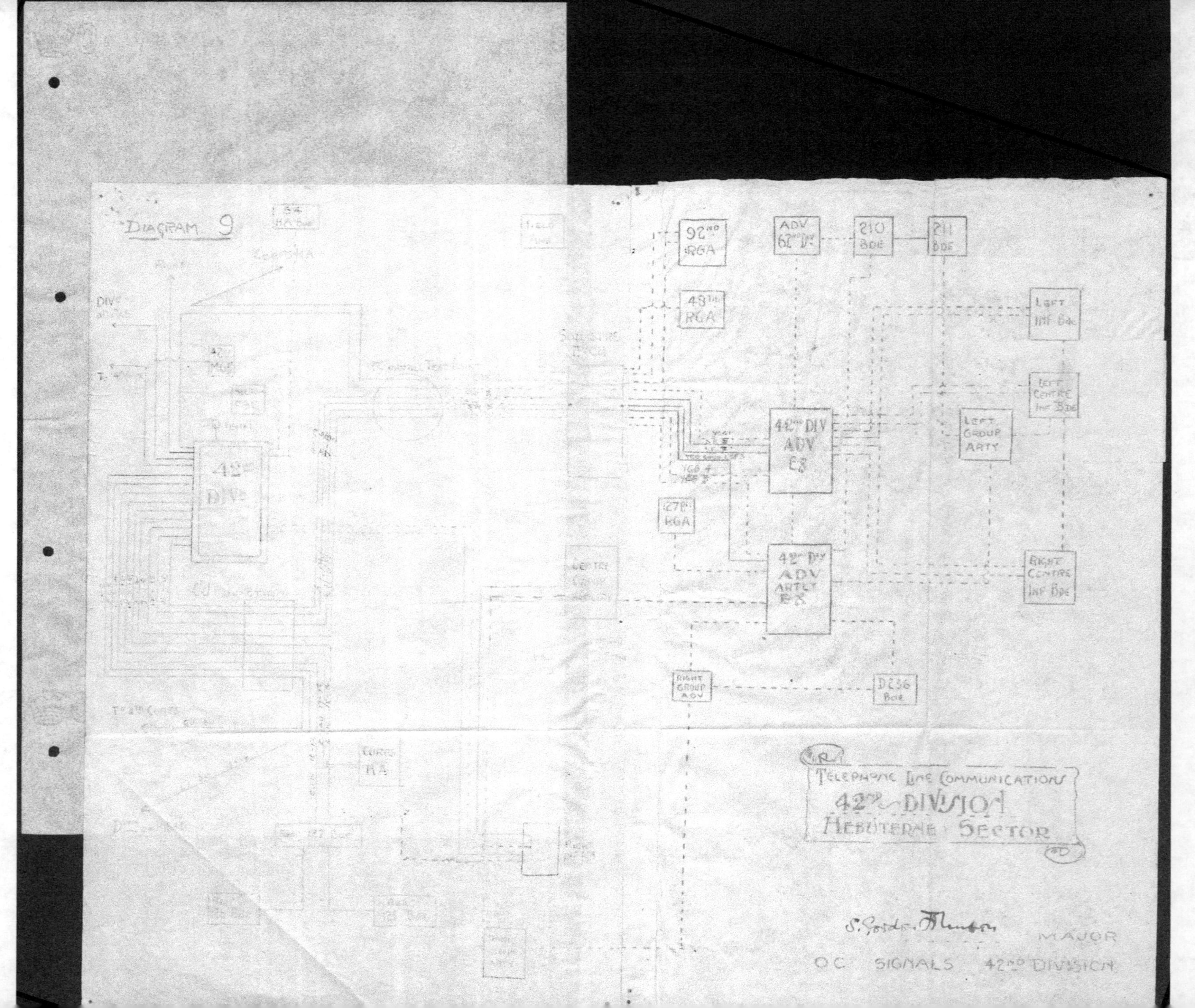

DIAGRAM 9
34 HA Bde
92ND RGA
48TH RGA
127TH RGA
ADV 62ND DN
210 BDE
211 BDE
LEFT INF BDE
LEFT CENTRE INF BDE
LEFT GROUP ARTY
42ND DIV ADV EX
42ND DIV ADV ARTLY EX
RIGHT CENTRE INF BDE
RIGHT GROUP ADV
D236 BDE
42ND DIVN
CORPS RA
TELEPHONE LINE COMMUNICATIONS
42ND DIVISION
HEBUTERNE SECTOR
S. Gordon Flumber
MAJOR
OC SIGNALS 42ND DIVISION

DIAGRAM II.

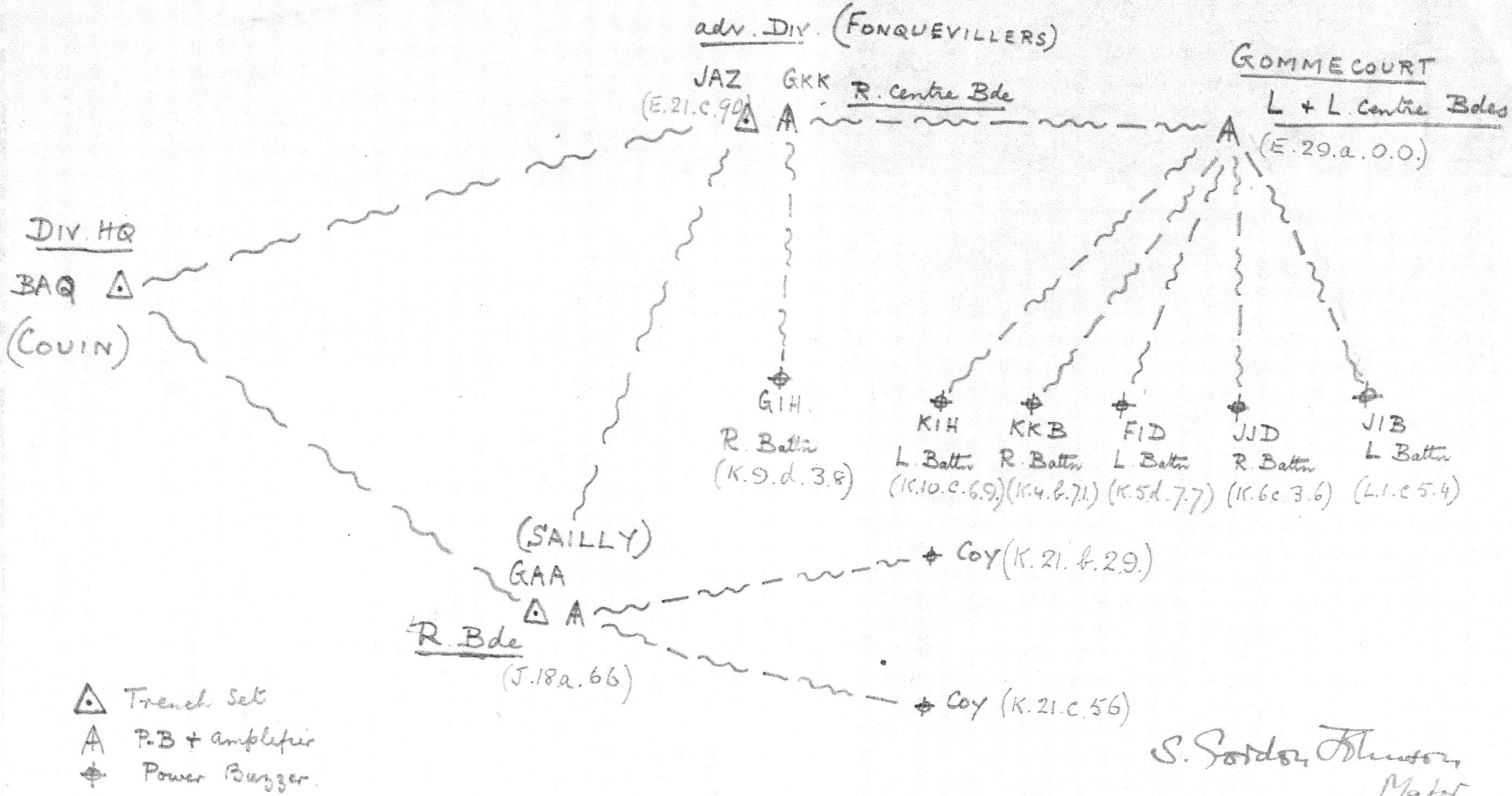

S. Gordon Johnston,
Major.

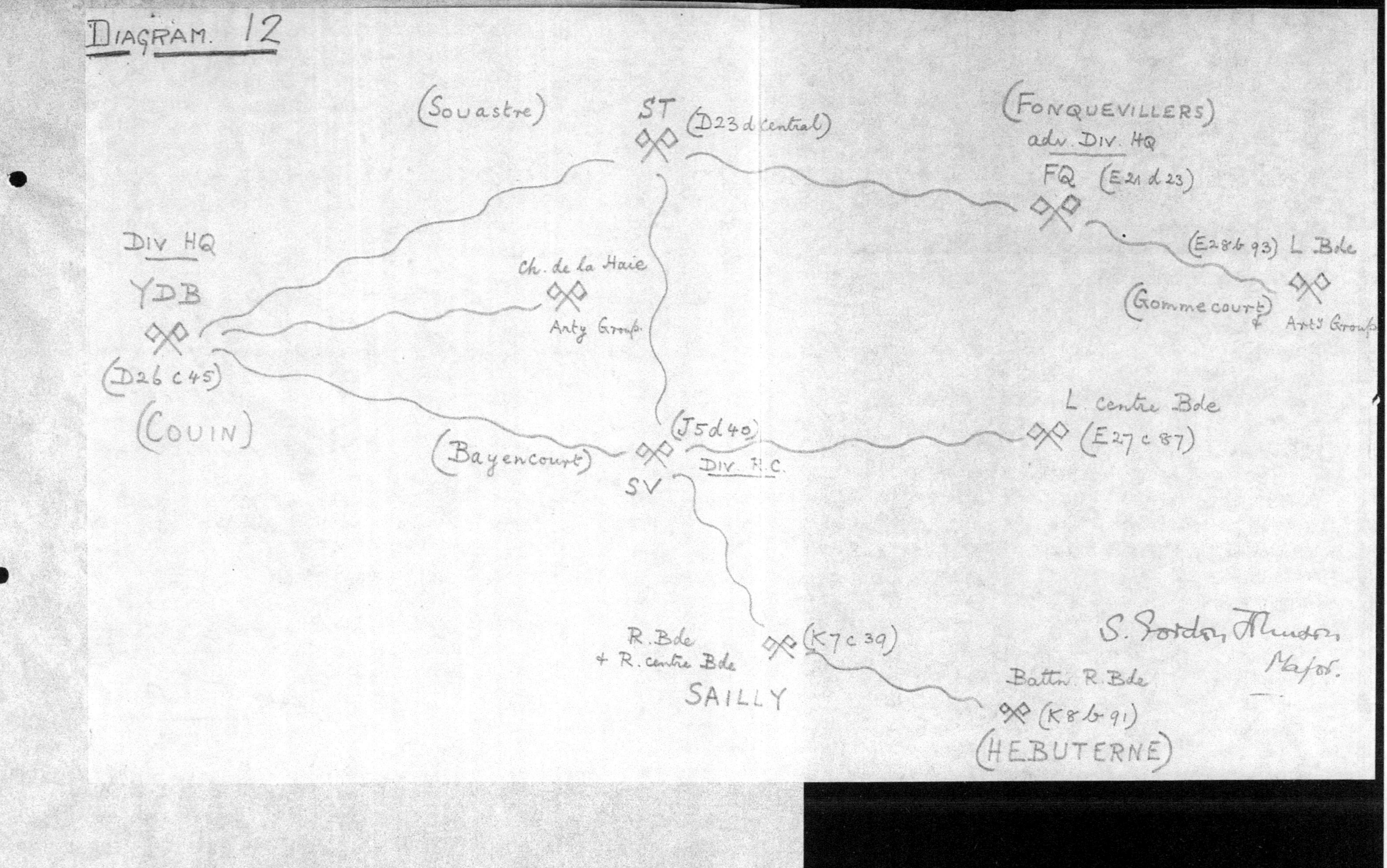

DIAGRAM. 12
(Souastre)
ST
(D23 d central)
(FONQUEVILLERS)
adv. DIV. HQ
FQ
(E21 d 23)
(E28 b 93) L. Bde
(Gommecourt)
& Arty Group
DIV HQ
YDB
(D26 c 45)
(COUIN)
Ch. de la Haie
Arty Group
L. centre Bde
(E27 c 87)
(J5 d 40)
DIV. H.C.
(Bayencourt)
SV
R. Bde
+ R. centre Bde
SAILLY
(K7 c 39)
Battn. R. Bde
(K8 b 91)
(HEBUTERNE)
S. Gordon Thunder
Major.

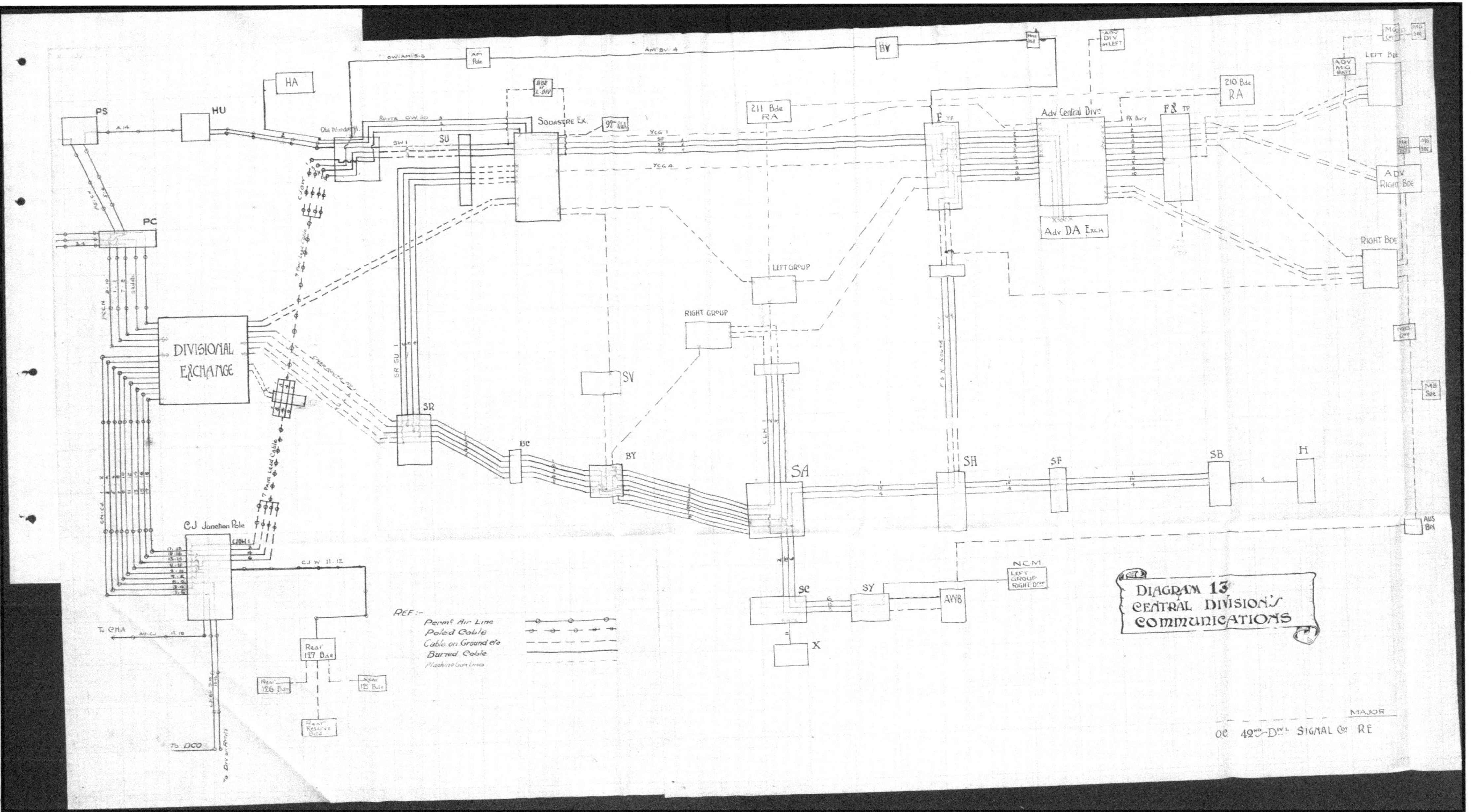
DIAGRAM 13
CENTRAL DIVISION'S
COMMUNICATIONS
DIVISIONAL EXCHANGE
C.J. Junction Pole
PS
PC
HU
HA
Old Windmill
SU
Soudastre Ex.
97th RGA
AM Pole
BV
211 Bde RA
210 Bde RA
F TP
FX TP
Adv Central Divn
Adv DA Exch
ADV DIV on LEFT
LEFT Bde
ADV RIGHT Bde
RIGHT Bde
ADV MG BATT
MG Coy
MG Sec
LEFT GROUP
RIGHT GROUP
SV
SR
BC
BY
SA
SH
SF
SB
H
SC
SY
AWB
X
AUS BN
N.C.M. LEFT GROUP RIGHT Divn
Rear 127 Bde
Rear 126 Bde
Rear 125 Bde
Rear Reserve Bde
To CHA
To DCO
To Div on Right
CJ W 11. 12
YCG 1
YCG 4
SR SU
REF:-
Permt Air Line
Poled Cable
Cable on Ground etc
Buried Cable
Machine Gun Lines
MAJOR
OC 42nd Divl SIGNAL Coy RE

Diagram 13

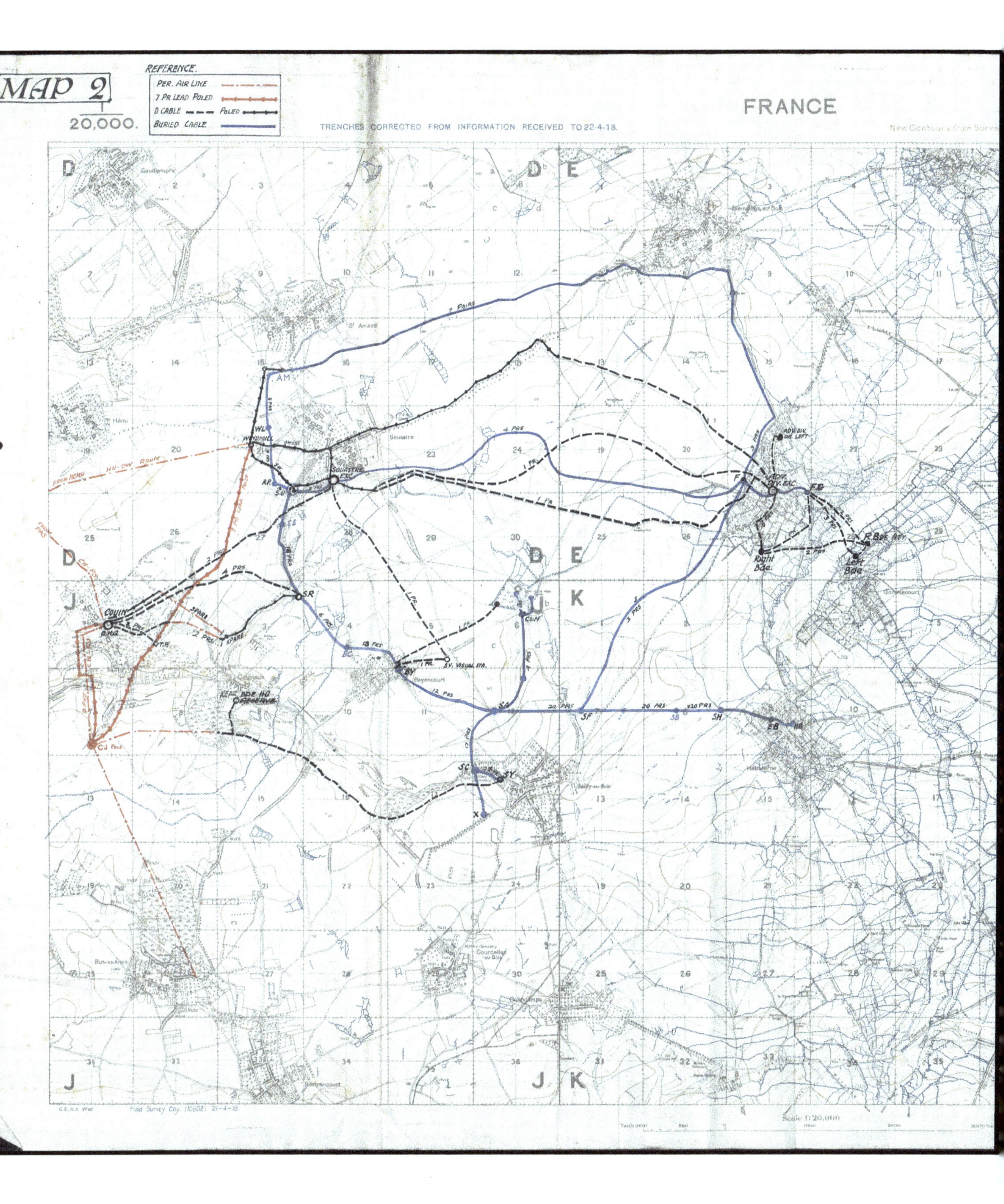

MAP 2
1/20,000.
REFERENCE.
PER. AIR LINE
7 PR LEAD POLED
D CABLE
POLED
BURIED CABLE
TRENCHES CORRECTED FROM INFORMATION RECEIVED TO 22-4-18.
FRANCE
COUIN
SOUSTRE
WINDMILL
ADV. DIV. EXC.
Right Bde.
Left Bde.
Bayencourt
Field Survey Coy. (10502) 21-4-18
Scale 1:20,000

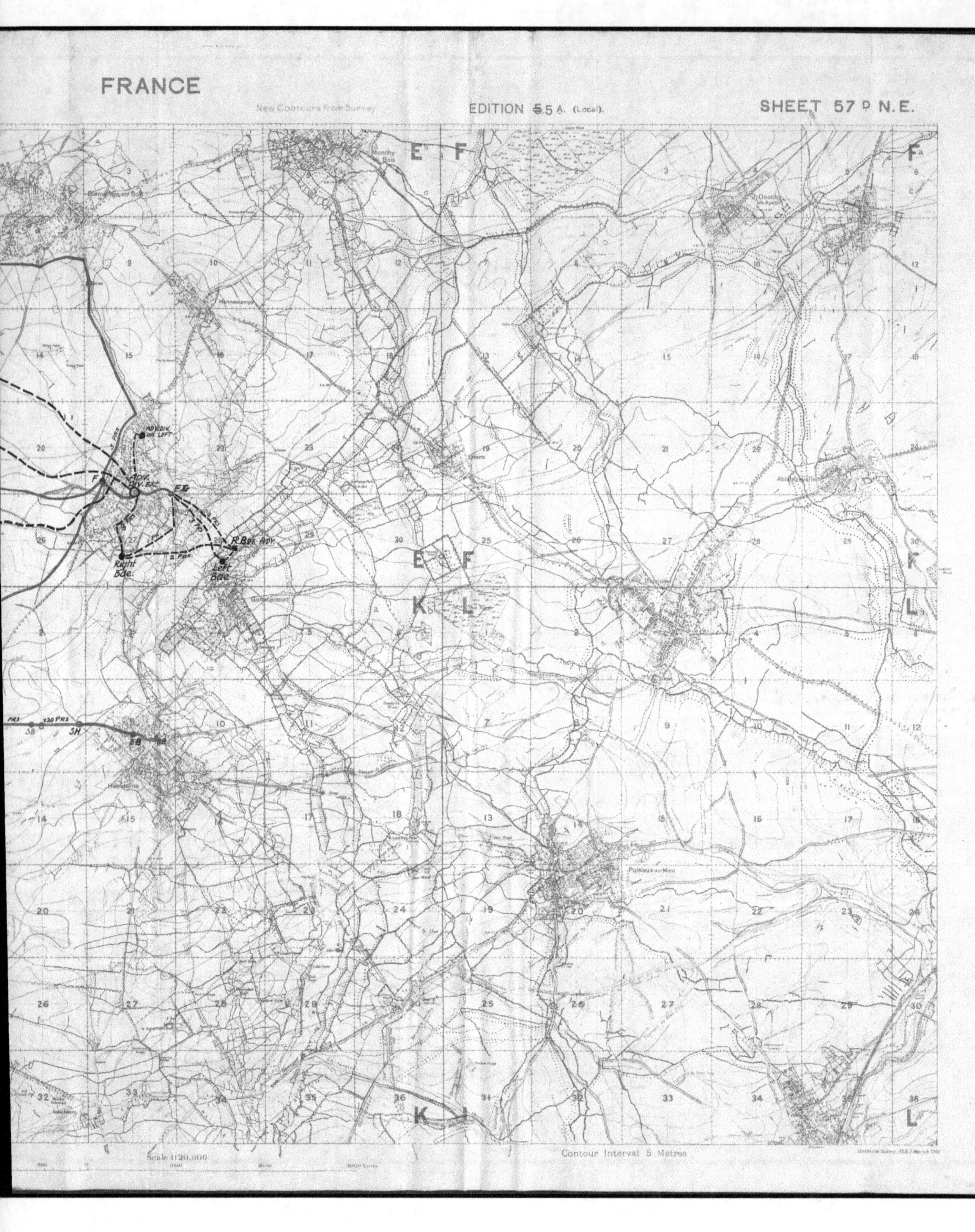

FRANCE
New Contours from Survey
EDITION 5A (Local)
SHEET 57D N.E.
E F
K L
Hannescamps
Gommecourt
Hebuterne
Puisieux-au-Mont
Adv. Div. Exc.
Right Bde.
Left Bde.
R.Bde Adv.
Scale 1:20,000
Contour Interval 5 Metres

Sub. Appendix

A.1.

[illegible] SIGNAL [illegible] ORDER No. 1a. Copy No. 7.
by Major [illegible] Johnson, [illegible]

Ref. [illegible], Sheet 57[illegible].

Red Line. 1. The [illegible] Division will hold the Red Line.

H.Q's. 2. Headquarters will be as follows:-
Divisional H.Q. [illegible]
125th Infy. Bde. Cross Roads, I.10.c.8.8.
126th Infy. Bde. [illegible] (COUIN)
127th Infy. Bde. I.[illegible] Central ([illegible])
Divisional H.Q. will, however, remain at PAS for a period after the units of the Division have taken up positions on the Red Line.

[illegible] to PAS. 3. (a) Line communication will be as shown in Diagram "A" while Divisional H.Q. is at PAS.

Wireless & Visual to PAS. (b) Lieut. [illegible] will establish Visual and Wireless communication as shown in Diagram "B" for communication while Divisional H.Q. is at PAS.

Cable Sections. 4. (a) When orders are given for the occupation of the Red Line,
(i) Captain [illegible] will proceed to the proposed position of Advanced Divisional H.Q. (I.14 Central) with one Cable Detachment and the necessary personnel and instruments for that office.
(ii) Lieut. [illegible] will proceed to 125th Bde. H.Q., COUIN with one Cable Detachment.
(iii) Lieut. [illegible] will proceed to 127 Bde. H.Q., [illegible] with one Cable Detachment.

Cable to [illegible]. (b) When orders are given that Divisional H.Q. will move to [illegible],
(i) Captain [illegible] will establish an Advanced Divisional Office at I.14 Central and will send his detachment to lay a one pair cable line from that point to Divisional H.Q. in [illegible].
(ii) Lieut. [illegible] will lay a one pair cable line from 125th Bde. H.Q. via 126th Bde. H.Q. to Advanced Division Office.
(iii) Lieut. [illegible] will lay a one pair cable line from 127th Inf. Bde. to Advanced Division Office.
Cable communication will then be as in Diagram "C".

Wireless & Visual to [illegible]. (c) When Divisional H.Q. moves to [illegible], Lieut. [illegible] will move the Divisional H.Q. Wireless Station from PAS to [illegible] and establish wireless and visual communication as shown in Diagram "D".

D.R's & Runners. 5. 12 Runners and [illegible] Motor Cyclist D.R's will be sent to Advanced Divisional Headquarters, the remainder will remain at Divisional H.Q.

[illegible] [signature] Major.
O.C. 42nd Div'l Signal Coy., R.E.

Issued by [illegible] at 11.0 a.m. [illegible]

Copies to 1. [illegible], 125th Bde. — Copy No. 5. [illegible]
2. [illegible], 126th Bde. — 6. [illegible]
3. [illegible], 127th Bde. — 7. War Diary.
4. [illegible] — 8. File.

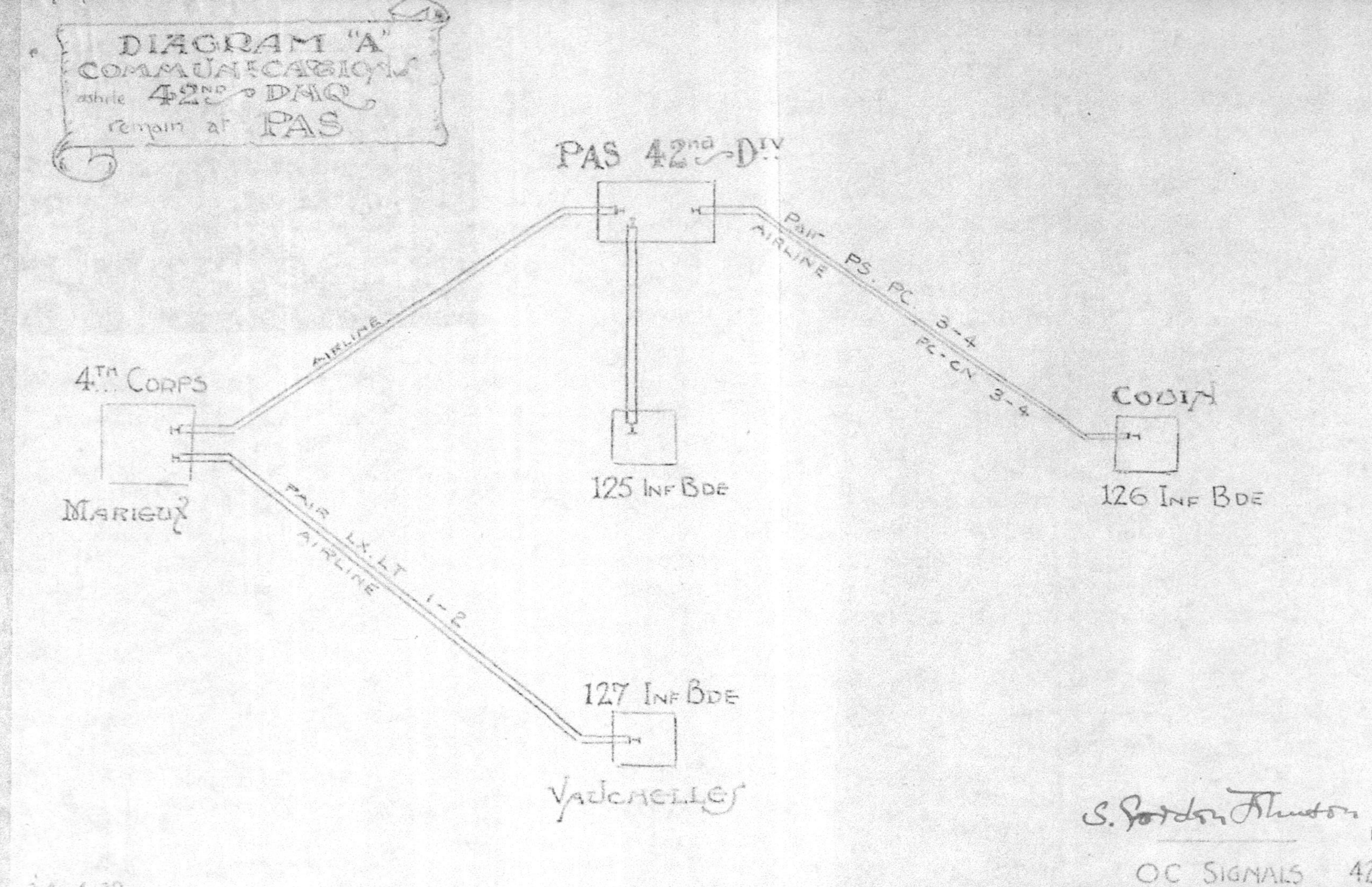
DIAGRAM "A"
COMMUNICATIONS
while 42ND DHQ
remain at PAS
PAS 42ND DIV
4TH CORPS
MARIEUX
AIRLINE
PAIR LX. LT 1-2
AIRLINE
125 INF BDE
PAIR PS. PC. 3-4
AIRLINE
PC-CN 3-4
COUIN
126 INF BDE
127 INF BDE
VAUCHELLES
S. Gordon Blunton
MAJOR
OC SIGNALS 42ND DIVN
14.4.18

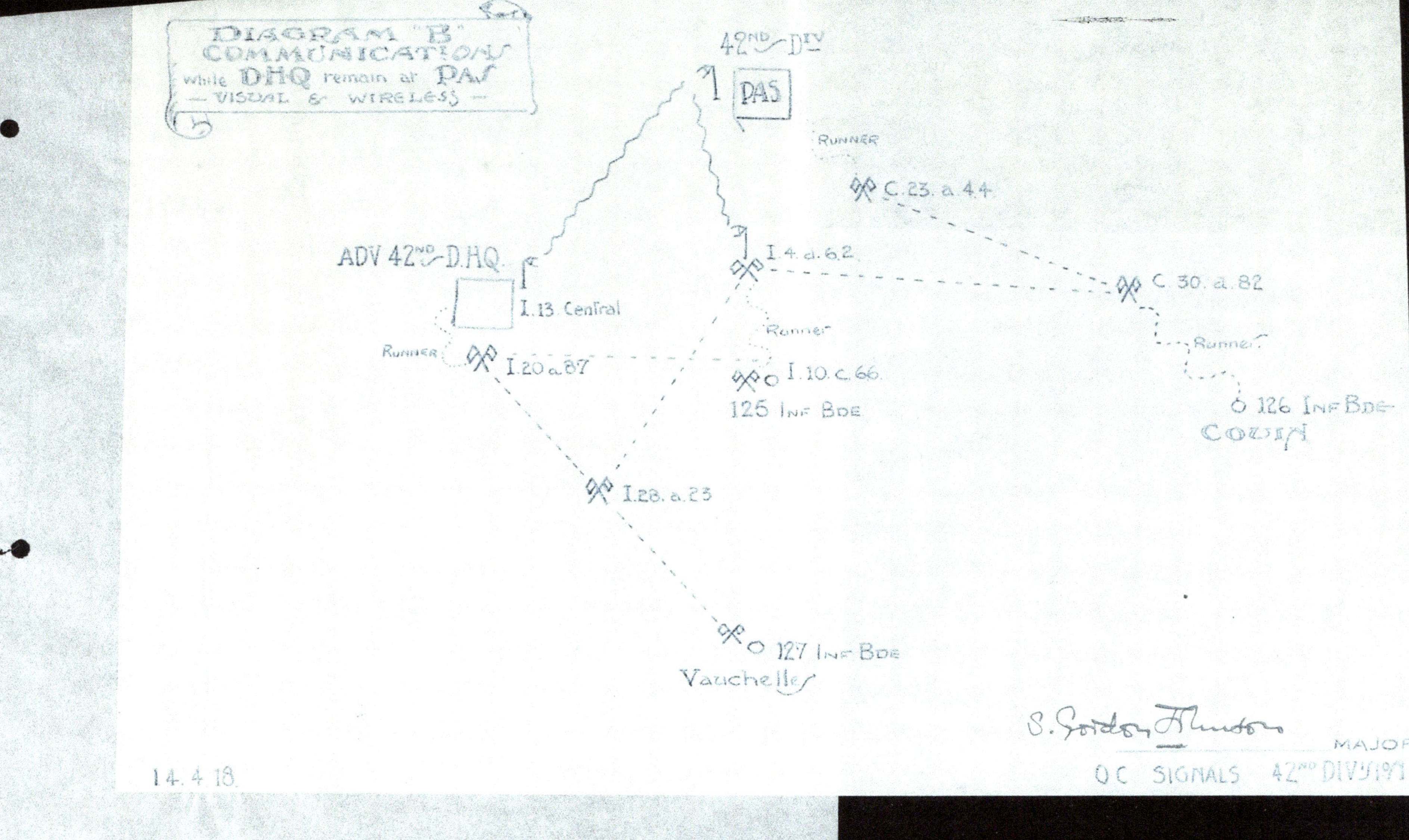
DIAGRAM "B"
COMMUNICATIONS
while DHQ remain at PAS
— VISUAL & WIRELESS —
42ND DIV
PAS
RUNNER
C.23. a. 4.4
ADV 42ND D.HQ.
I.4. d. 6.2
C. 30. a. 82
I.13. Central
Runner
Runner
RUNNER
I.20 a. 87
I.10. c. 66.
125 INF BDE
126 INF BDE
COUIN
I.28. a. 23
127 INF BDE
Vauchelles
S. Gordon Fllunsor
MAJOR
14. 4. 18.
O.C. SIGNALS 42ND DIVISION

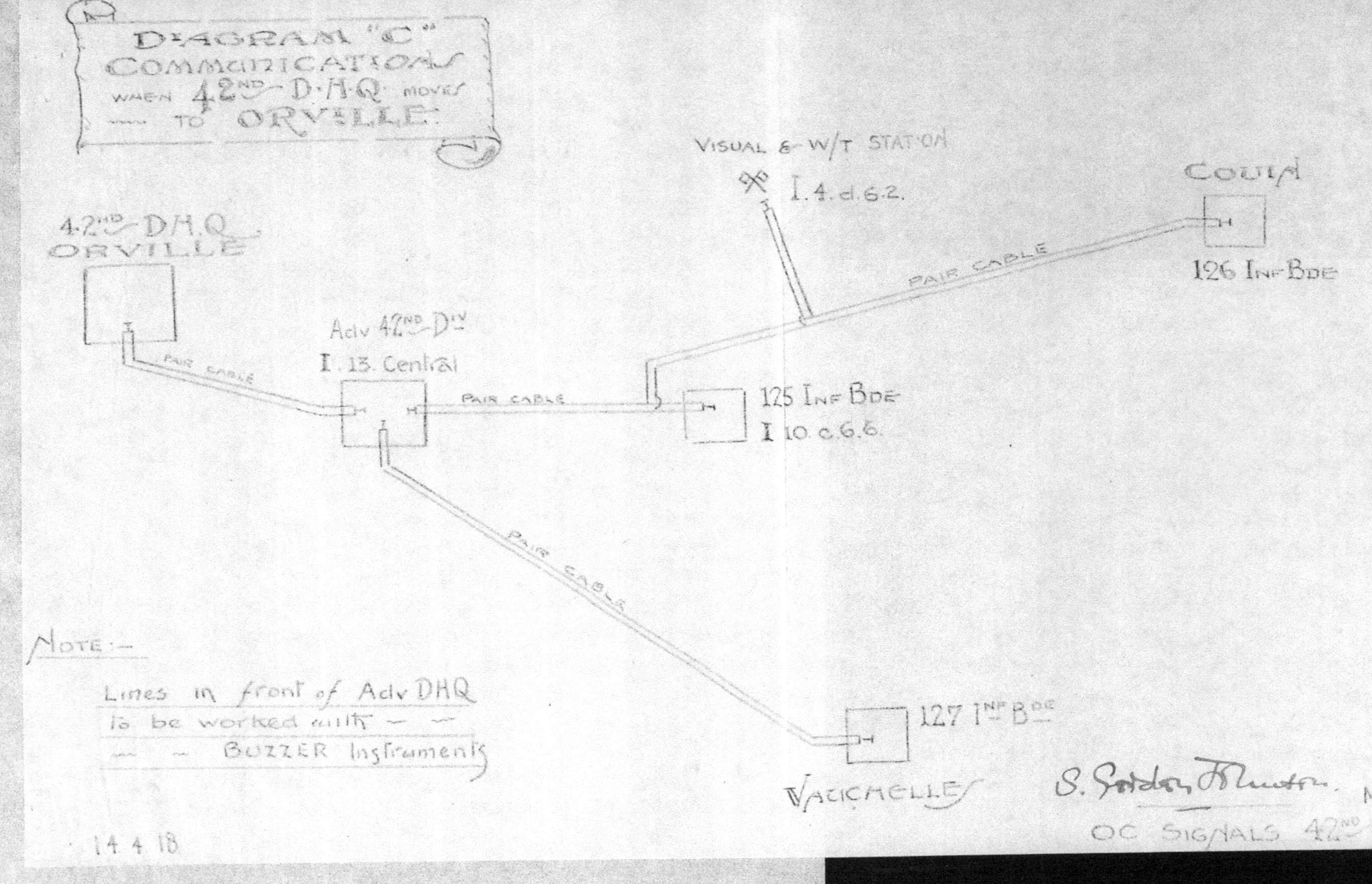
DIAGRAM "C"
COMMUNICATIONS
WHEN 42ND D.H.Q MOVES
TO ORVILLE.
42ND DHQ
ORVILLE
PAIR CABLE
Adv 42ND DIV
I. 13. Central
PAIR CABLE
VISUAL & W/T STATION
I. 4. d. 6 2.
COUIN
PAIR CABLE
126 INF BDE
125 INF BDE
I 10 c 6.6.
PAIR CABLE
127 INF BDE
VAUCHELLES
NOTE:-
Lines in front of Adv DHQ
to be worked with
BUZZER Instruments
14 4 18
S. Gordon Johnston. MAJOR
OC SIGNALS 42ND DIVN

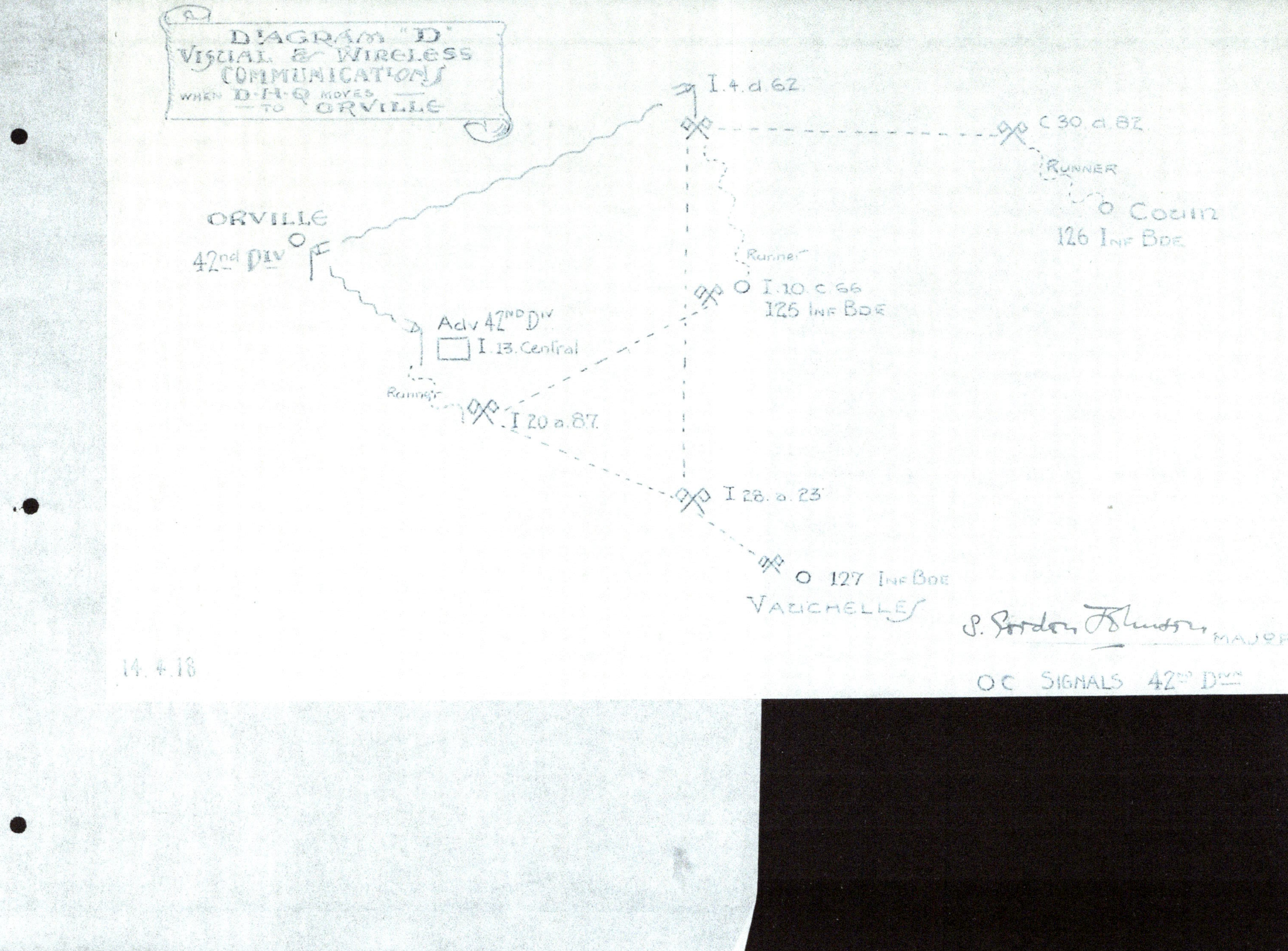

DIAGRAM "D"
VISUAL & WIRELESS COMMUNICATIONS
WHEN D·H·Q MOVES TO ORVILLE
ORVILLE
42nd DIV
Adv 42ND DIV
I. 13. Central
Runner
I 20 a. 87.
I. 4. d. 62
C 30. d. 82
RUNNER
COUIN
126 INF BDE
Runner
I. 10. c. 66
125 INF BDE
I 28. a. 23
127 INF BDE
VAUCHELLES
S. Gordon Johnson
MAJOR
OC SIGNALS 42nd DIVN
14. 4. 18

SUB-APPENDIX. A.2

SECRET.

42nd DIVISIONAL DEFENCE SCHEME.

COMMUNICATIONS IN THE GOMMECOURT SECTOR.

1. Buried Cable Routes.
2. Airline Routes.
3. Cable Routes.
4. Telephone Exchanges.
5. Instruments in use.
6. Wireless Stations.
7. Power Buzzer and Amplifier Stations.
8. Visual communications.
9. Despatch Rider Service, and Runners.
10. Artillery communications.
11. Machine Gun communications.
12. Divisional Battle Headquarters.

Diagrams.

A. Line communications.

B. Wireless, Power Buzzer-Amplifier communications.

C. Visual, Despatch Rider, Mounted Orderlies, and Runner communications.

Appendix.I.

Offices connected to Exchanges.

II.
D.R.L.S. Time Table.

COMMUNICATIONS.

Buried cable Routes. (1). The following buried cables are in use:-

(a). Three pairs direct from SOUASTRE Exchange to Advanced Divisional Exchange at FONQUEVILLERS.
(b). Two pairs from SR Test point (J.3.b8.8) to Advanced Divisional Exchange via BAYENCOURT.
(c). Two pairs from SR Test point to Right and Left Groups at CHATEAU DE LA HAIE (J.6.b.5.7).

All the above are old buries and with the exception of the portion between SR and SA Test Points are earthy.

Airline Routes. (2). There are 9 pairs from Divisional Headquarters at COUIN to CJ Junction pole (J.7.c.9.2) and 4 pairs forward to the Windmill Test Point Near SOUASTRE.

Cable Routes. (3). 2 Pairs direct COUIN to SOUASTRE.
2 Pairs direct SOUASTRE to FONQUEVILLERS.
3 Pairs FONQUEVILLERS to Left Brigade (E.28.d.1.6).
3 " " " Right " (E.27.c.3.7).
2 Pairs to Advanced Right Brigade.
4 Pairs from COUIN to SR Test Point.
4 " " SOUASTRE Exchange to SR Test Point.

These latter four pairs are left dis at SOUASTRE Exchange end for use in case lines go between Divisional Headquarters and SR-TP.

All cable Routes are poled in places where there is heavy traffic.

Telephone Exchanges. (4).(a). The Divisional Exchange is in a cellar of the Chateau at COUIN. The Reserve Brigade is connected to this Exchange.
(b). There is an Exchange at SOUASTRE serving Artillery and Local Units in that area.
(c). The Advanced Divisional Exchange is at FONQUEVILLERS. Both Brigades in the Line and Artillery Groups are on this Exchange, also the Advanced Dressing Station.
(d). Rear Brigade Headquarters are all connected to a small Exchange at COIGNEUX.

Instruments in use. (5). Sounders are used to Corps and Advanced Divisional Exchange. Fullerphones from Advanced Divisional Exchange to Right and Left Brigades. Also from Divisional Headquarters to Reserve Brigade and Artillery Groups.

Wireless Stations. (6). There is a Trench Set at Advanced Division at FONQUEVILLERS and also at the Divisional Visual Station and Report Centre at J.5.d.40. These can both send to and receive from a Wilson Set at Divisional Headquarters COUIN.

They can also work direct to one another if necessary. The Wilson Set is in direct communication with the Corps Directing Station at Corps Headquarters.

Power Buzzer and Amplifier Stations. (7). There are three Power Buzzer and Amplifier Stations on the Divisional front.
(a). At Advanced Division at FONQUEVILLERS.
(b). At Right Brigade Headquarters.
(c). At Right Brigade Report Centre.

(a). Provides communication with (b) and (c), and (a) and (b) have also communication with each other.

All of these three Stations can send to and receive messages from one another.

(c). Is quite close to the Left Brigade Visual Station and is linked up to both Brigades by telephone.

This latter Station can receive messages from Power Buzzers at all four Battalions in the line. The Right Battalion Right Brigade is also in communication with the Amplifier at Right Brigade Headquarters. Thus each Brigade is in

communication with its two Battalions in the line.
Each of the seven Stations has a special time for working allotted to it, so as to reduce jamming. S.O.S. messages can, however be sent by any Station at any time.
A test message is sent through each evening by Power Buzzer to the Amplifier at Advanced Division and thence transmitted by Wireless to Divisional Headquarters

Visual communications. (8). There is a Visual Station near Divisional Headquarters at J.26.c.54. connected by telephone to the Divisional Exchange. This is in direct communication with the two Divisional Transmitting Stations at J.5.d.40. and D.23.d central and also with the two Artillery Groups at CHATEAU DE LA HAIE.
The Station at D.23.d central is in direct communication with the Visual Station at Advanced Divisionat FONCQUEVILLERS, which is in direct communication with the Left Brigade Visual Station at E.28.b.95.
The Station at J.5.d.40 is in direct communication with the Right Brigade Visual Station close to Right Brigade Headquarters, and also with the two Artillery Groups at CHATEAU DE LA HAIE.
Thus each Brigade is linked up to Divisional Headquarters by a chain of Stations.
A test message is sent each evening from each Brigade in the line to Divisional Headquarters.
The Divisional Visual Stations are manned daily for work from 5 a.m. to 10 a.m. and again at 6 p.m. for the test message
Orders have also been issued that they are to be manned immediately in case of a breakdown in telephone communication

Despatch Rider Service. (a). (9). Infantry Brigades. There are three posts per day by Despatch Rider to Advanced Divisional Headquarters (FQ) at FONCQUEVILLERS; Each Brigade in the line sending despatches to FQ by Runner to meet the above Despatch Riders, the Runners returning to their Brigades with outgoing despatches.
Three Despatch Riders are maintained at FQ for use in case of "Specials" only.
Runners at FQ deliver to detached units in that vicinity.
Despatch Riders on return journey from FQ call at Rear Brigade Headquarters at COIGNEUX.
Artillery Groups. There are three posts per day to the Headquarters of Right and Left Groups R.F.A. at CHATEAU DE LA HAIE.
Corps. Five posts from and to Corps Headquarters daily.
The Time Table is given in appendix II.

Runners. (b) There are 12 Runners at Advanced Divisional FONCQUEVILLERS who are used for taking D.R.L.S. to each of the Brigades in the line.
They will also be used for taking Messages in case of a breakdown in other methods of communication.
A reserve of runners is maintained at Divisional Headquarters. These are normally employed as orderlies at the Signal Office.
Should the Divisional Report Centre be opened at J.5.d.4.0, six runners will be sent to this Station, also three mounted despatch riders will be sent by the Camp Commandant.

Artillery Communications. (10) (a) Division to Groups. There is a direct buried line from Divisional Artillery Exchange to each Group.
Alternative means of communication are provided as follows:-
(i) An Advance Divisional Artillery Exchange is established in FONCQUEVILLERS with lines to D.A. and each Group.
(ii) Left Group is connected to the Divisional Exchange in SOUASTRE which has a line to D.A.
(iii) Left and Right Groups are connected by means of a lateral line.

Artillery Communications (Cont'd)

(10) (b). Groups to Batteries. Direct lines from Groups (or Brigades in case of Left Group) to Batteries are provided in as many cases as the supply of cable has permitted. Where these direct lines do not exist, communication is obtained by means of a system of laterals giving alternative routes.

(c) O.P. Communication. Batteries are connected up as far as possible to an O.P. by direct line. In other cases the O.P. is obtained through a neighbouring battery. Forward O.P's where they exist are connected to the rear O.P's.

(d) Liaison with Infantry. Each Group has a direct line to the Infantry brigade whose front it covers.

Communication to Battalion Liaison Officers is obtained by means of lines reserved for Artillery use when possible, but which are for general use when rendered necessary by the breakdown of other lines.

(e) Liaison with Heavy Artillery. The 48th and 92nd H.A. Brigades are connected to SOUASTRE Exchange. 127th Heavy Battery has a line to Advanced Divisional Artillery Exchange. Heavy Artillery O.P's are connected laterally to Field Artillery O.P's and to the nearest Field Artillery Batteries.

Two O.P's on the Divisional Front are to be manned both by Heavy and Field Artillery Observers, who will have direct communication to Heavy and Field Batteries.

(f) Visual. Visual is established throughout from Division forward, wherever the nature of the ground permits.

Each Group has Visual to a Divisional Station and to every possible battery.

All O.P's except two which are hidden by GOMMECOURT, have Visual communication.

Machine Gun Communications.

(11) (a) The Machine Gun Battalion Headquarters are on the Divisional Exchange at COUIN.

(b) The Advanced Machine Gun Battalion Headquarters are at E.28.d.27., and are connected to the Left Brigade Exchange and also to the Right Brigade Report Centre.

(c) The Left Machine Gun Company at E.29.c.1.9 is connected direct to the Machine Gun Battalion Advanced Headquarters. This Company also has a line and Visual Communication to a Section.

(d) The Centre Machine Gun Company is at the Advanced Machine Gun Battalion Headquarters. They get communication with a section through the battalion of the Right Brigade at E.28.d.5.1.

(e) The Right Machine Gun Company have a direct line to the Right Brigade and also a line to the Left Battalion of the Right Division.

They have a direct line to a Section

(f) The Company in Reserve is connected by Runner.

Divisional Battle Headquarters.

(12) The Advanced Divisional Report Centre is at J.5.d.4.0. In the event of "Precautionary Measures" being received, three additional pairs of cables will be laid to 'BY' Test Point. At present there is one pair of cables to SOUASTRE Exchange and one pair connected to the buried cable route at 'BY' Test Point, giving telephone communication by alternative routes to Brigades in the Line.

S. Gordon Johnston
Major.

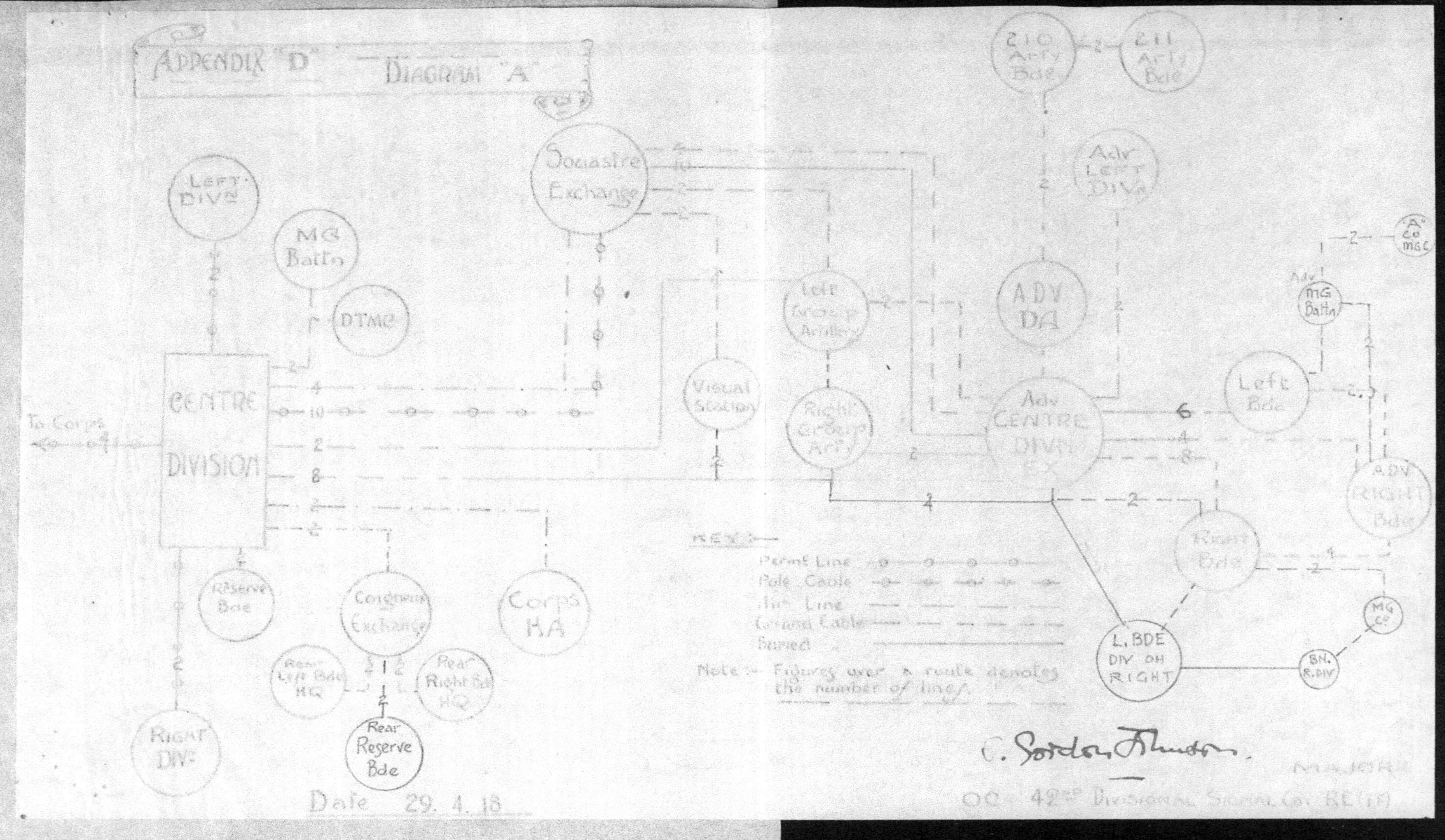

APPENDIX "D"
DIAGRAM "A"
Left Divn
MG Battn
DTMO
Centre Division
To Corps
Reserve Bde
Right Divn
Coigneux Exchange
Rear Left Bde HQ
Rear Right Bde HQ
Rear Reserve Bde
Corps HA
Souastre Exchange
Visual Station
Left Group Artillery
Right Group Arty
210 Arty Bde
211 Arty Bde
Adv Left Divn
ADV DA
Adv Centre Divn Ex
Adv MG Battn
"A" Co MGC
Left Bde
ADV Right Bde
Right Bde
MG Co
BN. R.DIV
L. BDE DIV ON RIGHT
KEY:-
Perm Line
Pole Cable
Air Line
Ground Cable
Buried
Note:- Figures over a route denotes the number of lines.
Date 29. 4. 18
C. Gordon Thunder.
MAJOR
OC 42nd Divisional Signal Co. RE (TF)

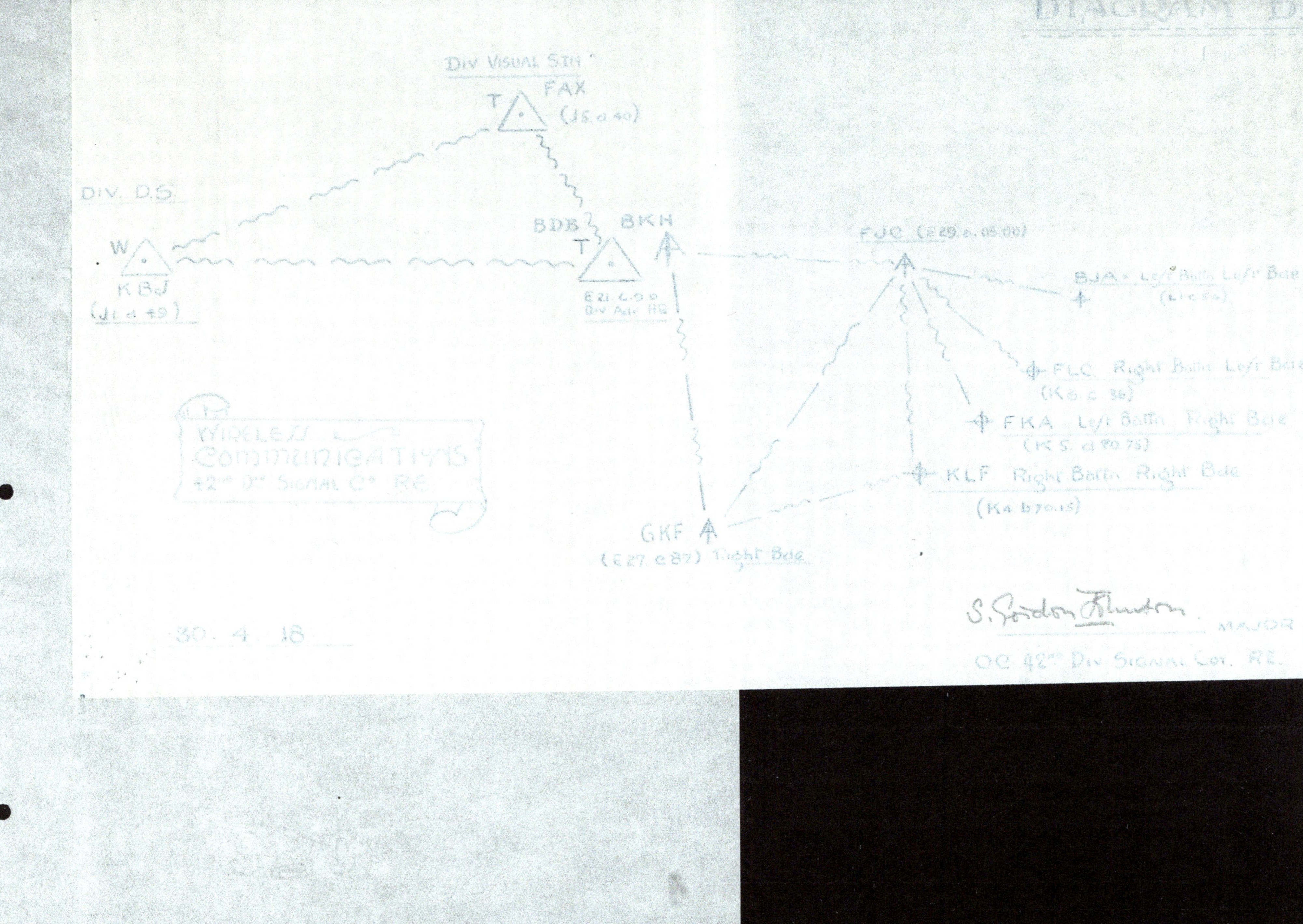
DIAGRAM "B"
DIV VISUAL STN
FAX
(J6.d.40)
DIV. D.S.
W
KBJ
(J1.d.49)
T
BDB
BKH
E21.c.9.0
Div Adv HQ
FJC (E29.a.05.00)
BJA Left Batt. Left Bde
FLC Right Batt. Left Bde
(K6.c.30)
FKA Left Batt. Right Bde
(K5.d.90.75)
KLF Right Batt. Right Bde
(K4.b.70.15)
GKF
(E27.c.87) Right Bde
WIRELESS COMMUNICATIONS
42nd Dn SIGNAL Co RE
30. 4. 18
S. Gordon Johnston
MAJOR
OC 42nd Div SIGNAL Coy. RE.

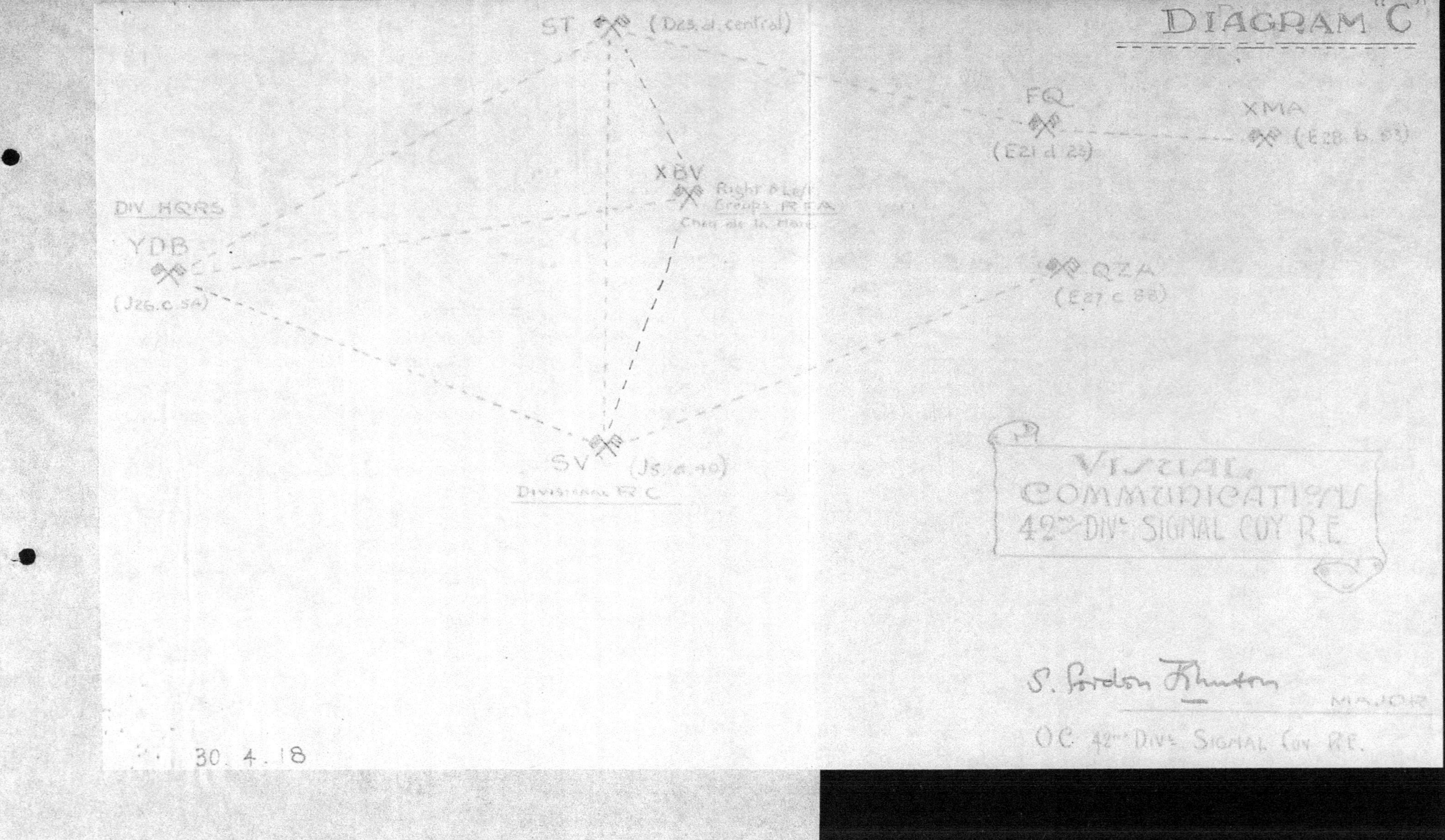
DIAGRAM "C"
ST (D23.d.central)
FQ
(E21.d.23)
XMA
(E28.b.83)
XBV
Right & Left Groups R.F.A.
DIV HQRS
YDB
(J26.c.54)
QZA
(E27.c.88)
SV
(J5.a.40)
Divisional R.C.
VISUAL COMMUNICATIONS
42ND DIVL SIGNAL COY R.E.
S. Gordon Johnston
MAJOR
O.C. 42ND DIVL SIGNAL COY R.E.
30.4.18

APPENDIX I.

42ND DIVISIONAL H.Q. EXCHANGE.

30 line Board.

1. Divisional Train. (Billet 27).
2. 42nd Machine Gun Battalion. (Billet 40).
3. S.A.A. and Signals Camp.
4. A.D.M.S. (Hut near Church).
5. D.A.D.O.S. (Billet 66).
6. Signals Orderly Room (Chateau Grounds).
7. C.R.E.)
8. 'A'.)
9. 'G'.) Chateau.
10. G.O.C.,)
11. Wireless, YDB.)
12. 'Q'.)
13.
14. G.S.O.1. (Chateau).
15. O.C., Signals. (No. 11 Room, Chateau).
16.
17. Messages.
18. Supervisor.
19. IV Corps.
20. SOUASTRE.
21. Right Division.
22. FONCQUEVILLERS.
23. Visual (YDB).
24. 170th Brigade.
25. Brigades Rear H.Q's.
26.
27. Brigade on Right.
28. FONCQUEVILLERS.
29. Left Division.
30. Reserve Brigade.

42ND DIVISIONAL ARTILLERY EXCHANGE.

20 line Board.

1. Reserve Brigade.
2. A.P.M., (Billet 28).
3. Mechanics Repair Shop.
4. 'R' Section, Field Survey.
5. Brigade Major, Div. Art'y.
6. Staff Captain, " "
7. R.A. Mess - Brigade Major - Night.
8. 47th D.A.C. (Billet 49).
9. SOUASTRE.
10. Buzzer Unit.
11. Corps Heavies.
12. R.A. Advanced.
13. SOUASTRE.
14. IV Corps.
15.
16.
17. Ammunition Refilling Point.
18. Left Group.
19. SOUASTRE.
20. Right Group.

Buzzer Unit.

Local A. Junction to Fullerphone.
1. (Visual, SV) Right Brigade, FONCQUEVILLERS.
2.)
3.) Connected to Test Panel for plugging
4.) through to any subscriber.
5.)
6. Connected to No. 10 on Div'l Artillery Exchange for working Fullerphone to Right and Left Groups.

SOUASTRE EXCHANGE.

16 line Exchange.

1. 48th Brigade R.G.A.
2. Centre Division.
3. Centre Division.
4. FONQUEVILLERS.
5. 92nd Brigade R.G.A.
6. Left Group.
7. Superintendent's Phone.
8. FONQUEVILLERS.
9. R.E. DUMP.
10. Divisional Artillery.
11. Centre Division.
12.
13. Visual Station ('SS')
14. " " ('SV')
15.
16. Field Ambulance, SOUASTRE.

FONQUEVILLERS EXCHANGE – ('FQ').

10 line Cordless.

1. Centre Division.
2. Right Brigade.
3. SOUASTRE Exchange.
4. Advanced Dressing Station.
5. Centre Division.
6. Junction to Buzzer Unit.
7. Right Brigade.
8. Advanced Divisional Artillery.
9. Advanced Division on Left.
10. Left Brigade.

Buzzer Unit.

1. Visual Station ('SV').
2. Centre Division, Right Brigade, Left Brigade of Right Division.
3. Advance Right Brigade.
4. Left Brigade.
5. Right Brigade.
6. Junction to Cordless Exchange.
7. W/T. Station. (WBPA).

COIGNEUX EXCHANGE.

Magneto Unit.

1. Pioneer Battalion.
2. Reserve Brigade, Rear.
3. Left Brigade, Rear.
4. Right Brigade, Rear.
5. Centre Division.

42nd Division.

D. R. L. S. TIME TABLE.

APPENDIX II.

LEAVE.		CALL AT.					R.A.		RETURN.	
D.H.Q.	IV Corps.	D.H.Q.	Local Units.	Left Brigade.	Right Brigade.	REAR BDE HQ'S.	Left Group.	Right Group.	D.H.Q.	IV Corps.
	6.0 am.	7.0 am								8.0 a.m.
9.0 am.			10 am.	10 am.	10 a.m.	9.30 a.m.	10 a.m.	10 a.m.	11.30 a.m.	
	12 noon.	1.0 pm.								2.0 p.m.
1.0 pm.			2.0. p.m.	2.0. p.m.	2.0. p.m.	1.30 p.m.	2.0. p.m.	2.0. p.m.	3.30. p.m.	
	3.0 pm.	4.0 pm.								5.0 p.m.
	6.0 pm.	7.0 pm.								8.0 p.m.
7.30 p.m.			8.30 p.m.	8.30 p.m.	8.30 p.m.	8.0 p.m.	8.30 p.m.	8.30 p.m.	9.30 p.m.	
	9.0 pm.	10 pm.								11.0 pm.

APPENDIX. "B" APRIL 1918.

WAR DIARY.

HONOURS AND AWARDS.

The Field Marshal Commanding-in -Chief has, under authority granted by His Majesty the King, awarded the following decorations to the undermentioned Officers:-

BAR TO THE MILITARY CROSS.

Captain A. Roberts. M.C.

MILITARY CROSS.

Lieut. H. Horner.
" A.G.Brown.
" H.T.P.Moore.
2/Lieut.A.J.Ellis.

The Fourth Corps Commander has, under authority granted by His Majesty the King, awarded the following decorations to the undermentioned N.C.O's and men:-

DISTINGUISHED CONDUCT MEDAL.

No.444610 2/Cpl Williams,W.
No.443933 Pnr Gray,A.S.

BAR TO MILITARY MEDAL.

No.444566 Cpl Fielding,J.

MILITARY MEDAL.

No.444003 Cpl Rhodes,F.
No.444241 MC Cpl Baldwin.A.O.
No.444246 " " Gregson.W.
No.444453 " " Roscoe,E.
No.444211 " " Flaws,L.R.
No. 86709 2/Cpl Hart.M.
No.443929 Pnr Kirkman,J.
No.444598 Cpl Riding,T.E.
No.441922 2/Cpl Thompson.J.
No.443968 Pnr Reeder,R.H.
No.444058 2/Cpl Duffy.J.
No.443973 Pnr Phillips,H.H.

S. Gordon Johnston.
Major.
O.C. 42nd Divisional Signal Co. R.E.

APPENDIX. "C" APRIL 1918.

WAR DIARY.

WEEKLY STRENGTHS, CASUALTIES, REINFORCEMENTS.

Weekly Strengths.

	O.	O.R.
Week ending April 6th	10	272
" " " 13th	11	276
" " " 20th	11	288
" " " 27th	11	288

Casualties.

		O.	O.R.
Killed.		-	9
Wounded.	Ø	2	7
Gassed.		-	15
Sick to hospital.		1	19
To Base Depot.		-	1
		3	51

/Ø 1 Attached supernunerary.
1 Attached.

Reinforcements.

		O.	O.R.
From Third Army.	X	2	-
" Signal Depot.		-	50
" Hospital.		1	3
Transferred from Infantry etc.		-	14
		3	67

X Attached supernumerary.

S. Gordon Johnston
Major.
O.C. 42nd Divisional Signal Co. R.E.

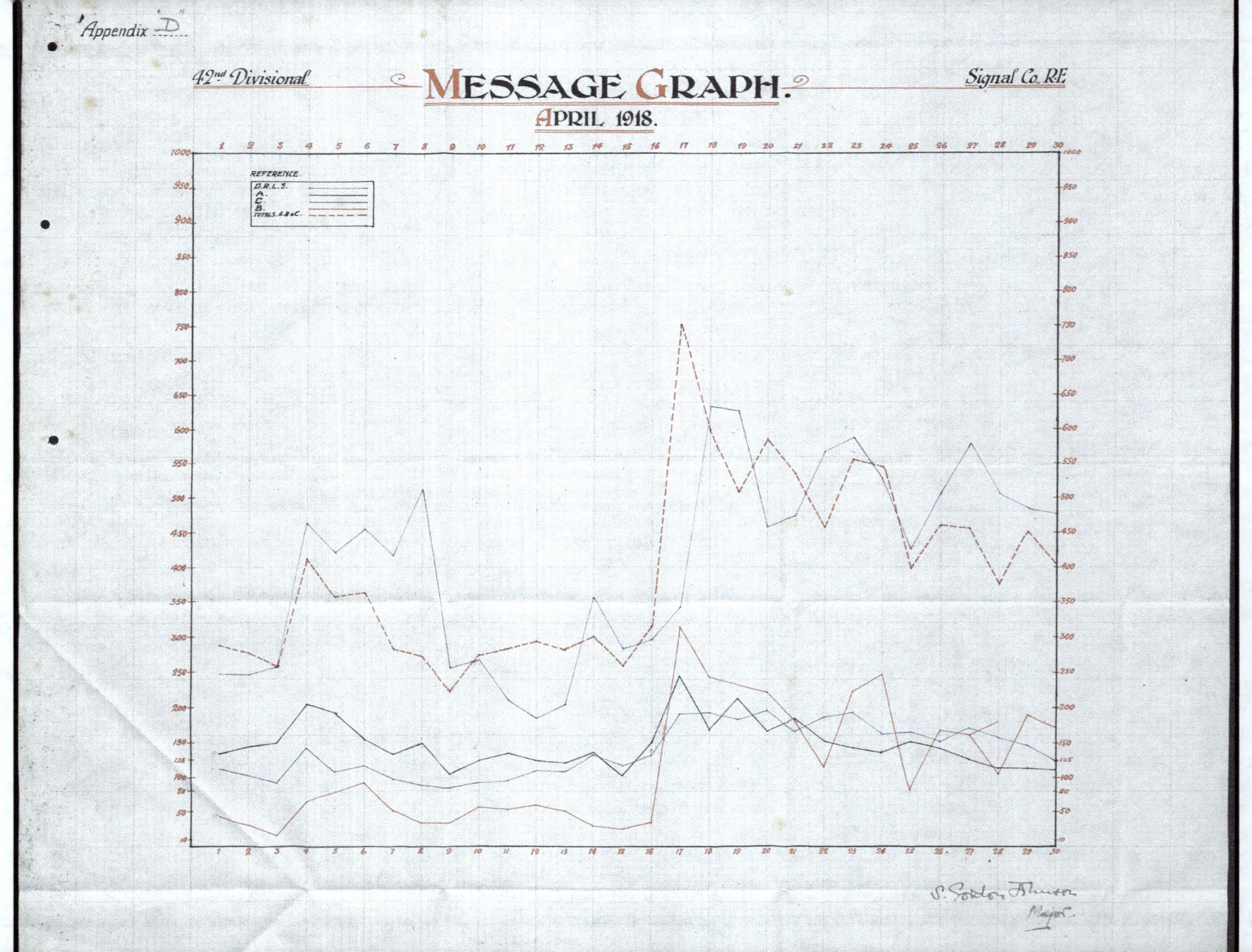

"Appendix D"
42nd Divisional
MESSAGE GRAPH.
Signal Co. RE
APRIL 1918.
REFERENCE.
D.R.L.S.
A.
C.
B.
TOTALS. A.B & C.
1 2 3 4 5 6 7 8 9 10 11 12 13 14 15 16 17 18 19 20 21 22 23 24 25 26 27 28 29 30
1000 950 900 850 800 750 700 650 600 550 500 450 400 350 300 250 200 150 125 100 80 50 10
Major.

Appendix ....

WAR DIARY.

SECRET

Vol 15

WAR DIARY.

42ND DIVISIONAL SIGNAL COY. R.E.

CHAPTER XIX. MAY 1918.

4.6.18

A Roberts. Capt RE.

for. O.C. 42ND DIVL. SIGNAL COY. R.E.

Instructions regarding War Diaries and Intelligence Summaries are contained in F. S. Regs., Part II. and the Staff Manual respectively. Title pages will be prepared in manuscript.

WAR DIARY
or
~~INTELLIGENCE SUMMARY.~~
(Erase heading not required.)

Army Form C. 2118.

Place	Date	Hour	Summary of Events and Information	Remarks and references to Appendices
			Map reference .FRANCE. 1/40,000 BUCQUOY. Combined sheet. FRANCE 1/40,000 Sheet 57 D	
			CHAPTER XIX. MAY 1918. 42nd (East Lancs) Divisional Signal Co.R.E.(T.F).	
COUIN.	1.5.18.		42nd Division holding the front line in the Centre Sector of 4th Corps Front. Divisional Headquarters and Signal Company Headquarters at COUIN Chateau. Communications were as described in previous Chapter and as shown in Diagram 13 of that chapter.	
PAS.	6.5.18.		The Division was relieved in the line by 57th Division and went into Army Reserve with Headquarters at PAS. Divisional Headquarters closed at COUIN at 4 p.m. and reopened at PAS same hour. The move to PAS was carried out in accordance with Company Order No. 16. The Company took over the lines and billets occupied by 57th Division in PAS Chateau grounds. Whilst in reserve the Division was held ready to man the RED LINE in case of attack. Communications as described in Appendix "A" and Diagrams 1 and 2.	APPENDIX "A".
	8.5.18.		The Divisional Signal Class commenced training at BEAUREPAIRE. The Twelfth Course consisting of approximately 220 men, mostly untrained, drawn from the Artillery and Infantry Units of the Division, and 20 men from the 4th Corps Heavy Artillery. On 29.5.18. the Divisional Signal Class moved to HALLOY. During the period in this area a number of the Signal personnel of the 307 (American) Infantry Regiment were attached to the Company for training and instruction.	
	31.5.18.		The Company remained at PAS for the remainder of this month, occupying the time in re-equipping and training.	

APPENDICES TO THIS DIARY.

(A). Communications.
(B). Communications for Left Division holding the RED LINE.
(C). Honours and Rewards.
(D). Casualties, Weekly Strengths, & Reinforcements.
(E). Monthly Message Chart.

3.6.18.

A Roberts Capt RE for Major.
O.C. 42nd Divisional Signal Co. R.E.

A7092). Wt. W12839/M1297 750,000. 1/17. D. D & L., Ltd. Forms/C2118/14.

SECRET. Copy No. 6

42nd DIVISIONAL SIGNAL COMPANY
ORDER No. 16.

---

1. The Company will hand over to the 57th Divisional Signal Coy. on May 6th, and will move to PAS CHATEAU taking over Offices, billets, and area occupied by the 57th Signals.

2. 42nd Divisional Headquarters will close at COUIN at 4 p.m. May 6th and open at PAS at the same hour.

3. Advance parties will proceed as follows:-
May 5th- One N.C.O. Supervisor and 2 Linemen from FONQUEVILLERS Office will proceed at 12 noon to 57th Divisional Advanced Headquarters Office at HENU.
One Telegraph Clerk, one Switchboard operator, one Lineman and 2 Orderlies from Divisional Headquarters Office will proceed to 57th Divisional Headquarters Office at PAS, arriving there at 2 p.m.

4. A complete Signal Office relief will proceed to PAS by Motor lorry leaving at 9.30 a.m. on May 6th.

5. Company Headquarters and transport will parade at 3 p.m. and move off at 3.15 p.m. on May 6th for PAS.

6. Detail of transport for May 6th & 7th as per attached sheet.

7. Cable wagon detachment as detailed will remain at COUIN, attached to the 57th Division.

8. Signal Office personnel as detailed will remain at COUIN until morning of May 7th when it will join the Company at PAS.

Issued at p.m. 5.5.18.

R. S. Newton
Captain.
for O.C. 42nd Div'l Signal Co. R.E.

Copy No. 1. "T" Officer.
" " 2. "A" Officer.
" " 3. CSM & CQMS.
" " 4. Signalmaster.
" " 5. Sgt. Harrison.
" " 6. War Diary. ✓
" " 7. File.

SPECIAL DETAIL OF TRANSPORT.

May 6th.

1. The P.E.L. Lorry will leave at 9.30 a.m. on arrival of the 57 Div. P.E.L. Lorry and will proceed to PAS CHATEAU.

2. Light Motor lorry will leave at 9.30 a.m. with Technical equipment, Q.M. Stores, and other Baggage for 57th Divisional Signal Lines.
A party of 1 N.C.O. and 3 men and a complete Signal Office relief will accompany this Lorry.
This Lorry will return to COUIN by 1.30 p.m.

3. Limbered wagon with Cook's Stores, and Cooks will leave for PAS at 2 p.m.

4. 3 Ton Motor Lorry with "Bluebirds" equipment, Technical Stores, Orderly Room Stores and Officers Kits and Mess Stores will leave for PAS at 2.15 p.m. Escort 1 N.C.O. and 3 men.

5. Light Motor Lorry will leave at 5 p.m. for PAS with Signal Office and W/T equipment and remainder of baggage. Escort 1 N.C.O. and 3 men.

6. One G.S. Wagon will be detailed to be at FONQUEVILLERS(FQ)at 4 p.m. to bring Stores direct to PAS.

7. One limbered wagon will be detailed to be at SV (BAYENCOURT) Visual Station at 3 p.m. to bring Stores direct to PAS. This wagon will call at SOUASTRE Exchange for Stores on return journey.

May 7th.

1. One G.S. Wagon will be detailed to be at FONQUEVILLERS (FQ) at 7 a.m. to bring Stores direct to PAS.

R. S. Newton
Captain.
5.5.18. for O.C. 42nd Divisional Signal Co. R.E.

WAR DIARY

42nd DIVISIONAL SIGNAL COMPANY.R.E.

ORDER No. 17 .

ON RECEIPT OF ORDER "BATTLE POSITIONS".

1. All ranks will immediately "stand to" with kits packed and equipment ready to move off.

2. Cooks will prepare tea for personnel moving out (if time permits).

3. Officers' chargers will be saddled up, and the three cable detachmentsx horses harnessed and ready to hook in.

4. Cable detachments will stand by ready to move off on receipt of orders. (Sgt. Borland responsible for this).

5. The 3 ton Motor Lorry will be ready to proceed to Advanced Divisional Headquarters Signal Office HENU (D.19.b.28) with the following:-

Stores and stationery for Advanced Signal Office.
(As detailed by Cpl ~~Meakins~~) Moores.
One complete Signal Office relief including 5 Runners.
(As detailed by Sgt. McCarthy).
Four Visyal Sigignallers.) For TR Station.
Four Runners.) (as detailed by Cpl Meakins).
Three W/T men and Stores for DS Station.) As detailed
All Stores for 3 Divisional Visual Stations.) by Cpl Meakins)

The N.C.O. i/c Signal Office relief will be in charge of this Lorry, its personnel and stores.

6. The following personnel (as detailed by Cpl Meakins) will be ready to proceed as follows:-

4 Visual Signallers.) YDB Visual Station HENU, D.14.c.05.
4 Runners.)
6 Visual Signallers.) PT Visual Station near HENU.D.19.d.80.
4 Runners.)
9 W/T men to 127th Brigade Advanced Headquarters.D.17.a.84.
9 W/T men to 125th Brigade. " " D.28.c.23.
6 W/T men to 126th Brigade " " D.26.d.24.

7. Six Motor Cyclist D.R's. will be ready to proceed to Advanced Divisional Signal Office HENU. (Detailed by Sgt.Harrison).

Two D.R's will report to Signals, 42nd Divisional Artillery as arranged by Signals, 42nd Divisional Artillery, with Sgt. Harrison.

8. N.C.O's. concerned will detail the above transport and parties each night to be ready to move at daybreak the following day.

9. One days' rations and full water bottles will be carried. The C.Q.M.S. will see that this is arranged each night.

10. The Motor Lorry and limbered Wagons detailed above will (unless otherwise ordered) return to Company Headquarters PAS on completing their respective journeys.

11. The above parties and transport will be ready to move off without any delay. The N.C.O's named below are responsible and will see that their detachments turn out quickly and parade fully equipped with rations ready to move off, reporting this to the senior Officer present or if no officer is present, the Sergt.-Major.

Sgt. Borland..............	Three cable detachments.
N.C.O. i/c Signal Office relief..................	Motor lorry personnel and Stores.
Cpl Meakins.............	The W/T and Visual detachments.
Sgt.Harrison............	D.R's.

R. S. Newton
Captain.

10.5.18. for O.C. 42nd Divisional Signal Co.R.E.

APPENDIX "A". WAR DIARY. MAY 1918.

Reference sheet 57 D.
Edition 2.

COMMUNICATIONS.

1.5.18. Until the Division was relieved on the 6th May the system of communications remained unchanged. General maintainence was carried out and various ground cables were poled to prevent being damaged by traffic.

4.5.18. The enemy scored a direct hit on the S.F. buried route between SOUASTRE and FONQUEVILLERS, three working lines being "dis".

5.5.18. S.F. Bury through.

6.5.18. Diagram 1 shows the communication which existed on the 6th May when the Division moved into Army Reserve with Divisional Headquarters at PAS (C.16.d.5.3). The Division was ordered to be prepared to occupy the RED LINE at an hours notice.

The Battle Headquarters of the Infantry Brigades were connected to the Divisional Battle Headquarters with one pair of lines. The Signal Office at the Divisional Headquarters was in a cellar near the Church at HENU.

As the village would probably be shelled heavily if the enemy attacked, arrangements were made to move the Signal Office to a dug-out at D.13.d.6.5. and build poled cable routes across country to each Infantry Brigade Battle Headquarters.

11.5.18. This work was commenced on the 11th May and with the exception of the dug-out was completed by the 18th. Pending the completion of the dug-out the Signal Office was established in a Tent Telegraph in the Wood near by.

18.5.18. Diagram 2 shows the communication which then existed until the end of the month.

On the 18th May the Division held a Battle practice Scheme and notes on communications during the scheme are attached.

A Roberts Capt RE.
for Major.

3.6.18. O.C. 42nd Divisional Signal Co. R.E.

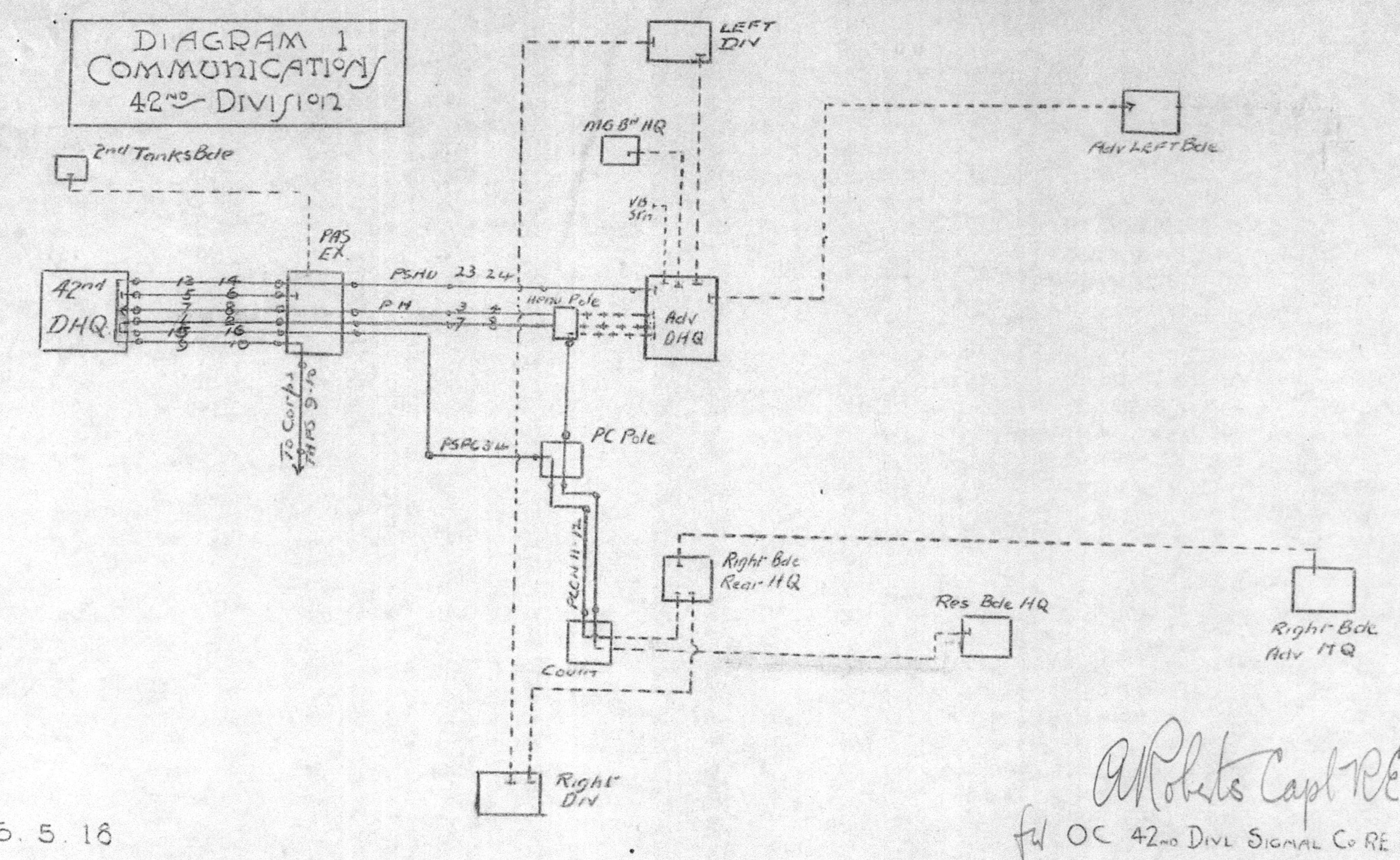
DIAGRAM 1
COMMUNICATIONS
42ND DIVISION
2nd Tanks Bde
42nd DHQ
PAS EX.
To Corps
PSHU 23 24
PM 3 4
7 8
PSPC 3 4
PC Pole
LEFT DIV
MG Bn HQ
VB + Stn
Adv DHQ
Adv LEFT Bde
Right Bde Rear HQ
Res Bde HQ
Right Bde Adv HQ
Right DIV
6. 5. 18
A Roberts Capt RE
for OC 42ND DIVL SIGNAL Co RE

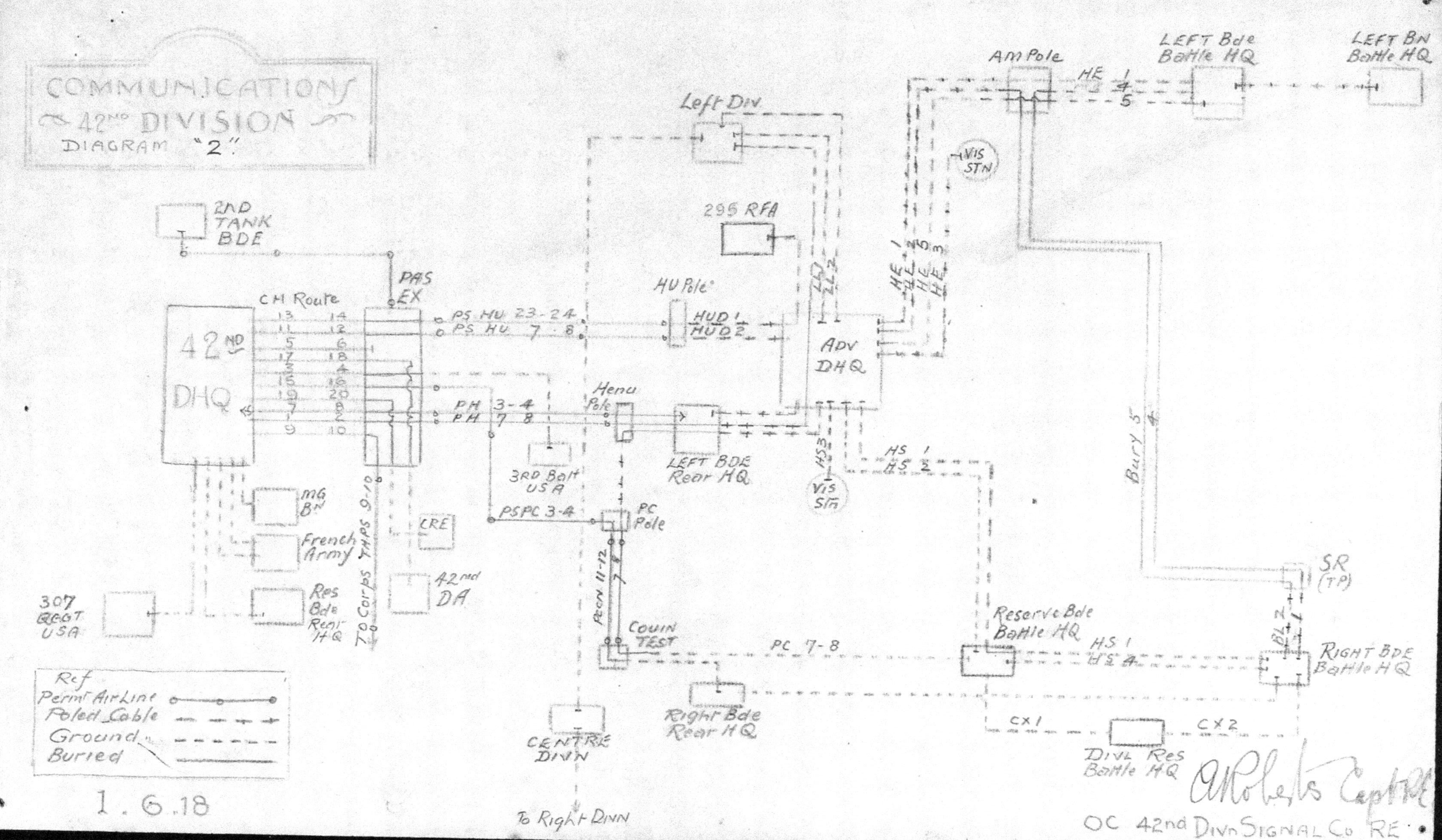
COMMUNICATIONS
42ND DIVISION
DIAGRAM "2"
2ND TANK BDE
PAS EX
CH Route
42ND DHQ
PS HU 23-24
PS HU 7-8
PH 3-4
PH 7 8
PSPC 3-4
HU Pole
HUD 1
HUD 2
Left Div
295 RFA
LL 1
LL 2
ADV DHQ
HE 1
HE 2
HE 5
HE 3
VIS STN
AM Pole
HE 1
4
5
LEFT Bde Battle HQ
LEFT BN Battle HQ
Henu Pole
LEFT BDE Rear HQ
HS3
VIS STN
HS 1
HS 2
3RD Batt USA
PC Pole
Rcon 11-12
7 8
Couin TEST
PC 7-8
Bury 5 4
SR (TP)
BL 2 1
Reserve Bde Battle HQ
HS 1
HS 4
RIGHT BDE Battle HQ
Right Bde Rear HQ
CENTRE DIVN
To Right DIVN
CX 1
CX 2
DIVL Res Battle HQ
MG BN
French Army
Res Bde Rear HQ
CRE
42nd DA
To Corps THPS 9-10
307 REGT USA
Ref
Perm^t AirLine
Poled Cable
Ground
Buried
1.6.18
A Roberts Capt RE
OC 42nd Divn Signal Co RE

APPENDIX "A"   War Diary

NOTES ON COMMUNICATIONS DURING SCHEME, 18/5/18.

1. WARNING ORDER. The Warning Order was received in the Signal Office at 7.8 a.m.

2. ADVANCE DIVISIONAL OFFICE. The Advance Divisional Office was opened at HENU at 8.15 a.m. in communication to Rear Divisional Headquarters and Corps.

Communication was established to Brigades as follows:-

Brigade.	Telephone.	Visual.	Wireless.
125th.	8.30 a.m.	8.51 a.m.	9.35 a.m.
126th.	10.0 a.m.	10.4 a.m.	No.set.
127th.	9.25 a.m.	9.25 a.m.	Set faulty.

3. NO. OF MESSAGES DEALT WITH AT ADVANCE DIVISION.

Messages forwarded.	13.
" transmitted.	26.
" received.	72.
Total.	111.

4. D.R.L.S. Six D.R's reported for duty at Advanced Divisional Office 32 minutes after the Warning Order was received at PAS.

Packets despatched.	Nil.
" received.	10.
Total.	10.

5. MOUNTED ORDERLIES. The three mounted orderlies to be detailed by the Camp Commandant for the Advanced Divisional Headquarter Office were not forthcoming.

6. PRACTICE. Originators of Messages failed to insert the word 'Practice' in the text. A certain amount of difficulty was experienced by operators in dealing with such messages as it was not always quite clear whether it was a real message or not.

7. VISUAL. Visual Communication throughout the Division was good, but signallers require further training in Station Duties.

Over 40 messages were dealt with by three Division Visual Stations. Helio was largely used and proved very successful in spite of the fact that signallers were naturally out of practice in this branch of signalling. The common fault of the sender not watching his spot closely was noticeable in many cases.

The Divisional Visual Station at D.19.d.8.0 was unable to cope with all the work demanded of it. This was chiefly due to the fact that Battalions and M.G.Coys were sending messages addressed direct to Division, which would not normally be the case. About 20 such messages sent by Visual to 125th Brigade were cleared to Division by runner, when it was realised that it would be impossible to get them throughby Visual the whole way.

8. WIRELESS. The uncertainties of Wireless were again illustrated by the fact that the trench set at the 127th Brigade was unable to receive, though it had been completely overhauled and tested the previous day. This set was able to send 4 messages to Advance Division but only one was correctly received owing to the Directing Station being hopelessly jammed by the Wilson Set at the 62nd D.H.Q.

14 messages were disposed of between Advance D.H.Q. and 125th Brigade.

8. WIRELESS (CONT'D)

Similarly the rear loop set at D.19.d.8.0 was unable to receive though able to transmit. The forward loop set at J.5.b.6.4 could both receive and send. Two days previously this communication under precisely similar circumstances had worked well both ways.

Amplifiers at Brigades got to work quickly, but were badly jammed as soon as telephone and buzzer communication started. This, again, is almost unavoidable.

One Battalion moved their Power Buzzer without orders from the Brigade and in consequence got no messages through by it.

9. POPHAM PANEL. The following notes on the use of the Popham Panel are important :-

(i) Men must stand well clear of panels, otherwise they cannot be read. This was not always done.

(ii) All panels should be laid out with the tops of the 'T' facing East. This also was not done in all cases and made it difficult for the observer to read.

(iii) One Battalion sent a message of thirtysix letters. Long messages like this should never be sent.

One message took two minutes from the time it was sent to the time it was received.

10. In all cases communication with the Brigades was established some considerable time before the Brigade Staffs sent messages so that the time that the first message was received from each Brigade is no indication as to the time communication was established.

The total number of messages dealt with by the Brigades and Division and exclusive of Companies and Battalions, was as follows :-

125th Brigade.	92.
126th Brigade.	81.
127th Brigade.	108.
42nd Division.	173.
Total.	454

APPENDIX "B".

SECRET.

COMMUNICATIONS FOR LEFT DIVISION HOLDING THE RED LINE.

The Rear Headquarters of Units are as follows:-

Rear Headquarters. (1). Division and Divisional Artillery at CHATEAU, PAS. Infantry Brigades at PAS, HENU, and COUIN. These Headquarters are all connected to Divisional Headquarters at PAS.

Battle Headquarters. (2). The Battle Headquarters for holding the RED LINE are as follows:-
Division and Divisional Artillery at the Mairie, HENU.
The PAS Brigade at D.26.d.2.4. near COUIN.
The HENU Brigade at D.17.a.7.4. in Sunken Road North East of SOUASTRE.
The COUIN Brigade at D.28.c.2.3 near the Watering Point.
The Divisional Reserve with Headquarters at D.3.c.2.5.
All these Headquarters are connected to the Divisional Battle Headquarters at HENU with one pair of lines. An additional pair will be laid immediately orders are received to hold the RED LINE.

Diagrams. (3). Diagram "A" shows the Line communications at Rear and Battle Headquarters.
Diagram "B" shows the Wireless, Power Buzzer, Amplifier and Loop Set communication.
Diagram "C" shows the Visual, Runner, and Mounted Orderly communications.

Visual communications. (4). The Brigades will test all Visual communications with Battalions and Machine Gun Companies, etc, and will fix routes for lines in case the RED LINE is held. But no lines will be run until the Division is ordered to hold the RED LINE.

Communicat- to Tanks. (5). The Brigade at D.28.c.23 is responsible for laying lines and getting visual to "C" Company, 10th Tank Battalion.

Communication in case of Counterattacks. (6). In case the Brigade at D.17.a.7.4. Counter-attacks, forward communications can be obtained through the Advanced Signal Offices at either the Left or Centre Division at FONQUEVILLERS and a Visual Station placed at D.23.d. central can obtain a Visual Station in the Tower at FONQUEVILLERS, and the latter can obtain any position forward up to and including GOMMECOURT WOOD.
In case of the Brigade at D.26.d.2.4. counter-attacking forward the Visual communications can be obtained through the Visual Station at J.5.d.2.0 up to the Eastern edge of HEBUTERNE, S.E. edge of GOMMECOURT PARK and the Southern end of FONQUEVILLERS.

Signal Office for Administrative Units. (7). The PAS Divisional Office will be kept open for Administrative Units.

Artillery communications. (8). The Reserve Artillery Brigade will run lines to the nearest Infantry Brigades Advanced Headquarters when they move into position for holding the RED LINE or counter-attacking. The Visual communication established will be used by this Brigade and they will connect the O.P. at J.11.b.99 to the Visual Station at J.5.d.20.

Divisional Dropping Station. (9). Divisional Dropping Station will be situated at ~~D.19.d.48~~ R B d.4.4, Brigades and Battalions will lay out their signs; care is to be taken to screen them when enemy planes are overhead.

DIAGRAM "B"

W Wilson Set
T Trench Set
Amplifier
Power Buzzer

D.17.a.74 (Adv Bde)

D.23.b.88 (L.Bn)

(D.13.b. Adv D[illegible])

D.27.b.41 (R.Bn)

D.28.c.23 (Adv Bde)

D.29.c.92 (L.Bn)

D.28.[illegible].24 (Adv Bde)

J.c.343 (L.Bn)

(J.E.[illegible].91)(R.B)

J.12.[illegible] (R.Bn)

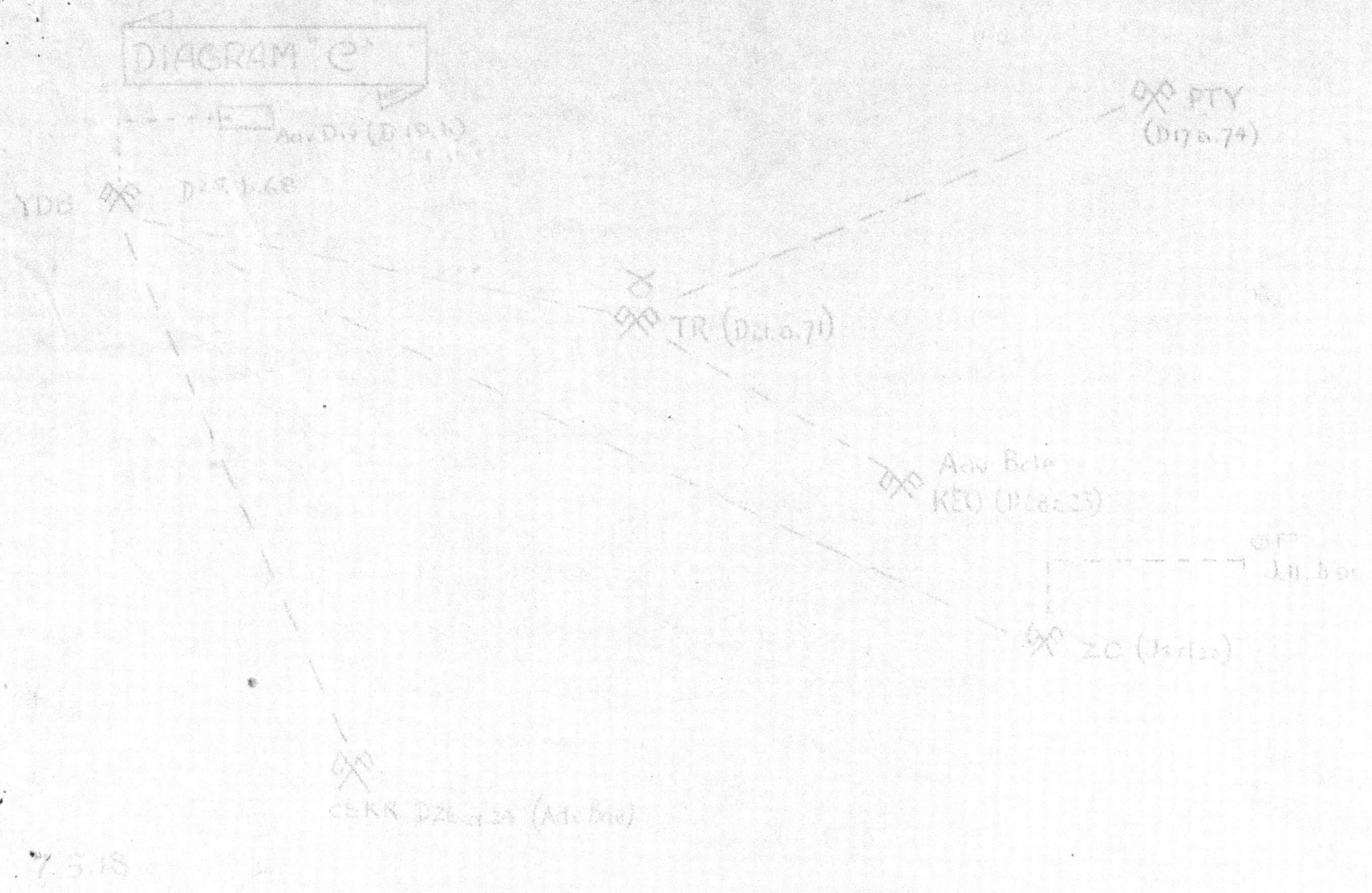

DIAGRAM "C"

Adv Div (D 10.b)

YDB

D25.1.68

TR (D21.a.71)

PTY (D17.a.74)

Adv Bde
KED (D26.2.23)

ZC

CSKR D26.7.34 (Adv Bde)

APPENDIX "C". WAR DIARY. MAY 1918.

HONOURS and AWARDS.

The IV Corps Commander has, under authority granted by His Majesty the King, awarded the following decorations to the undermentioned N.C.O. and man.:-

MILITARY MEDAL.

No.444601 Sgt. H.Pinder, D.C.M.
No.443926 Pnr F.Gregory.

MENTIONED in Field Marshal Sir Douglas Haig's Despatch dated 7.4.18.:-

Major S.G.JOHNSON.,M.C.
Lieut.A.J.ELLIS.,M.C.

No.444354 L/Cpl Fox,G.

ARoberts Capt RE
for Major.

3.6.18. O.C. 42nd Divisional Signal Co. R.E.

APPENDIX "D".   WAR DIARY.6   MAY 1918.

WEEKLY STRENGTHS, CASUALTIES, REINFORCEMENTS.

Weekly Strengths.	Officers.	O.R.
Week ending May 4th.	11	299
" " " 11th.	11	298
" " " 18th	11	295
" " " 25th.	11	305

Casualties.		
Killed.	-	-
Wounded.	-	1
Sick.	-	12
To Base.	-	2
Total.	-	15.

Reinforcements.		
From hospital.	-	1
" Depot.	-	15
" 4th Corps Signal Company.	-	1
Transferred from M.G.C.	-	7
Total.	-	24.

A Roberts Capt RE
for Major.

3.6.18.   O.C. 42nd Divisional Signal Co. R.E.

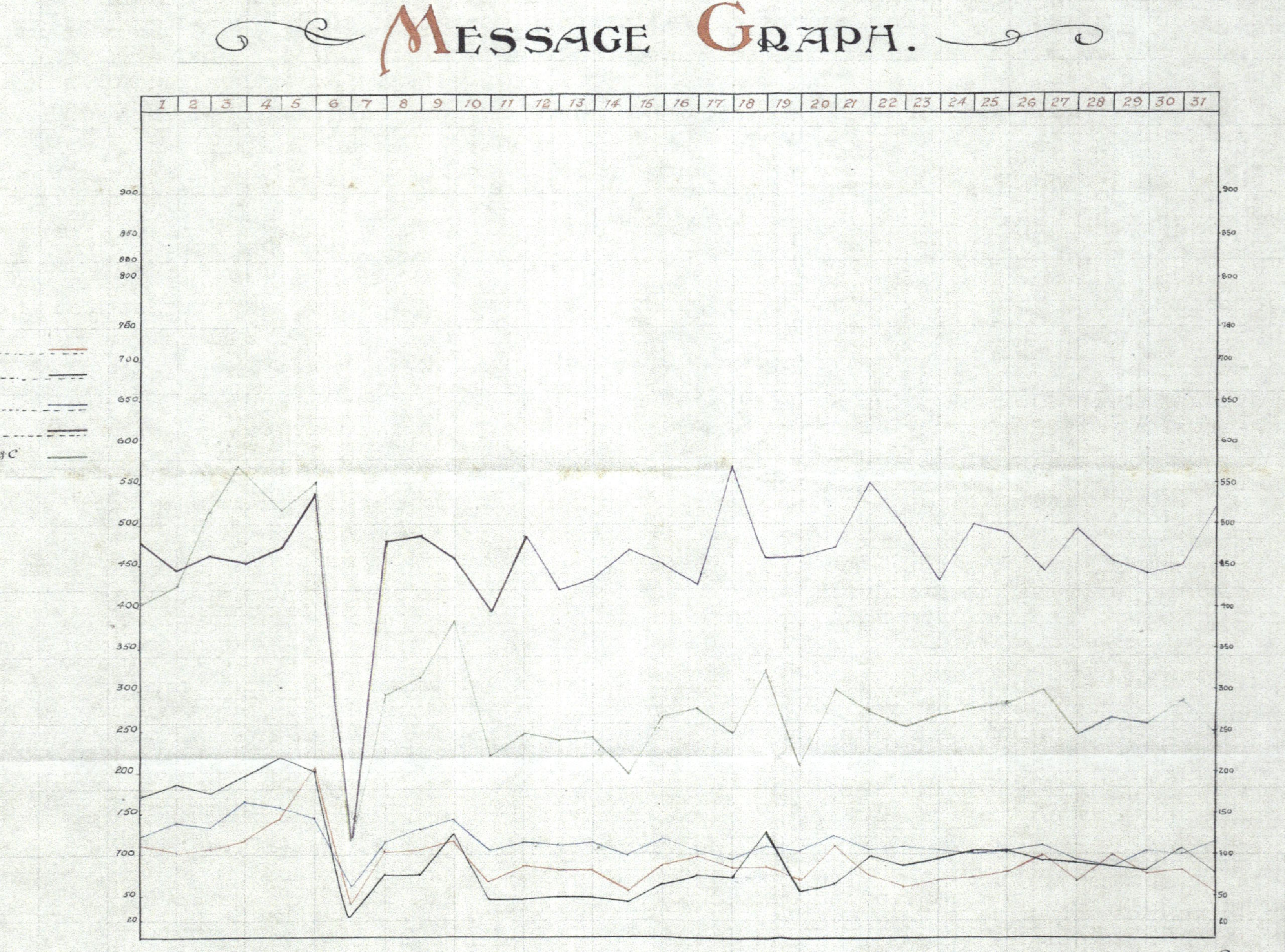
DIAGRAM 'E'
MESSAGE GRAPH.
1
2
3
4
5
6
7
8
9
10
11
12
13
14
15
16
17
18
19
20
21
22
23
24
25
26
27
28
29
30
31
A
B
C
DRLS
Total of A B & C
MAY. 1918.
A. Roberts Capt R.E.
O.C. 42nd Divisional Signal Coy. R.E.

Message Graph

Appendix "E"

Vol 16

SECRET.

WAR DIARY.

42ND DIVISIONAL SIGNAL COY. R.E.

CHAPTER XX

4th July 1918.

A Roberts. Capt. R.E.
O.C. 42nd DIVISIONAL SIGNAL COY. R.E.

Army Form C. 2118.

Instructions regarding War Diaries and Intelligence Summaries are contained in F. S. Regs., Part II. and the Staff Manual respectively. Title pages will be prepared in manuscript.

WAR DIARY
or
~~INTELLIGENCE SUMMARY.~~
(Erase heading not required.)

Place	Date	Hour	Summary of Events and Information.	Remarks and references to Appendices
			42nd (East Lancs) Divisional Signal Co.R.E.	
			CHAPTER XX. JUNE 1918. Reference Map, FRANCE 1/40,000.Sheet 57.D	
PAS.	1.6.1918.		42nd Division in Army Reserve. Divisional Headquarters and Signal Company Headquarters at PAS Chateau. Communications as described in previous Chapter.	
BUS.	7.6.1918.		The Division took over the Right Sector of the Fourth Corps front from the New Zealand Division. Divisional Headquarters closed at PAS at 4 p.m. and re-opened at BUS-LES-ARTOIS at same hour. The move to BUS-les-ARTOIS was carried out in accordance with Company Order No.18. The Company took over area and billets occupied by New Zealand Signal Company. Communications as described in Appendix 'A'. Divisional Signal Class continued training of the Twelfth Course mentioned in previous Chapter, at HALLOY.	APPENDIX 'A'.
			APPENDICES TO THIS DIARY. (A). Communications, Telephone and Telegraph. (B). Subsidiary communications. (C). Honours and Rewards. (D). Casualties, Weekly strengths, and Reinforcements. (E). Monthly Message Chart.	
	4.7.18.		A Roberts Captain. R.E for O.C. 42nd Divisional Signal Co. R.E.	

A7092). Wt. W12839/M1293 750,000. 1/17. D. D & L., Ltd. Forms/C2118/14.

APPENDIX 'A'. JUNE 1918.

WAR DIARY.

COMMUNICATIONS (Telephone and Telegraph).

1.6.18. to 6.6.18. During the period the Division remained in Reserve the communications were as described in Chapter XIX.

7.6.18. The Division relieved the New Zealand Division in the Right Sector of the Fourth Corps front and the communications were as shown in Diagrams 'A' and 'B'. The latter Diagram shows all Test Boxes mentioned below.
Buried cable routes varying in depth from 3 to 7 feet provided the principal means of communication.

7.6.18. to 19.6.18. Maintenance was carried out during the dates mentioned, Test boxes were strengthened and lines labelled.

20.6.18. W - Q bury 'dis'.

21.6.18. Work begun on W - Q bury 'dis' near Q point. 25 pair paper core cable found to be faulty and wet. 60 yards new cable put in. Depth 6 feet.

22.6.18. W - Q bury through - 24 pairs tested and proved 'O.K'.

23.6.18.to 27.6.18. Maintenance work continued and 4 pairs on an old bury from M - H Test points put through.

28.6.18. A new bury (25 pairs consisting of three 7 pair Brass Sheathed and two Quad G.P. Armoured) from CH-to FB Test points, commenced, depth 7 feet. Infantry Working party (110 shovels) provided. Task set 70 cubic feet per man.

29.6.18. Work continued on CH - FB bury.Infantry Working Party of 120.

30.6.18. Work continued on CH - FB bury and RT - RB buried cable routes (25 pairs - three 7 pair Lead Covered. Two Quad G.P. Armoured). Working Party of 120 Infantrymen. ½ mile completed on CH-FB bury, joints made and all lines tested through.

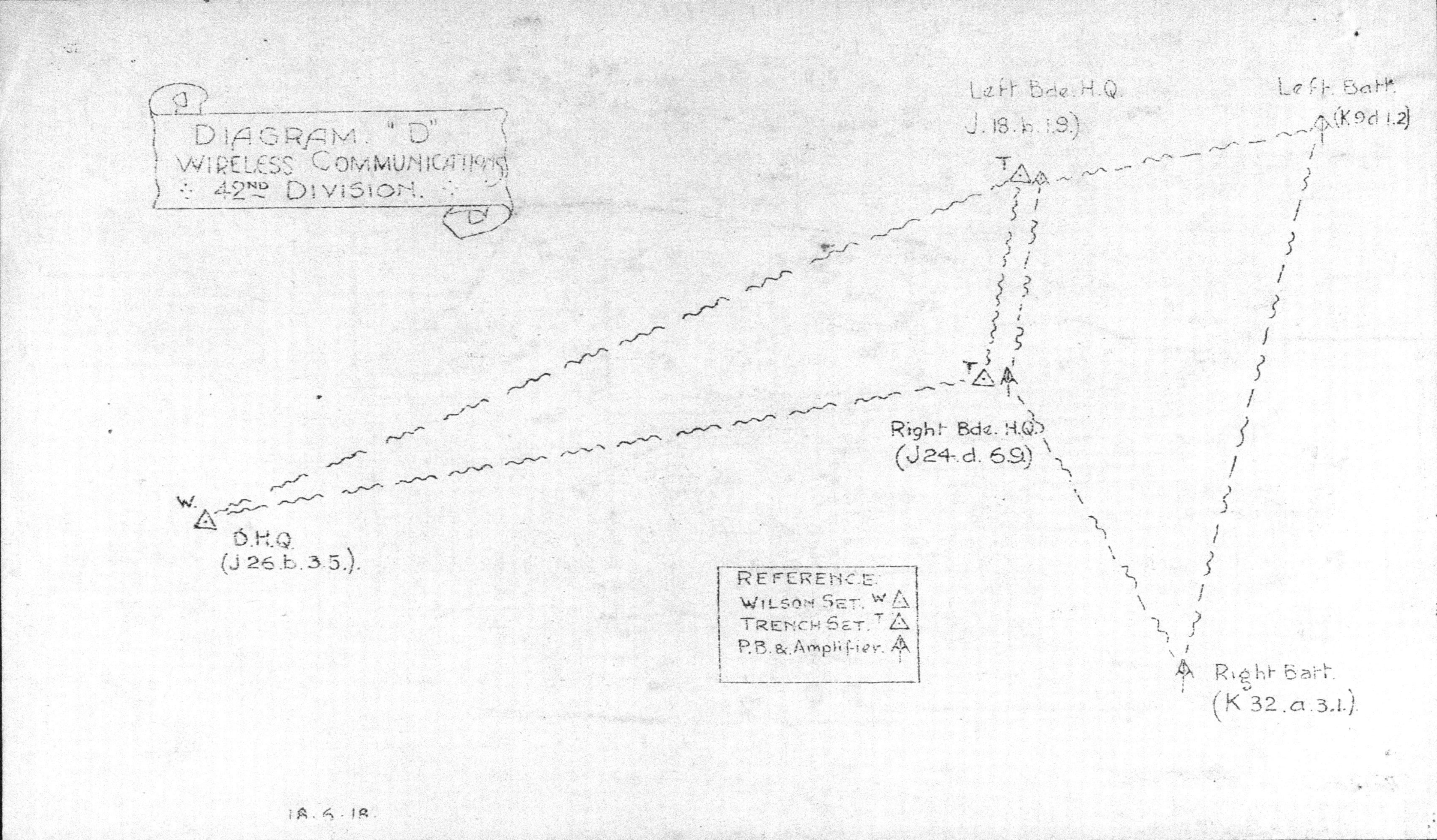

DIAGRAM. "D"
WIRELESS COMMUNICATIONS
42ND DIVISION.

Left Bde. H.Q.
J. 18. b. 1.9.)

Left Batt.
(K 9 d 1.2)

Right Bde. H.Q.
(J 24. d. 6.9)

D.H.Q.
(J 26. b. 3.5.).

Right Batt.
(K 32. a. 3.1.)

REFERENCE:
WILSON SET. W △
TRENCH SET. T △
P.B. & Amplifier.

18.6.18.

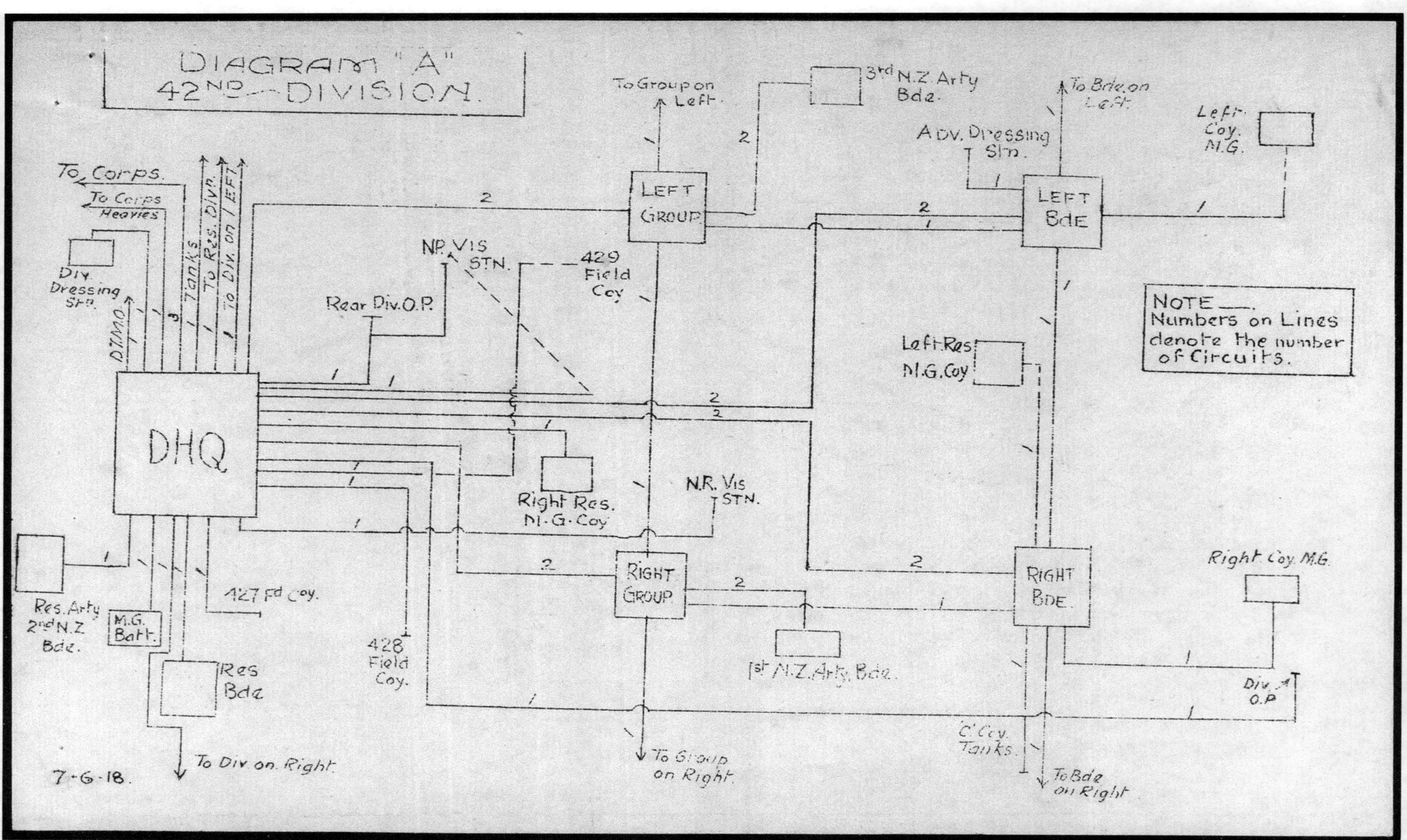
DIAGRAM "A"
42ND DIVISION.
To Corps.
To Corps Heavies
Tanks
To Res. Divn.
To Div. on LEFT
Div. Dressing Stn.
D.T.M.O.
DHQ
Rear Div. O.P.
NR. Vis STN.
429 Field Coy
To Group on Left.
LEFT GROUP
3rd N.Z. Arty Bde.
To Bde. on Left.
A Dv. Dressing Stn.
LEFT BdE
Left Coy. M.G.
NOTE___. Numbers on Lines denote the number of Circuits.
Left Res M.G. Coy
Right Res. M.G. Coy
N.R. Vis STN.
Res. Arty 2nd N.Z Bde.
M.G. Batt.
427 Fd Coy.
428 Field Coy.
Res Bde
RIGHT GROUP
1st N.Z. Arty Bde.
RIGHT BDE.
Right Coy. M.G.
Div. O.P.
'C' Coy. Tanks.
To Div. on Right.
To Group on Right.
To Bde on Right
7-6-18.

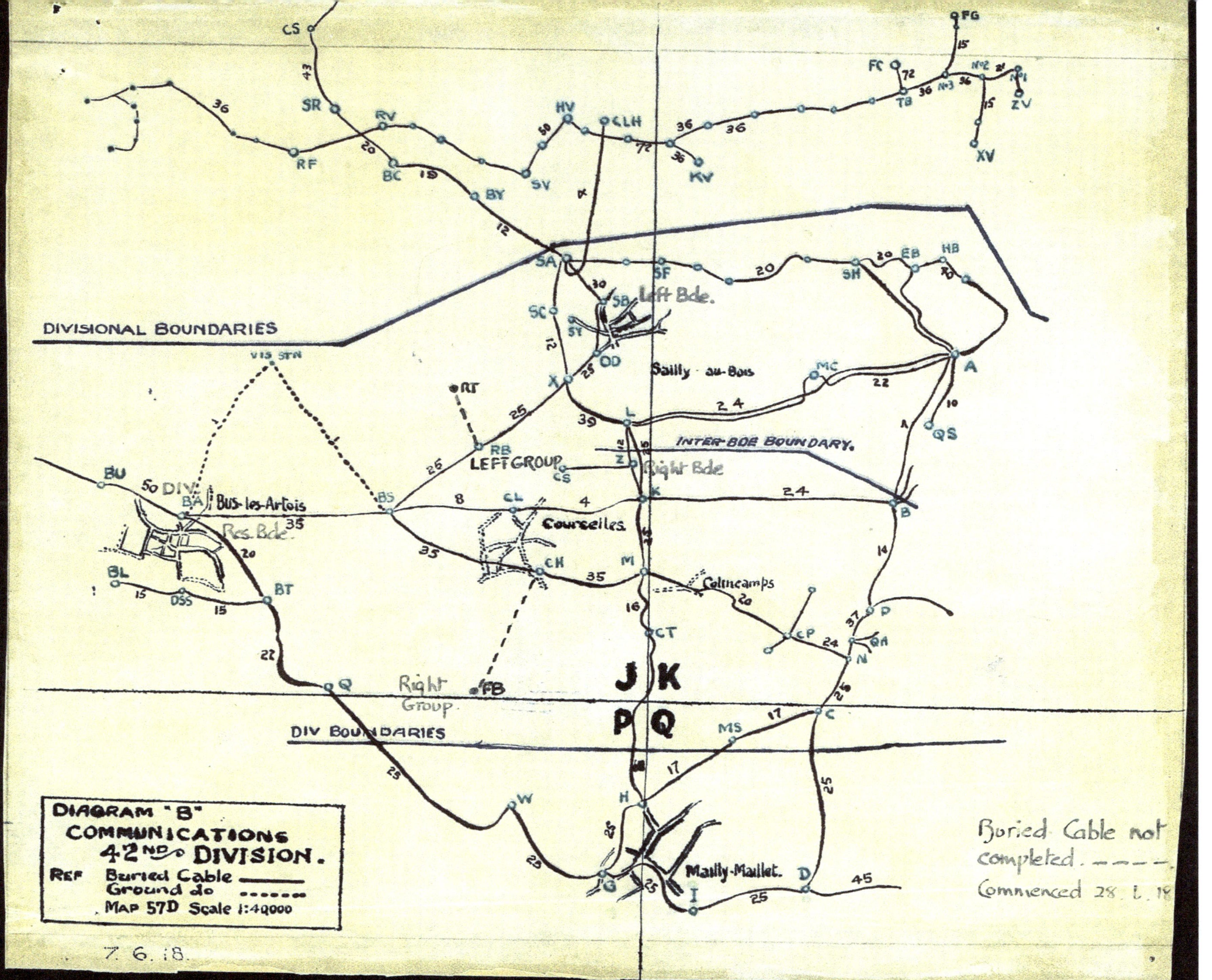
DIAGRAM "B"
COMMUNICATIONS
42ND DIVISION.
REF Buried Cable
Ground do
Map 57D Scale 1:40000
7. 6. 18.
Buried Cable not completed.
Commenced 28. 1. 18
DIVISIONAL BOUNDARIES
DIV BOUNDARIES
INTER-BDE BOUNDARY.
Sailly-au-Bois
Left Bde.
Right Bde
LEFT GROUP
Right Group
Courcelles
Colincamps
Bus-les-Artois
Res. Bde.
50 DIV.
Mailly-Maillet.
VIS STN
J K
P Q
CS
SR
RV
RF
BC
BY
SV
HV
CLH
KV
TB
FC
FG
ZV
XV
SA
SF
SB
SC
ST
OD
X
SH
EB
HB
A
QS
MC
L
Z
K
B
RB
RT
BS
CL
CH
M
CT
CP
P
N
C
MS
H
G
I
D
W
Q
FB
BU
BA
BL
DSS
BT

SECRET. Copy No. 6

42nd DIVISIONAL SIGNAL COMPANY. R.E.
ORDER No. 18.

1. Company Headquarters will move to BUS tomorrow, June 7th and take over billets and lines from the N.Z. Divisional Signal Company.R.E.

2. 42nd Divisional Headquarters will close at PAS at 4 p.m. June 7th and open at BUS at the same hour.

3. The 3 Ton Motor Lorry will leave at 8 a.m. for BUS with complete Signal Office relief in charge of L/Cpl Strathdee and Technical Stores. Four W/T men will proceed on this lorry. After unloading the lorry will return to PAS.

4. The P.E.L. lorry will leave for BUS at 10 a.m.

5. The 3 ton Motor Lorry will leave for BUS at 2 p.m. with Signal Office Stores, Orderly Room Stores, Officers' Mess Stores and remainder of baggage. These stores will be dumped outside Q.M. Stores at 1.30 p.m.

6. Transport and dismounted men will leave at 1.30 p.m.

7. One Signal Office relief and one lineman will remain at PAS until 6.30 a.m. on June 8th when they will proceed to BUS on Motor lorry.

8. Sgt. Harrison will make all necessary arrangements for taking over D.R.L.S. from N.Z. Division and will be responsible that any unallotted bicycles are ridden to BUS.

R. S. Newton
Captain.
for O.C. 42nd Divisional Signal Co. R.E.

Issued at p.m. 6.6.18.

Copy No. 1 "T" Officer.
" " 2 "A" Officer.
" " 3 C.S.M. & C.Q.M.S.
" " 4 Signalmaster.
" " 5 Sgt. Harrison.
" " 6 War Diary.
" " 7 File.

APPENDIX 'B'. JUNE 1918.

WAR DIARY.

SUBSIDIARY COMMUNICATIONS.

May 1 - 6. Same as in Chapter XIX.

May 7. Division moved into the line in Right Sector of Fourth Corps. D.H.Q. at BUS.

Wireless. Wilson set established at D.H.Q., and Trench Sets at Right and Left Brigade H.Q.

Combined Power Buzzer-Amplifiers put in at Right and Left Brigades working to similar instruments at Left Battalion Left Brigade, and Right Battalion Right Brigade and also to one another. Owing to the poor quality of the crystals now supplied the experiment was tried of working the Trench Sets on French Amplifiers, cutting out the crystal. This gave louder signals and proved far more reliable.

Visual. A Divisional Visual Station NR was established at J.28.a.69, working forward to Infantry and Artillery Brigades and back to NC Station in the Chateau at BUS.

Pigeons. Six birds brought up by Corps D.R. daily for each of the two Infantry Brigades in the line and distributed by Brigades to Battalions.

14.6.18. NC Visual Station was closed down.

18.6.18. NP Visual Station established at J.15.c.66.

To this Station direct communication could be obtained by a Lamp placed in the dug-out entrance at each Brigade and protected by sandbags.

NR Station still kept open as an emergency Station.

Two forward Loop Sets set up at each Brigade to duplicate the Trench Set communication, working back to a rear Loop Set at NP. At Left Brigade Loop worked from foot of dug-out steps 20 feet below ground, while at Right Brigade the Loop was erected at entrance to dug-out protected by sandbags.

NOTE. Diagram 'C' shows the Visual communications, and Diagram 'D' the Wireless communications.

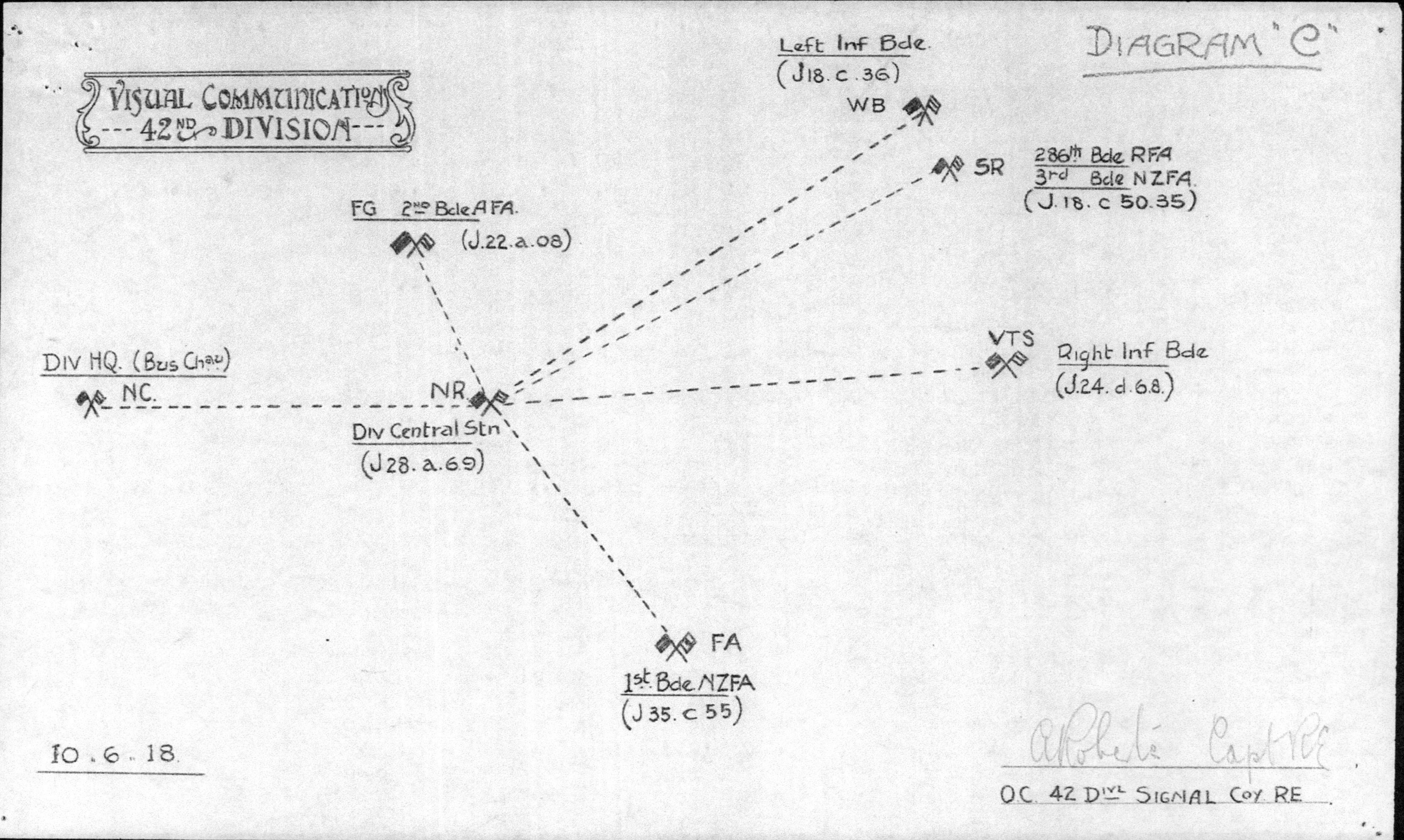

Diagram "C"

Visual Communications 42nd Division

Left Inf Bde.
(J18. c. 36)
WB

SR
286th Bde RFA
3rd Bde NZFA.
(J. 18. c 50.35)

FG 2nd Bde AFA.
(J.22.a.08)

VTS
Right Inf Bde
(J.24. d. 6.8.)

Div HQ. (Bus Chau)
NC.

NR.
Div Central Stn
(J28. a.69)

FA
1st Bde NZFA
(J35. c 55)

10.6.18.

O.C. 42 Div[l] Signal Coy RE.

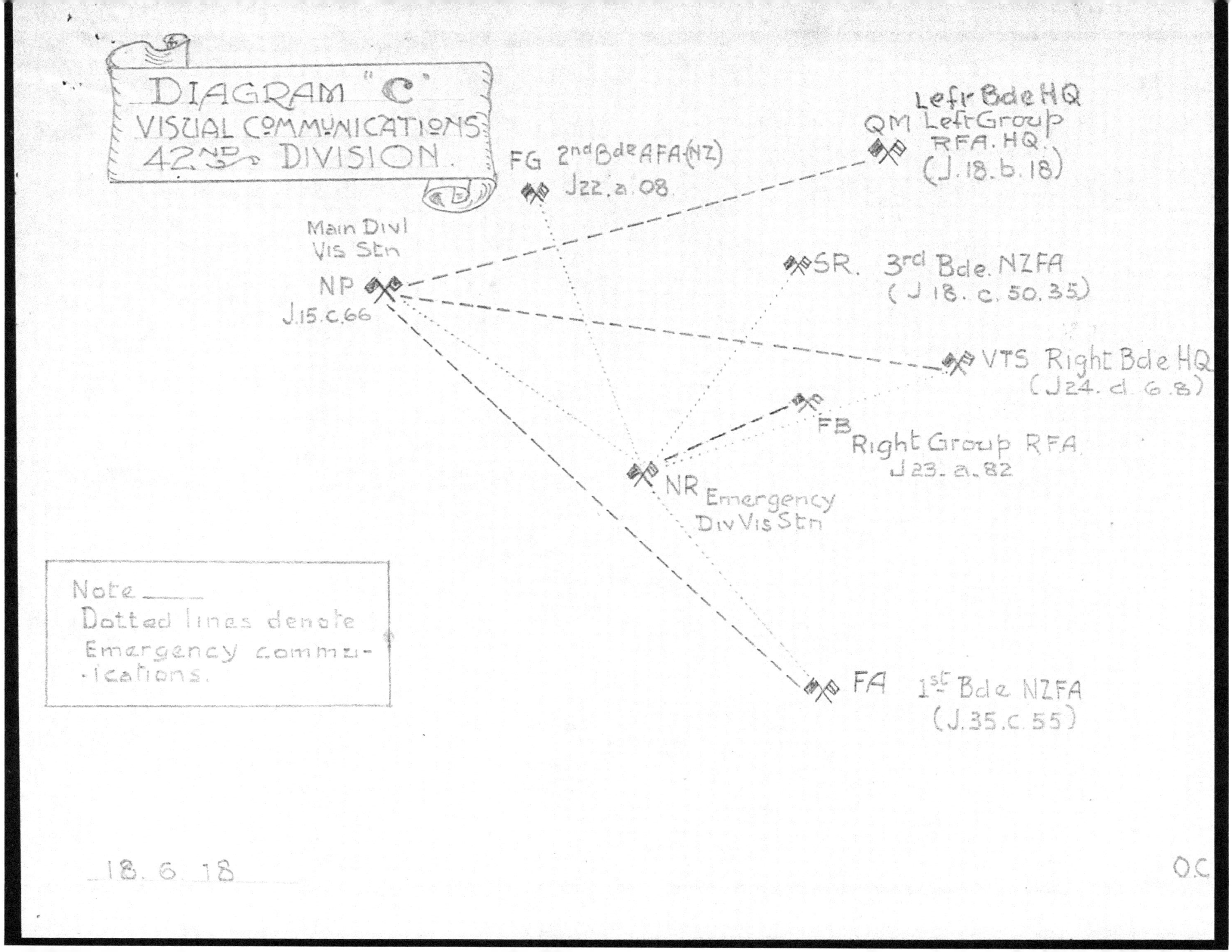

DIAGRAM "C"
VISUAL COMMUNICATIONS
42ND DIVISION.

FG 2nd Bde AFA (NZ)
J22. a. 08

QM Left Bde HQ
Left Group
RFA. HQ.
(J.18.b.18)

Main Divl
Vis Stn
NP
J.15.c.66

SR. 3rd Bde. NZFA
(J 18. c. 50.35)

VTS Right Bde HQ
(J24. d. 6.8)

FB
Right Group RFA
J23. a. 82

NR Emergency
Div Vis Stn

FA 1st Bde NZFA
(J.35.c.55)

Note ____
Dotted lines denote
Emergency commun-
-ications.

18. 6. 18

O.C

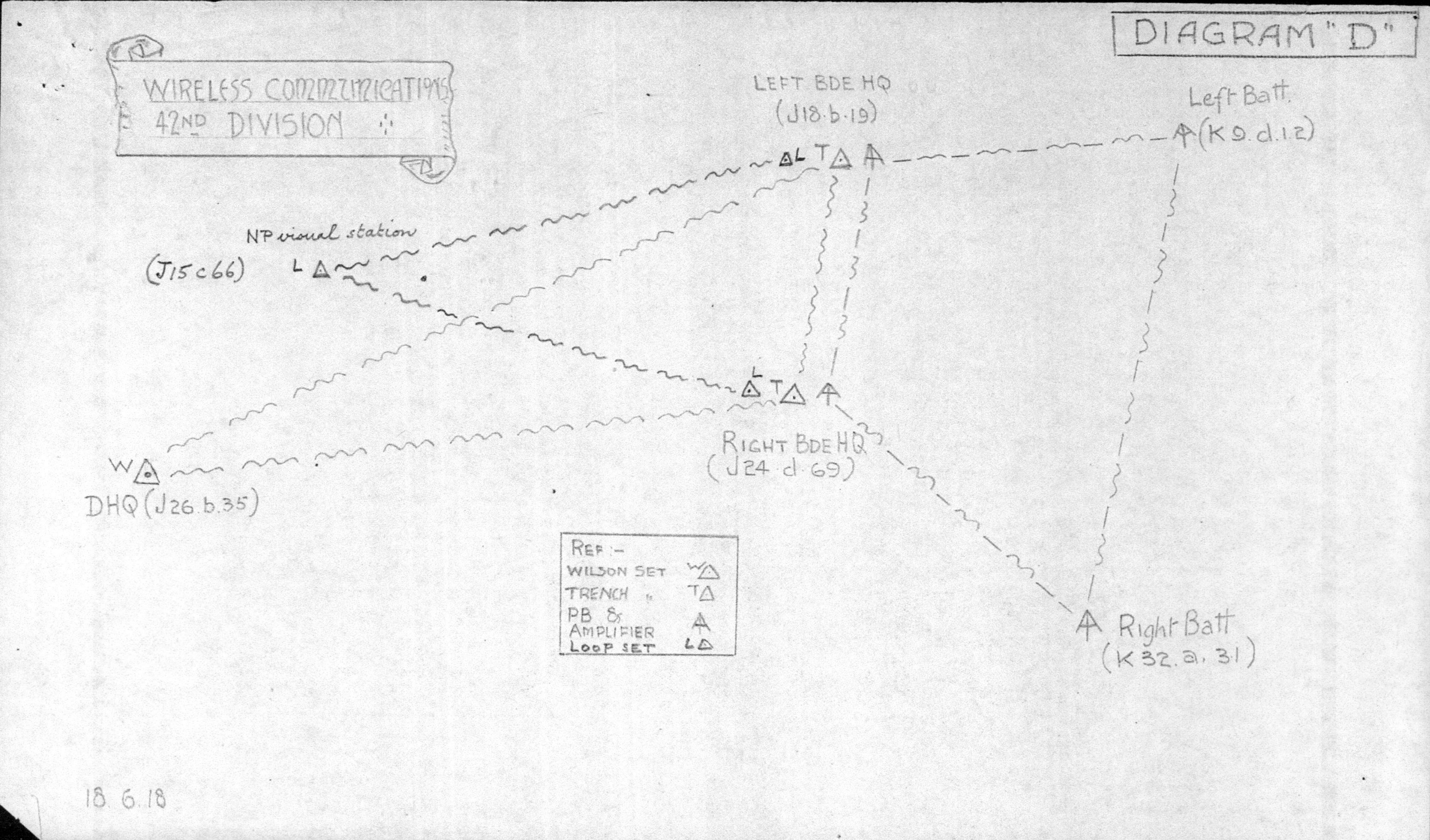

DIAGRAM "D"

WIRELESS COMMUNICATIONS
42ND DIVISION

LEFT BDE HQ
(J18.b.19)

Left Batt.
(K9.d.12)

NP visual station
(J15 c 66)

RIGHT BDE HQ
(J24 d 69)

Right Batt
(K32.a.31)

DHQ (J26.b.35)

REF :-	
WILSON SET	W△
TRENCH "	T△
PB & AMPLIFIER	A
LOOP SET	L△

18.6.18

APPENDIX 'C'. JUNE 1918.

WAR DIARY.

HONOURS and AWARDS.

Awarded the

DISTINGUISHED SERVICE ORDER

(Field Marshal Sir Douglas Haig's Despatch dated 7.4.18.)

MAJOR S.G.JOHNSON.,M.C.

Awarded the

MERITORIOUS SERVICE MEDAL

(Field Marshal Sir Douglas Haig's Despatch dated 7.4.18).

No.444324 Sgt. W.H.Shimmin.,M.M.
No.444349 2/Cpl A.T.Folwell.
No.444277 Spr H. Rowlands.

A Roberts
Captain.R.E.

4.7.18. O.C. 42nd Divisional Signal Co. R.E.

APPENDIX 'D'. WAR DIARY. JUNE 1918.

WEEKLY STRENGTHS, CASUALTIES, REINFORCEMENTS.

Weekly Strengths.	Officers.	O.R.
Week ending June 1st.............	11	307
" " " 8th............	11	304
" " " 15th............	11	302
" " " 22nd............	11	298
" " " 29th............	11	297

Casualties.	Officers	O.R.
Killed..........................	-	-
Wounded.........................	-	1
Sick............................	-	17
	-	18

Reinforcements.	Officers	O.R.
From hospital.....................	-	2
" Depot.........................	-	5
	-	7

A Roberts

Captain.R.E.

4.7.18. for O.C. 42nd Divisional Signal Co.R.E.

APPENDIX "E"

Message Chart

Reference :-

"A"

"B"

"C"

Totals of AB&C

DRLS

1 2 3 4 5 6 7 8 9 10 11 12 13 14 15 16 17 18 19 20 21 22 23 24 25 26 27 28 29 30

950 900 850 800 750 700 650 600 550 500 450 400 350 300 250 200 150 100 50

June 1918.

A Roberts Capt RE

O.C 42ND Divisional Signal Coy R.E.

SECRET

Vol 17

WAR DIARY

42ND DIVISIONAL SIGNAL COY

CHAPTER XXI

S. Gordon Johnston.
MAJOR

AUGUST 1918

O.C. 42ND DIVL SIGNAL COY R.E.

Instructions regarding War Diaries and Intelligence Summaries are contained in F. S. Regs., Part II. and the Staff Manual respectively. Title pages will be prepared in manuscript.

WAR DIARY
or
~~INTELLIGENCE SUMMARY.~~
(Erase heading not required.)

Army Form C. 2118.

Place	Date	Hour	Summary of Events and Information	Remarks and references to Appendices
			CHAPTER XXI. JULY 1918. 42nd (East Lans) Divisional Signal Co. R.E.	
			Reference Map FRANCE 1/40,000. Sheet 57D.	
BUS.	1.7.18.		42nd Division holding the front line in the Right Sector IV Corps front. Divisional Headquarters and Signal Company Headquarters at CHATEAU, BUS-LES-ARTOIS. (J.26. central) Communications as described in Appendices 'A' and 'B' of Chapter XX.	
HALLOY.	4.7.18.		Twelfth Course at the Divisional Signal School dispersed. For reports of training see Appendix 'C'.	APPENDIX "C"
	5.7.18.		Signal School moved from HALLOY (B.17.c) to BEAUREPAIRE (B.9.c).	
BEAUREPAIRE.	6.7.18.		The Thirteenth Course, approximately 100 other ranks drawn from units of the Division, assembled at BEAUREPAIRE and continued training throughout the month.	
	9.7.18.		Orders received that Divisional Headquarters would move, Battle Headquarters to dugouts at I.23.central. and rear Headquarters to SARTON (H.11.d).	
	10.7.18.		Divisional Headquarters closed at BUS 11.0 a.m. and opened at I.23.central same hour. Changes in communications were as described in Appendices 'A' and 'B'. The move of the Company to SARTON and I.23.central was carried out in accordance with Company Order No. 19.	
SARTON.	15.7.18.		Orders received that Divisional Headquarters would move to AUTHIE (I.16.a)	
AUTHIE.	16.7.18.		Advanced D.H.Q. closed I.23.central 6.0 p.m. and opened at AUTHIE same hour. For changes in communications see Appendices 'A' and 'B'.	
"	31.7.18.		Move of Company from I.23.central and SARTON to AUTHIE was carried out in accordance with Company Order No. 20.	
			The Division remained in Right Sector to the end of the month. Communications were as described in Appendix 'A' (Diagrams 'A' and 'B') and Appendix	APPENDIX 'A'.

A7092). Wt. W12839/M1293 750,000. 1/17. D. D & L., Ltd. Forms/C2118/14.

Army Form C. 2118.

Instructions regarding War Diaries and Intelligence Summaries are contained in F. S. Regs., Part II. and the Staff Manual respectively. Title pages will be prepared in manuscript.

WAR DIARY

or

~~INTELLIGENCE SUMMARY.~~

(Erase heading not required.)

Place	Date	Hour	Summary of Events and Information	Remarks and references to Appendices
			(Continued.)	
			'B' (Diagrams 'C' and 'D').	APPENDIX

APPENDICES TO THIS DIARY.

(A). Communications, telephone and telegraph.

(B). Subsidiary communications.

(C). Report on 12th Course at the Divisional Signal Class.

(D). Honours and Awards.

(E). Casualties, Weekly Strengths, & Reinforcements.

(F). Monthly Message Chart.

S. Gordon Johnston
Major.

4.8.18. O.C. 42nd Divisional Signal Co. R.E.

A7092). Wt. W12839/M1297 750,000. 1/17. D. D & L., Ltd. Forms/C2118/14.

SECRET. War Diary. Copy No...

42nd DIVISIONAL SIGNAL COMPANY.R.E.
ORDER No. 19.

1. The Company will move to SARTON tomorrow, July 10th with the exception of personnel on Lists 1 andd 2.
Those on No. 1 List will proceed to new Divisional H.Q. at I.23. central, those on No. 2 List will remain at BUS or on 'out Stations'.

2. 42nd Divisional H.Q. will close at BUS at 11 a.m. July 10th and open at I.23. central at same hour.

3. A complete Signal Office relief in charge of L/Cpl Burne will proceed by march route to I.23. central at 9 0 a.m.

4. The P.E.L. Lorry with Wireless Stores will leave for I.23. central at 10 a.m.

5. The 3 Ton Motor Lorry will leave with Stores for SARTON, billet No. 66 at 6 a.m., after unloading, the Lorry will return to BUS
The lorry will leave BUS again for SARTON at 9 a.m. with Orderly Room Stores, etc, will return at once, after unloading, to refilling point, draw rations, proceed to BUS, collect Officer's Mess Stores, and remainder of baggage, and then proceed to SARTON.
Personnel will accompany Lorry as detailed. All stores to be dumped in Chateau Yard half an hour before the departure of the Lorry.

6. Transport and dismounted men will leave at 10 a.m.

7. One complete cable detachment with one cable wagon, two limbers, a watercart, and the box car will remain at BUS.
This transport will deal with the removal of all stores etc., from BUS to I.23.central.

8. Sgt. Harrison will make all necessary arrangements for D.R.L.S and will be responsible that any unallotted bicycles are ridden to SARTON.

Issued at p.m.

P C Fletcher
Lieut. R.E.
for O.C. 42nd Divisional Signal Co. R.E.

Copy No. 1 'T' Officer.
2 'A' Officer.
3. Captain Roberts.
4. C.S.M. & C.Q.M.S.
5. Signalmaster.
6. Sgt. Harrison.
7. War Diary.
8. File.

SECRET.

Copy No..7...

42nd DIVISIONAL SIGNAL COMPANY.R.E.
ORDER No. 20.

---

1. The Company with the exception of the personnel at BUS and forward stations will move to AUTHIE tomorrow July 16th.

2. 42nd Rear Divisional Headquarters will close at SARTON at noon July, 16th and open at AUTHIE same hour.
42nd Divisional Battle Headquarters will move from I.23. central to AUTHIE at 6 p.m.

3. Captain Gill will arrange all details of office reliefs and move of personnel and stores from I.23.central to AUTHIE. The box car and the transport at BUS will be available for this.

4. Sgt. Harrison will make all necessary arrangements for D.R.L.S. and bicycles.

5. The Company will take over at AUTHIE all billets, horse lines, etc. lately vacated by the 57th Divisional Signal Company.

6. Cpl Fuller will see that all electric lighting arrangements at AUTHIE are completed by 6 p.m.

7. The telegraph office at SARTON will close at 9 a.m. Messages for units of 42nd Rear Headquarters will be sent over the telephone through SARTON exchange from 9 a.m. - noon.

8. Transport and dismounted men will leave SARTON for AUTHIE at 9.30 a.m. i/c 2/Lieut.Abell.

9. The 3 ton lorry will leave SARTON for AUTHIE at 6.30 a.m. return to SARTON at once after unloading, and proceed again to AUTHIE at 9 a.m. with Officers kits and mess stores, Orderly Room Stores, Company Cooks, and remainder of baggage and personnel as detailed.

P.C.Fletcher Lieut.R.E.
Issued at 7 p.m. for O.C. 42nd Divisional Signal Co. R.E.

Copy No. 1 Capt. Roberts.
2 Capt. Gill.
3 'A' Officer.
4 C.S.M. & C.Q.M.S.
5 Sgt. Harrison.
6 Signalmaster.
7 War Diary.
8 File.
9 Cpl Fuller.

APPENDIX 'A'. WAR DIARY. JULY 1918.

(CHAPTER XXI).

COMMUNICATIONS. (Telephone and Telegraph).

1.7.18. Communications as shown in Diagrams 'A' and 'B' Chapter XX. Work continued on CH-FB and RT-RB buried routes.
Eight pairs D.8 cable laid overland from RT to RB and two pairs f from RT to X. These cables are for use of Left Brigade on moving to RT from SB until buried route RT-RB is completed.

2.7.18. No working party available owing to Infantry Brigade reliefs. Left Brigade moved from SB to RT. Communication uninterrupted.

3.7.18. No working party available owing to Infantry Brigade reliefs.

4.7.18.)
)
6.7.18.) Work continued on RT-RB bury. Infantry working party of 150 shovels. Task set 60 cubic feet per man. Digging hard owing to flinty soil and great care needed in burying lead covered cables (25 pairs consisting of three 7 pair Lead covered and two Quads G.P. Armoured).

6.7.18. RT-RB route completed. All lines tested good.

7.7.18. Left Brigade (at RT) communications between RT-RB and RT-X transferred from overland cable routes to RT-RB bury. Overland cables RT-RB recovered. Work continued on CH-FB bury. Infantry working party of 150 shovels. Task set 70 cubic feet per man.
Digging normal. Clay soil and a little chalk.

8.7.18.)
9.7.18.) Work continued on CH-FB route.

9.7.18. MS-C bury 'dis' owing to a dug-out having been constructed on the route.

10.7.18. Work begun on MS-C route. No working party available for CH-FB route owing to Infantry Brigade relief.
D.H.Q. at BUS (BA) closed at 11 a.m. and moved to I.23.central (AT). Lines extended through BU and communication maintained throughout without interruption.

11.7.18. Diversion and repairs effected to MS-C route. All lines good. No digging party available for CH-FB route.

12.7.18.)
13.7.18.) Work continued on CH-FB route .(Digging party of 150 men).

14.7.18. CH-FB route completed (digging party of 20 men). All lines good.

15.7.18. Right Infantry Brigade (at Z) moved to FB. No interruption of communication. Lines extended through Z-K-M-CH-FB.

16.7.18. D.H.Q. (at AT) moved to AUTHIE (AE) at 6 p.m. Nine pairs of cable laid from AT to AE and six pairs allotted by Corps on existing AT-AE trestle route.

17.7.18.)
21.7.18.) General maintenance. Test boxes overhauled.

22.7.18. Left Artillery Group moved from SAILLY (OD) to J.23.a.5.3.(RB). Lines extended OD-X-RB. Communication maintained without interruption.

23.7.18.)
31.7.18.) General maintenance and salvage work carried out.

31.7.18. Communications as shown in Diagrams 'A' and 'B'. All test points mentioned above are shown in these Diagrams.

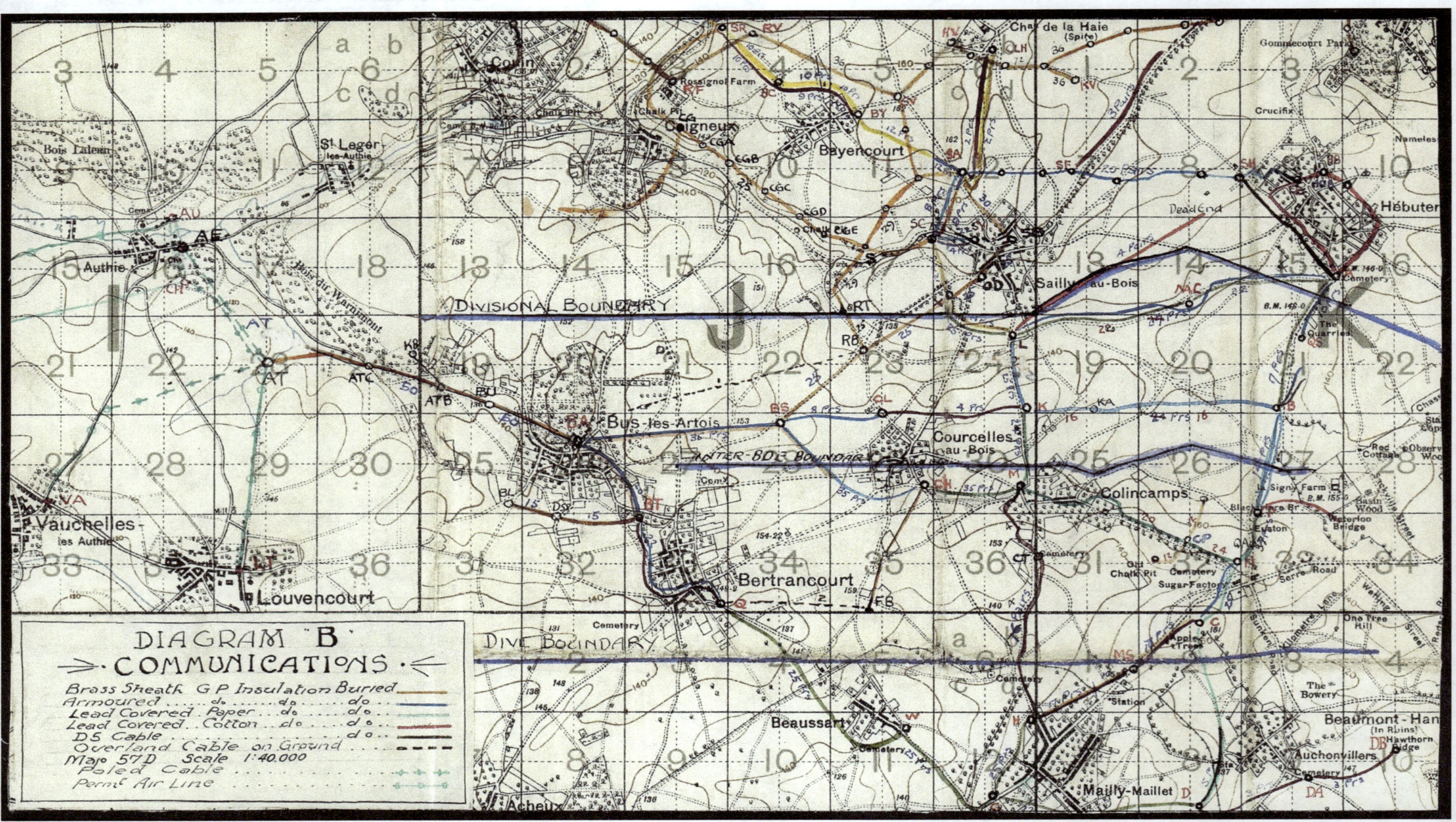
DIAGRAM "B"
COMMUNICATIONS
Brass Sheath G P Insulation Buried
Armoured do do do
Lead Covered Paper do do
Lead Covered Cotton do do
DS Cable do
Overland Cable on Ground
Map 57D Scale 1:40,000
Poled Cable
Permt Air Line
DIVISIONAL BOUNDARY
INTER-BDE BOUNDARY
DIVL BOUNDARY
Authie
Vauchelles les Authie
Louvencourt
St Leger les Authie
Bois du Warnimont
Bois Laleau
Couin
Coigneux
Rossignol Farm
Bayencourt
Chau de la Haie
Sailly au Bois
Bus-les-Artois
Courcelles au Bois
Colincamps
Bertrancourt
Beaussart
Mailly-Maillet
Auchonvillers
Beaumont-Ham
Hebuterne
Gommecourt Park
Dead End
Acheux

APPENDIX 'B'. WAR DIARY. JULY 1918.

SUBSIDARY COMMUNICATIONS.

June 1st. (Same as Chapter XX).

" 2nd. Left Brigade Headquarters moved from SAILLY to J.17.c.41.
Trench Set, Loop Set, and Power Buzzer-Amplifier moved from SAILLY to Left Brigade new Headquarters.
Power Buzzer & Amplifier moved to new Left Battalion Headquarters at K.14.d.26.
New Visual Station 'NR' established at 'BS' test point J.28.a.98 working to Right and Left Infantry Brigades and Right and Left Artillery Groups.
'NP' Station closed down for visual, but still kept open for Loop Set communication to Right and Left Infantry Brigades.

" 9th. Wireless Directing Station moved to new D.H.Q. at I.23.central.
'ML' Visual Station established at I.29.d.45.35. working back to 'NR'.
'NP' Station closed down.

" 10th. D.H.Q. moved from BUS to I.23.central with rear Headquarters at SARTON.

" 15th Trench Set moved to Right Brigade new Headquarters at Fort Bertha.
Both Trench Sets working well on Amplifiers as in Chapter XIX.

" 16th D.H.Q. moved to AUTHIE with Battle Headquarters at I.23.central.

" 26th Two pigeons were allotted to each Artillery Group thus reducing the number of birds assigned to two Infantry Brigades in the line to four each.

" 1st) to) " 31st) Loop Sets were established during this period at various points in the line, but proved very unreliable and unsatisfactory.

Message carrying rockets were frequently tested by Brigades in the line during this period and proved quite satisfactory.

Visual Communications as Diagrams "C"
Wireless do do. Diagrams "D"

DIAGRAM 'C'
VISUAL COMMUNICATIONS
42ND DIVISION

KP
(J17.c.43) Left Bde

SR
211 th Bde RFA
J18. c. 50.30

Div Emergency Stn
ML
I29. d. 24

NR
Div Vis Stn
(J28. a. 98)

FA
J35. c 55
{Right Bde
{210 Bde. RFA.

2.7.18.

S. Gordon Johnston
Major
O.C. 42ND Divisional Signals

VISUAL COMMUNICATIONS 42ND DIVISION

DIAGRAM "C"

LEFT BDE J.17.c.43
KP

LEFT GROUP J23.a.7.2
RB

DIVL VIS STN "BS" TEST PT. J. 28.a.9.7.
NR

DIVL BATTLE HQ I29.d.45.35.

RIGHT GROUP J.35.c.55.
FA

RIGHT BDE J35.c.4.2.
FB

N.B. All Two way working

26. 7. 1918.

Major O.C 42nd DIVISIONAL SIGNAL COY

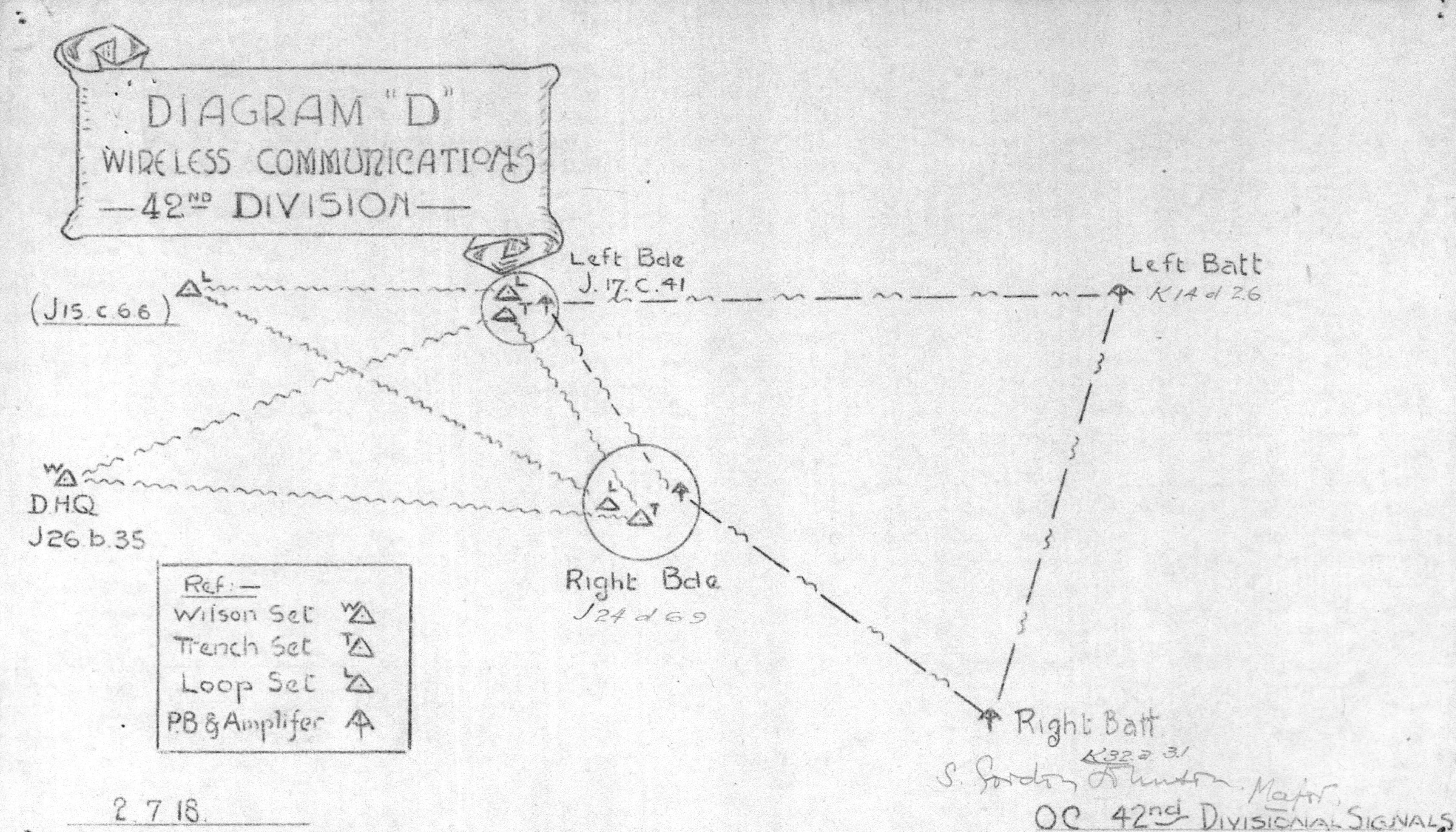
DIAGRAM "D"
WIRELESS COMMUNICATIONS
— 42ND DIVISION —
Left Bde
J. 17. C. 41
Left Batt
K 14 d 2.6
(J15. c. 6.6)
D.H.Q
J26. b. 35
Right Bde
J24 d 6.9
Right Batt
K32 a 31
Ref: —
Wilson Set
Trench Set
Loop Set
P.B & Amplifer
2. 7. 18.
S. Gordon Johnston Major
OC 42nd DIVISIONAL SIGNALS

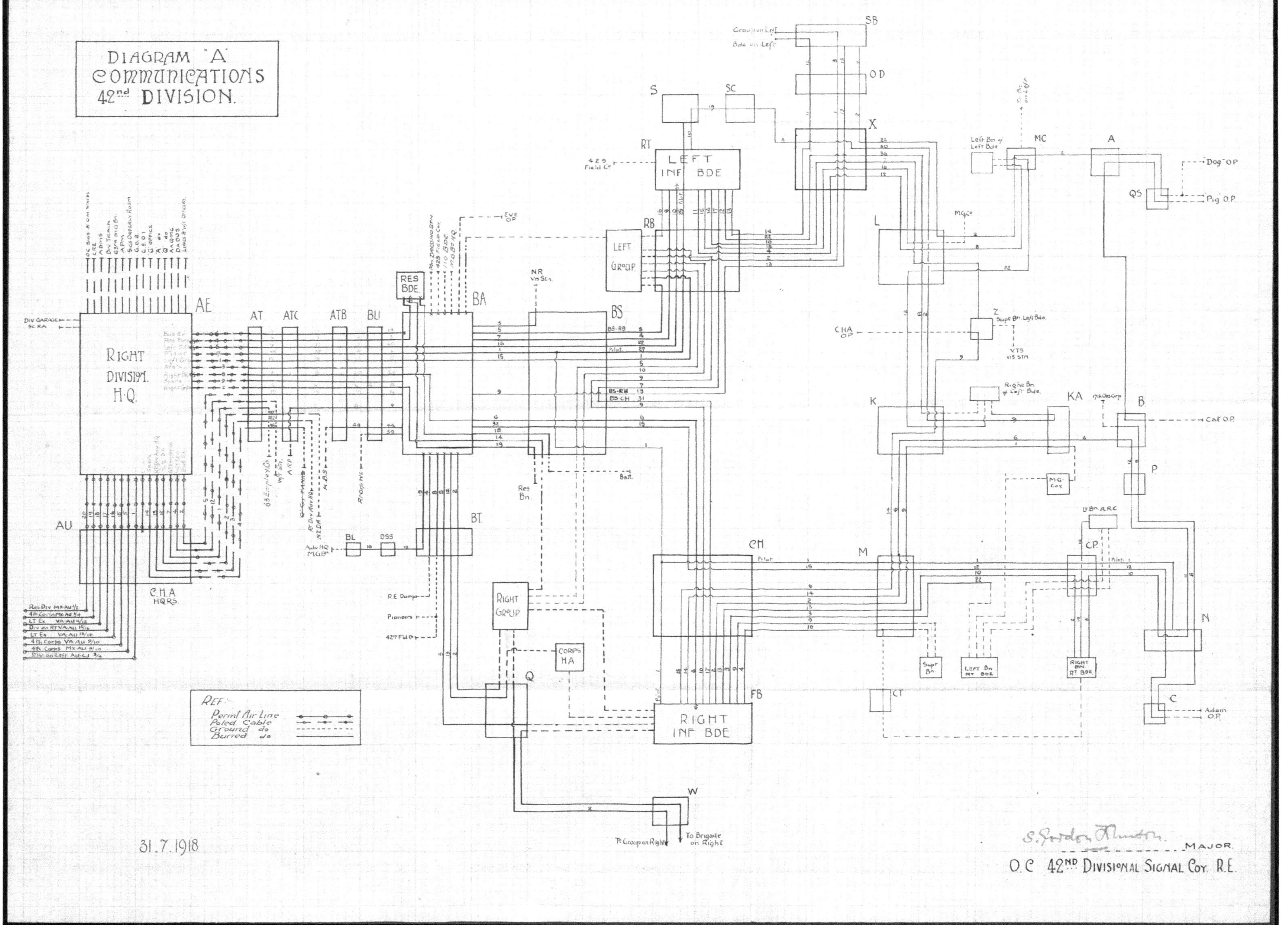

DIAGRAM 'A'
COMMUNICATIONS
42nd DIVISION.
RIGHT DIVISION H.Q.
AE
AT
ATC
ATB
BU
RES BDE
BA
BS
BT
BL
DSS
NR Vis Stn.
EVE OP
LEFT GROUP
RB
RT
LEFT INF BDE
S
SC
X
OD
SB
Group on Left
Bde on Left
429 Field Co
L
MC
A
QS
Dog O.P.
Pig O.P.
Left Bn of Left Bde
MGCo
Z
Supt Bn Left Bde.
VTS Vis Stn
CHA OP
Right Bn of Left Bde.
K
KA
B
Cat O.P.
P
MG Coy
CH
M
CP
N
C
Adam O.P.
Supt Bn.
Left Bn Rt Bde
Right Bn Rt Bde
CT
FB
RIGHT INF BDE
RIGHT GROUP
CORPS HA
Q
W
To Group on Right
To Brigade on Right
Res Bn.
Batt.
R.E. Dump
Pioneers
427 Fld Co
Adv HQ MGBn
AU
C.H.A HQRS.
Div Garage SC RA
Res Div MX-AU 1/2
4th Corps MX AU 3/4
LT Ex VA-AU 11/12
Div on Rt VA-AU 15/16
LT Ex VA-AU 13/14
4th Corps VA-AU 9/10
4th Corps MX-AU 9/10
Div on Left AU-CJ 3/4
REF:-
Permt Air Line
Poled Cable
Ground do
Buried do
31.7.1918
S. Gordon Thurston
MAJOR.
O.C 42ND DIVISIONAL SIGNAL COY. R.E.

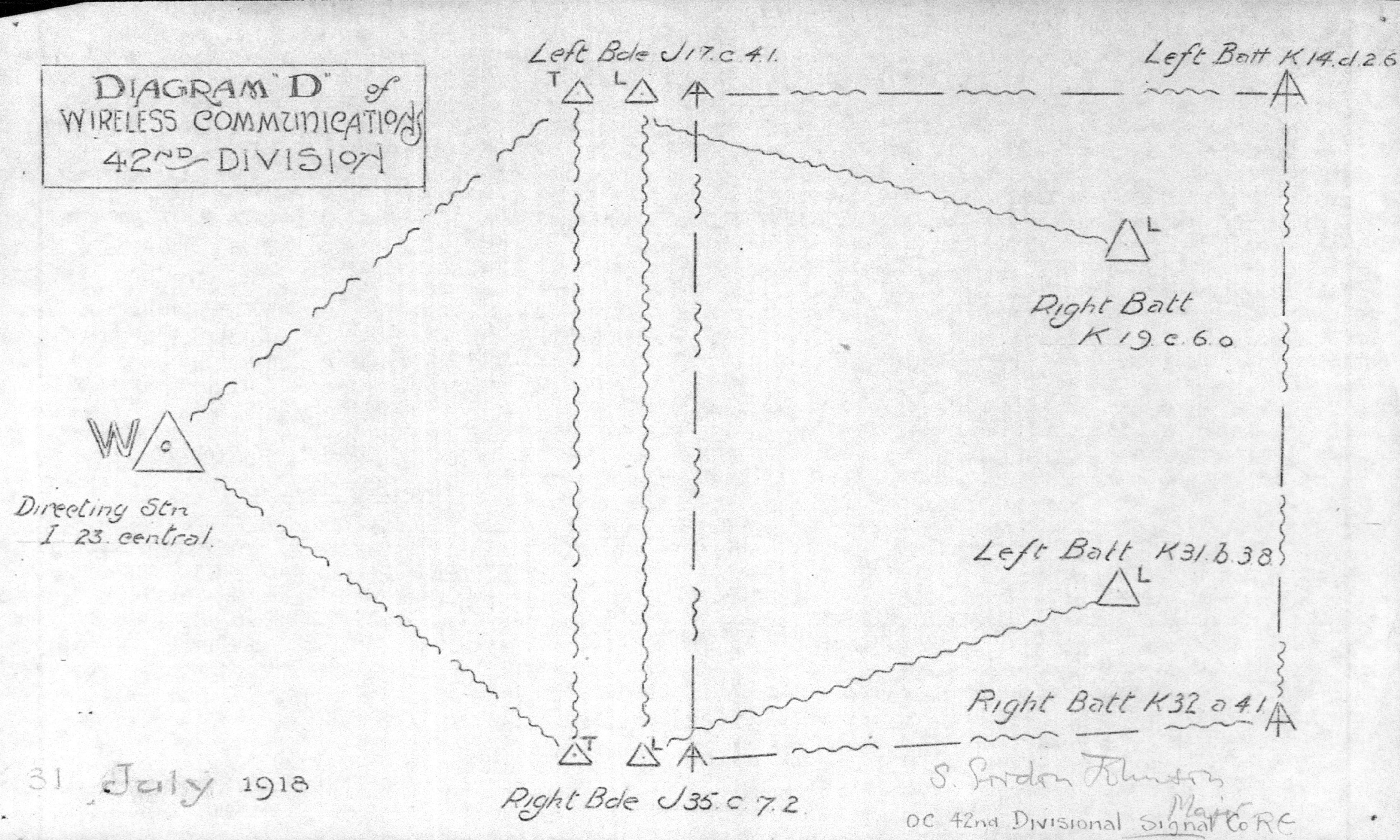
DIAGRAM "D" of
WIRELESS COMMUNICATIONS
42ND DIVISION
Left Bde J17.c 4.1.
T
L
Left Batt K 14.d.2.6
L
Right Batt
K 19.c.6.0
W
Directing Stn
I 23. central.
Left Batt K31.b.3.8
L
Right Batt K32 a 4.1
T
L
Right Bde J35.c 7.2
31 July 1918
S. Gordon Johnston
Major
OC 42nd Divisional Signal Co RE

T.

APPENDIX 'C'

REPORT ON TRAINING AND RESULTS
of the
TWELFTH (BEGINNERS) COURSE.
42nd Divisional Signal Class.

Course commenced at BEAUREPAIRE 8.5.18. and was concluded at HALLOY 4.7.18.

The Course consisted chiefly of beginners from nearly all units in the Division, and also a small party of Fourth Corps R.G.A. who joined 14 days after the commencement.

The Officers N.C.O's. and men attending the Course on the whole showed interest and keenness in their work. A large number of men were sent back to their units during the Course as unlikely to become efficient Signallers owing to the standard of the men sent by Battalions not being quite up to the standard required for a Battalion Signaller and to the large number attending this Course (274) sufficient individual attention could not be given to very backward men.

The flag drill improved very much towards the end of the Course and was of a high standard.

On the whole the results were satisfactory. The R.F.A. were particularly good. The R.G.A. were older men and for the most part rather slow, but had they had another 14 days their results would have been much better.

Full instruction was given in the following subjects.

Flag Drill.
Sending and Receiving on-
- D.III Telephone and Vibrator.
- Fullerphone.
- Lucas Lamp.
- Shutter.

Lectures and Practical work on:-
- Message Form.
- Buzzer Unit.
- Signal Office Routine.
- Intercommunication by D.III & Fullerphone.
- Intercommunication in the Field by Lamp & Shutter, D.R.L.S. and Runners.
- Lineman's duties. Labels and knots & jointing.
- Writing.

Partial Instruction was given in:-
- Map reading.
- Elemantary Magnetism & Electricity.
- Theory, connections and care of instruments.
- Circuit diagrams.
- Forward communications in battle.
- Power Buzzer.
- Pigeon Service.

Signal Office Work.

All except the very backward men have spent several days on Traffic Scheme, consisting of small offices equipped with D.III Telephones & Fullerphones, representing Brigade and Battalion communications. All men in turn performed Signalmasters duties.

Visual Station work.

Several small schemes were carried out and one large

scheme for all Infantry. The latter also introduced communication by cable with D.III's.

Artillery.

All R.F.A. took part in a scheme under Artillery Assistant Instructors representing a Brigade in action in open warfare.

Very good results were obtained in these schemes especially in the combined Infantry Scheme, and the final Artillery Scheme.

Tables are attached showing numbers of personnel who attended or left the Course and who qualified or failed in each unit.

S. S. J.

Major.

July 12th 1918. O.C. 42nd Divisional Signal Co. R.E.

APPENDIX 'D'. WAR DIARY. JULY 1918.

HONOURS AND AWARDS.

NIL.

S. Gordon Johnston
Major.

4.8.18. O.C. 42nd Divisional Signal Company.R.E.

APPENDIX 'E'. WAR DIARY. JULY 1918.

WEEKLY STRENGTHS, CASUALTIES, REINFORCEMENTS.

Weekly Strengths.	Officers.	O.R.
Week ending July 6th.	11	302
" " " 13th	11	298
" " " 20th	11	294
" " " 27th	12	309

Casualties.		
Killed.	-	-
Wounded.	-	-
Sick.	2	17
To Base.	-	4
Total.	-	21

Reinforcements.		
From hospital.	-	2
" Depot.	-	19
" 4th Corps Signal Co.	-	7
" Third Army Signal Co.	ø 2	-
Total.	2	28

ø / Attached supernumerary.

S. Gordon Johnston

Major.

4.8.18. O.C. 42nd Divisional Signal Co.R.E.

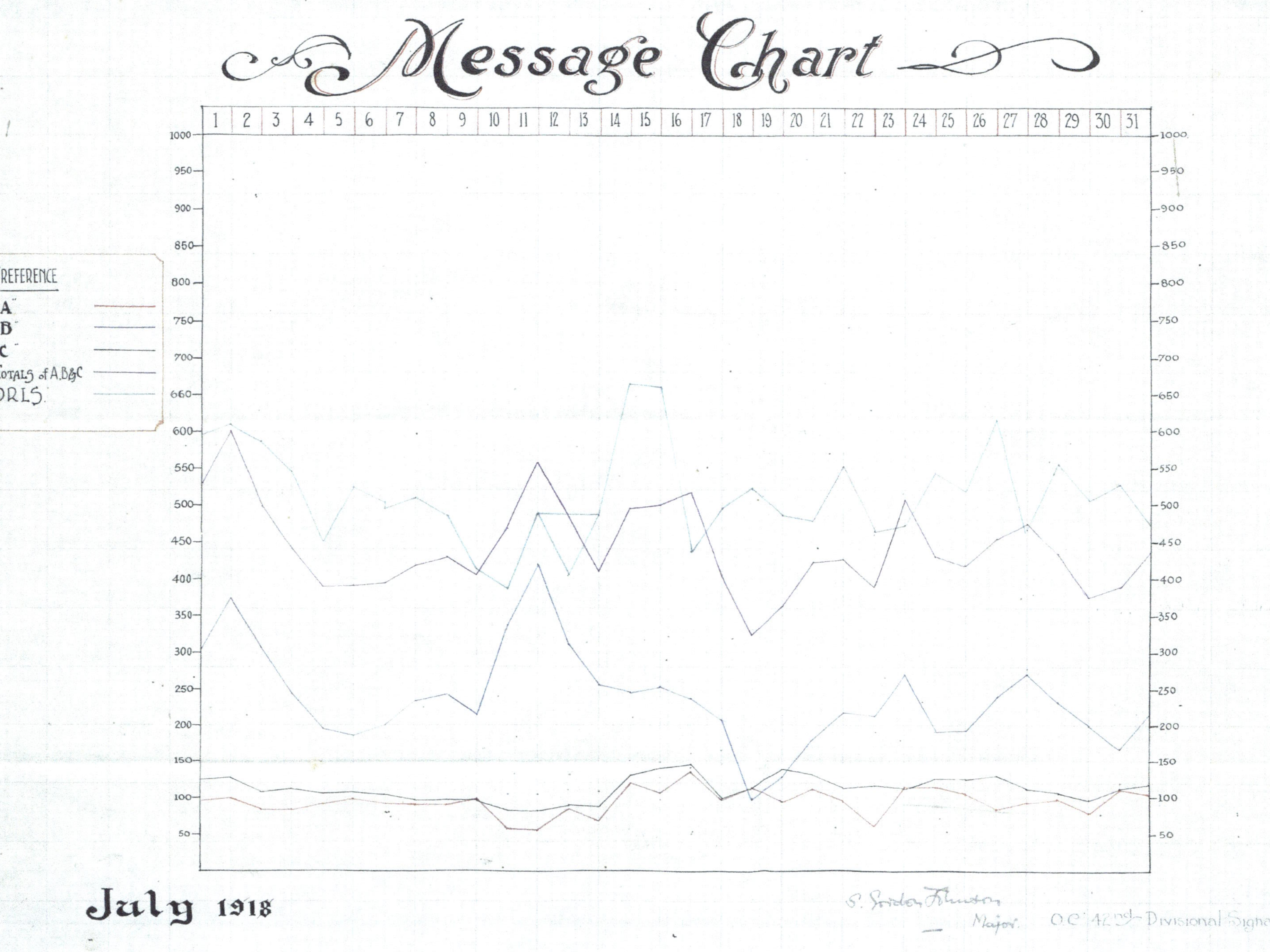
Message Chart
1 2 3 4 5 6 7 8 9 10 11 12 13 14 15 16 17 18 19 20 21 22 23 24 25 26 27 28 29 30 31
1000 950 900 850 800 750 700 660 600 550 500 450 400 350 300 250 200 150 100 50
1000 950 900 850 800 750 700 650 600 550 500 450 400 350 300 250 200 150 100 50
REFERENCE
"A"
"B"
"C"
TOTALS of A.B&C
DRLS.
July 1918
Major.
O.C. 42nd Divisional Signal Coy R.E.

APPENDIX "F"

Vol 18

SECRET

WAR DIARY.

42ND DIVISIONAL SIGNAL COY. R.E.

CHAPTER XXII

P. A. Ford

Major

Sept 1918.

O.C. 42ND DIVISIONAL SIGNAL COY R.E.

Instructions regarding War Diaries and Intelligence Summaries are contained in F. S. Regs., Part II. and the Staff Manual respectively. Title pages will be prepared in manuscript.

WAR DIARY
or
~~INTELLIGENCE SUMMARY.~~
(Erase heading not required.)

Army Form C. 2118.

Place	Date	Hour	Summary of Events and Information	Remarks and references to Appendices
			CHAPTER XXII. AUGUST 1918. 42nd (East Lancs.) Divisional Signal Co. R.E. (T). Reference Map, FRANCE. 1/40,000. Sheet 57D. 1/40,000. Sheet 57C.	
AUTHIE.	1.8.18.		42nd Division holding the front line in the Right Sector, IV Corps front. Divisional Headquarters and Signal Company Headquarters at AUTHIE (57D.I.16.a).	
			Communications as described in Appendix A.	APPENDIX 'A'
BUS-les-ARTOIS.	15.8.18.		Divisional Headquarters closed at AUTHIE at 2 p.m. and reopened at BUS-les-ARTOIS (57D.J.26.b) at the same hour. Signal Company handed over billets, etc., to 62nd Division Signal Co. R.E. and moved to BUS-les-ARTOIS in accordance with Company Order No.21 (Appendix C.)	APPENDIX 'C'
	19.8.18.		'AW' Cable Section from V Corps attached to this Company.	
	24.8.18.		Advanced Divisional Signal Office formed at the Chalk Pits (57D.32.a.41) COLINCAMPS. Cable Section and necessary Signal Office Staff moved forward. Orderly Room and rest of Company remained at BUS. Communications as described in Appendix A.	APPENDIX 'A'
COLINCAMPS.	25.8.18.		Remainder of Company moved at 5.30 a.m. from BUS-les-ARTOIS to Advanced Divisional Headquarters at the Chalk Pits, COLINCAMPS.	
	27.8.18.		Divisional Headquarters closed at the Chalk Pits, COLINCAMPS at 5.30 p.m. and reopened 5.30 p.m. at 57D.L.4.d. near BUCQUOY. Company moved in accordance with Company Order No. 23. (Appendix C). The rear Signal Office at BUS-les-ARTOIS closed at 12 noon, and personnel and stores were brought by Motor Lorry to Company Headquarters,	APPENDIX 'C'
BUCQUOY.	28.8.18.		Divisional and Signal Company Headquarters lines were moved about 500 yards to a more favourable position. Divisional Signal School moved from BEAUREPAIRE. to BUS-les-ARTOIS. Communications as described in Appendix 'A'.	APPENDIX 'A'

Contd/.

A7092). Wt. W12839/M1297 750,000. 1/17. D. D & L., Ltd. Forms/C2118/14.

Instructions regarding War Diaries and Intelligence Summaries are contained in F. S. Regs., Part II. and the Staff Manual respectively. Title pages will be prepared in manuscript.

WAR DIARY
or
~~INTELLIGENCE SUMMARY.~~
(Erase heading not required.)

Army Form C. 2118.

Place	Date	Hour	Summary of Events and Information	Remarks and references to Appendices
			Contd/	
BUCQUOY.	30.8.18.		Divisional and Signal Company Headquarters moved from L.10.a. (BUCQUOY) to 57C.G.29.b. central near GREVILLERS. Divisional Headquarters closed at BUCQUOY at 12 noon and reopened at GREVILLERS at same hour. 'AW' Cable Section remained at BUCQUOY for work under IV Corps.	
GREVILLERS.	31.8.18.		Communications as described in Appendix A.	APPENDIX 'A'

APPENDICES TO THIS DIARY.

(A). Communications, Telephone & Telegraph.
(B). " Subsidiary.
(C). Company Movement & Operation Orders.
(D). Honours and Awards.
(E). Casualties, Weekly Strengths, & Reinforcements.
(F). Monthly Message Chart.

Pe?ott
Major R.E.
6/9/18

A7092). Wt. W12839/M1293. 750,000. 1/17. D, D & L., Ltd. Forms/C2118/14.

APPENDIX 'A'.

COMMUNICATIONS (TELEPHONE and TELEGRAPH).

1.8.18. Work begun on CH Test point which required strengthening. Decided to sink box six feet below ground level.

2.8.18. to 5.8.18. Work continued and completed on CH Test point.

6.8.18. CH - M buried route 'dis'. Earth Fault located 50 yards from CH Box. Caused by bad joint. Reported to Corps and necessary stores indented for in the event of the Corps Area Detachment not being available for repairing the route.
All lines from FB - M via CH diverted via BS - RB and X boxes.

7.8.18. Stores for repairing CH -M Route received and work begun.
8.8.18. Work completed on CH-M route. All lines O.K.
9.8.18. Work begun on new Test point mid-way between M and CP Boxes in order to provide buried cable communication from Right Brigade at FB to Battalion Headquarters at K.31.b.4.8. and Battalions to Companies.

10.8.18. 11.8.18. Work continued on new Test Box. Unable to complete owing to stores not being available.

12.8.18. M.T. Company at HALLOY connected to D.H.Q. Exchange. Existing airline used except for a distance of 500 yards. D8 twisted used to complete.

13.8.18. Infantry working parties of 10 and 20 shovels supplied to fill up RT - RB and CH - FB routes which had sunk below ground level due to heavy rains.
Work completed.

14.8.18. General maintenance and tidying up of local lines in AUTHIE

15.8.18. D.H.Q. moved to BUS. Communications uninterrupted.

16.8.18. Right Brigade moved to CHALK PITS, COLINCAMPS (K.32.a.4.1).
Lines extended via CH - M and CP. Two pairs D8 twisted laid from B Test Point to K.29.c.8.8. Left Brigade R.C. near SERRE.
M - CP route earthy. Two pairs D8 twisted cable laid overground from M Box to Right Brigade.

17.8.18. Advanced Divisional Signal Office established in a dugout in COUNTRY TRENCH (J.24.b.5.1) 50 yards from K Test Box. Ten pairs overground cables laid from K. Box to Advanced D.H.Q.

18.8.18. Two pairs D8 twisted laid from N Box to Right Brigade R.C. at K.35.c.0.2. and one lateral pair connecting this Headquarters with the Left Brigade R.C. near SERRE.

19.8.18. Four pairs D8 twisted cable laid from M Test Box to new Right Brigade Headquarters at K.31.b.4.8. Also four pairs D8 twisted cable from K.A. Test Box.

20.8.18. Left Infantry Brigade and Left Group of Artillery moved to K.31.b.4.8. Communications via BS - RB diverted at BS Box via CH - M and overground to Brigade Headquarters. Brigades to Battalions lines via KA and B.

21.8.18. Maintenance work carried out, special attention being paid to forward overground cables. These were poled where considered liable to damage from traffic.

22.8.18. Two additional pairs D8 twisted cabele laid from B Test Box to Left Brigade forward Station at K.29.c.8.8.

23.8.18. General maintenance.

24.8.18. Advanced D.H.Q. opened at CHALK PITS , COLINCAMPS.
Advanced Divisional Signal Office near K Test box closed.down and Signal Office of Right Brigade taken over at noon. Advanced D.H.Q. opened at 5 p.m..
Right Brigade moved to K.29.c.8.8.

25.8.18. Light Cable wagons attached to 126th and 127th Infantry Brigades with orders to extend Divisional lines in event of Brigades moving forward.
Divisional Report Centre established at BEAUREGARD DOVECOT.
All Infantry Brigades and Artillery Groups connected direct to Divisional Report Centre.
Division withdrawn into Corps reserve. H.Q. remained unchanged.

26.8.18. No change in communications. Sounder working to Report Centre and Fullerphone forward to Brigades.
Generxal maintenance carried out.

27.8.18. Rear D.H.Q. at BUS closed at 12 noon and a Public Call and D.R.L.S. Office established. One line on to Corps Exchange and one line to Advanced D.H.Q. at COLINCAMPS until 5.30 p.m. when Advanced D.H.Q. closed down and moved to L.10.a. near BUCQUOY.
Two pairs of D.3 twisted and one pair D.8. twisted laid from new D.H.Q. at BUCQUOY to Report Centre at BEAUREGARD DOVECOT.
Three pairs twisted D.3 laid from Report Centre to new Report Centre at G.28.c.6.4. near LOUPART WOOD.
The line communications at midnight 27th/28th were as follows:-
D.H.Q. to 125 Brigade and 126 Brigade via BEAUREGARD DOVECOT Exchange. 127 Brigade via new Report Centre at LOUPART WOOD, also both Artillery Groups.
Division relieved 63rd Division at midnight.

28.8.18. D.H.Q. moved about 300 yards - off the sky line. Signal Office not moved- local lines extended.
Direct lines laid from Report Centre at LOUPART WOOD to 125 Brigade at PYS (M.2.d.4.5) and 126 Brigade at M.9.a.9.9.
Report Centre Signal Office moved 500 yards North, the old Office being too near battery positions.
Communications uninterrupted.

29.8.18. All forward lines improved- poled- buried and labelled.

30.8.18. D.H.Q. closed at BUCQUOY at 12 noon and opened at GREVILLERS at the same hour. Seven pair brass sheathed cable laid from Report Centre to new D.H.Q. also two pairs D3. twisted cable.
Report Centre closed down and lines put through.
Old lines via DOVECOT EXCHANGE reeled up.

31.8.18. Recovered old lines between BUCQUOY and LOUPART WOOD.
Forward lines improved.

APPENDIX 'B'.

SUBSIDIARY COMMUNICATIONS.

August.
1 - 15 As on 31.7.18 in Chapter XXI.
Power Buzzers and Trench Sets working well.
Loop Sets very erratic.

15 Division moved to BUS-les-ARTOIS. Directing Station moved to BUS. ML Visual Station closed.

16 Directing Station moved to J.28.a.88.

18 Directing Station moved to Advanced Division. J.30.b.88.
BS closed down.
Terminal Visual Station VTS established in concrete O.P. near Advanced D.H.Q. in communicationwith Left Brigade Visual Station at K.21.c.83 and Right Brigade Visual Station at K.33.b.23.
Loop Set working between this point and SERRE.

20 Loop Set also working from SERRE to K.30.c.62 for the attack.

21 Attack bagan. Left Brigade Trench Set moved to SERRE.

23 Directing Station moved to K.21.c.83 on top of ridge working to SERRE and Right Brigade.
VTS Visual Station moved to K.21.c.83 and SERRE Visual Station taken over.

24 D.H.Q. moved to COLINCAMPS.
All Loop Sets and Power-Buzzer-Amplifiers called in owing to difficulties of transport and accumulators.

25 Directing Station moved to SERRE.
One pack animal with two panniers attached to each of the two forward Brigades for transport of Trench Set equipment.
Visual Stations established at SERRE, LOZENGE HILL, and BEAUREGARD DOVECOT near new Divisional R.C.

26 Main Visual Station established at BEAUREGARD DOVECOT in communication with three forward Brigades. Rear Stations closed. W/T communication with Right and Left Brigades E. of PYS for nearly 8000 yards.

27 D.H.Q. moved to near BUCQUOY.
Directing Station established at D.H.Q. working to both forward Brigades.
Visual communication BEAUREGARD DOVECOT to new D.H.Q, and also to Brigades and Station near new Divisional R.C. N. of LOUPART WOOD.

29 Visual Station at BEAUREGARD DOVECOT closed down.
Terminal Visual Station established near Divisional R.C. working through a chain to two forward Brigades.

30 D.H.Q. moved to GREVILLERS. Directing Station moved to new D.H.Q. chain of Visual Stations established between new D.H.Q. and two forward Brigades.

18 - 31 During this period pigeons were delivered by Corps D.R. at D.H.Q. and sent by Divisional D.R. to Brigades in stock basket lent by Corps. Difficulty was found in supplying Battalions with sufficient Infantry pattern baskets owing to losses during the frequent moves.

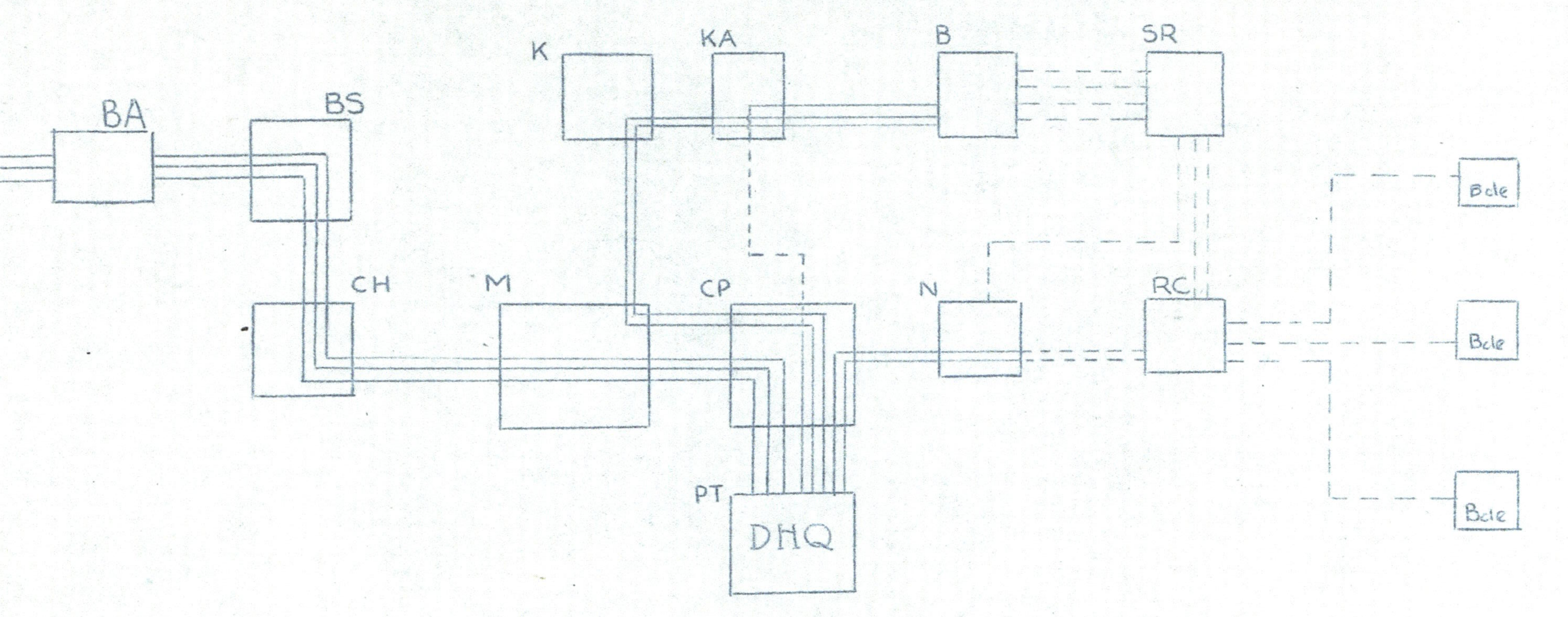
COMMUNICATIONS
42ND DIVISION
TO
IV CORPS
BA
BS
CH
M
K
KA
CP
PT
DHQ
B
SR
N
RC
Bde
Bde
Bde
26.8.18
42ND DIVL SIGNAL COY RE

COMMUNICATIONS
42nd DIVISION

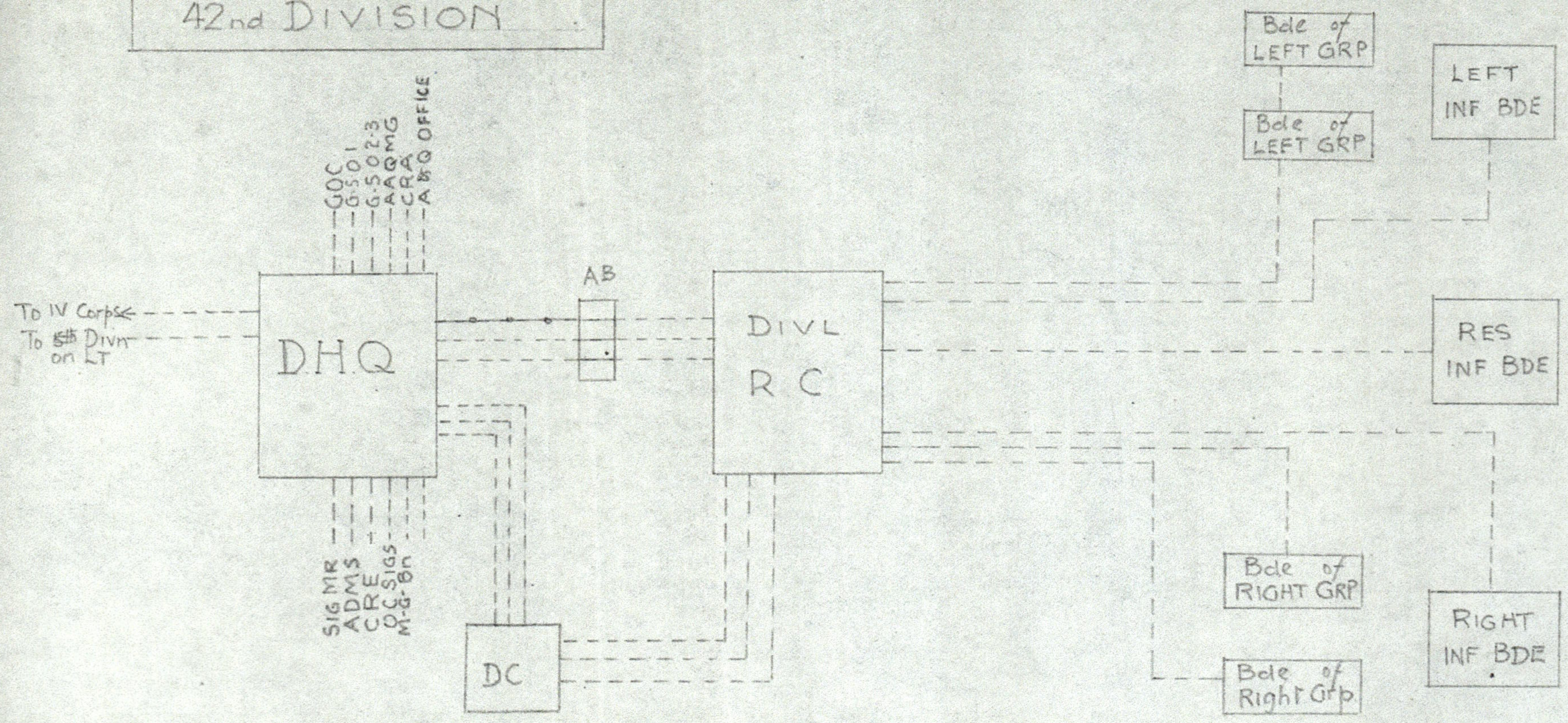

29. 8. 18

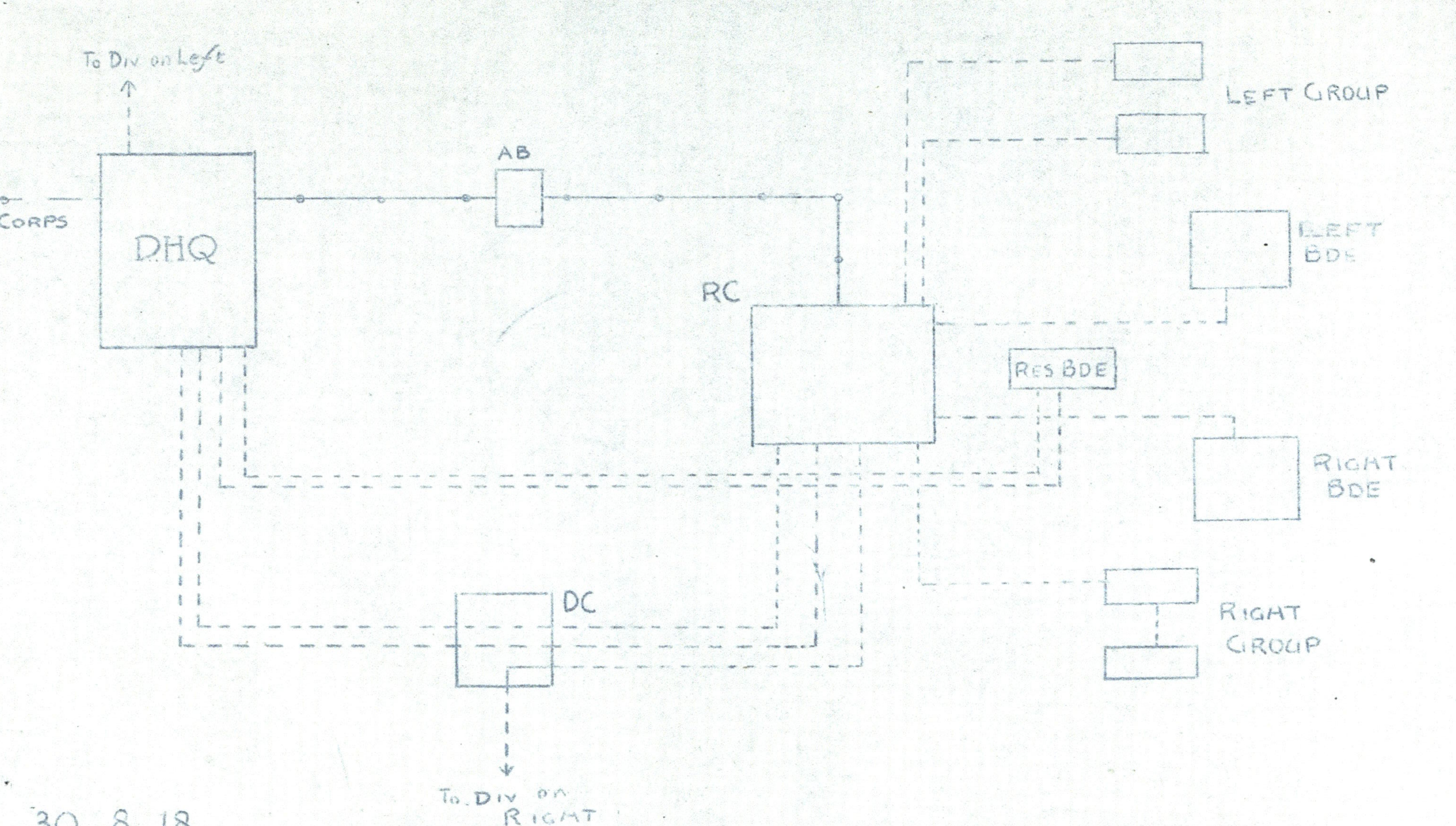
To Div on Left
To Corps
DHQ
AB
RC
Left Group
Left Bde
Res Bde
Right Bde
Right Group
DC
To Div on Right
30.8.18.

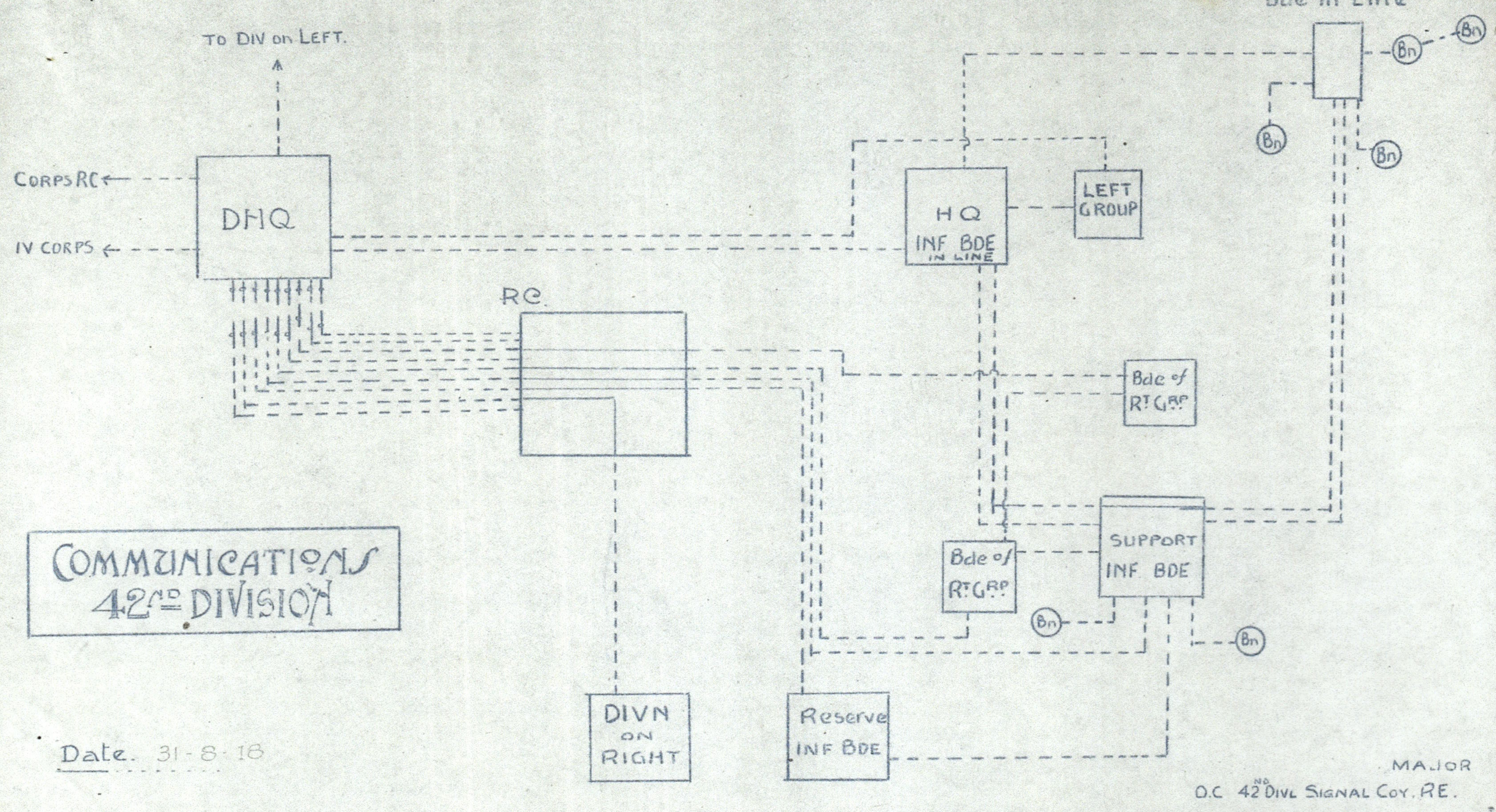
Adv HQ of
Bde in Line
Bn
Bn
Bn
Bn
TO DIV on LEFT.
CORPS RC
IV CORPS
DHQ
HQ
INF BDE
IN LINE
LEFT
GROUP
RC.
Bde of
R^T G^RP
Bde of
R^T G^RP
SUPPORT
INF BDE
Bn
Bn
COMMUNICATIONS
42ND DIVISION
DIVN
ON
RIGHT
Reserve
INF BDE
Date. 31-8-18
MAJOR
O.C 42ND DIVL SIGNAL COY. RE.

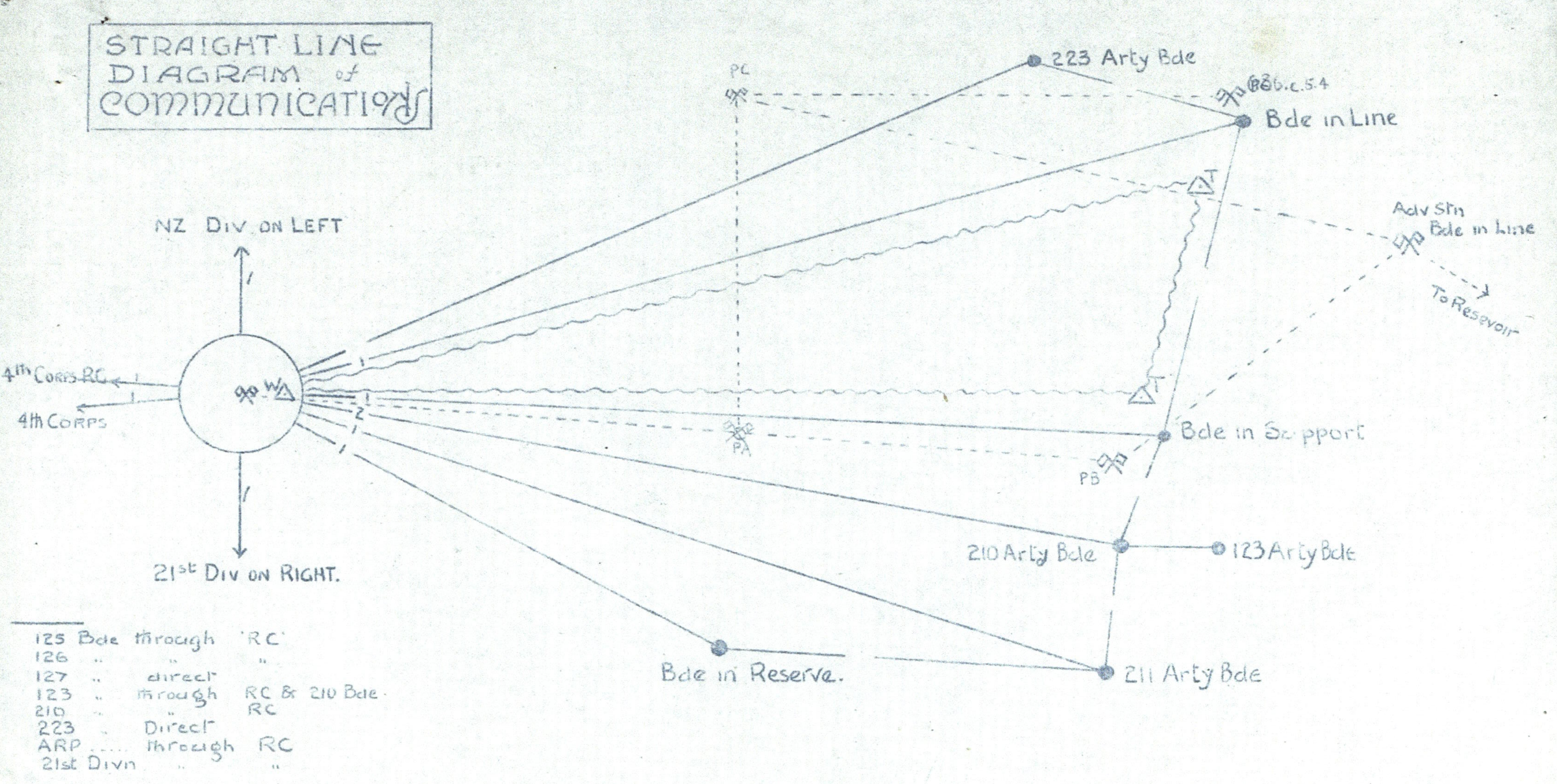

STRAIGHT LINE DIAGRAM of COMMUNICATIONS
NZ DIV ON LEFT
21st DIV ON RIGHT.
4th CORPS RC
4th CORPS
223 Arty Bde
Bde in Line
Adv Stn Bde in Line
To Resevoir
PC
PA
PB
Bde in Support
210 Arty Bde
123 Arty Bde
211 Arty Bde
Bde in Reserve.
125 Bde through 'RC'
126 " " "
127 " direct
123 " through RC & 210 Bde
210 " " RC
223 " Direct
ARP ..... through RC
21st Divn " "
31. 8. 1918.

APPENDIX 'C'.

SECRET. Copy No. 9

42nd DIVISIONAL SIGNAL COMPANY. R.E.
ORDER No. 21.

---

1. The Company will move to BUS Chateau grounds tomorrow, August 15th. D.H.Q. will close at AUTHIE at 2.0 p.m. and reopen BUS at same hour. D.H.Q. will be clear of AUTHIE by 3.0 p.m.

2. 6 a.m.- Motor Lorry will leave for BUS with technical and D.R. stores, Sgt. McQuigan i/c. Spr Davenport, Cpl Baldwin, and 3 W/T men will travel on this lorry.

Lorry will return to AUTHIE after unloading.

8.0 a.m.- Box Car will proceed to Directing Station i/c Sgt. Meakins returning to AUTHIE on completion of duty.

9.0 a.m. - P.S.L. lorry under Cpl Fuller and Sapper Whittaker with A.B.C' Set will leave for BUS.

11.0 a.m.- Motor Lorry will leave for BUS with Cooks' Stores, Orderly Room and Officers' Mess Stores and Officers' Kits.

The following will travel on this lorry- L/Cpl Parkinson, Spr Hayes, Pnr Foster, Dvr Ellis, Dvr Bent,J. and 'C' Signal Office relief. Signal Office Orderlies of this relief will proceed on bicycles.

3. The Company and transport under 2/Lieut.Abell will parade at 10.45 a.m. and move off for BUS at 11.0 a.m.

4. Sgt. Harrison will make all necessary arrangements for transfer of D.R's Motor Cycles and bicycles and the maintenance of D.R.L.S.

5. Surplus baggage as detailed by C.Q.M.S. will be left at AUTHIE in charge of two men to be detailed by C.S.M.

R. S. Newton
Captain.
for O.C. 42nd Divisional Signal Co. R.E.

Issued at 10.30 p.m.

Copy No. 1 O.C.
2. 'A' Officer.
3. Lines Officer.
4. Officers' Mess.
5. C.S.M. & C.Q.M.S.
6. Sgt. Harrison.
7. Signalmaster.
8. War Diary.
9. File.

APPENDIX 'C'

Copy. SECRET.

42nd DIVISIONAL SIGNAL COMPANY. R.E.
ORDER No. 23.

27.8.18.

Relief.	1. The 42nd Division will relieve the 63rd Division in the Right Sector of the Fourth Corps at midnight on the 27th August.
Location of Headquarters.	2. The Location of Headquarters of various units and the Divisional Report Centre will be notified later.
BUS Signal Office. Sgt. McGuigan.	3. At 12 noon 27th August the BUS Office will be closed and the personnel and stores will move to the new Advanced D.H.Q. with the exception of the two men with ringing telephone who will remain in charge of the Public Call and D.R.L.S. Office. They will be established in the BUS Chateau.
Advanced D.H.Q. Colincamps. Capt. Gill.	4. The Advanced D.H.Q. will close down at 4 p.m. and personnel and stores will move to the new Advanced D.H.Q.
Serre Signal Office. 2/Lieut.Abell.	5. The Signal Office at SERRE will close down at 10 a.m. 27.8.18. and all Linemen's Test Boxes will be established. O. i/c will detail two Linemen to remain behind until 4 p.m. and the remainder will go to the new Report Centre. The two Linemen will also go at 4 p.m. to the New Report Centre.
Dovecot Report Centre. Cpl Burne.	6. Stores and personnel of the Report Centre will move to the new Report Centre at 4 p.m.
Signal Compy. Capt.Newton. M.C.	7. The Signal Company under Capt. Newton.,M.C. will start for the new Advanced D.H.Q. at 1 p.m.
Cable Detachments. C.S.M.Willcock.	8. (a) 'B'2 Detachment under C.S.M.Willcock will start for the Report Centre at 1 p.m. and will await Orders there ready to la lay a pair to the Advanced D.H.Q.
Cable Detachment. Sgt. McCarthy.	(b). The two Cable Detachments going to advanced D.H.Q. on arrival will be ready to lay lines to the report Centre.
'AW' Cable Sec 2/Lieut.Davie.	(c). 'AW' Cable Section will start at 1 p.m. for the new Advanced D.H.Q. and await orders ready to lay lines.
Cable Detachments attached to Brigades.	(d). Cable Detachments attached to Brigades will go to the new Report Centre at 1 p.m. and then lay lines to the new Brigade H.Q.
Wireless. Cpl Holton.	9. The Directing Station at Serre will start for the new Advanced D.H.Q. at 10 a.m.
Brigade Wireless Stations.	10. Trench Wireless Sets attached to Brigades will start for the new Brigade H.Q. immediately they are known and erect Stations.
Visual Stations Cpl Hill.	11. Cpl Hill will establish a Central Visual Station (as near as possible to the Report Centre) in touch with each Brigade and Advanced Division.
D.R's.	12. Six mounted Orderlies will go to the Report Centre at 1 p.m. Four D.E's will report at the new Advanced D.H.Q. by 4.30 p.m. The remaining D.R's will start for Advanced Div. at 5 p.m.
Pigeons. Lt.Fletcher.	13. Lieut. Fletcher will arrange with the Corps to deliver pigeons at Advanced D.H.Q. and from there will distribute to Infantry Brigades, in the line.

APPENDIX 'C'

Transport.
Capt. Newton., M.C.

14. Capt. Newton will arrange for the transport of BUS, COLINCAMPS, SERRE, and DOVECOT Offices and the 'Wireless Directing Station' at SERRE to move to the new positions and will issue orders as to the routes to be takem.

Cable Dump.
Lieut. Ayles.

15. A Cable Dump will be established at the Report Centre.
The necessary transport will be provided by Capt. Newton. Brigades will wire requirements to Advanced Division and on obtaining sanction may draw from the Dump.

(Sgd). S.Gordon Johnson.

Major.
O.C. 42nd Divisional Signal Co. R.E.

Issued by Special D.R. at 9 a.m. 27th August 1918.

APPENDIX 'D'. WAR DIARY. AUGUST 1918.

HONOURS AND AWARDS.

NIL.

Patol.

Major.R.E.

O.C. 42nd Divisional Signal Company.R.E.

APPENDIX 'E'. AUGUST 1918.

WAR DIARY.

WEEKLY STRENGTHS, CASUALTIES, REINFORCEMENTS.

Weekly Strengths.	Officers.	O.R.
Week ending Aug. 3rd.	12	313
" " " 10th	12	312
" " " 17th	12	315
" " " 24th	13	313
" " " 31st	12	315

Casualties.		
Killed.	-	1
Wounded.	-	4
Sick.	-	6
To Base.	-	1
" Fifth Army Signal School.	-	2
	-	14

Reinforcements.		
From Hospital.	-	1
From Depot.	-	12
" 9th Corps Signal Co.R.E.	-	1
	-	14

Paton

Major.R.E.

10.9.18. O.C. 42nd Divisional Signal Co.R.E.

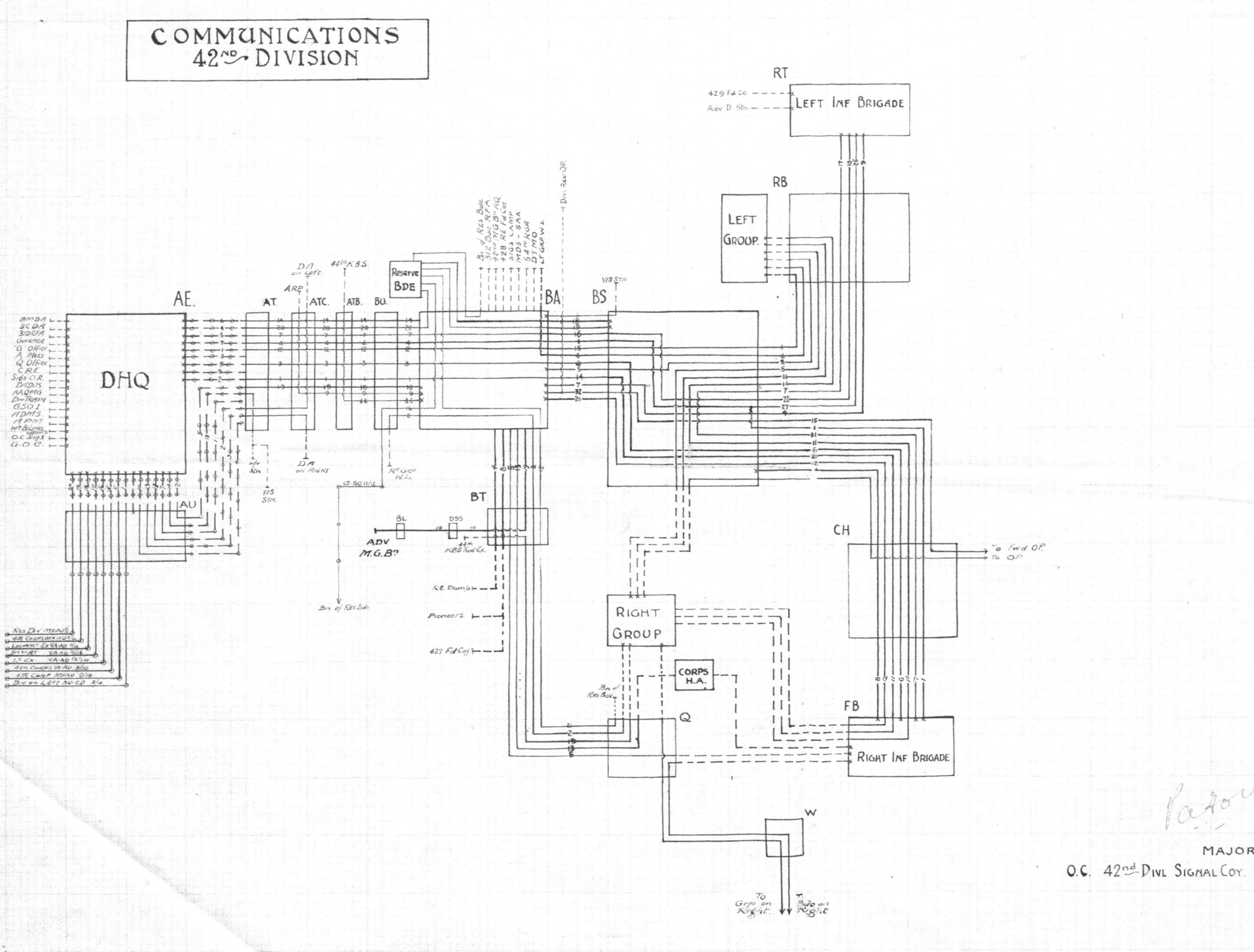
COMMUNICATIONS
42ND DIVISION
DHQ
AE.
AU
AT.
ATC.
ATB.
BU.
Reserve BDE
BA
BS
BT
ADV M.G.Bn
RT
LEFT INF BRIGADE
RB
LEFT GROUP.
CH
RIGHT GROUP
CORPS H.A.
Q
FB
RIGHT INF BRIGADE
W
MAJOR. R.E
O.C. 42nd DIVL SIGNAL COY. R.E.

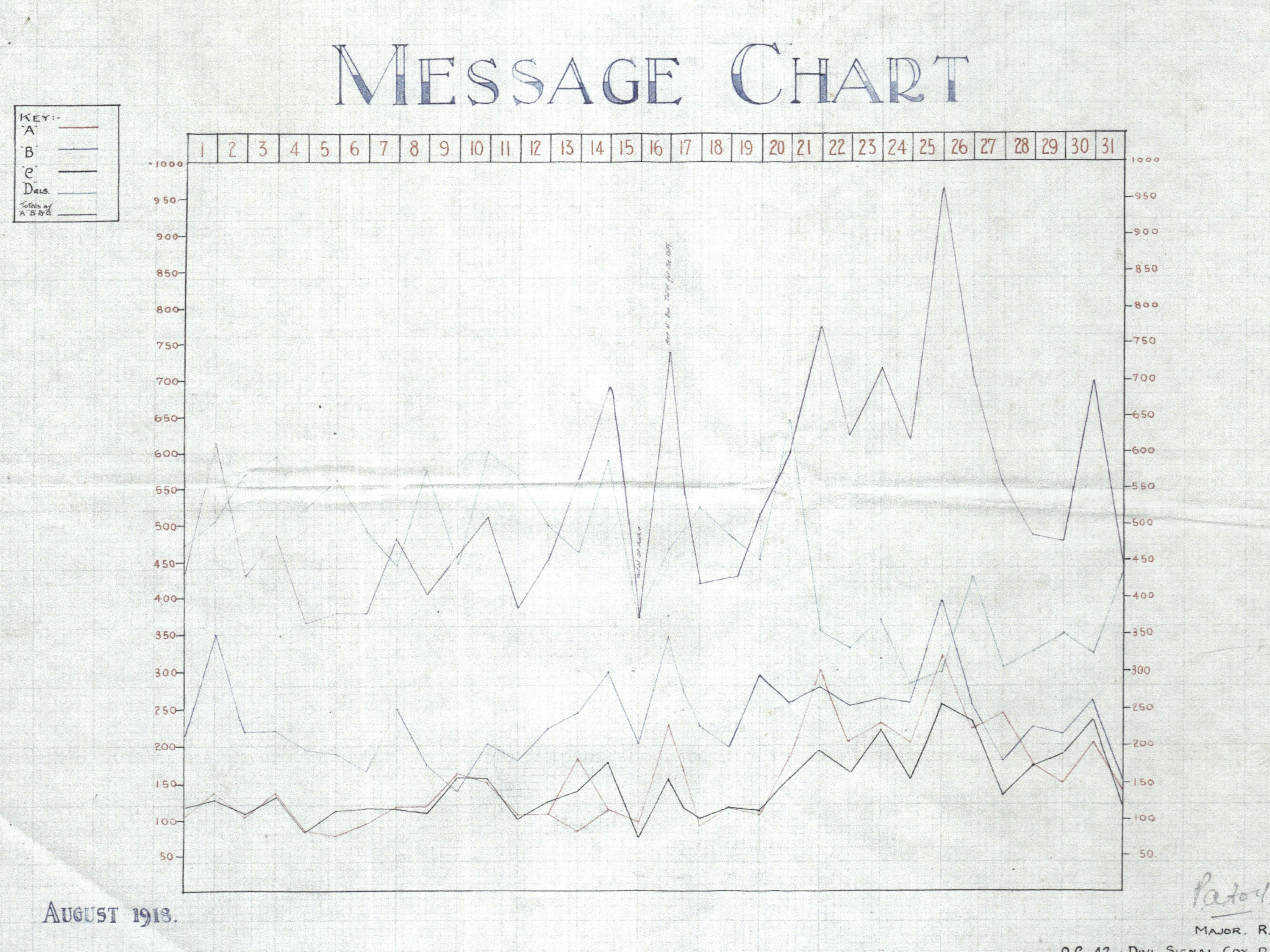
MESSAGE CHART
KEY:-
'A'
'B'
'C'
D.R.s.
Totals of 'A' 'B' & 'C'
1 2 3 4 5 6 7 8 9 10 11 12 13 14 15 16 17 18 19 20 21 22 23 24 25 26 27 28 29 30 31
1000 950 900 850 800 750 700 650 600 550 500 450 400 350 300 250 200 150 100 50
AUGUST 1918.
Paton
MAJOR. R.E.
O.C. 42nd DIVL SIGNAL COY R.E.

Sep/18

VR 19

Secret

War Diary

42nd Divisional Signal Company R.E.

Chapter XXIII.

4th Oct 1918.

Paton
Major
O.C. 42nd Divisional Signal Coy R.E.

Army Form C. 2118.

Instructions regarding War Diaries and Intelligence Summaries are contained in F. S. Regs., Part II, and the Staff Manual respectively. Title pages will be prepared in manuscript.

WAR DIARY

or

~~INTELLIGENCE SUMMARY.~~

(Erase heading not required.)

Place	Date	Hour	Summary of Events and Information	Remarks and references to Appendices
			42nd (East Lancs.) Divisional Signal Co.R.E.(T).	
			CHAPTER XXIII. SEPTEMBER 1918. Reference Map, 1/40,000. FRANCE. Sheet 57C.	
GREVILLERS.	1.9.18.		42nd Division holding the Right Sector of the IV Corps front. Divisional Headquareers and Signal Company Headquarters at G.30.c.5.7. One pair (D.8 twisted) laid from Divisional Headquarters to 127 Brigade Headquarters in G.36.a.3.9. Two Detachments recovering cables in vicinity of LOUPART WOOD.	
	2.9.18.		Two pairs (D.8 twisted) laid - one from 127 Brigade Headquarters to new Brigade Headquarters at N.3.a. and one from Divisional Headquarters to 210 Brigade at N.5.c. Two Detachments recovering cables in rear areas.	DIAGRAM 1.
	3.9.18.		Divisional Report Centre established at N.5.c. Near REINCOURT. Single D.5 cables laid from Report Centre to 125 Brigade at BARASTRE, 126 Brigade at VILLERS -au- FLOS, and 127 Brigade at N.3.a. Three horses killed and two wounded owing to one of the Cable wagons' team of six kicking a bomb.	
Nr REINCOURT les-BAPAUME.	4.9.18.		Divisional Headquarters and Company Headquarters moved to N.5.c. closing down at 10.0 a.m. and reopening at new position same hour. IV Corps and 21st Division (in reserve) lines strapped through at old Headquarters to two existing pairs to N.5.c. Single D.2 cable run to 17th Division on Right and single D.5 cables from 126 Brigade Headquarters to 56 H.A.Brigade (about 1000 yards away) 126 Brigade to 125 Brigade and 125 Brigade to the Brigade Forward Station at BUS.	DIAGRAM 2.
	5.9.18.		Single D.5 cable laid to N.Z.Division on Left. Two Detachments recovering cables in back areas.	
	6.9.18.		Existing lines to PYS, WARLENCOURT, and LE BARQUES areas diverted and extended for use of Infantry Brigades moving into relief into these areas.	DIAGRAM 3.
	7.9.18.		Poled lines to Brigades and recovered cables between Divisional Headquarters and GREVILLERS.	

A7092). Wt. W12839/M1297 750,000. 1/17. D. D & L., Ltd. Forms/C2118/14.

Instructions regarding War Diaries and Intelligence Summaries are contained in F. S. Regs., Part II. and the Staff Manual respectively. Title pages will be prepared in manuscript.

WAR DIARY

or

~~INTELLIGENCE SUMMARY.~~

(Erase heading not required.)

Army Form C. 2118.

Place	Date	Hour	Summary of Events and Information	Remarks and references to Appendices
	8.9.18.		Two Detachments recovering cable, remainder overhauling and checking stores.etc.	
	9.9.18. to 20.9.18.		This period was devoted to refitting, training and physical exercise.	
VELU WOOD.	21.9.18.		Divisional Headquarters and Company Headquarters moved to VELU WOOD (I.36.d.8.2) in accordance with Company Order No.24 (Appendix A) and took over area and billets previously occupied by 37th Division. The Signal Company Transport lines being located at LEBUCQUIERE (I.24.d.5.4). 42nd Division relieved 37th Division in the Left Sector of the IV Corps front at 12 midnight. (See Diagram 4).	APPENDIX 'A'
	22.9.18.		127 Brigade (in Support) moved from P.11.central to BERTINCOURT. Existing ground lines from Divisional Headquarters to this Brigade running near this place were split and diverted thus giving two pairs back to Divisional Headquarters and two pairs forward to Advanced Brigade Headquarters at P.11.central. A Divisional Report Centre was also established in the same dug-out at this place. Work begun on old bury system between K-KJ-B-P and R test boxes (See Diagram 5). Seven pairs put through between K and B boxes.	
	23.9.18.		Work continued on bury. 20 pairs put through between B and R boxes enabling Brigade in line to use bury cable to Battalions in line. Infantry Working party cleared open trench between M and K boxes in HAVRINCOURT WOOD. Enemy shelled Wood once dispersing the party. Two pairs D.8 twisted cable laid in trench and 150 yards of old bury from railway to K test box tested - 7 pairs found O.K.	
	24.9.18.		Two pairs D.8 twisted laid in trench between M and K boxes. General maintenance - lines labelled and poled.	
	25.9.18.		Tanks moving into position caused considerable trouble, frequently breaking cables, especially those on short poled (stakes about 3' high) routes.	
	26.9.18.		Support and Reserve Brigade moved forward to P and R boxes becoming Left and Right Brigades respectively. Left and Right Artillery Group were established at the same Headquarters.	

A7092). Wt. W12839/M1293 750,000. 1/17. D. D & L., Ltd. Forms/C2118/14.

Army Form C. 2118.

Instructions regarding War Diaries and Intelligence Summaries are contained in F. S. Regs., Part II. and the Staff Manual respectively. Title pages will be prepared in manuscript.

WAR DIARY

or

~~INTELLIGENCE SUMMARY.~~

(Erase heading not required.)

Place	Date	Hour	Summary of Events and Information	Remarks and references to Appendices
			- 3 -	
			Brigade in line became Reserve Brigade and remained at PLACE MORTEMART, about 300 yards from KJ test box. Communications as shown in Diagrams 5 and 6 and described in Appendix 'B'.	APPENDIX 'B'.
	27.9.18.		42nd Division attacked enemy's positions. All lines working at Zero hour. Direct line communication maintained all day. Little shelling, Supply Tanks caused slight trouble rear of Divisional Report Centre.	
	28.9.18.		7 pairs put through R-Q bury. Two pairs laid from Q box to R.36.central. Reserve Brigade and Left Artillery Group moved to K.36.central. Speaking very faint between Divisional Headquarters and these Headquarters due to earthy bury between KJ -K boxes. Fullerphone worked well. 126 Brigade Headquarters returned to PLACE MORTEMART. Light Cable wagon, two mules and one rider, lost due to enemy bombing.	
	29.9.18.		N.Z.Division relieved 42nd Division at 3.0 a.m. Two pairs from BERTINCOURT to K.36. central. handed over to N.Z.Division. Report Centre closed down at 5.0 p.m. 125 Brigade moved to old bury Left Brigade position at Q.3.b. and 127 Brigade to P.11.central. Divisional Headquarters remained at VELU WOOD. Communications as shown in Diagram 7.	
	30.9.18.		Communications unchanged. Horses and personnel rested as much as possible.	

APPENDICES TO THIS DIARY.

(A). Company Order No.24.
(B). Signal Communications.
(C). Honours and Awards.
(D). Weekly Strengths, Casualties, Reinforcements, etc.
(E). Monthly Message Chart.

4.10.18.

Major. R.E.

O.C. 42nd Divisional Signal Co. R.E.

A7092). Wt. W12839/M1293 750,000. 1/17. D. D & L., Ltd. Forms/C2118/14.

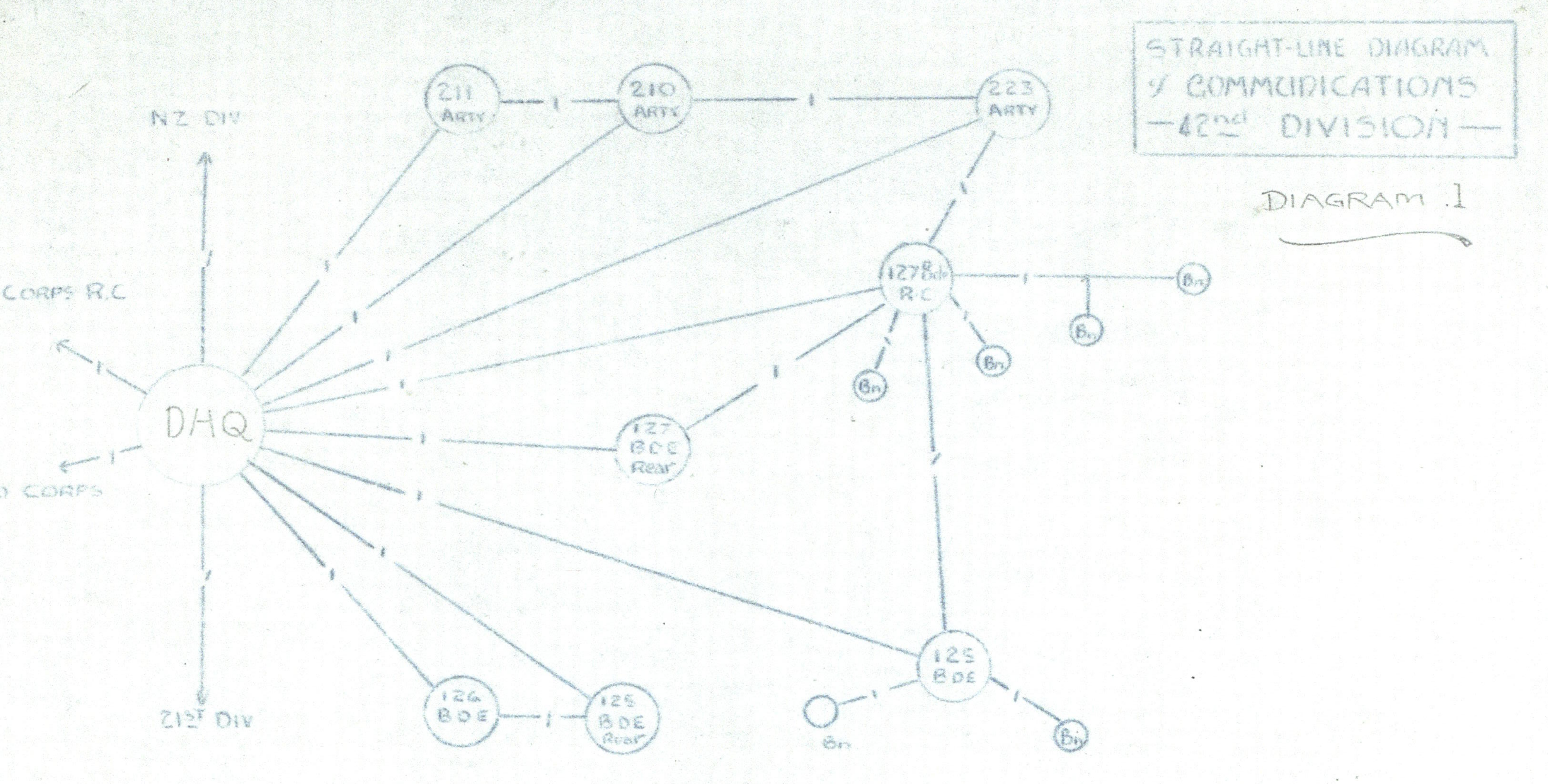
STRAIGHT-LINE DIAGRAM
of COMMUNICATIONS
—42nd DIVISION—
DIAGRAM 1
211 ARTY
210 ARTY
223 ARTY
NZ DIV
TO CORPS R.C
TO CORPS
21ST DIV
DHQ
127 Bde R.C
Bn
Bn
Bn
Bn
127 BDE Rear
125 BDE
Bn
Bn
126 BDE
125 BDE Rear
Date 2.9.18

DIAGRAM 2

COMMUNICATIONS

42nd Division

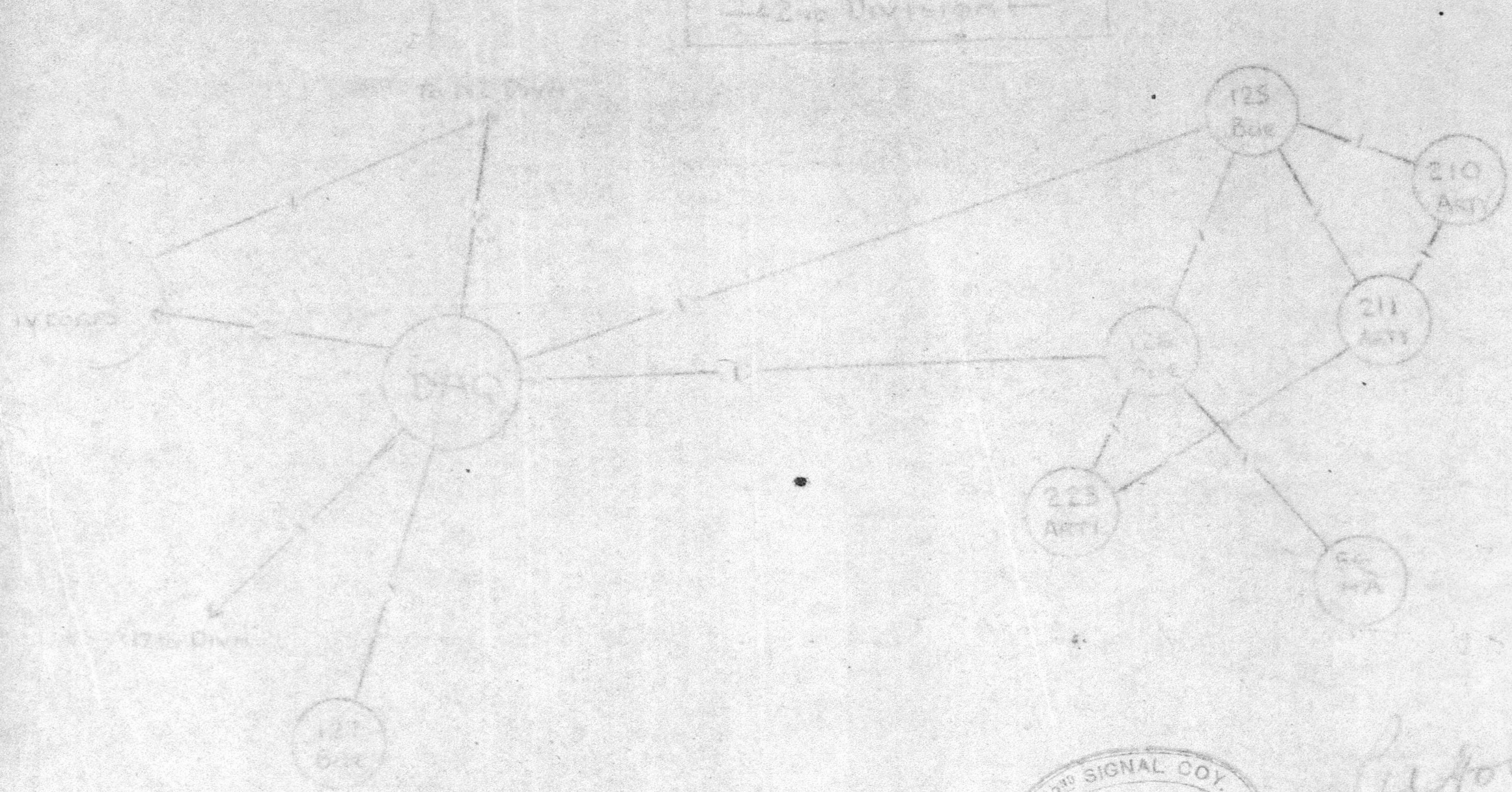

125 Bde

210 Arty

211 Arty

223 Arty

DIAGRAM 3

COMMUNICATIONS
→·42nd DIVISION·←

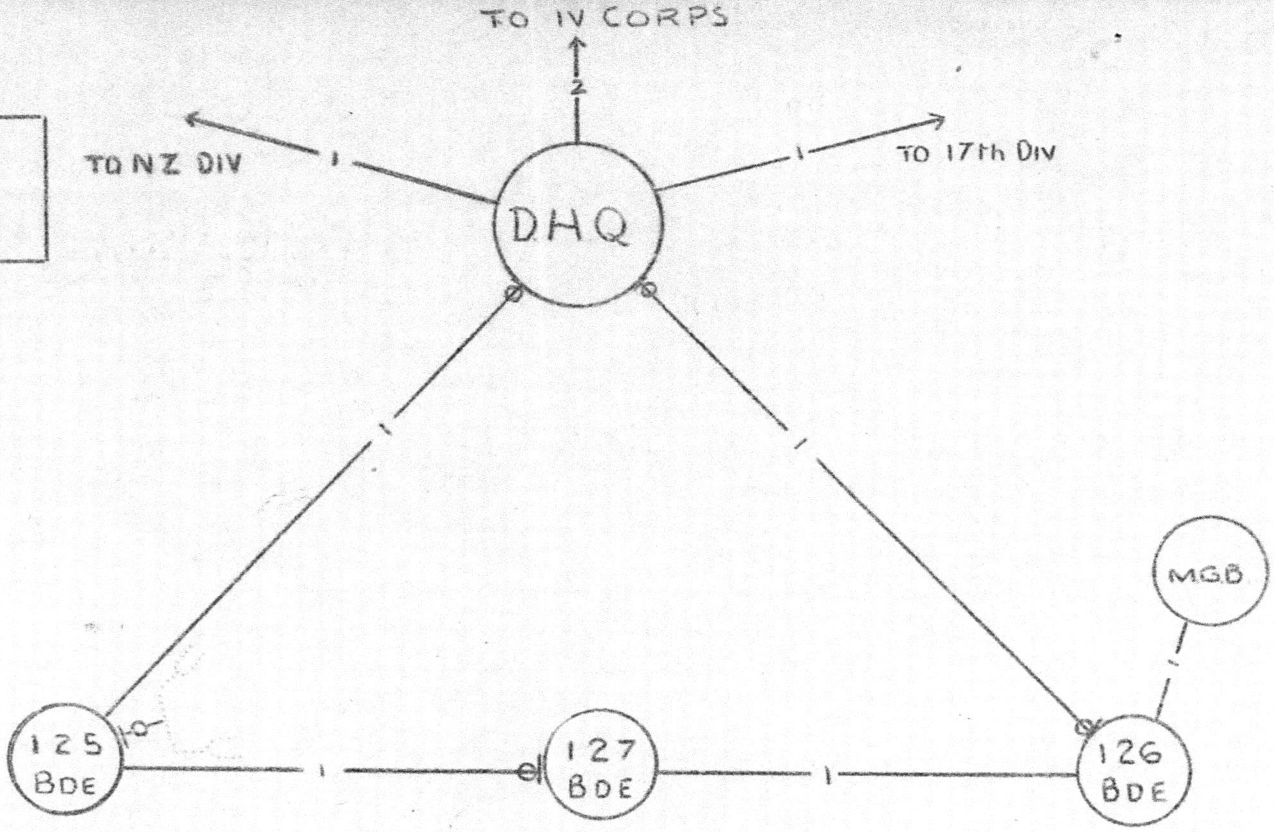

TO IV CORPS

TO NZ DIV

TO 17th DIV

DHQ

MGB

125 BDE

127 BDE

126 BDE

MAJOR

Date 6.9.18

⊢o— Fullerphone

O.C 42nd DIVL SIGNAL COY R.E.

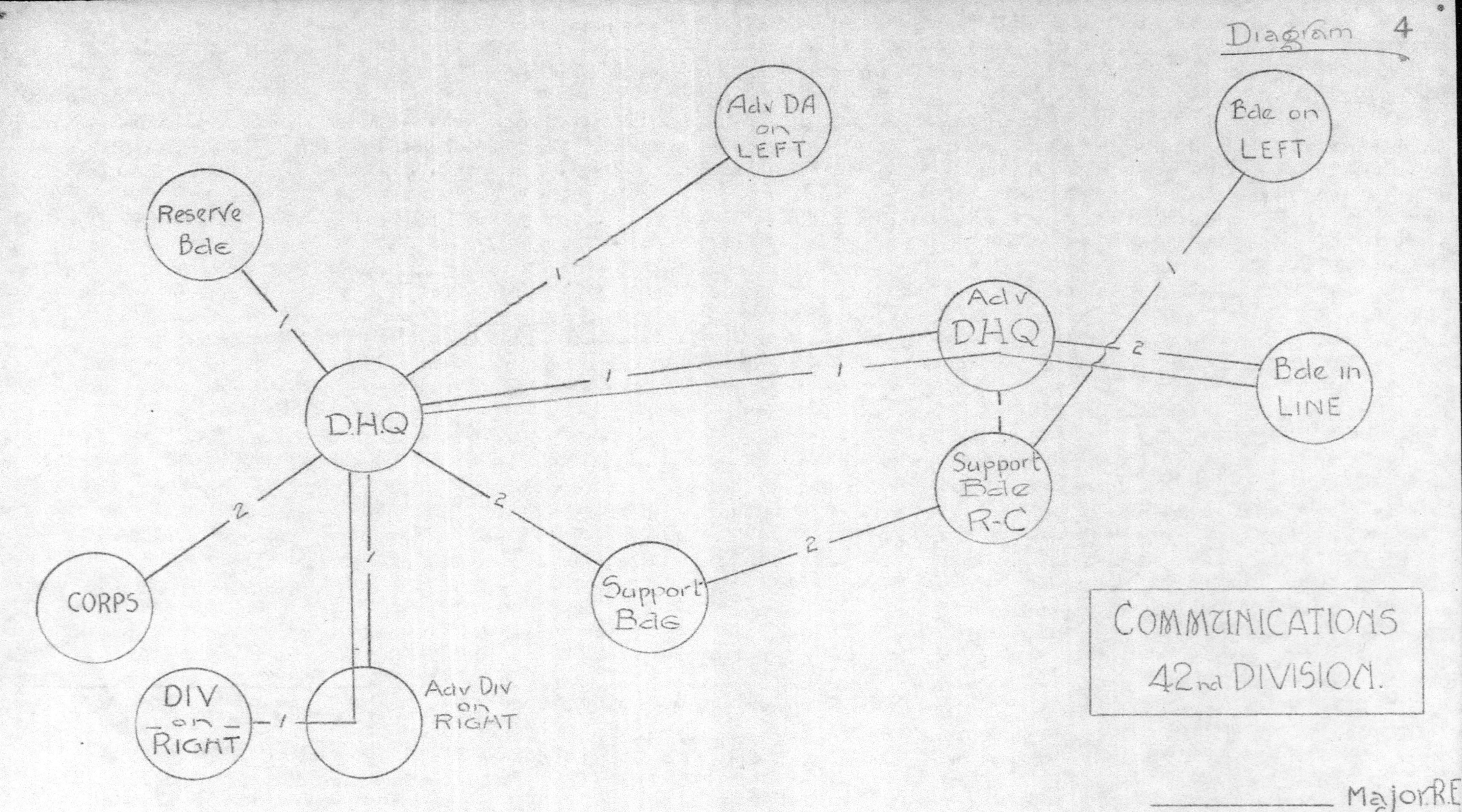
Diagram 4
Adv DA on LEFT
Bde on LEFT
Reserve Bde
Adv DHQ
Bde in LINE
D.H.Q
Support Bde R-C
CORPS
Support Bde
COMMUNICATIONS
42nd DIVISION.
DIV on RIGHT
Adv Div on RIGHT
1
1
1
1
2
1
1
2
2
2
1
1
Major R.E
Date 22.9.18.
O.C. 42nd Divl Signal Coy. R.E.

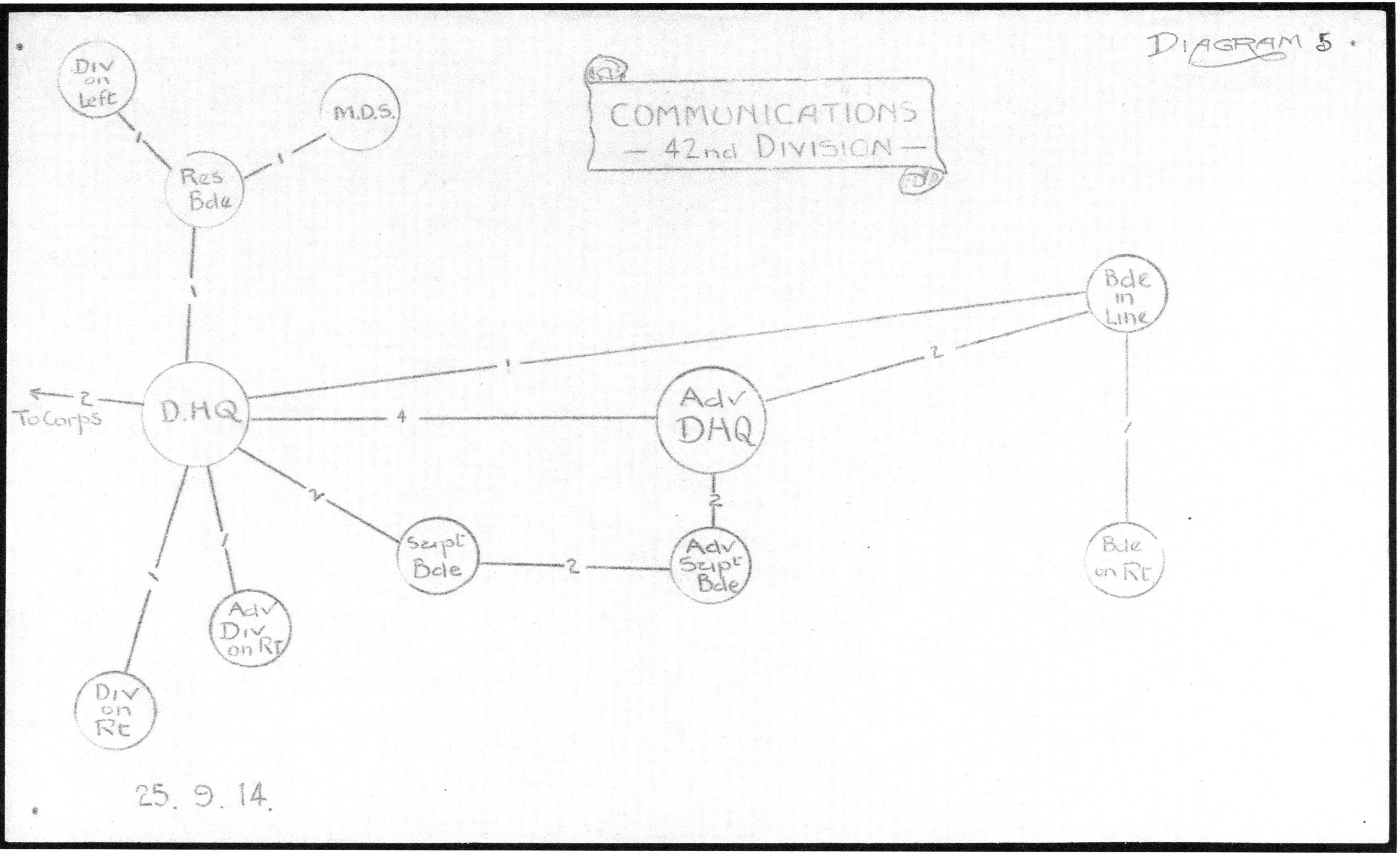

DIAGRAM 5.

COMMUNICATIONS
— 42nd DIVISION —

Div on Left
M.D.S.
Res Bde
D.HQ
To Corps
Adv DHQ
Bde in Line
Bde on Rt
Szipt Bde
Adv Szipt Bde
Adv Div on Rt
Div on Rt
1
1
1
2
1
4
2
2
2
2
1
1
1

25. 9. 14.

DIAGRAM 6

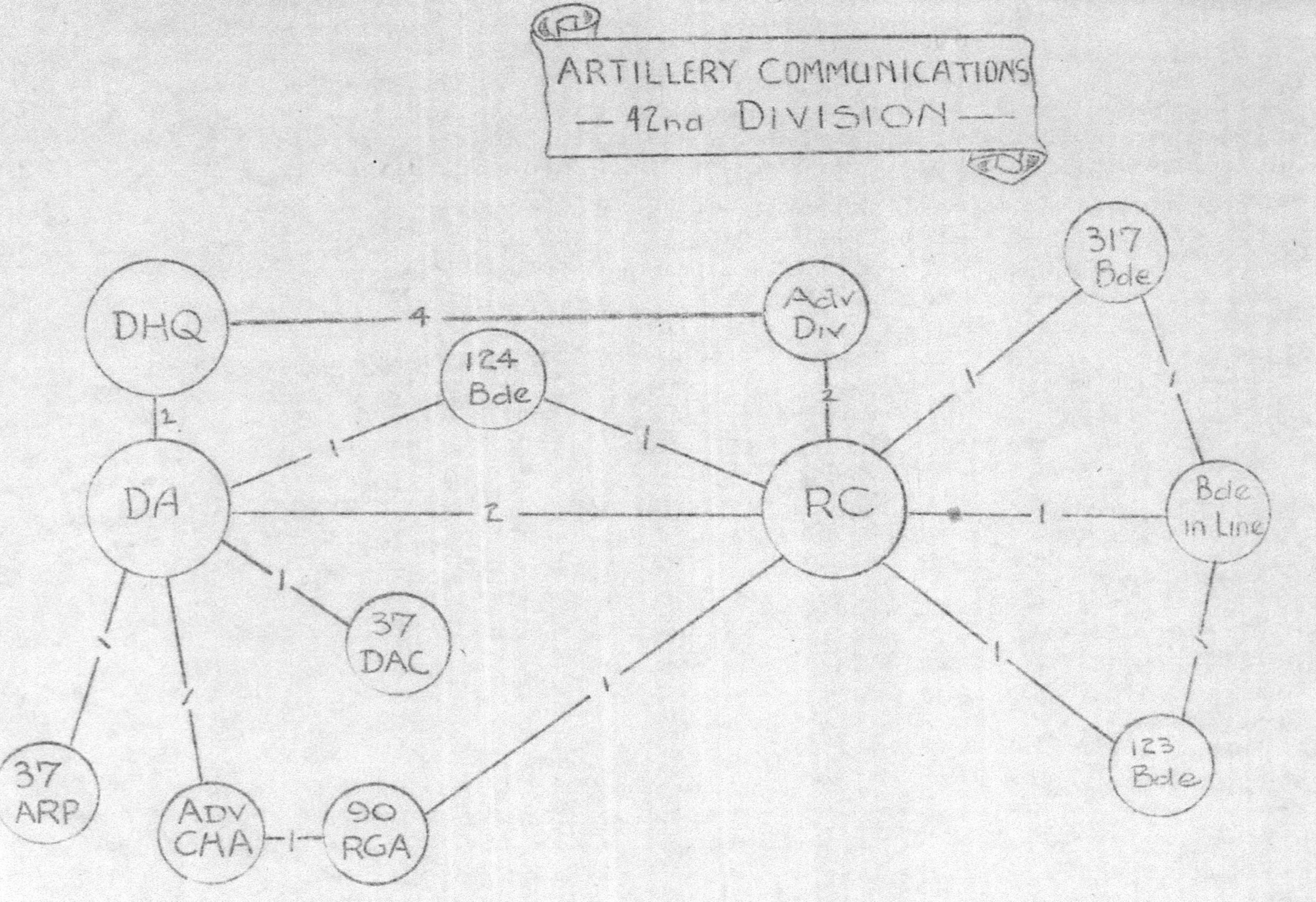
ARTILLERY COMMUNICATIONS
— 42nd DIVISION —
DHQ
4
Adv Div
124 Bde
317 Bde
2
DA
2
RC
1
Bde in Line
1
1
1
1
1
1
37 DAC
1
1
123 Bde
37 ARP
Adv CHA
1
90 RGA
25.9.18.

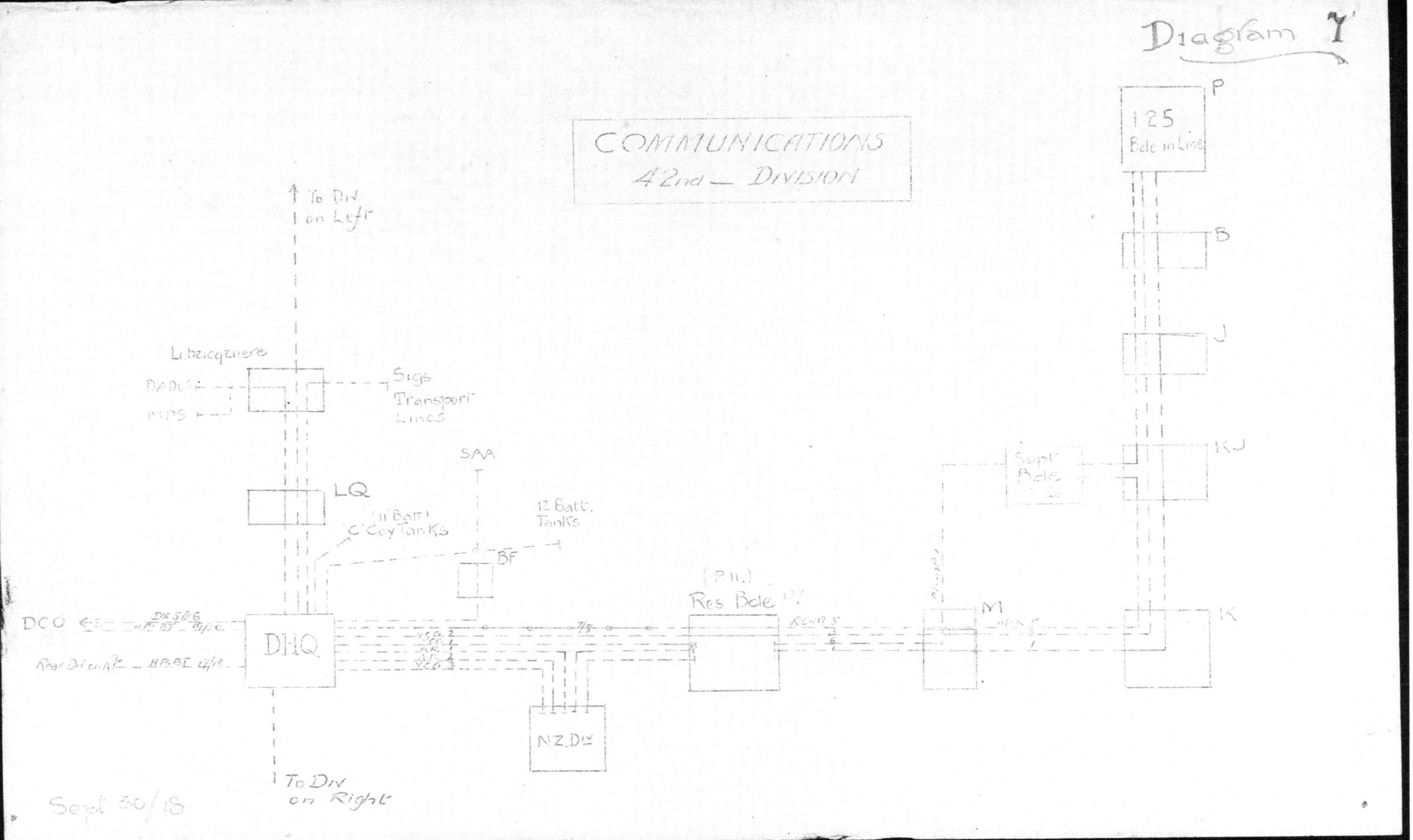

Diagram Y

COMMUNICATIONS
42nd — DIVISION

P
125
Bde in Line

B

J

KJ

Supt Bde

K

M

(P.11.)
Res Bde

NZ Div

To Div on Left

Lebucquiere

DADOS

MDS

Sigs Transport Lines

LQ

SAA

(11 Batt) C Coy Tanks

12 Batt. Tanks

BF

DCO

DHQ

Rear Div

To Div on Right

Sept 30/18

APPENDIX 'A'

SECRET.

42nd DIVISIONAL SIGNAL COMPANY. R.E.
ORDER No. 24.

Copy No. 11

Divisional Headquarters closes at N.5.c. at 5 p.m. Septr 21st 1918, and opens at I.36.d.8.2. at the same hour.

The Company will move and prepare to assume duties on arrival under the following arrangements:-

1. Lorry Schedule.
2. Signal Office.
3. Lines.
4. D.R.L.S.
5. P.E.L.
6. Visual.
   Wireless.
7. Company Transport, personnel, stores, etc.

---

1. Lorry Schedule. The lorry will run to the following time-table as far as possible.

A.	7.30 a.m.	Signal Office relief.
B.	11.30 a.m.	Wireless Directing Station and other stores.
C.	4.0 p.m.	Signal Office Relief.

2. Signal Office The closing and opening of both offices is under the direction of Lieut. Ellis.

One office relief, complete with instruments, less that which has been sent today, will proceed by lorry 'A'. On arrival steps will be taken immediately to change over personnel and instruments gradually, in order that all signals at 37th Divnl Headquarters may be manned by us by 2.0 p.m.

Change of command does not take place until midnight 21st/22nd; and Signals, 37th Division are leaving one Superintendent until that hour.

The aeroplane dropping station will be in position by 5.0 a.m. on the 22nd.

One relief, and the office as running at present, less any instruments not required, will remain at N.5.c. until 2.0 p.m., when it will be relieved by Signals, 37th Division. This relief and office equipment will proceed to the new headquarters by lorry 'C'.

The third office relief will march with the Company at 2.0 p.m.

3. (a) Lines. The responsibility for completing out-station linemen and for taking over line communications rests with Lieut. Ellis. Lorry 'A' can take a limited number of linemen. Arrangements will be made for taking over the dump of cable at the Support Brigade, and for receiving the cable which will be sent up on the 22nd inst.

A pencil diagram of lines will be made out on 22nd inst and submitted to O.C., Company.

(b) Arrangements for establishing new and taking over existing R.A. lines rests with Lieut. Abell, who will apply to O.C., Company for necessary assistance.

4. Sergt. Harrison will submit his D.R.L.S. Time Table to O.C., Company at 6.0 p.m., 21st.

Four D.R's will proceed to new Headquarters at 2.0 p.m. The remainder at 5.0 p.m.

The Artificer and his shop will proceed by the P.E.L. Lorry (See 5.)

5. The P.E.L. Lorry will leave at 9.0 a.m. Sergt. Harrison is responsible that all lights are stripped and lighting cable recovered, and the P.E.L. lorry and personnel are ready to move off by that hour.

5 (Cont'd)

On arrival at the new headquarters, the existing wiring will be taken over, and an equivalent length given to 37th Signals in return. Steps will be taken at once to replace fittings, and any necessary alterations will be made in order that lighting may commence at the usual hour.

6. Visual and Wireless Lieut. Fletcher is responsible for the effective establishment and relief of Visual and Wireless Stations.

The Box-car will make journeys at :-

(a) 8.0 a.m.
(b) 11.0 a.m.
(c) 2.0 p.m.

(a) may take 4 Visual signallers and equipment and 3 W/T men and equipment.
(b) may take 7 W/T men and equipment.
(c) is at Captain Newton's disposal.

The Directing Station and personnel will proceed by lorry 'B'.

8 bicycles are available for Visual purposes.

A combined Visual and Wireless diagram will be submitted to O.C., Company by 6.0 p.m., 22nd.

7. The move of personnel, transport, stores, etc., are under the supervision of Captain Newton.

The Company will move off at 2.0 p.m.

Lorry 'B', except as already detailed, will be loaded with technical stores and equipment which may be required within 24 hours of arrival.

Lorry 'C' will be completed with stores as far as practicable.

Cable as verbally detailed and any stores for which transport has not been available, will be left behind under a guard, and will be fetched by lorry on 22nd inst.

All personnel, except as detailed by other officers, will move under Captain Newton's arrangements.

The camp, horse lines, all billets and offices will be left quite clean.

Paton.

Major. R.E.

20.9.18. O.C., 42nd Div'l Signal Coy., R.E.

Issued by orderly at p.m., 20.9.18.

Copy No 1. Captain Newton.
2. Lieut. Fletcher.
3. Lieut. Ellis.
4. Lieut. Abell.
5. C.S.M.
6. C.Q.M.S.
7. Sgt. McGuigan.
8. Sgt. Harrison.
9. O.C., Signals, 37th Divn. (For information).
10. File.
11. War Diary.

SECRET. APPENDIX B Diary.

42nd DIVISION.

BATTLE INSTRUCTIONS No.1 .

SIGNAL COMMUNICATIONS.

I. General.
II. Telephone and Telegraph.
III. Visual.

IV. Wireless.
V. Message carrying Agencies.
   (1). Runners, Mounted Officers and Orderlies, and D.R's.
   (2). Pigeons.
   (3). Message carrying Rockets.
VI. Signalling to Aeroplanes.
VII. Miscellaneous.

APPENDIX - Diagrams.

I. GENERAL.

Position of Headquarters.

1. Divisional Headquarters. — I.36.d.8.1.
   Divisional Report Centre. — P.11 Central.
   Right Brigade.) Right Group.) — Q.10 Central.
   Left Brigade.) Left Group.) — Q.3.b.3.1.
   Reserve Brigade. — PLACE MORTEMARE.

2. Diagrams of existing cable, visual and wireless communications as existing on Y/Z night are appended. (See appendices I and II)

3. The Left Brigade and Left Group Hdqrs. will move to about K.35.a.8.4. after the final objective has been captured. The Headquarters of the Right Brigade and Group Hdqrs. will remain at Q.10 Central throughout the operation.

II. TELEPHONE AND TELEGRAPH.

Appendix III shews the only portion of the old buried system which can be used for the operation.

A certain number of pairs will be available as far forward as 'R' Test point. The minimum allotment of these will be one pair per infantry brigade, one pair per artillery group.

The allotment will be increased according to the number of pairs it is possible to repair in time.

COMMUNICATIONS DURING THE ATTACK.

Infantry.

1. Each Brigade will select a Brigade forward station :-
   Right Brigade in the vicinity of R.7.a.
   Left Brigade in the vicinity of K.36.b.2.3.
   These forward stations will accept messages from all units whether infantry, artillery or Machine Guns, and will be marked by a blue and white flag.

2. Brigade forward parties, on lines laid down in S.S.191, Section 9, will be formed.

Detachments 'A' (Each under a Battalion Signalling Officer) of these parties, will go forward immediately behind the attacking infantry and will consist of personnel and equipment to open up communication by visual, runner, pigeons and message carrying rockets.

Detachments 'B' will consist of personnel and equipment for laying and maintaining one main circuit forward from the burried cable head to the Brigade forward Station, and will include the forward station of the Loop Set for working back to the rear station at Brigade Hqrs.

This detachment should not go over with the infantry, but should delay with a view to selecting, if possible, gaps in the enemy's barrage.

3. The main circuit will be laid via, or near by, the position selected for the move forward of Brigade Hdqrs, in order that, after the move, the rear portion may be used for communication back to the Division.

Only twisted cable will be laid by infantry brigade sections. The mobile establishment of both infantry and artillery will be kept intact with a view to a further advance. A dump of cable of all classes for infantry and artillery will be established at the Divisional Report Centre - P.11 Central. Demands will be made on O.C., Signals.

Brigades will arrange to supplement the personnel of Brigade Sections by battalion signallers where necessary.

Artillery.

The Headquarters of Officers commanding Artillery Groups will remain with Hdqrs of Infantry Brigades to which they are affiliated and will move forward with those hdqrs. One F.O.O. per Brigade and one F.I.O. (Forward Intelligence Officer) per Group will be sent forward with the attacking infantry and will be accompanied by personnel and equipment for opening up telephone, visual, pigeon and runner communication.

The main forward circuit for each Group will be that run for the F.I.O. and will be laid by one Brigade Section officer selected from each Group. This circuit will, if possible, be laid via or near to the position selected for the move forward of Group Hdqrs. F.I.O's and F.O.O's may use single cable; but in the event of new positions of Artillery Brigade Hdqrs and batteries being taken up, only twisted cable will be laid.

III. VISUAL.

1. A Divisional Visual station, call 'DV', in touch with Divisional Headquarters via the BEETROOT FACTORY, has been established at K.25.d.5.8, in the trench at SQUARE COPSE.

Appendices IV, V and VI shew that this station can see our present front line, Right Brigade Hdqrs and the high ground in the area to be attacked, including HIGHLAND RIDGE.

2. Infantry Brigades will arrange Visual by lamp between Brigade forward station and Brigade Hdqrs, and by flapper between Companies and Battalions and Brigade Forward Station.

3. 126th Brigade will arrange to man a visual transmitting station at the O.P., Q.9.a.1.7. This point is a Test point on the buried route in direct communication with 126th Brigade Headquarters. This station is in direct visual communication with the Divisional Visual Station and can see the whole of the present front.

4. 126th Brigade will arrange to test visual communication between one company in Right, Centre and Left Battalion now in the line and the Divisional Visual Station, and will hand this over as a working proposition to Right and Left Brigades on taking over.

5. The Brigade Forward visual party, attacking infantry, F.I.O's and F.O.O's will send information direct by visual to the Divisional Visual Station when practicable, and in the event of their own chain not having been established. Each Brigade forward station will carry a heliograph for this purpose.

V. WIRELESS.

1. Stations will be located as follows:-

(a) Divisional Hdqrs. - Directing Station.
(b) Divnl. Report Centre, P.11 Central - Trench Set.
(c) Right Brigade Hdqrs. - Trench Set.
(d) Left Brigade Hdqrs. - Trench Set.

(d) will advance with Brigade Hdqrs., and will open up communication immediately on arrival at new hdqrs. Spare masts will be carried by both these sets.

2. Power Buzzer - Amplifiers will be established at Right, Left and 126th Brigade Hdqrs and at the Divisional Report Centre.

3. One Loop Set complete with personnel, will be allotted to Right and Left infantry Brigades. The forward station of each Loop Set will accompany 'A' Detachment of the Brigade forward party and will be established at the Brigade forward station to work back to Brigade Hdqrs.

V. MESSAGE CARRYING AGENCIES.

1.

(a) Runners. In the event of complete interruption of communications between Division and the Right Brigade and Group Hdqrs, messages may be sent by runner to 126th Brigade Hdqrs. 126th Brigade will be prepared to establish a Runner system between their Headquarters and Right Brigade Headquarters.

(b). Mounted Officers and Orderlies. Each Infantry Brigade Headquarters will have:-

I. Mounted Officers for communication with flanking Brigades.
ii. Four mounted Orderlies for inter Brigade communication.

Six ~~Sixx~~ mounted Orderlies will be posted at Divisional Report Centre, P.11 central, for communication with Right and Left Brigades and Groups.

(c). Despatch Riders Before zero Motor Cyclist D.R's. will deliver despatches from Divisional Headquarters for both Right and Left Brigades and Groups to the O.P. Dug-out in Quadrangle Trench. Q.9.a.0.5, wher Brigades and Groups will arrange to have orderlies to receive the despatches and take them on to their Headquarters.

After zero, Motor Cyclist D.R's. will deliver direct to the Left Brigade and Group Headquarters, and to about Q.10.a.0.0. for the Right Brigade and Group who will arrange to receive at that point.

When the Left Brigade and Group move to K.35.a.8.4 they will arrange to receive D.R. packets at Q.3.b.3.1, and to take them on to their new Headquarters, until a D.R. route is reconnoitred.

Endeavour to deliver direct by mounted Orderly from Divisional Report Centre will also be made.

2. Pigeons. IV Corps will endeavour to supply 24 pigeons for the whole Division. These will be delivered to:-
   i. Infantry Brigades - eight birds.
   ii. Artillery Groups. - four birds.

for distribution as follows:-

Battalions.	2 each.
Right Brigade Forward Stations.	2 each.
F.I.O's.	2 each.
F.O.O's. (1 Bde per Group).	2 each.

3. Message carrying Rockets.
IV Corps will endeavour to supply 12 Rockets. These will be distributed 6 to each Infantry Brigade Forward Station, and will be carried forward by 'A' Detachment and will be used for communication back to Brigade Headquarters. They will have to be fired at their maximum range, 2000 - 2300 yards; and, in the case of the Left Brigade, a look out Station will be established at about K.35.c.0.0. in order to receive the rocket and convey the message back to Brigade Headquarters by Runner.

VI. SIGNALLING TO AEROPLANES.

1. The Contact Aerpplane will fly over the Battlefield at

Zero+220.	Red Line Objective.
Zero+300.	Brown and Brown dotted line objective.
Zero+420.	Blue line objective.

2. When the plane wishes to locate the forward Infantry, it will sound its Klaxon horn.
The Infantry will signal their position-
(a). By flashing tin discs in the sun.
(b). By lighting flares.
(c). By waving tin hats and handkerchiefs.
(b). Flares will be lighted in groups of 3 or 4, approximately every thirty yards along the front.

3. Code letters for communicating to the plane will be the four letter Code Calls at present in use by the Division.

4. Signalling to the plane will be done by means of the Popham Panel.
Each Brigade Headquarters and all Battalion Headquarters will take Popham Panels and will expose them when wishing to Signal to the Contact Plane.
Ground signal sheets will be exposed by Brigade Headquarters and Battalion Headquarters when the Contact Plane is flying overhead.

5. The Divisional dropping Station will be established at Divisional Headquarters; I.36.d.3.6.

VII. SYNCHRONISATION.

1. Correct time will be taken round to Right and Left Brigade and Group Headquarters by an Officer at an hour and date to be notified later.

2. Watches will not be synchronised by telephone in the area East of a line drawn North and South through PLACE MORTHARE

[signature]

Lt.- Colonel.
General Staff.
42nd Division.

September 25th 1918.

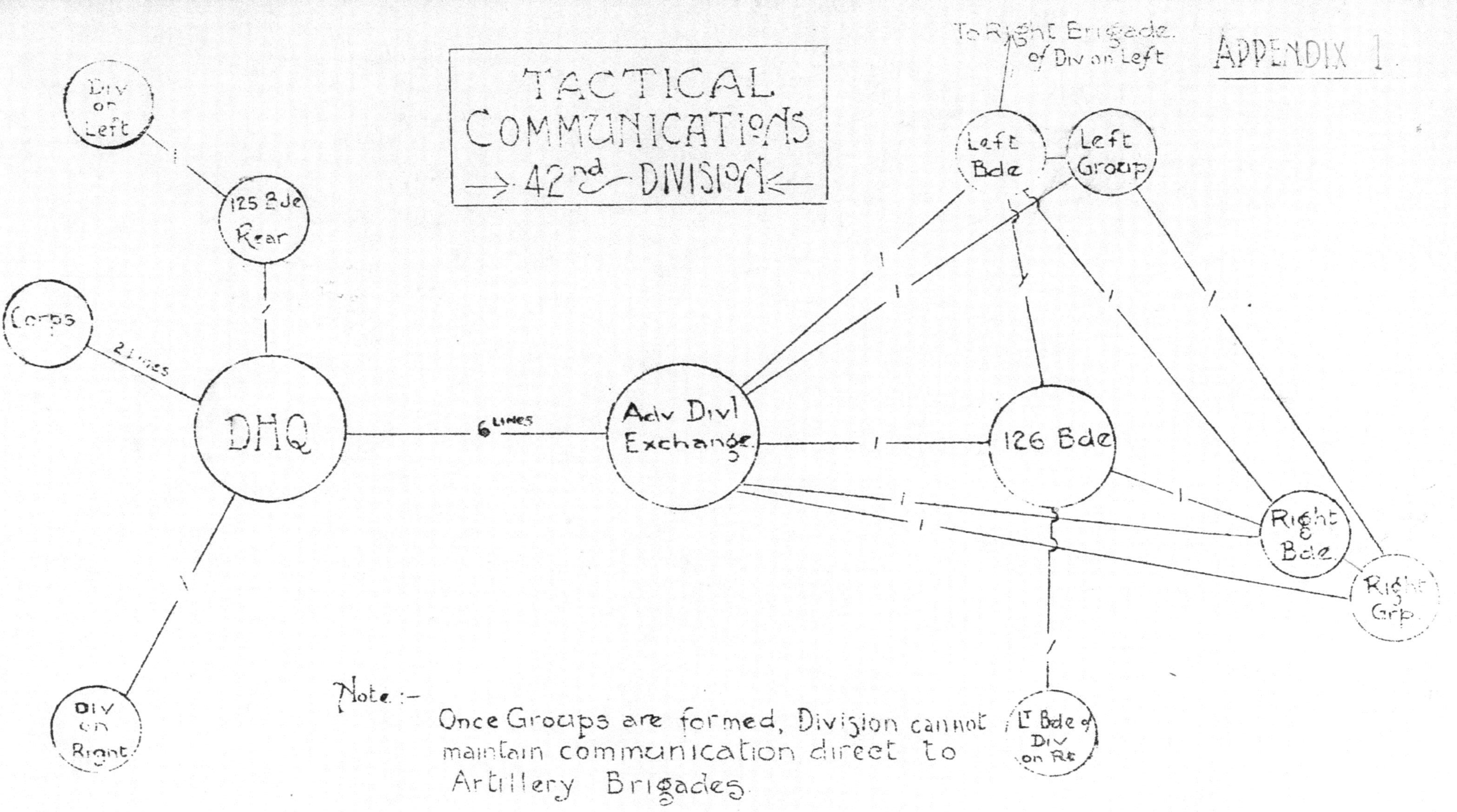
APPENDIX 1.
TACTICAL COMMUNICATIONS
→ 42nd DIVISION ←
To Right Brigade of Div on Left
Div on Left
125 Bde Rear
Corps
2 Lines
DHQ
6 LINES
Adv Divl Exchange
Left Bde
Left Group
126 Bde
Right Bde
Right Grp.
Div on Right
Lt Bde of Div on Rt
Note :- Once Groups are formed, Division cannot maintain communication direct to Artillery Brigades.
Date 26.9.18.

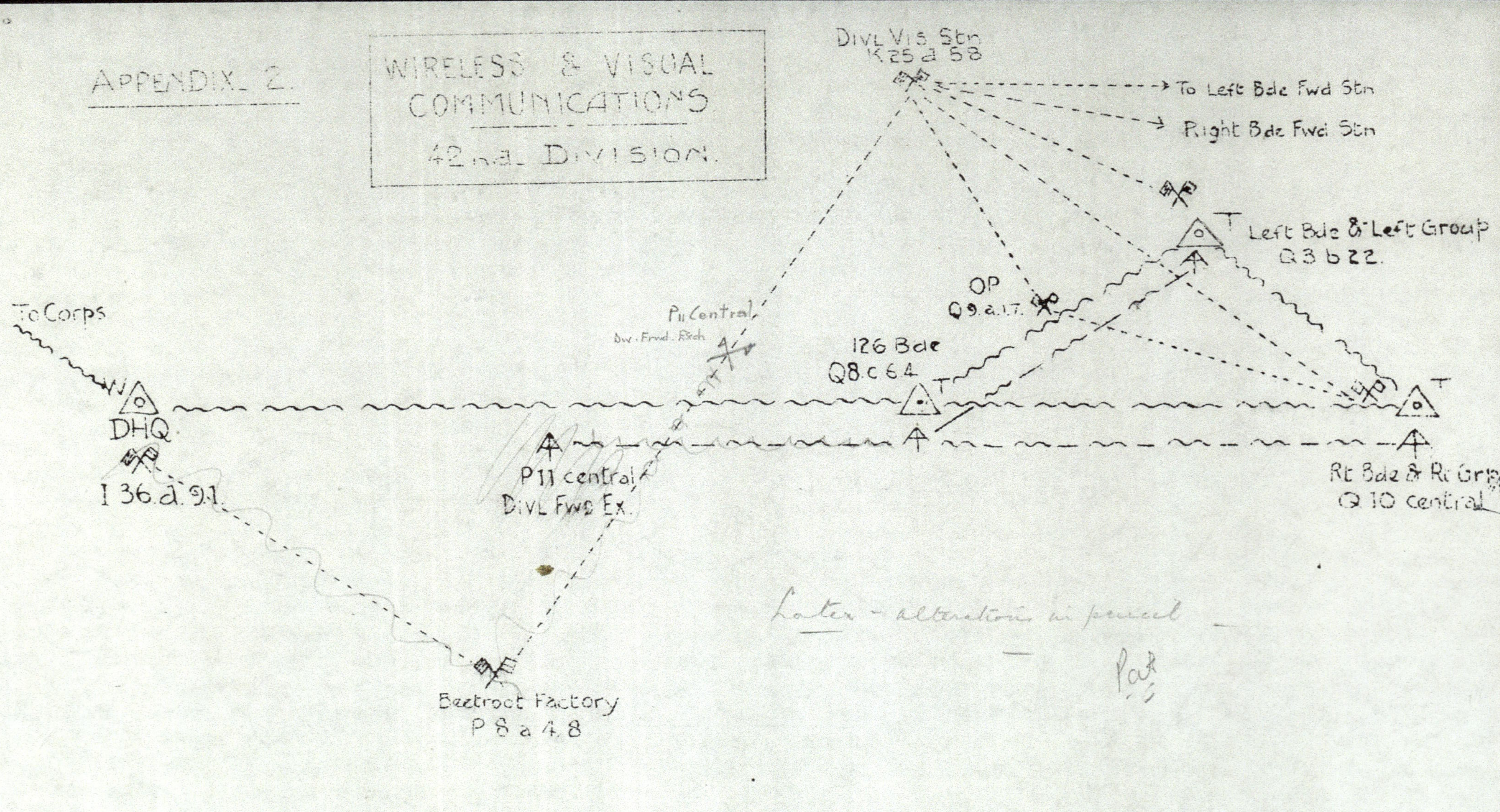

APPENDIX 2.
WIRELESS & VISUAL COMMUNICATIONS
42nd. DIVISION.
Divl Vis Stn
K25 d 58
To Left Bde Fwd Stn
Right Bde Fwd Stn
Left Bde & Left Group
Q3 b 22.
OP
Q9.a.1.7.
126 Bde
Q8 c 6 4
To Corps
W
DHQ
I 36.d.9.1.
P11 Central
Div. Fwd. Exch
P11 central
DIVL Fwd Ex.
Rt Bde & Rt Grp
Q 10 central
Beetroot Factory
P 8 a 4.8
Later – alterations in pencil
26. 9. 18.

APPENDIX . C

SEPTEMBER 1918.

WAR DIARY.

HONOURS AND AWARDS.

The Corps Commander, under authority granted by His Majesty the King, has awarded the following decoration to the under-mentioned man:-

MILITARY MEDAL.

No.249176 Pnr Pugh,F.J.

Patey

Major. R.E.

4.10.18.

O.C. 42nd Divisional Signal Co.R.E.

APPENDIX . D SEPTEMBER 1918.

WAR DIARY.

WEEKLY STRENGTHS, CASUALTIES, REINFORCEMENTS.

Weekly Strengths.

	Officers.	O.R.
Week ending Sept. 7th.	12	316
" " " 14th.	12	311
" " " 21st.	12	308
" " " 28th.	12	301.

Casualties.

Killed.	-	3
Wounded and gassed.	-	7
Hospital.	-	10
To Depot.	-	5
	-	25

Reinforcements.

From hospital.	-	3
From Depot.	-	7
	-	10

Paton

Major.R.E.

4.10.18. O.C. 42nd Divisional Signal Co.R.E.

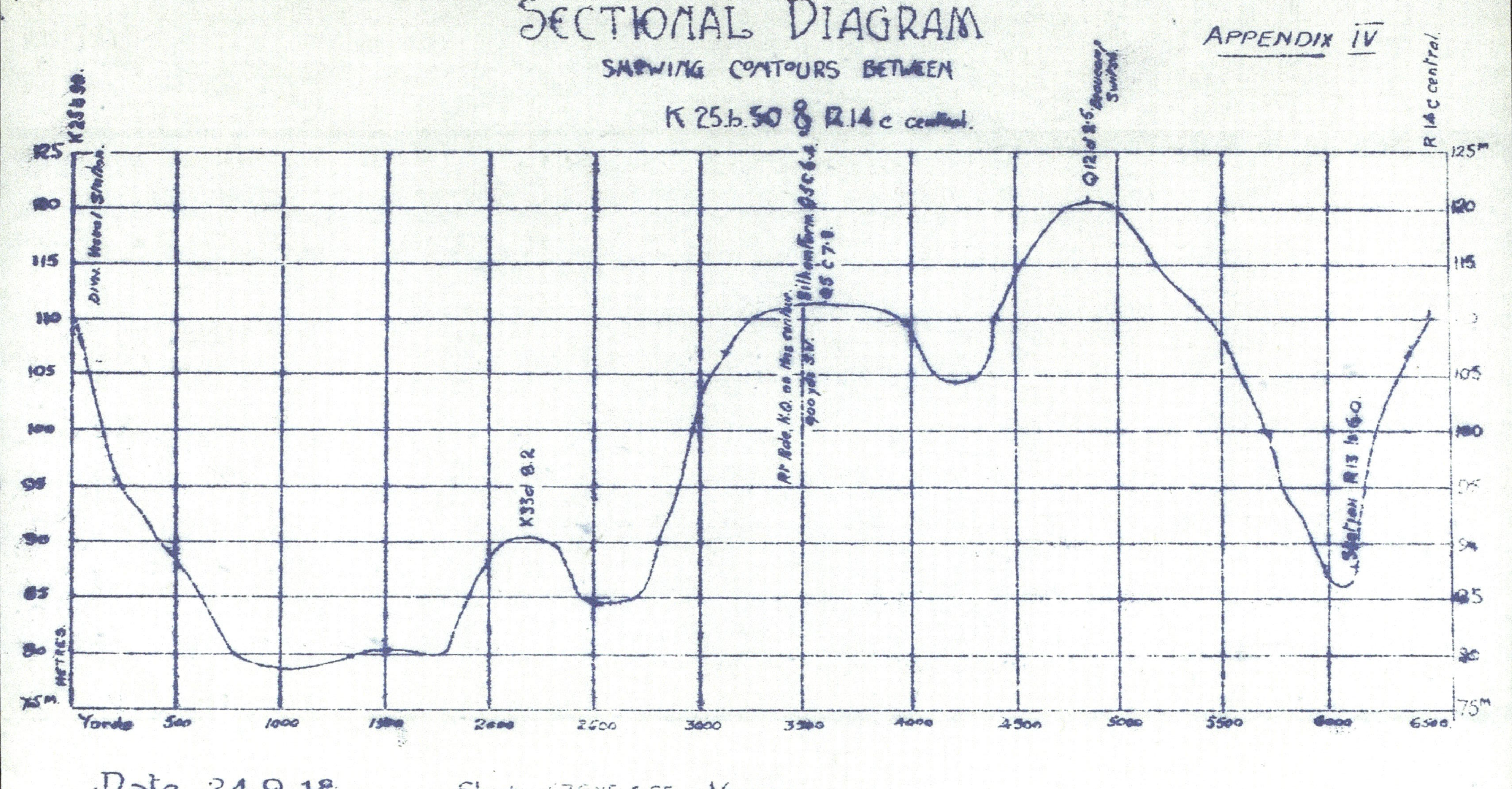
SECTIONAL DIAGRAM
SHOWING CONTOURS BETWEEN
K 25.b.50 & R.14 c central.
APPENDIX IV
K25b90.
Divn. Wood/Station.
K33d 8.2
Rt Bde. H.Q. on this contour. 900 yds S.W.
Bilhem Farm Q5c6.4.
Q5 c 7.8.
Q12d 8.5. Beaucamp Switch
Station R13 b 6.0.
R 14 c central.
METRES.
Yards 500 1000 1500 2000 2500 3000 3500 4000 4500 5000 5500 6000 6500.
125 120 115 110 105 100 95 90 85 80 75m
Date 24.9.18.
Sheets 57c NE & SE. 1/20000.

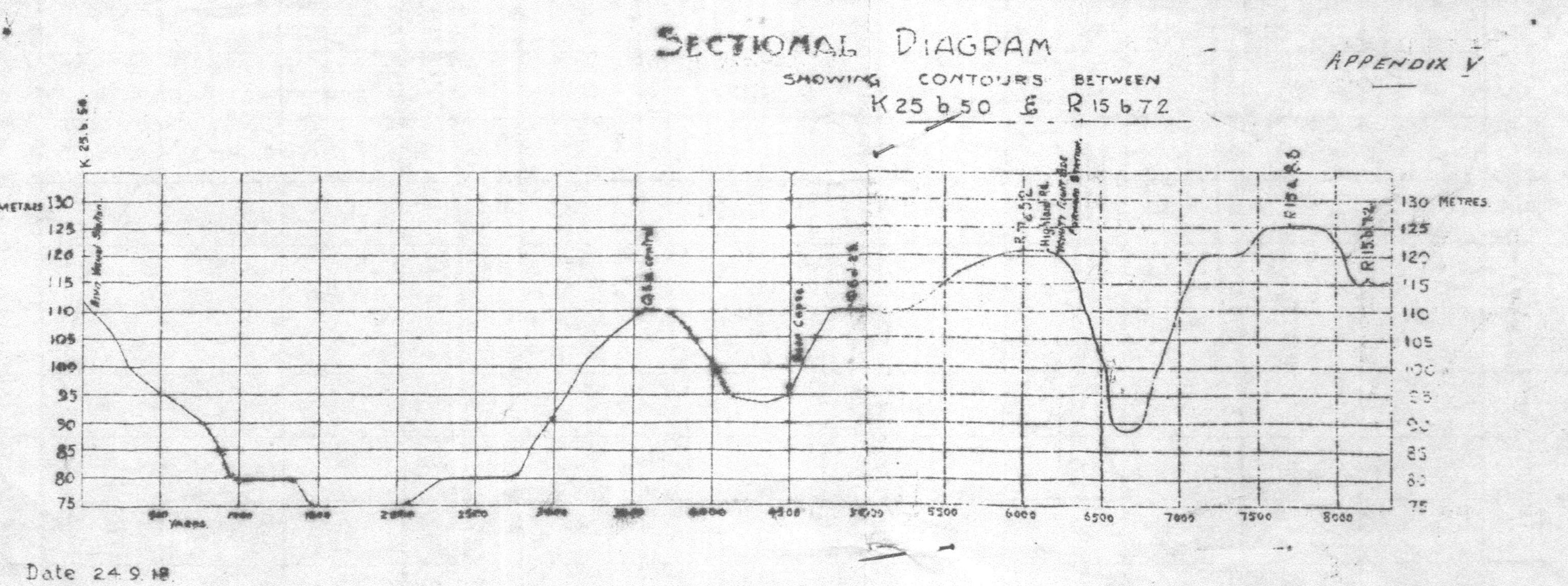

SECTIONAL DIAGRAM
SHOWING CONTOURS BETWEEN
K 25 b 50 & R 15 b 72
APPENDIX V
METRES
130
125
120
115
110
105
100
95
90
85
80
75
130 METRES
YARDS
5500
6000
6500
7000
7500
8000
Date 24.9.18.

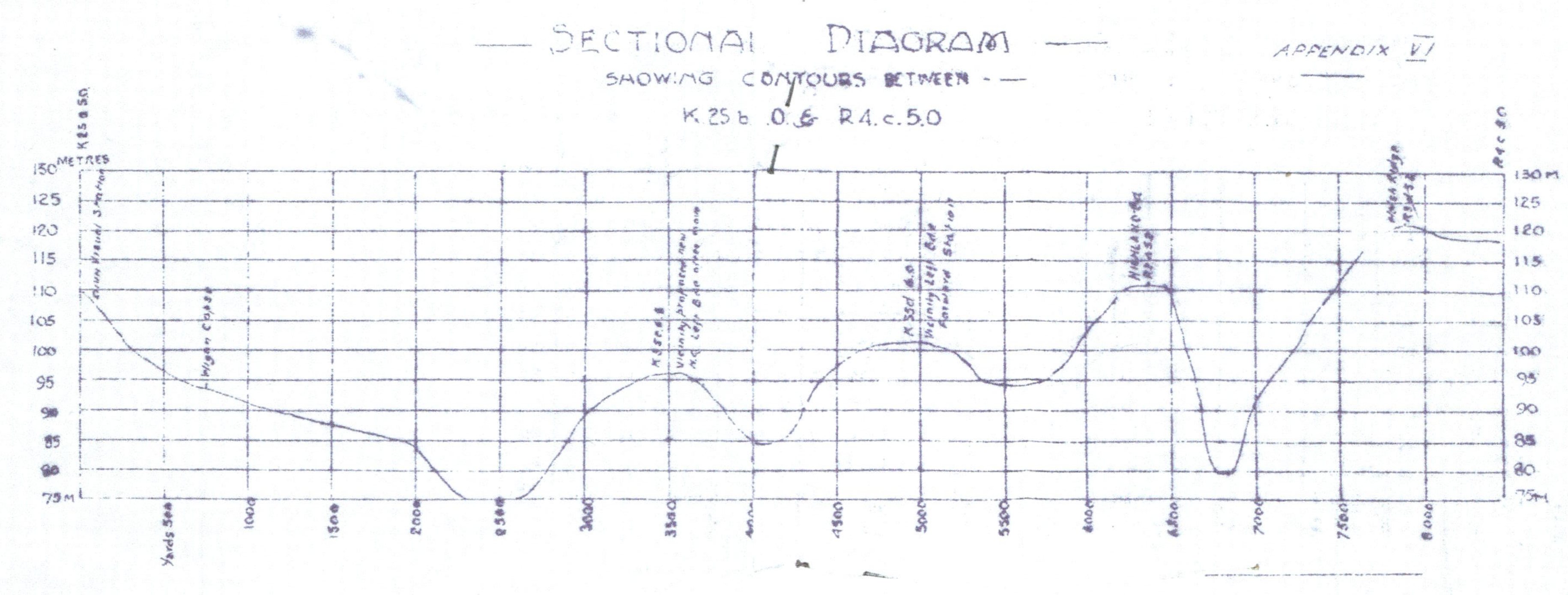
APPENDIX VI
SECTIONAL DIAGRAM
SHOWING CONTOURS BETWEEN
K.25 b .0.5 & R4.c.5.0
METRES
130
125
120
115
110
105
100
95
90
85
80
75M
130M
Wigan Copse
Yards 500
1000
1500
2000
2500
3000
3500
4500
5000
5500
6000
6500
7000
7500
8000

Appendix E

Message Chart

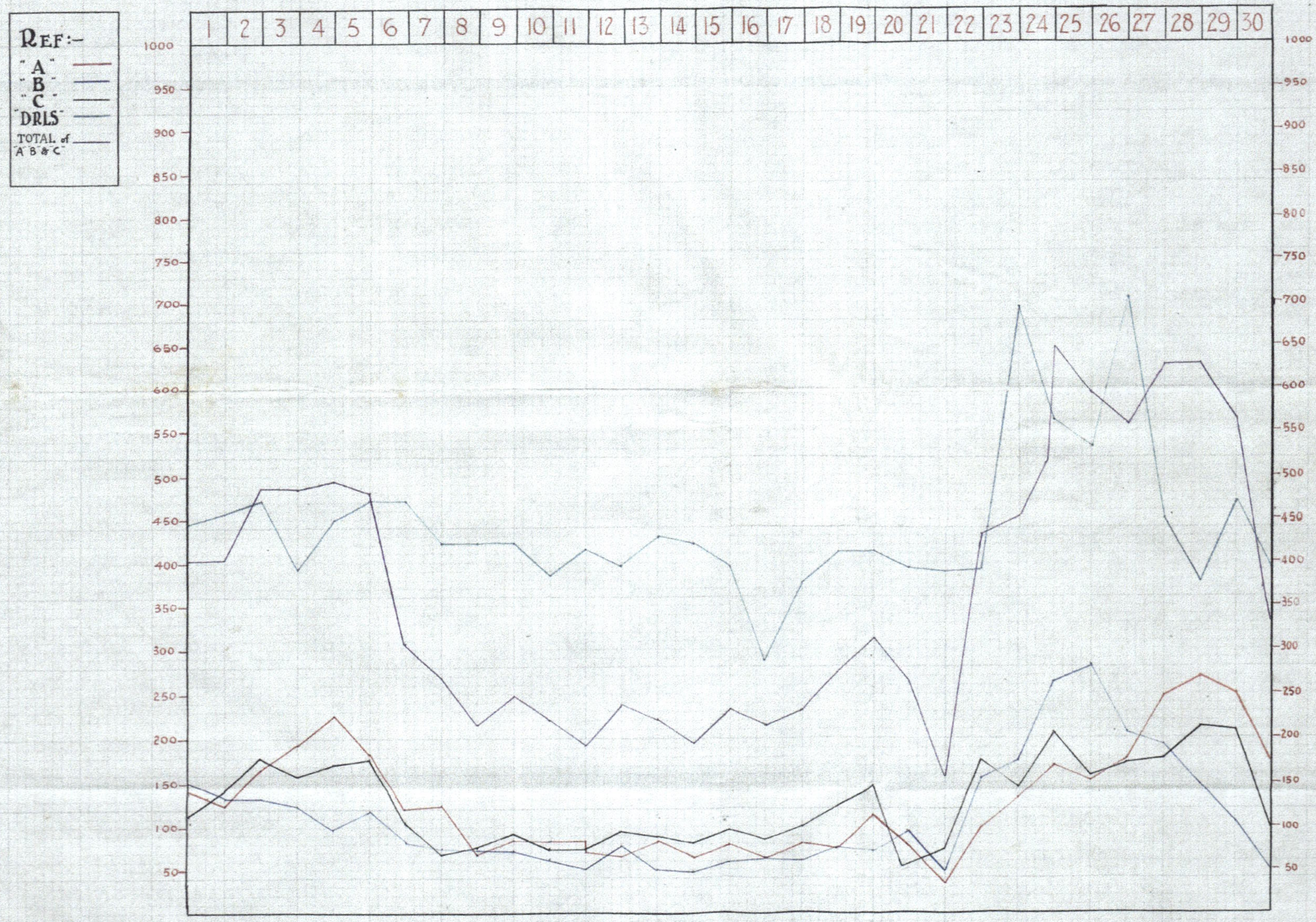

Ref:-
"A"
"B"
"C"
"DRLS"
Total of "A B & C"

1 2 3 4 5 6 7 8 9 10 11 12 13 14 15 16 17 18 19 20 21 22 23 24 25 26 27 28 29 30

1000 950 900 850 800 750 700 650 600 550 500 450 400 350 300 250 200 150 100 50

September 1918.

Major: R.E.
O.C. 42nd Divisional Signal Company R.E.

APPENDIX "E"

APPENDIX E

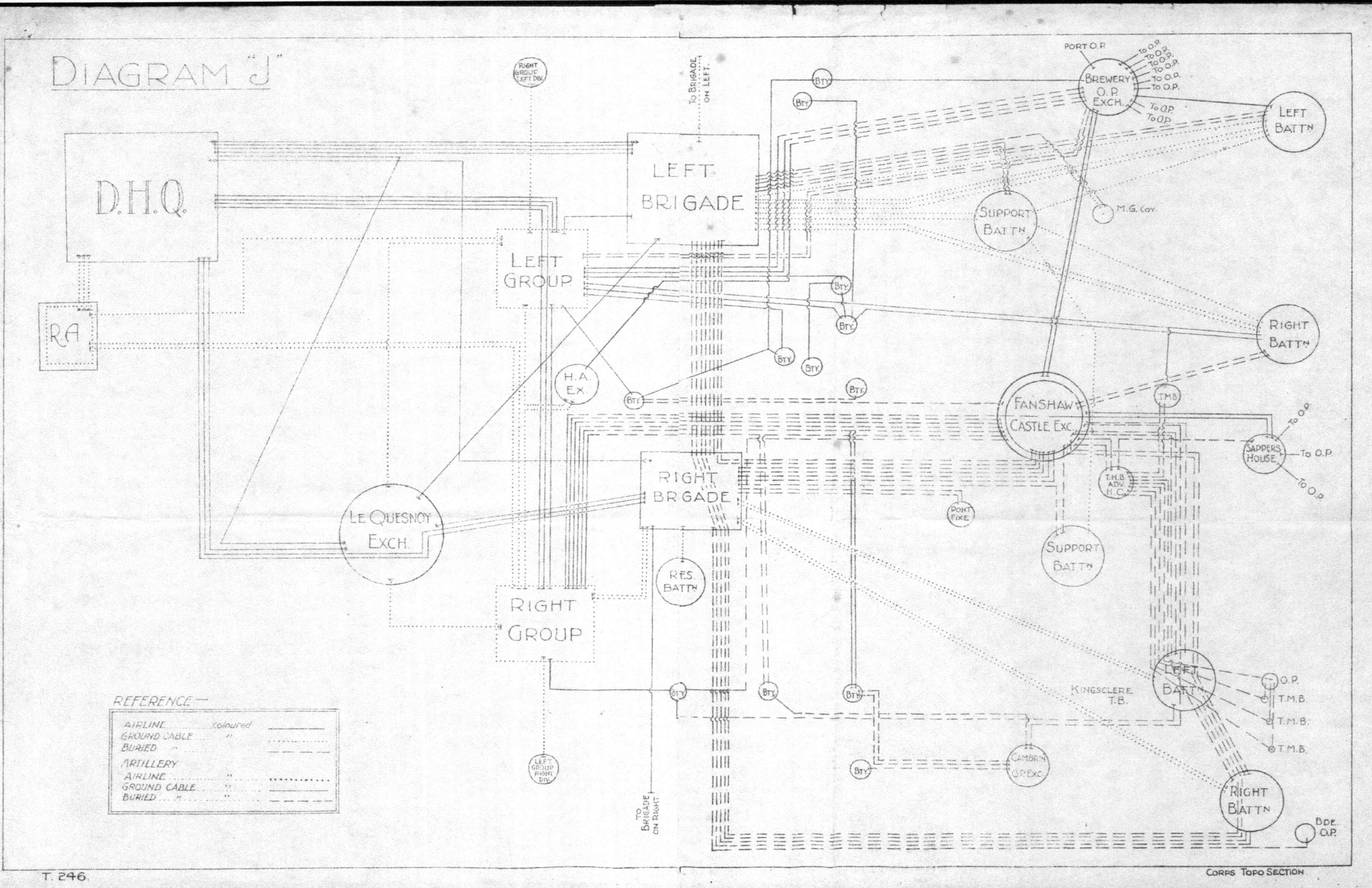

DIAGRAM "J"
D.H.Q.
R.A.
LEFT BRIGADE
RIGHT BRIGADE
LEFT GROUP
RIGHT GROUP
LE QUESNOY EXCH.
H.A. EX.
RES. BATTN
RIGHT GROUP LEFT DIV.
LEFT GROUP RIGHT DIV.
TO BRIGADE ON LEFT.
TO BRIGADE ON RIGHT
BTY.
PORT O.P.
BREWERY O.P. EXCH.
TO O.P.
LEFT BATTN
SUPPORT BATTN
M.G. COY.
RIGHT BATTN
FANSHAW CASTLE EXC.
T.M.B.
SAPPERS HOUSE
T.M.B. ADV. H.C.
PONT FIXE
SUPPORT BATTN
KINGSCLERE T.B.
LEFT BATTN
O.P.
T.M.B.
CAMBRIN O.P. EXC.
RIGHT BATTN
BDE. O.P.
REFERENCE—
AIRLINE .... coloured
GROUND CABLE ...... "
BURIED ...... "
ARTILLERY
AIRLINE .... "
GROUND CABLE ...... "
BURIED ...... "
T. 246.
CORPS TOPO SECTION

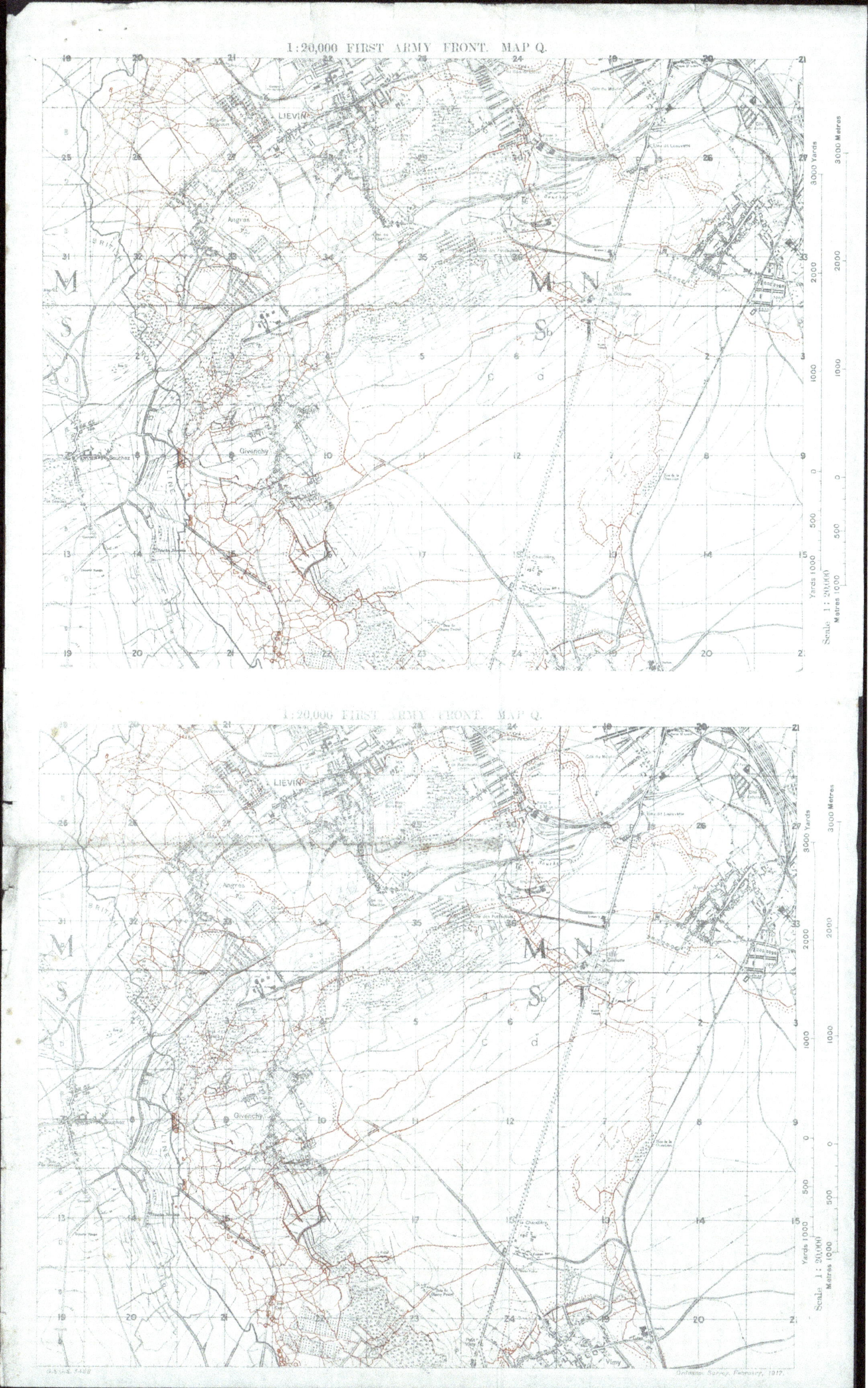

1:20,000 FIRST ARMY FRONT. MAP Q.
LIEVIN
Angres
Givenchy
Souchez
M
N
S
T
Scale 1 : 20,000
Yards 1000
Metres 1000
3000 Yards
3000 Metres
1:20,000 FIRST ARMY FRONT. MAP Q.
LIEVIN
Angres
Givenchy
Souchez
Vimy
M
N
S
T
Scale 1 : 20,000
Yards 1000
Metres 1000
3000 Yards
3000 Metres
Ordnance Survey, February, 1917.

Secret

Vol 20

WAR DIARY

42nd DIVISIONAL SIGNAL COY. R.E.

CHAPTER XXIV

4th Nov. 1918.

Paton.
Major R.E.
O.C. 42nd Divl Signal Coy. R.E.

Instructions regarding War Diaries and Intelligence Summaries are contained in F. S. Regs., Part II. and the Staff Manual respectively. Title pages will be prepared in manuscript.

WAR DIARY
or
INTELLIGENCE SUMMARY.
(Erase heading not required.)

Army Form C. 2118.

Place	Date	Hour	Summary of Events and Information	Remarks and references to Appendices
			42ND (East Lancs) Divisional Signal Coy. R.E. (TF) Reference Map FRANCE, 1/40,000, Sheets 57.B. and 57.C. CHAPTER XXIV. OCTOBER 1918.	
VELU WOOD.	1.10.18.		42nd Division in reserve. Communications as shown in diagram 1. Overhauling cable and stores, cleaning and refitting.	
	2.10.18.		Divisional Commander inspected the Company at 2 p.m. and presented medal ribbons to several N.C.O's. and men.	
	3.10.18.		All Detachments working recovering cable.	
	4.10.18.		Two Detachments recovering cable, one Detachment improving and labelling existing lines and the other overhauling cable.	
	5.10.18.		One Detachment recovering cable - remainder overhauling cable. M.T. Company connected to Divisional Exchange.	
	6.10.18.		All available men on running through recovered cable. Mobile Workshops at VELU connected to Divisional Exchange.	
	7.10.18.		Cable from Signal Office to road at P1A8.2 NR BERTINCOURT recovered and line (Division to 126 Brigade) put through on permanent route. Company transport moved from LEBUCQUIRE to VELU WOOD. C & D Cable Detachments moved complete to Q.10.central - Rear N.Z.Division H.Q.	
Q.10.CENTRAL.	8.10.18.		D.H.Q. and Company moved to Q.10.central. Communications as shown in diagram 2.	
ESNES.	9.10.18.		D.H.Q. and Company moved to ESNES. No lines laid to Brigades. Communication by Despatch Rider.	
	10.10.18.		Cables (D.8.twisted) laid to 126 Brigade at Brisseux (N10c 2.2) and 127 Brigade at le Grand Pont Nr ESNES.	

A7092). Wt. W12839/M1293 750,000. 1/17. D. D & L., Ltd. Forms/C2118/14.

Army Form C. 2118.

WAR DIARY

or

~~INTELLIGENCE-SUMMARY~~.

(Erase heading not required.)

Instructions regarding War Diaries and Intelligence Summaries are contained in F. S. Regs., Part II. and the Staff Manual respectively. Title pages will be prepared in manuscript.

Place	Date	Hour	Summary of Events and Information	Remarks and references to Appendices
ESNES.	11.10.18.		Communications as shown in diagram 3 (APPENDIX 'A')	
BEAUVOIS-en-CAMBRESIS	12.10.18.		Move in accordance with Order No.25./ Communications as shown in diagram 4.	APPENDIX 'A'
	13.10.18. to 16.10.18.		Improved existing communications - labelling, strengthening lines to Brigades and flanking Divisions.	
	17.10.18.		Laid two pairs poled cable (D.8 twisted) from AULICOURT FARM to cellar of Ruined Cottage at D.27.a.3.8.- proposed place for Divisional Forward Exchange.	
	18.10.18.		Three pairs (D.8. twisted) laid from D.27.a.3.8. to proposed Battle Headquarters for two Infantry Brigades and Main Artillery Group at D.22.a.6.6. Also one pair (D.3. twisted) from PRAYELLE to J.4.b.1.9.(Sub-Group Artillery Headquarters).	
	19.10.18.		One pair (D.3.twisted) laid from PRAYELLE to Brigade of Division on Left at QUIEVY. Two pairs (D.8.twisted) laid from D.27.a.3.8. to PRAYELLE. All lines patrolled, poled where necessary, and labelled. Lines from Division connected through at D.27.a.3.8 to PRAYELLE - Battle Headquarters of 126 and 127 Infantry Brigades and Main Group of Artillery.	
	20.10.18.		Division attacked. Communications as outlined in Battle Instructions No. 1 Appendix B. Messenger dogs used successfully between Battalion HQ and Brigade Report Centre. Line communications to Brigades and Artillery Group maintained throughout the operations.	APPENDIX 'B'
	21.10.18.		Two pairs (D.8.twisted) laid from D.22.a.6.6. to E.19.a.3.4. new Headquarters of 125 Infantry Brigade and Main Group of Artillery. Advanced Divisional Office established in cellar at D.27.a.3.8. Lines diverted and extended where necessary. Communications as shown in diagram 5. One pair (D.8.twisted) laid from D.22.a.3.8. to Right Group at VIESLY. Line to Brigade of 62 Division on left extended about 400 yards to 3rd Divisional Headquarters at QUIEVY. One pair on Corps open route which previously connected Brigade at PRAYELLE	

A7092). Wt. W12839/M1293 750,000. 1/17. D. D & L., Ltd. Forms/C2118/14.

Army Form C. 2118.

Instructions regarding War Diaries and Intelligence Summaries are contained in F. S. Regs., Part II. and the Staff Manual respectively. Title pages will be prepared in manuscript.

WAR DIARY
or
~~INTELLIGENCE SUMMARY.~~
(Erase heading not required.)

Place	Date	Hour	Summary of Events and Information	Remarks and references to Appendices
			to Division diverted to Advanced Divisional Office and forward portion of route used to connect Advanced Division to Forward Corps Exchange at BRIASTRE.	
	23.10.18.		Division attacked. Communications as shown in diagram 6. Line communication to attacking Brigade and Left Group at E.19.a.3.4. and Right Group 500 yards East of VIESLY maintained throughout the operations. Division relieved by N.Z. Division. Advanced Division closed at 3 p.m. Communications as described in diagram 7, Three Detachments recovering cable.	
	24.10.18. to 31.10.18.		During this period the Division remained in reserve with Headquarters at BEAUVOIS en-CAMBRESIS. Thirty miles of cable were recovered and overhauled. The mornings were devoted to drill, overhauling cable, stores, etc. cleaning equipment and refitting. The afternoons to recreation.	

APPENDICES TO THIS DIARY.

(A) Company Order No. 25.
(B) Battle Instructions No 1.
(C) Weekly strengths, Casualties, Reinforcements etc.
(D) Monthly Message Chart.

4.11.18.

Paton
Major. R.E.
O.C. 42nd Divisional Signal Co. R.E.

A7092). Wt. W12839/M1297 750,000. 1/17. D. D & L., Ltd. Forms/C2118/14.

Instructions regarding War Diaries and Intelligence Summaries are contained in F. S. Regs., Part II. and the Staff Manual respectively. Title pages will be prepared in manuscript.

Army Form C. 2118.

42

WAR DIARY
or
~~INTELLIGENCE SUMMARY.~~
(Erase heading not required.)

42 D Signals

22

Place	Date	Hour	Summary of Events and Information	Remarks and references to Appendices
			42nd (East Lancs) Divisional Signal Co. RE(TF) Reference Maps BELGIUM (Valenciennes) sheet 12.L.3. & BELGIUM. NAMUR. sheet 8. F.2.	
			DECEMBER 1918. CHAPTER	
HAUTMONT.	1.12.18		Signal Company Headquarters in billets at HAUTMONT, France.	
Move to BINCHE, Belgium.	14.12.18.		Transport and mounted men proceeded by march route to BINCHE and billeted there until 16.12.18.	
Move to CHARLEROI	16.12.18.		Transport and mounted men proceeded by march route to CHARLEROI. The remainder of the Company having arrived during the past three days by Motor lorry from HAUTMONT. Company Headquarters remained with Divisional Headquarters in billets in the town of CHARLEROI until the end of the month. Horse Lines being located at DAMPRENY.	
			The 14th Course of the Divisional Signal Class closed at HERPIGNY FARM near CAUDRY on December 10th, the personnel of staff and students returning to their units.	
			APPENDICES TO THIS DIARY.	
			(A). Honours and Awards.	
			(B). Weekly Strengths, Casualties, Reinforcements.	

16.1.19.

Paton
Major. R.E.
O.C. 42nd Divisional Signal Co. R.E.

A7092). Wt. W12839/M1293 750,000. 1/17. D. D & L., Ltd. Forms/C2118/14.

APPENDIX A .   DECEMBER 1918.

WAR DIARY.

HONOURS AND AWARDS.

The Field Marshal Commanding-in - Chief, under authority granted by His Majesty the King, has awarded the following decorations to the undermentioned Officers:-

MILITARY CROSS.

Lieut. G.H.OSMASTON.
Lieut. P.C.FLETCHER.

The Corps Commander, under authority granted by His Majesty the King, has awarded the following decoration to the undermentioned:-

DISTINGUISHED CONDUCT MEDAL.

No.444011 CSM. WILLCOCK,H.

Paton

Major. R.E.
16.1.19.   O.C. 42nd Divisional Signal Co. R.E.

APPENDIX B. DECEMBER. 1918.

WAR DIARY.

WEEKLY STRENGTHS, CASUALTIES, REINFORCEMENTS, etc.

Weekly strengths.	Officers.	O.R.
Week ending December 7th.	11	292
" " " 14th.	11	304
" " " 21st.	11	303
" " " 28th.	11	301

Casualties.		
Died.	-	1
Sick.	-	9
Demobilized.	-	9
Total.	-	19

Reinforcements.		
From Hospital.	-	3
" Depot.	-	47
Total.	-	50

Paton

Major. R.E.

16.1.19. O.C. 42nd Divisional Signal Co. R.E.

APPENDIX 'A'.

SECRET.

Copy No 2.

42nd DIVISIONAL SIGNAL COMPANY. R.E.(T.F). ORDER No. 25.

1. 42nd Division (less Artillery) will relieve the N.Z. Division in the line (Left Sector, IV Corps) on the night 12th/13th October, command passing to G.O.C. 42nd Division at 1830 hours, October 12th.

2. Divisional Headquarters will close at ESNES at 1000 hours, October 12th, opening at BEAUVOIS -EN - CAMBRESIS (I.9.d.2.2) at the same hour.

3. The Company will move under the following arrangements:-

Time.	Remarks.
0600.	Lorry with Technical Stores, Cable and Signal Office relief. N.C.O. i/c Sgt. Moores.
0630.	Box Car with Wireless and Visual equipment. N.C.O. i/c Cpl Campbell.
0700.	'A' and 'B' Cable Detachments. N.C.O. i/c Sgt. McCarthy.
0900.	Box Car with Officer's kits and Mess Stores. N.C.O. i/c L/Cpl Burne.
0900.	Lorry with Cable, Orderly Room, and Q.M. Stores. N.C.O. i/c Sgt. McGuigan.
0930.	All horse transport and personnel. Officer i/c Lieut. A.J.Ellis.,M.C.
0930.	P.E.L. lorry with D.R's. Stores, W/T Directing Station. N.C.O. i/c Cpl Fuller.
1130.	Lorry with remaining kits, Signal Office personnel and Stores. W.O. i/c C.S.M. Willcock.

4. The C.Q.M.S. will billet the Company at BEAUVOIS -EN- CAMBRESIS.

5. The C.S.M. will be responsible for seeing that the Camp, Horse Lines, all billets and Offices at ESNES, are left clean.

AJEllis
Lieut. R.E.
for O.C. 42nd Divisional Signal Co.R.E.

11.10.18.
Issued by

Copy No. 1. O.C.
2. War Diary.
3. File.
4. Captain Roberts.
5. Lieut. Ellis.
6. C.S.M.
7. C.Q.M.S.
8. Sgt. McGuigan.
9. Sgt. Harrison.
10. Sgt. Moores.

APPENDIX 'B'. SECRET.

42nd DIVISION.

BATTLE INSTRUCTIONS No. 1.

SIGNAL COMMUNICATIONS.

I. General.
II. Telephone and Telegraph.
III. Visual.
IV. Wireless.
V. Message carrying Agencies.
(1). Mounted Orderlies.
(2). Pigeons.
(3). Message carrying Rockets.
(4). Messenger Dogs.

APPENDICES I to V - Diagrams.

I. GENERAL.

1. Position of Headquarters.

Divisional Headquarters.	BEAUVOIS.
126th Bde. Headquarters.)	
127th Bde. Headquarters.)	PRAYELLE.
Main Group, R.F.A.)	
Sub-group. R.F.A.	J.4.b.1.9.
Reserve Brigade.	BEAUVOIS.
Advanced Report Centres of)	D.22.central.
126th and 127th Brigades.)	

2. 127th Infantry Brigade Headquarters and Main Group Headquarters will move to the vicinity of E.14.d. when the final objective has been captured.

3. The following diagrams are appended;-
Appendix I. Divisional cable Communications as existing on Y/Z night.
Appendix II. Visual and Wireless Communications as existing on Y/Z night.
Appendix III. 126th Inf. Bde. Communications at zero hour.
Appendix IV. Infantry Forward Communications to be established after zero hour when practicable.
Appendix V. Section of country, D.22.a. to E.10.d, showing visual possibilities.

II. TELEPHONE AND TELEGRAPH.

Communications during the attack.

Infantry.

1. For 126th Brigade Communications, see Appendices III and IV.
2. 127th Brigade Communications will be run on the lines laid down in S.S.191 and as circulated with 42nd Division G.S.116/73, d/7.10.18. See Appendix IV.
3. The Report Centre, (126th Brigade), to be established in D.23.d.5.7. and the Brigade Forward Station (127th Brigade) to be established in E.14.c. will both accept and transmit messages for all arms. The position selected at E.14.c. will be marked by a blue and white flag.

Artillery.

1. One Forward Intelligence Officer per Group and one Forward Observation Officer per Artillery Brigade will be sent forward with the attacking infantry, and will proceed, in the first place, to the high ground in E.14.b. and d., and later to the ridge in E.15.b and d. They will be accompanied by personnel and equipment to open up and maintain telephone, visual, rocket and runner communication back to Group and Brigade Hqrs respectively.

III. VISUAL.

Visual will be established as shown in Appendices II, III and IV.

IV. WIRELESS.

Wireless Communications will be established in accordance with Appendices II, III and IV.

Trench Sets, allotted to 126th and 127th Brigade Hqrs, will move forward with those Hqrs, and open up on arrival at new positions without delay.

V. MESSAGE CARRYING AGENCIES.

1. Mounted Orderlies. Four mounted orderlies will be stationed at Divisional Battle Hqrs, for carrying despatches to Brigade Hqrs if required.
2. Pigeons. Only 8 pigeons are available for the operation. These will be allotted to 127th Brigade.
3. Message Carrying Rockets. Rockets are being distributed as follows:-

126th Brigade.	12 rockets, 1 stand.
127th Brigade.	12 rockets, 1 stand.
Main Group.	12 rockets, 1 stand.
Sub-Group.	12 rockets, 1 stand.

and will be used as indicated in Appendices III and IV.

4. Messenger Dogs. Three messenger dogs will be allotted to 126th Brigade Hqrs, and will be used as indicated in Appendices III and IV.

R. G. Hay

Lt. Colonel,
General Staff,
42nd Division.

October 19th, 1918.

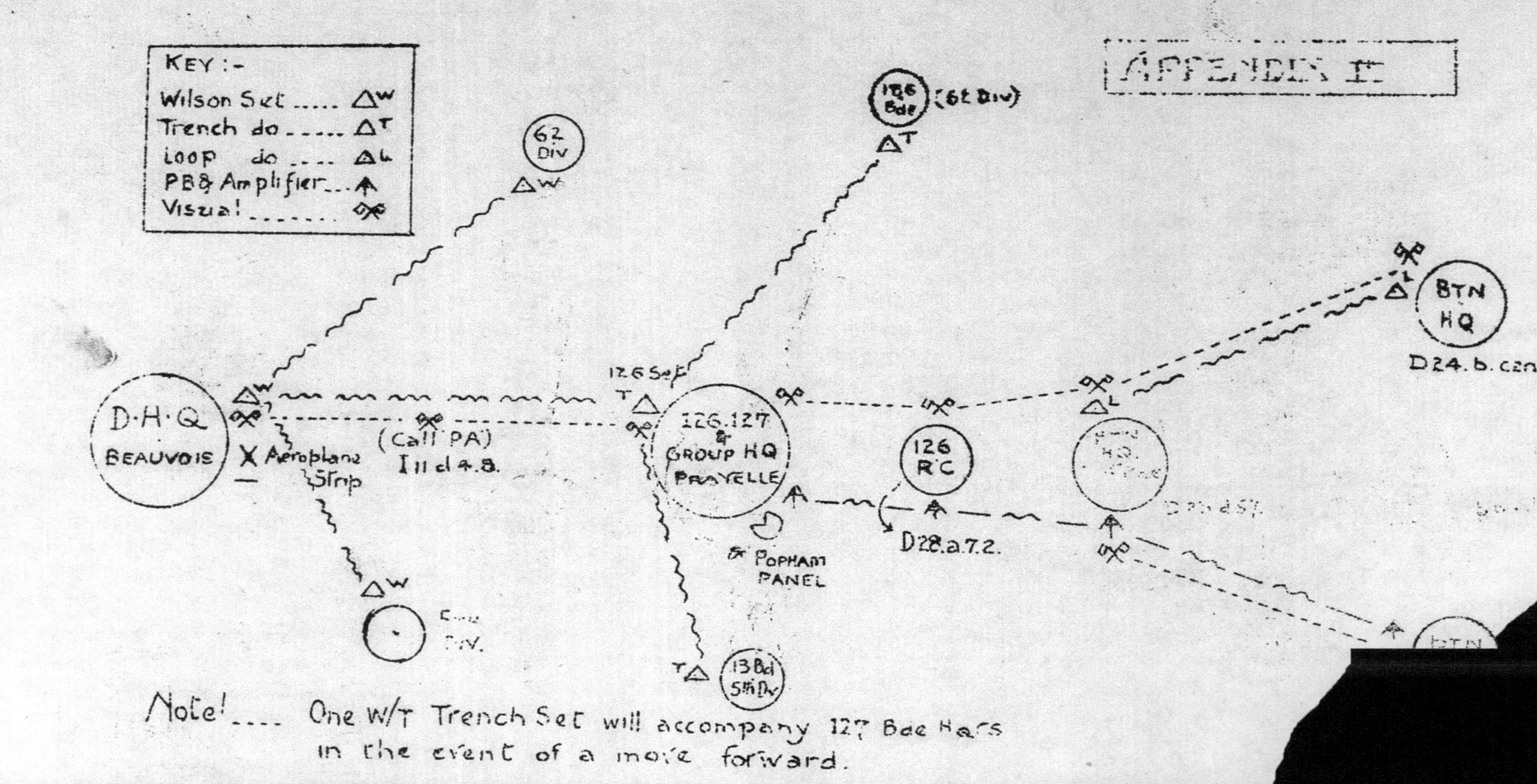
APPENDIX II
KEY :-
Wilson Set ..... △W
Trench do ..... △T
Loop do ..... △L
PB & Amplifier ...
Visual ....
62 DIV
126 Bde (62 Div)
D·H·Q BEAUVOIS
Aeroplane Strip
(Call PA)
I 11 d 4.8.
126 Set
126.127 & GROUP HQ PRAYELLE
126 R C
D28.a.7.2.
Popham Panel
13 Bd 5th Div
BTN HQ
D24.b.cent.
Note! .... One W/T Trench Set will accompany 127 Bde Hqrs
in the event of a move forward.

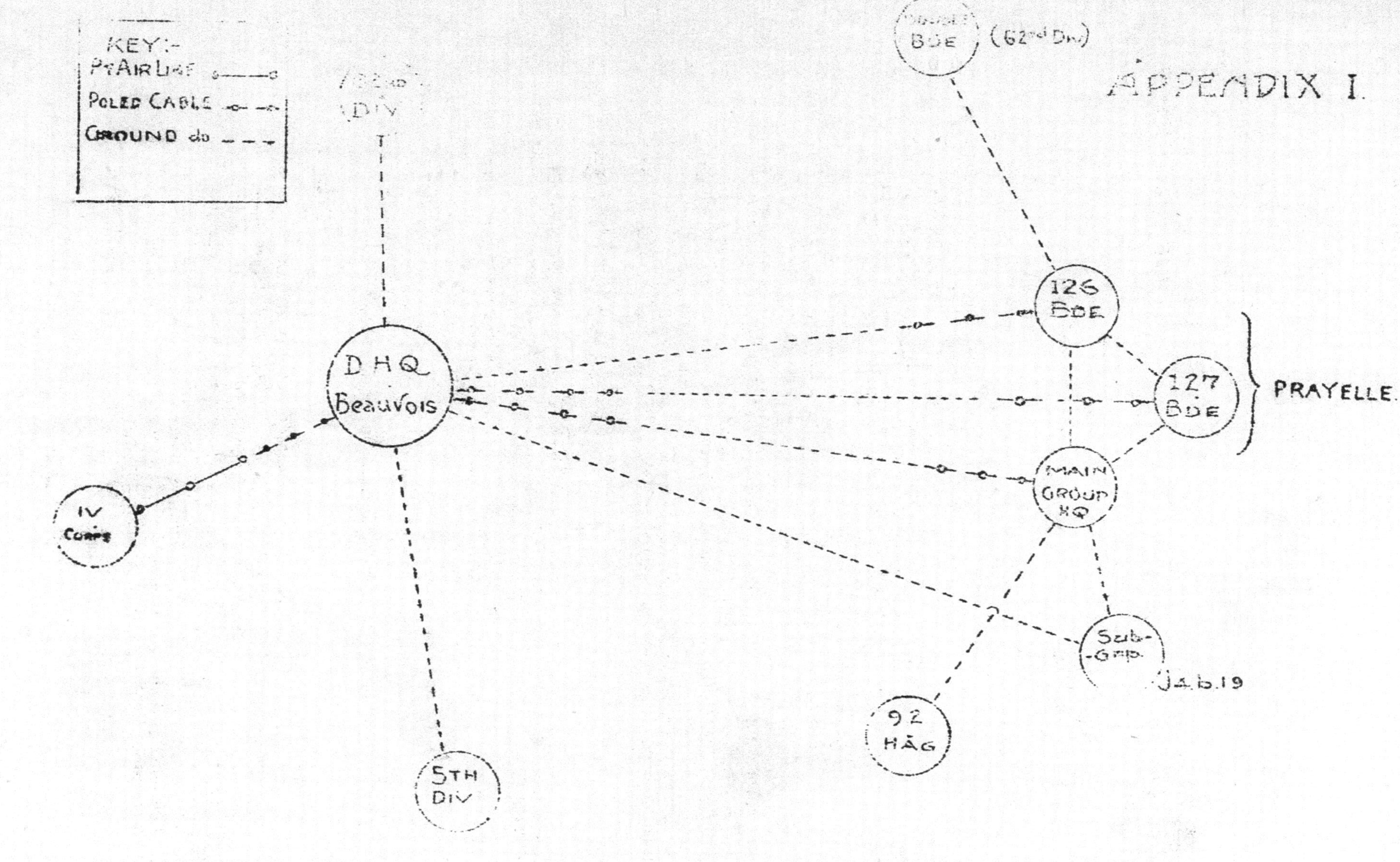
APPENDIX I.
KEY:-
PrAirLine
Poled Cable
Ground do
DIV
DHQ
Beauvois
IV
Corps
5TH
DIV
BDE
126
BDE
127
BDE
PRAYELLE.
MAIN
GROUP
HQ
Sub-
Grp.
92
HAG

APPENDIX IV

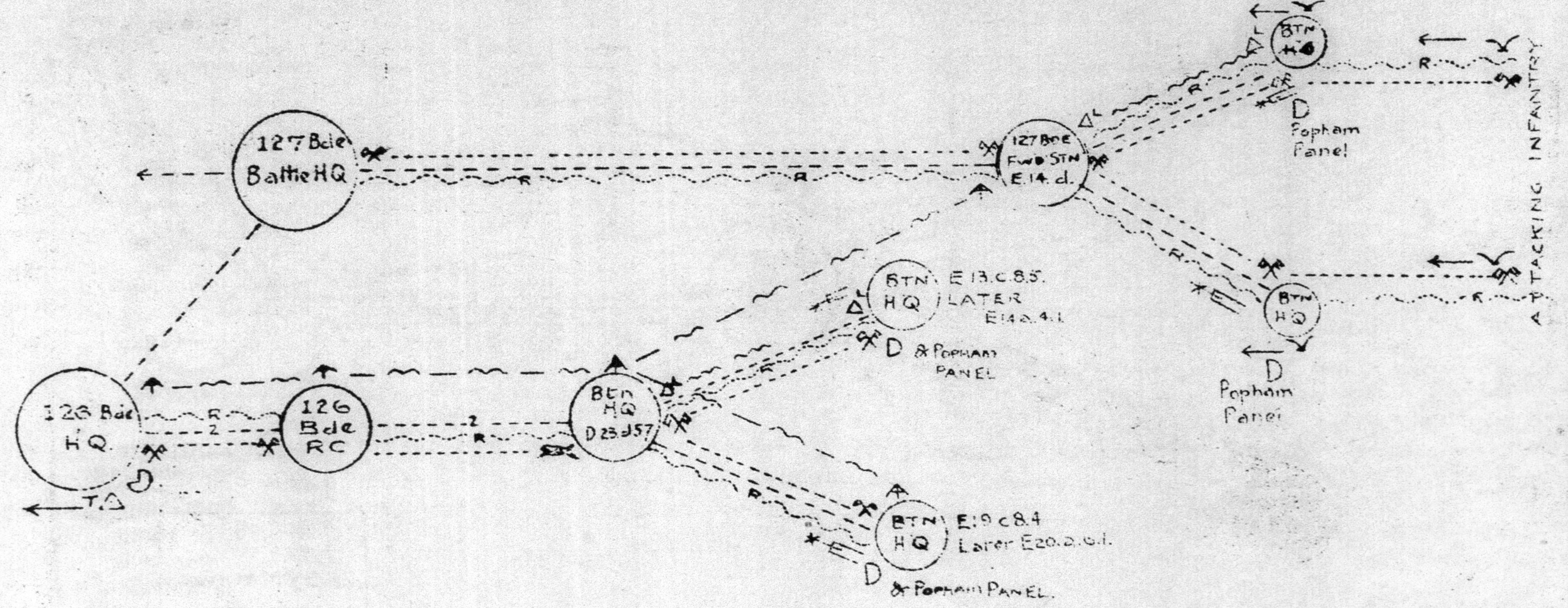

127 Bde Battle HQ

127 Bde Fwd Stn E.14.d.

Btn HQ

Popham Panel

Btn HQ

Popham Panel

Btn HQ E.13.c.8.5. Later E.14.a.4.1.

& Popham Panel

126 Bde HQ

126 Bde RC

Btn HQ D.23.d.5.7

Btn HQ E.19.c.8.4 Later E.20.a.0.1.

& Popham Panel.

Attacking Infantry

APPENDIX III

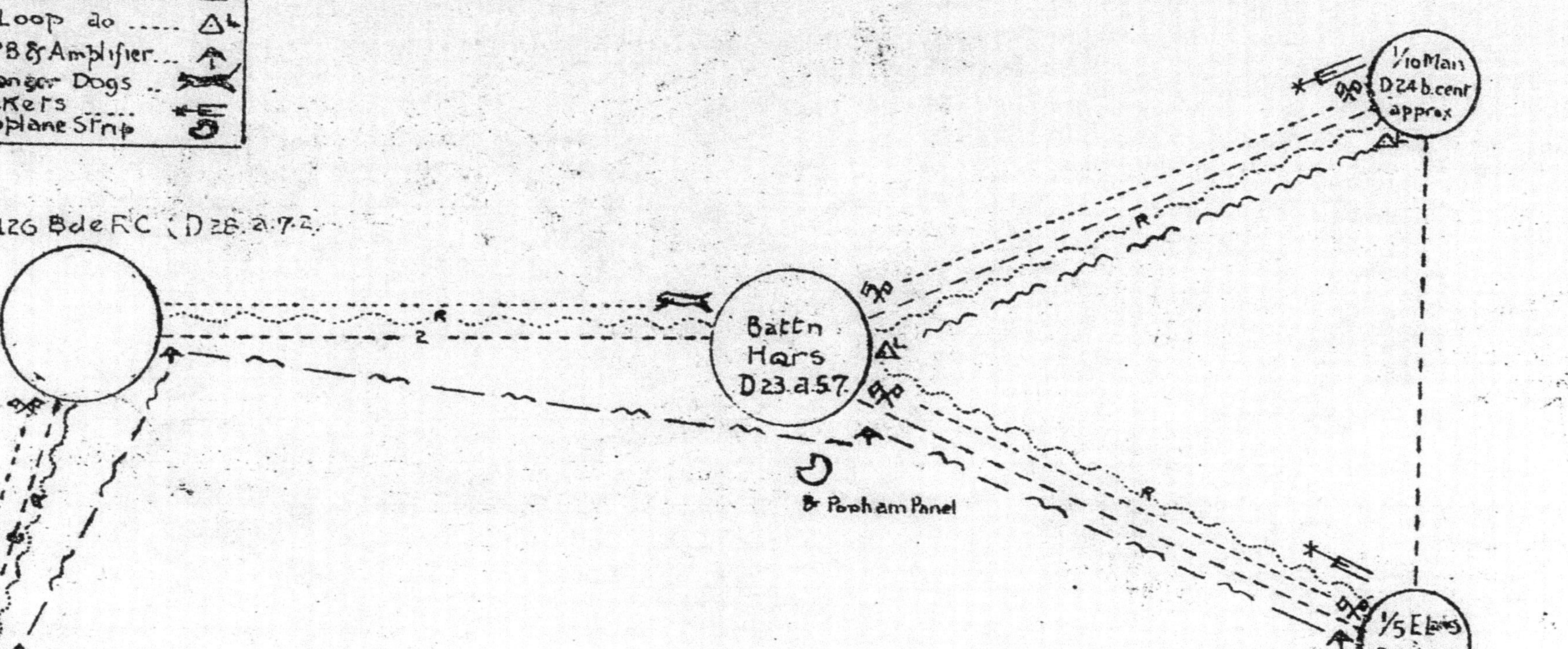

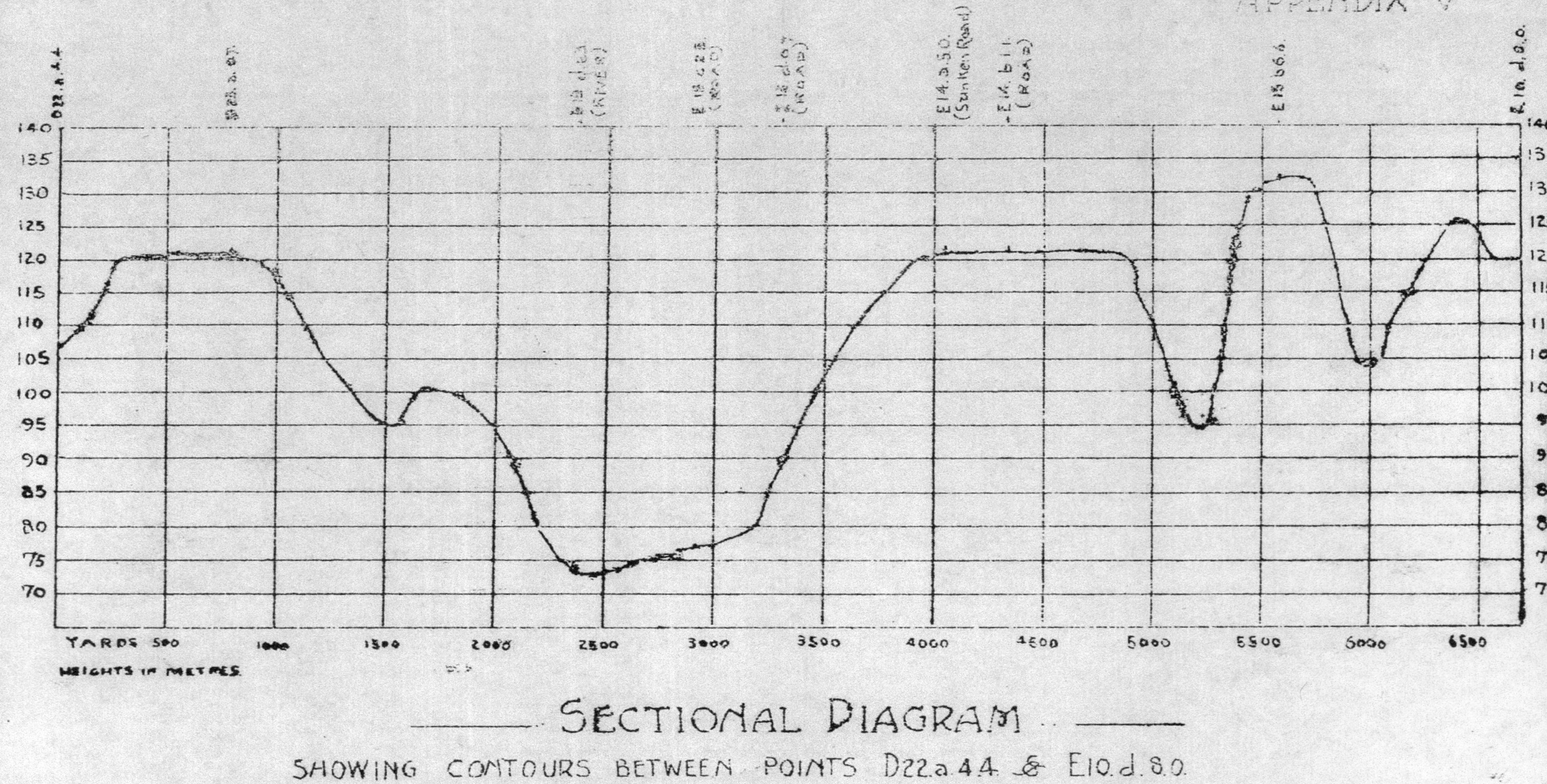
APPENDIX V
E14.a.5.0. (Sunken Road)
(RIVER)
(ROAD)
(ROAD)
(ROAD)
140
135
130
125
120
115
110
105
100
95
90
85
80
75
70
YARDS 500
1000
1500
2000
2500
3000
3500
4000
4500
5000
5500
6000
6500
HEIGHTS IN METRES
SECTIONAL DIAGRAM
SHOWING CONTOURS BETWEEN POINTS D22.a.4.4 & E10.d.8.0

WAR DIARY.

APPENDIX 'C'. OCTOBER, 1918.

WEEKLY STRENGTHS, CASUALTIES, REINFORCEMENTS.

Weekly Strengths.	Officers.	O.R.
Week ending Oct. 5th.	12.	296.
" " " 12th.	12.	305.
" " " 19th.	12.	311.
" " " 26th.	10.	303.

Casualties.		
Killed.		1.
Wounded & Gassed.		4.
Hospital.	1.	16.
To U,K.	1.	
	2.	21.

Reinforcements.		
From Base Signal Depot.		14.
From Hospital.		3.
From 37th Div Sig. Co.R.E.	1.	
From 3rd Army Signal Co R.E.	1.	
	2.	17.

[signature]

Major, R.E.

Nov, 4th, 1918. O.C., 42nd Div'l Signal Coy., R.E.

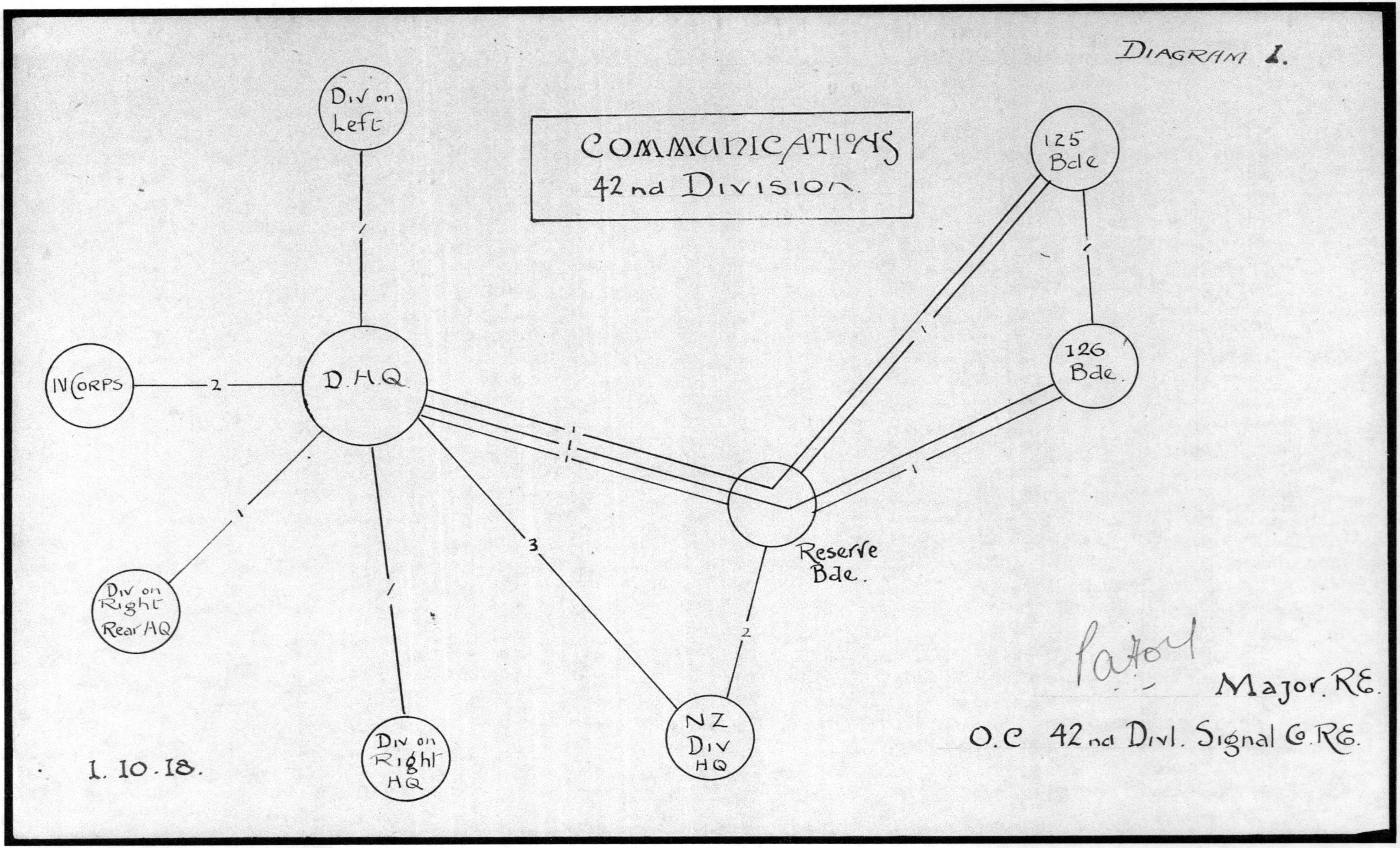

DIAGRAM 1.

COMMUNICATIONS
42nd DIVISION

Div on Left

IV CORPS

D.H.Q

Div on Right Rear HQ

Div on Right HQ

NZ Div HQ

Reserve Bde.

125 Bde

126 Bde.

1

2

1

1

3

2

II

1

1

1

1. 10. 18.

Paton

Major. R.E.

O.C 42nd Divl. Signal Co. R.E.

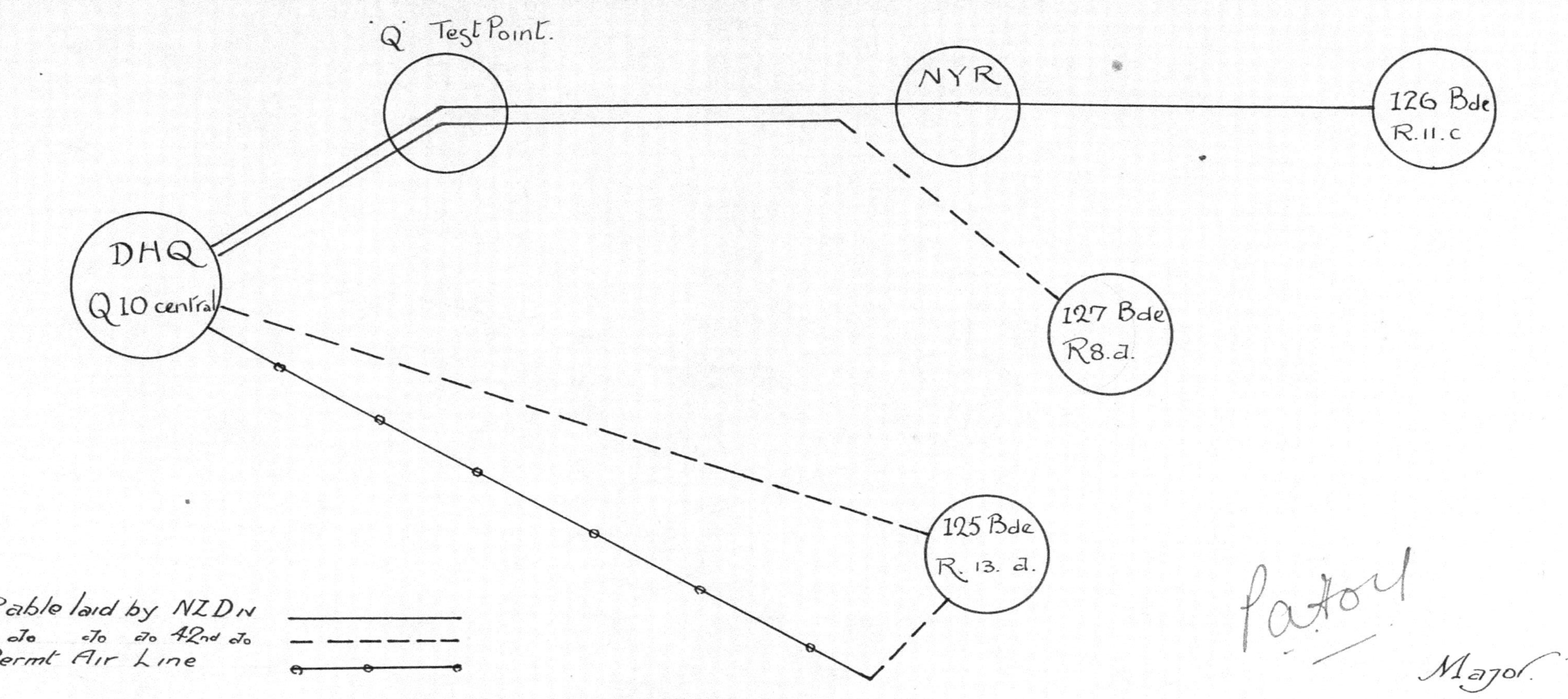
Diagram 2.
Communications
42nd Division
'Q' Test Point.
NYR
126 Bde
R.11.c
DHQ
Q 10 central
127 Bde
R8.d.
125 Bde
R. 13. d.
Cable laid by NZDn
do do do 42nd do
Perml Air Line
Paton
Major. R.E.
O.C. 42nd. Divl Signal Coy.
R.E.
8. 10. 18.

DIAGRAM. 3

COMMUNICATIONS
42ND DIVISION.

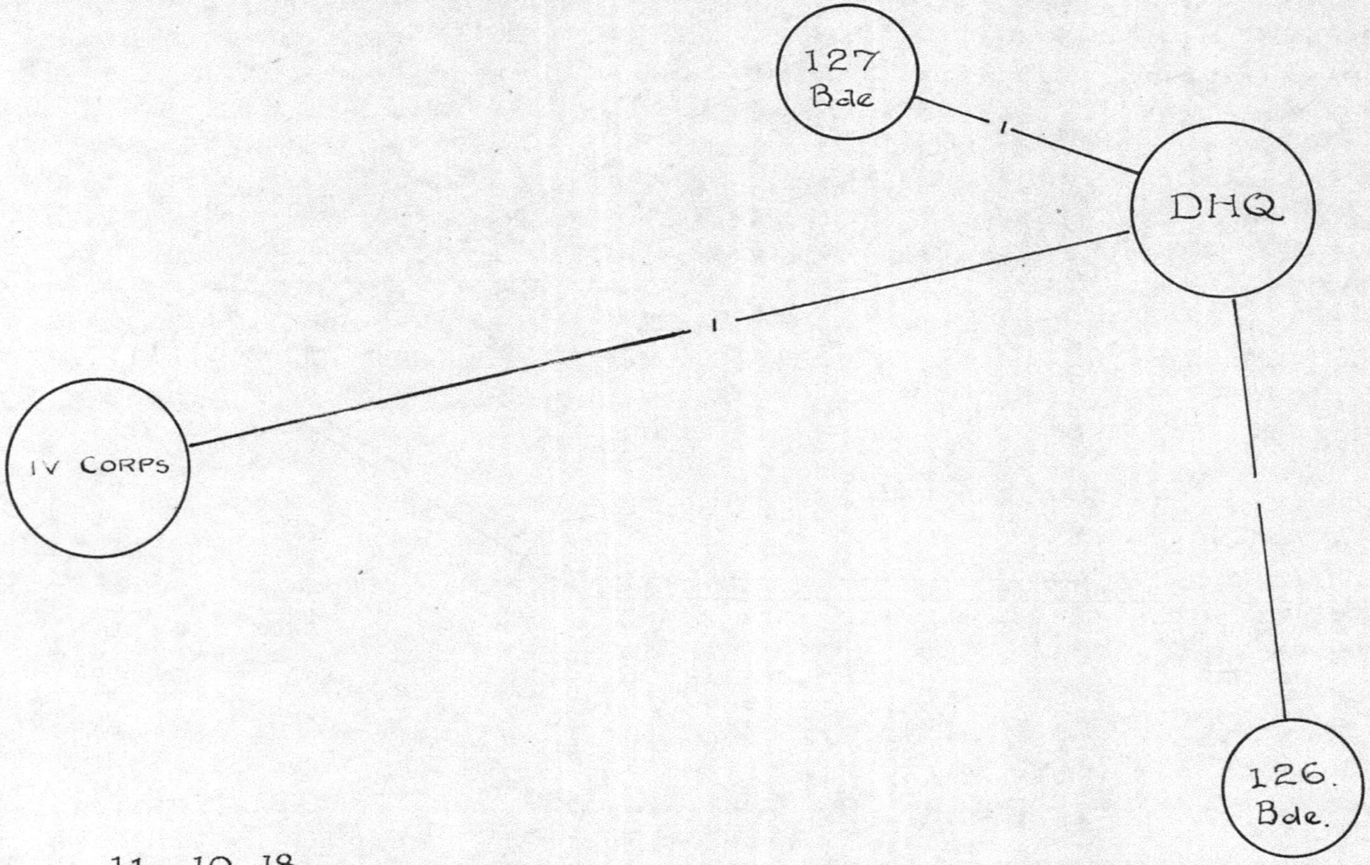

127
Bde

DHQ

IV CORPS

126.
Bde.

Paton

Major. R.E.

O.C. 42nd Divl Signal Coy R.E.

11. 10. 18.

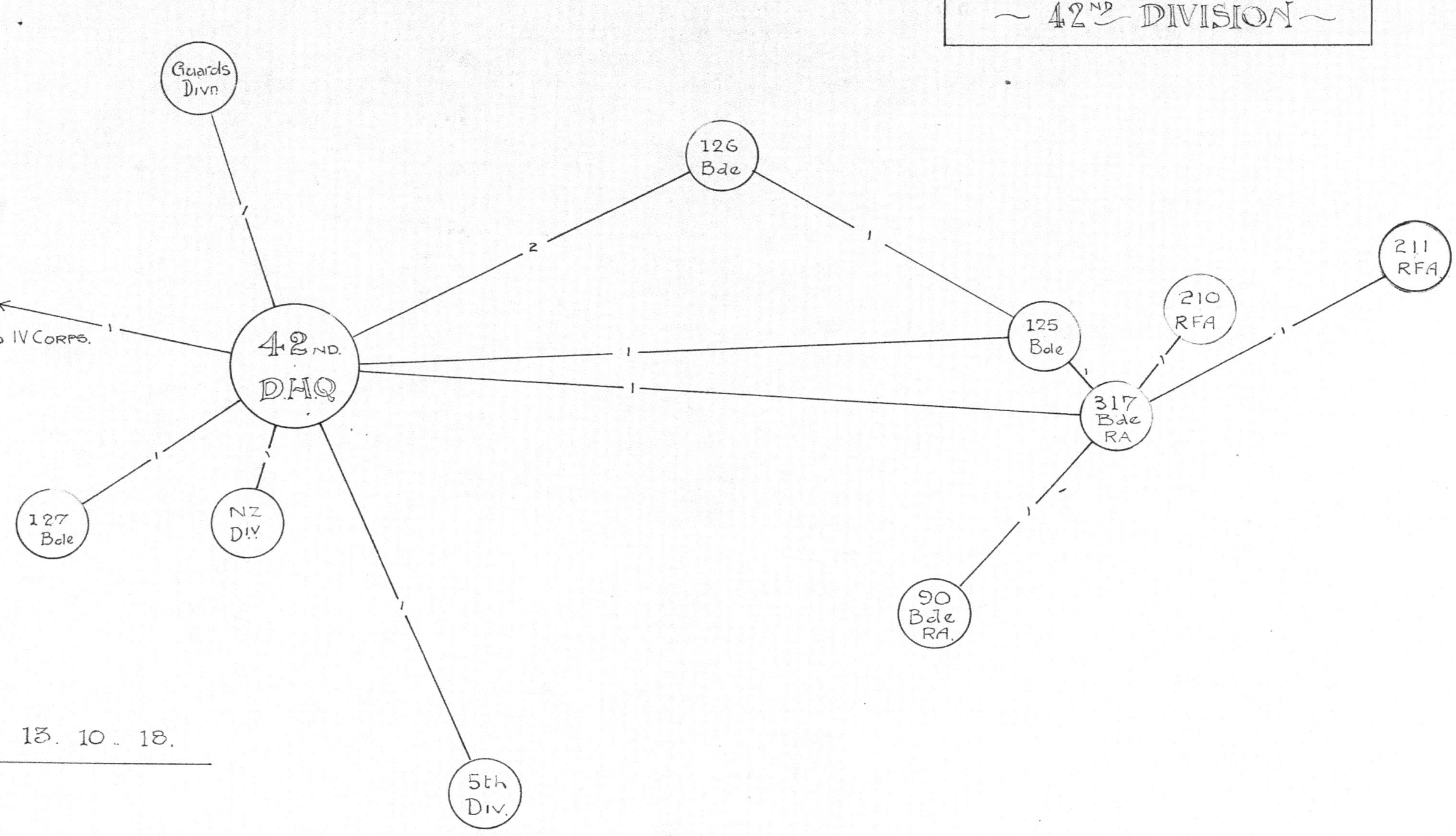

4
COMMUNICATIONS
~ 42ND DIVISION ~
42ND. D.H.Q
Guards Divn
To IV CORPS.
127 Bde
NZ DIV
5th DIV.
126 Bde
125 Bde
317 Bde RA
210 RFA
211 RFA
90 Bde RA.
2
1
13. 10. 18.

5

Communications
42nd Division

62nd Divn
Guards Divn
Corps
D.H.Q.
5th Div.
125 Bde.
Main Group (317)
Sub-Grp
126 Bde
127 Bde
Bde of Div on Left
Bde of Div on Left.

Paton

Major R.E.

O.C. 42nd. Divl Signal Co. R.E.

21. 10. 1918.

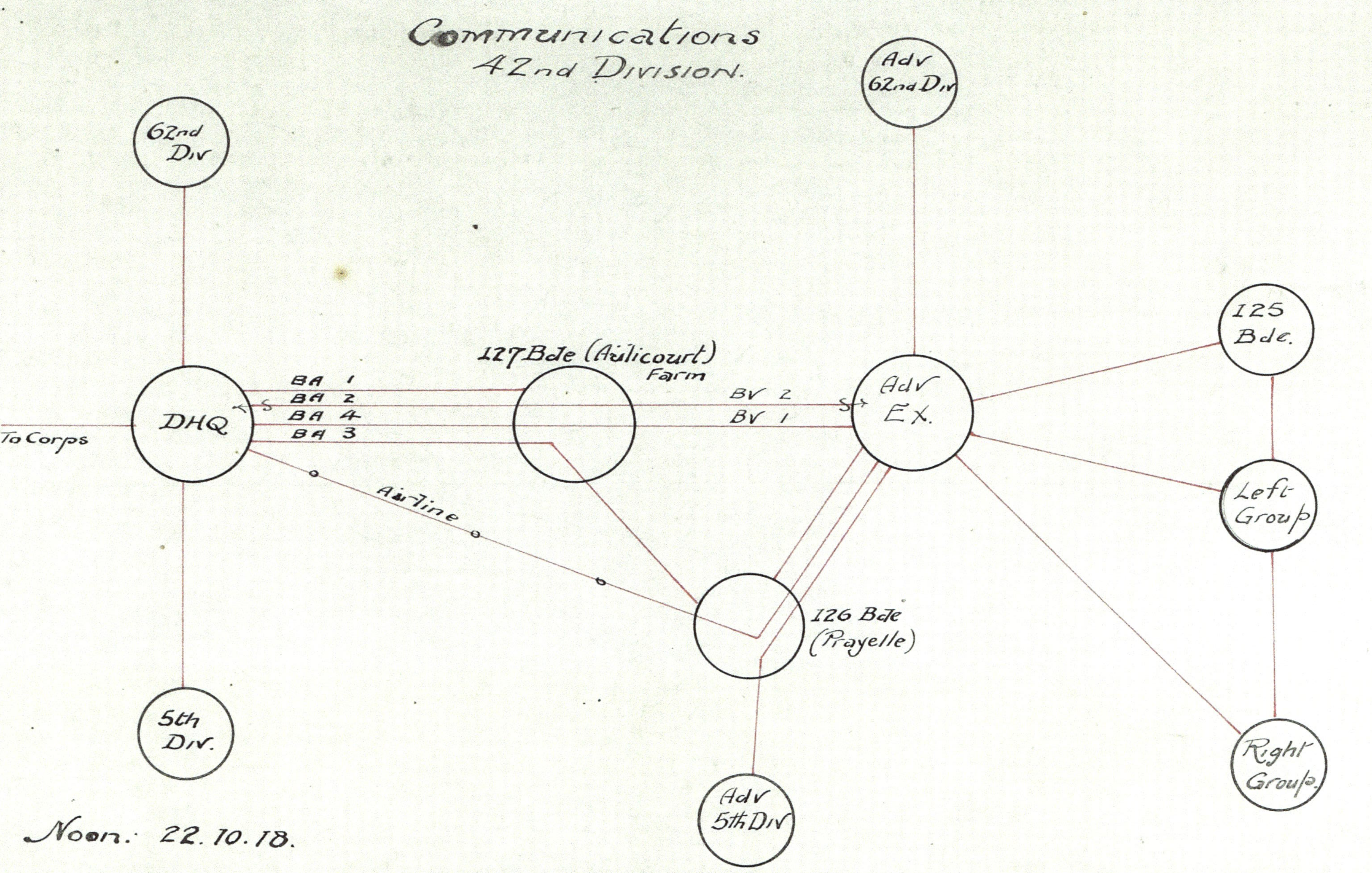
Communications
42nd Division.
6
62nd Div
Adv 62nd Div
DHQ
To Corps
5th Div.
127 Bde (Ailicourt) Farm
BA 1
BA 2
BA 4
BA 3
Airline
BV 2
BV 1
Adv Ex.
126 Bde (Prayelle)
Adv 5th Div
125 Bde.
Left Group
Right Group.
Noon: 22.10.18.

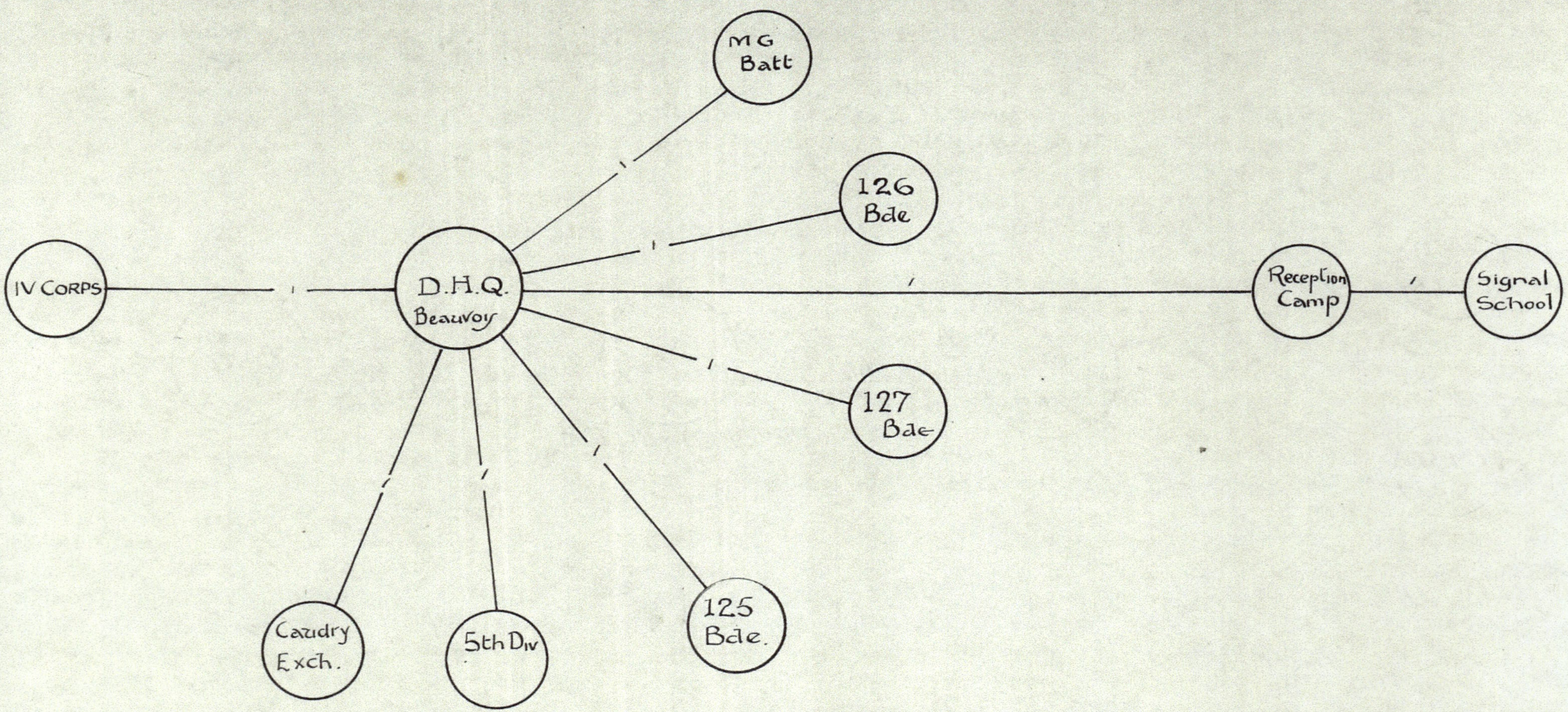

Y

MG Batt

126 Bde

IV CORPS

D.H.Q. Beauvois

Reception Camp

Signal School

127 Bde

Caudry Exch.

5th Div

125 Bde.

31. 10. 18.

APPENDIX D

MESSAGE GRAPH

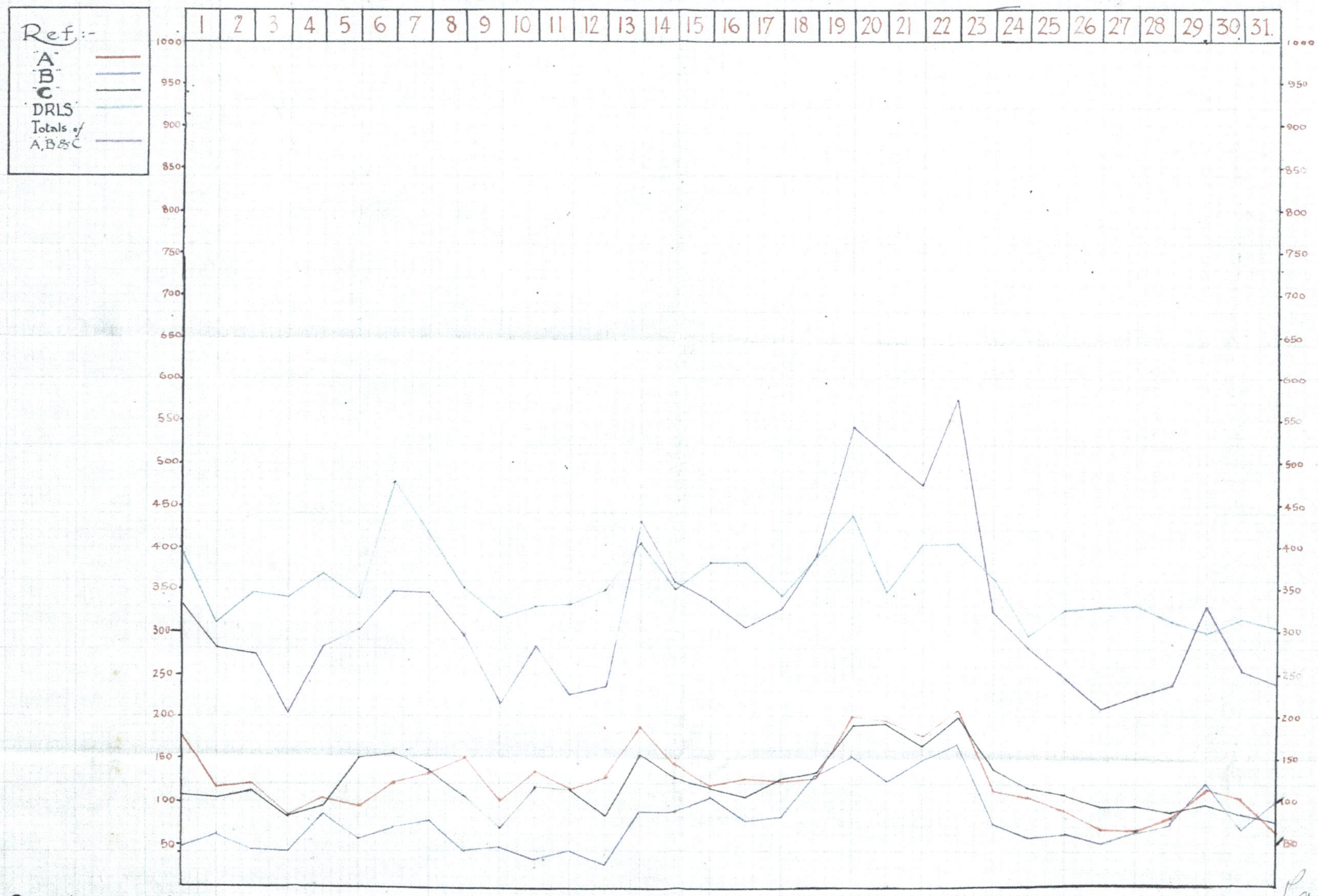

October 1918.

Patoy Major. R.E.
O.C. 42nd. Divl Signal Coy. R.E.

APPENDIX "D"

APPENDIX. "D"

War Diary.

MAP 2

COMMUNICATIONS

Secret.

9/8 21

War Diary

42nd Div. Signal Coy. R.E.

Chapter XXV

November 1918

1a404

4th December 1918.

Major R.E.

O.C. 42nd. Divl Signal Coy R.E.

APPENDIX III

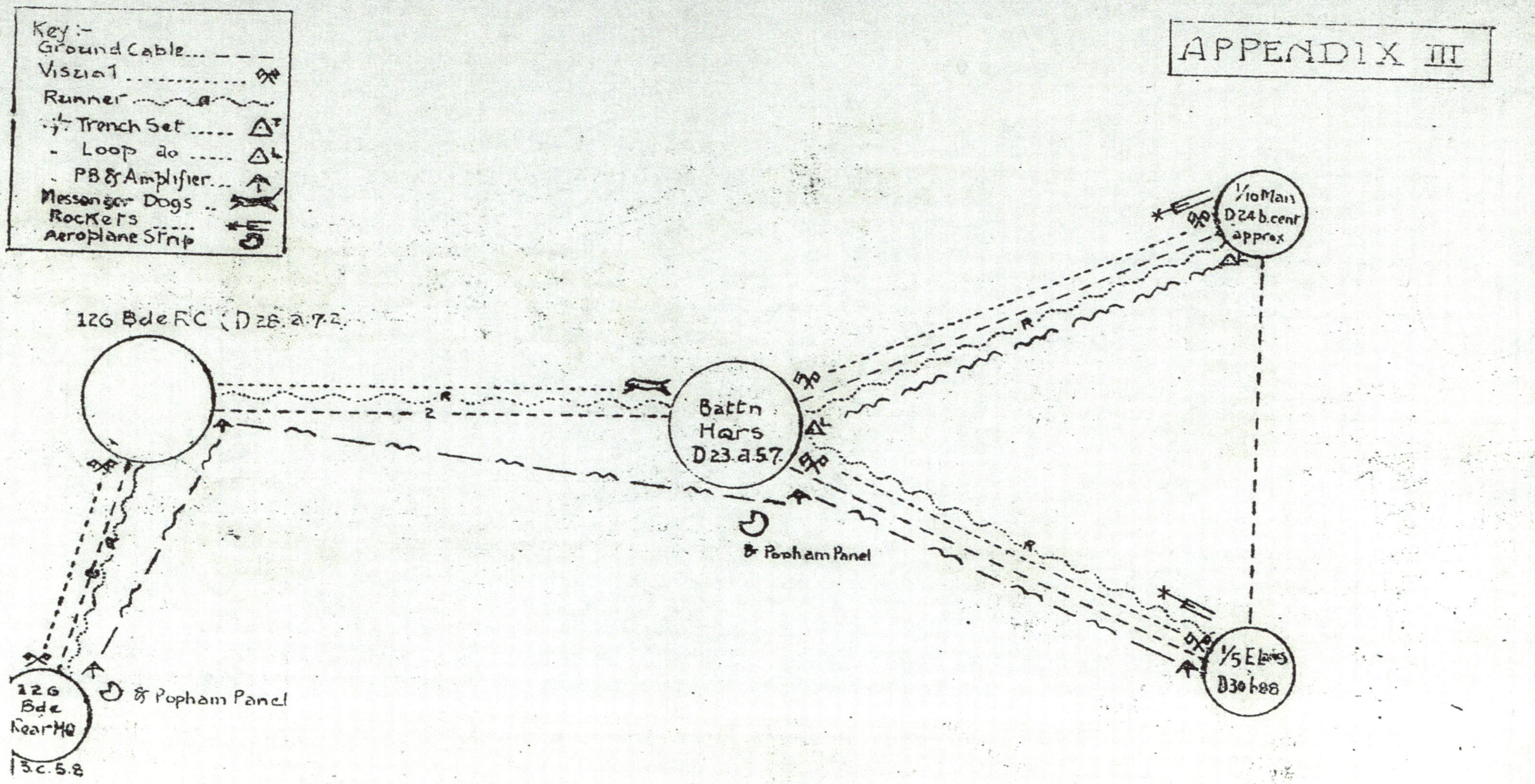

Key:-
Ground Cable
Visual
Runner
Trench Set
Loop do
PB & Amplifier
Messenger Dogs
Rockets
Aeroplane Strip

126 Bde F.C. (D28.a.7.2.)

Battn Hqrs D23.a.5.7.

1/10 Man D24.b.cent approx

1/5 E Lancs D30.b.8.8

126 Bde Rear HQ 3.c.5.8

Popham Panel

CHAPTER XXV.
NOVEMBER 1918.

Place	Date	Hour	Summary of Events and Information	Remarks
BEAUVOIS en CAMBRESIS.	1.11.18 - 3.11.18.		42nd Division in Fourth Corps Reserve remained in BEAUVOIS with Headquarters at I.9.d.22 (sheet 57B). Communications as at end of last month. (War Diary October Appendix A. Diagram 7).	
	3.11.18.		During day, 126th Infantry Brigade moved to SOLESMES into reserve of N.Z. Division in preparation for the next day's attack. Communication by telephone from 126th Brigade Headquarters to N.Z. Divisional Headquarters in SOLESMES established.	
	4.11.18.		Attack launched on Fourth Corps front. 42nd Division ordered to move forward in support of left (N.Z) Division. 126th Infantry Brigade moved to BEAUDIGNIES and telephone communication with advanced N.Z. Divisional Headquarters at X.2.a.65 (sheet 51A) established. 127th Infantry Brigade moved to VERTIGNEUL FARM with telephone communication with N.Z. (Rear) Headquarters at SOLESMES.	
		1000	Two complete cable Detachments moved from BEAUVOIS to SOLESMES in order to be in a position to move next day to new Headquarters of 42nd Division. Orders received in evening that Divisional Headquarters would move at 1000 from BEAUVOIS to BEAUDIGNIES.	See Appx D. (Coy. Order no. 26)
	5.11.18.	0830	Two cable Detachments moved from SOLESMES to BEAUDIGNIES. Preparations made to take over communications from N.Z. Division.	
		1100	Orders received that Divisional Headquarters would move to POTELLE CHATEAU (M.27.b.7.4. sheet 51) 126th Infantry Brigade Headquarters moved to FORRESTERS POST (N.20.c.sheet 51). 127th " " " " " HERBIGNIES. (M.30.c. " "). 125th " " " " " BEAUDIGNIES.	
POTELLE CHATEAU.			During afternoon Divisional Headquarters arrived at POTELLE CHATEAU and preparations were made to take over communications from N.Z. Divisional Signal Coy.	
		1830	G.O.C. 42nd Division took over command of Left Divisional Sector, Fourth Corps front.	

A7092). Wt. W12839/M1297 750,000. 1/17. D. D & L., Ltd. Forms/C2118/14.

Instructions regarding War Diaries and Intelligence Summaries are contained in F. S. Regs., Part II. and the Staff Manual respectively. Title pages will be prepared in manuscript.

WAR DIARY
or
~~INTELLIGENCE SUMMARY.~~
(Erase heading not required.)

Army Form C. 2118.

- 2 -

Place	Date	Hour	Summary of Events and Information	Remarks and references to Appendices
	Night. 5/6.11.18.		The Infantry Brigades of 42nd Division relieved Brigades of N.Z.Division in the line, dispositions being as follows:- Leading Brigade. ... 126th Infantry Brigade. Support Brigade. ... 127th Brigade. Reserve Brigade. ... 125th Brigade. The Artillery under the Divisional command, consisting of three Brigades R.F.A. was formed into a single group with Group Headquarters at the Headquarters of the leading Brigade. The communications taken over from the N.Z. Division consisted of one D.8. pair from Divisional Headquarters along main road through M.29.a & b. and HERBIGNIES to Cross Roads in N.31.a. thence N.E. along road to FORRESTER'S POST (126th Infantry Brigade and Artillery Group Headquarters). (See Diagram 1). One cable Detachment sent forward during the afternoon of November 5th carrying six miles D.8. cable was stationed at Headquarters of leading (126th) Infantry Brigade to lay cable forward in case of an advance of Headquarters by that Brigade.	DIAGRAM. 1.
	6.11.18.		It being anticipated that the leading Infantry Brigade would that day move Headquarters to FORESTERS HOUSE (N.36.a.7.6. sheet 51),	
		0630	A cable Detachment was sent from Divisional Headquarters to lay a D.8. pair from POTELLE CHATEAU via HERBIGNIES, MAISON ROUGE, Cross Roads in T.3.d. thence along road in M.3.b., N.34.d., N.35.c. to FORESTERS HOUSE where the leading (126th) Infantry Brigade had established an advanced exchange and had one pair D.8. cable from their Headquarters to that Exchange. Another Detachment was sent out to lay a single D.5. circuit from POTELLE CHATEAU by the same route to MAISON ROUGE then to go to FORESTERS POST to supply cable to the Detachment stationed there. Cable from this Detachment was also sent to complete the line mentioned above to FORESTERS HOUSE. Owing to the very bad weather and the congested state of the roads both these Detachments were out all day before their lines could be completed. Meanwhile owing to the state of the roads the move of the Company transport to POTELLE CHATEAU was proving very difficult. It was impossible to bring heavily loaded lorries and G.S. wagons up without considerable risk of their being bogged and the horses of the Company were very tired by the long distance and heavy work.	

A7092). Wt. W12839/M1293 750,000. 1/17. D. D & L., Ltd. Forms/C2118/14.

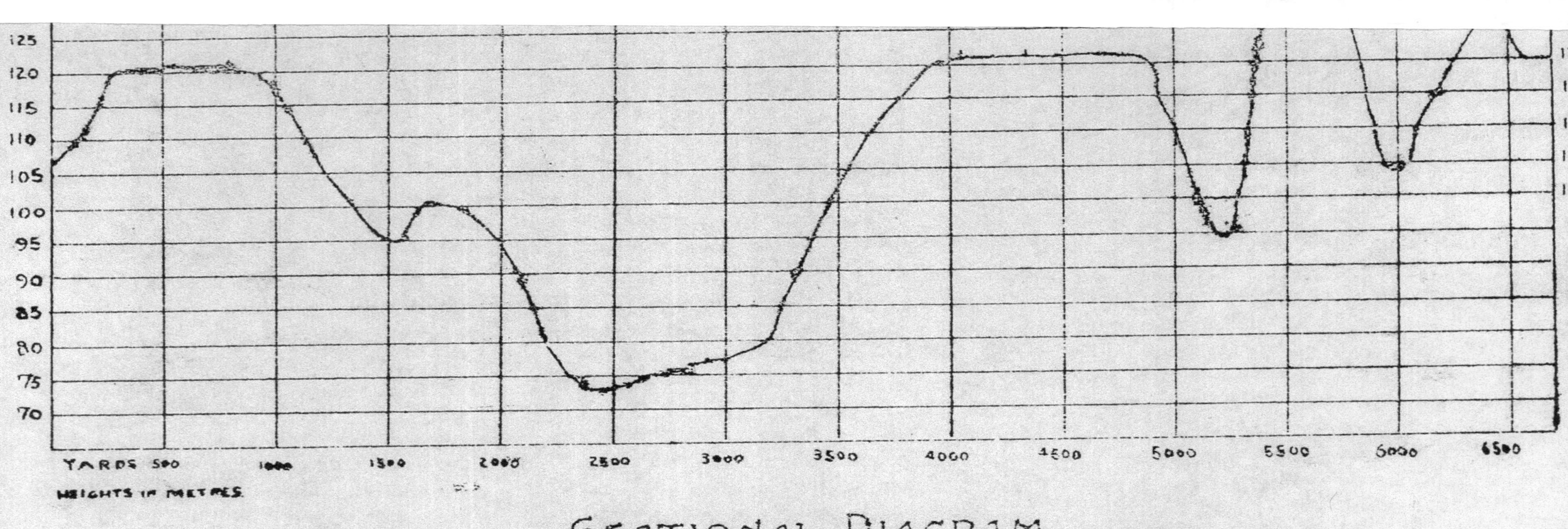

SECTIONAL DIAGRAM

SHOWING CONTOURS BETWEEN POINTS D22.a.4.4. & E10.d.8.0.

Army Form C. 2118.

Instructions regarding War Diaries and Intelligence Summaries are contained in F. S. Regs., Part II. and the Staff Manual respectively. Title pages will be prepared in manuscript.

WAR DIARY
or
~~INTELLIGENCE SUMMARY.~~
(Erase heading not required.)

Place	Date	Hour	Summary of Events and Information	Remarks and references to Appendices
	6.11.18.		Direct communication with Fourth Corps was not established until the early morning of November 6th. From the time when Divisional Headquarters was opened at POTELLE CHATEAU messages to and from Fourth Corps were transmitted by Advanced N.Z. Divisional Exchange (BEAUDIGNIES) and N.Z. Divisional Exchange (SOLESMES). Speech through this line was not possible. Owing to the situation on the left flank of the Division, the leading (126th) Infantry Brigade did not move its Headquarters from FORRESTERS POST. The support (127th) Infantry Brigade after moving forward through the FORET DE MORMAL returned and established Headquarters at MAISON ROUGE (N.31.a) and communication from Divisional Headquarters was established on the D.8. line laid earlier in the day from Divisional Headquarters to FORESTERS HOUSE. During the afternoon of November 5th the Reserve (125th) Infantry Brigade had moved up from BEAUDIGNIES and established Headquarters at HERBIGNIES, communication to its Headquarters from Divisional Headquarters being by the single D.5. cable laid earlier in the day. Communication to right flank Division (5th) was established about mid-day.	
	6/7.11.18.		Thus communication on the night 6th/7th November was as in Diagram 2. The role of Support Infantry Brigade was taken over by 125th Infantry Brigade from 127th Infantry Brigade, the latter becoming reserve Brigade. The advance was resumed on November 7th. The leading (126th) and Support (127th) Brigades Headquarters moved forwards to PETIT BAVAY. A D.8 pair cable was laid from the 126th Brigade advanced Exchange (FORESTERS HOUSE) to the new Headquarters. The Exchange at FORESTERS HOUSE was taken over as an Advanced Divisional Exchange. The Reserve (127th) Brigade Headquarters remained at MAISON ROUGE.	DIAGRAM. 2
	Night. 7/8.11.18.		Communications on the night 7th/8th November were as shown in Diagram 3 During the night the role of leading Brigade passed to 125th Infantry Brigade, 126th Brigade becoming Support Brigade.	DIAGRAM. 3.
LA HAUTE RUE.	8.11.18.		On the 8th November orders were received that Divisional Headquarters would move to LA HAUTE RUE in the afternoon.	

A7092). Wt. W12839/M1293 750,000. 1/17. D. D & L., Ltd. Forms/C2118/14.

Army Form C. 2118.

Instructions regarding War Diaries and Intelligence Summaries are contained in F. S. Regs., Part II. and the Staff Manual respectively. Title pages will be prepared in manuscript.

WAR DIARY
or
~~INTELLIGENCE - SUMMARY.~~

(Erase heading not required.)

Place	Date	Hour	Summary of Events and Information	Remarks and references to Appendices
			- 4 - The existing line from FORESTERS POST to PETIT BAVAY passed this point and was cut there. The Rear Office at POTELLE CHATEAU was kept open for communication with Fourth Corps and for Divisional 'Q' Office which remained there. On the completion of air-line through FORET DE MORMAL direct communication was established with Fourth Corps at 1900 hours, and the Divisional Exchange at FORESTERS HOUSE closed. Early in the afternoon the leading (125th) Infantry Brigade moved to BOUSSIERES and a D.8. pair cable was laid from PETIT BAVAY to its new Headquarters. The 127th Infantry Brigade moved to VIEUX MESNIL and a single D.5. cable was laid from Divisional Headquarters to that place. A lateral D.5. circuit was also laid from 127th Infantry Brigade Headquarters to 125th Infantry Brigade Headquarters at BOUSSIERES.	
	Night. 8/9.11.18.		Communication by cable with 5th Division on right was established during the afternoon. Thus communications on the night 8th/9th November were as shown in Diagram 4.	DIAGRAM 4
HAUTMONT.	9.11.18.		Orders were received that Divisional Headquarters would move to HAUTMONT (P.22.b.4.3 sheet51) in the afternoon of 9th November. A D.8 line was laid from BOUSSIERES to the new Divisional Headquarters for communication with 125th Infantry Brigade and through their Exchange to 127th Brigade Headquarters at VIEUX MESNIL. 126th Infantry Brigade moved to a Headquarters close to new Divisional Headquarters and no line was laid to that Brigade. As no communication existed from Fourth Corps Headquarters to HAUTMONT a Rear Divisional Exchange was left at LA HAUTE RUE through which messages for Corps were transmitted.	
	Night. 9/10.11.18.		Thus communication on night 9th/10th November were as shown in Diagram 5.	DIAGRAM 5
	10.11.18.		42nd Division took over the advance on the whole of Fourth Corps front. The leading (125th) Brigade moved to Headquarters on the Eastern outskirts of HAUTMONT, a line being laid through the Town from Divisional Headquarters to its new Headquarters. 127th Infantry Brigade moved Headquarters to BOUSSIERES. During the day lines to local Headquarters in HAUTMONT were laid. Orders were received that Sixth Corps were taking over the advance on Fourth Corps front and that the 42nd Division would stand fast.	

A7092). Wt. W12839/M1293 750,000. 1/17. D. D & L., Ltd. Forms/C2118/14.

Instructions regarding War Diaries and Intelligence Summaries are contained in F. S. Regs., Part II. and the Staff Manual respectively. Title pages will be prepared in manuscript.

WAR DIARY
or
~~INTELLIGENCE-SUMMARY~~.
(Erase heading not required.)

Army Form C. 2118.

Place	Date	Hour	Summary of Events and Information	Remarks and references to Appendices
			Direct communication to Fourth Corps was established at 1800 and the Rear Divisional Office at LA HAUTE RUE closed down.	
			Communications on the night 10th/11th November were as shown in Diagram 6.	DIAGRAM 6.
	11.11.18.		Orders were received that hostilities would cease at 1100.	
	12.11.18. to 30.11.18.		The Division was concentrated in and about HAUTMONT and communication consisted of short lines in the Town The Signal Company was rested and the transport and equipment cleaned and overhauled.	
			During the whole of the period from 1st November the Headquarters and No.1 Sections of the Signal Company were very severely crippled by the epidemic of influenza. Approximately 50% of the total strength of linemen and Drivers were sent sick to hospital in the period 1st - 10th November. In the No. 1 Section there were on 10th November no Officers and only one Corporal and one Lance Corporal effective. Unskilled Drivers from the Infantry Battalions and Signallers from the Pioneer Battalion of the Division were used to replace the skilled personnel. Owing to the lack of proper supervision and to the very bad weather the cable wagons and transport of the Company suffered considerably and a great deal of cleaning and overhauling was necessary when operations finished.	

APPENDICES TO THIS DIARY.

(A). Honours and Awards.
(B). Weekly Strengths, Casualties, Reinforcements, etc.
(C). Monthly Message Chart.
(D). Coy. ORDER. No. 26.

4.12.18.

Paton
Major. R.E.
O.C. 42nd Divisional Signal Co. R.E.

A7092). Wt. W12839/M1293 750,000. 1/17. D. D & L., Ltd. Forms/C2118/14.

Diagram 1

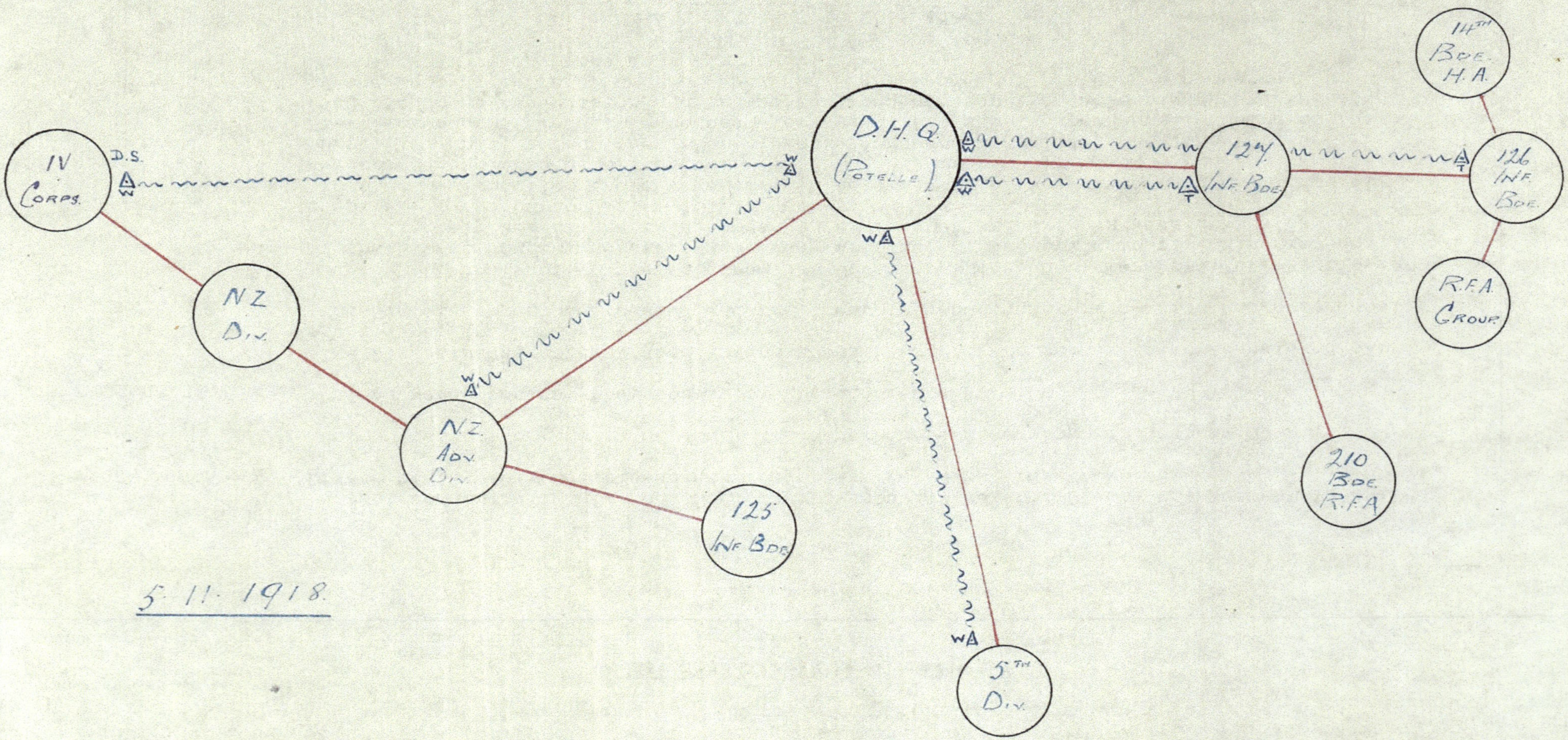

IV Corps.
D.S.
NZ Div.
NZ Adv. Div.
125 Inf Bde.
D.H.Q. (Potelle)
5th Div.
124 Inf Bde.
126 Inf. Bde.
114th Bde. H.A.
R.F.A. Group.
210 Bde. R.F.A.

5.11.1918.

Diagram 2.

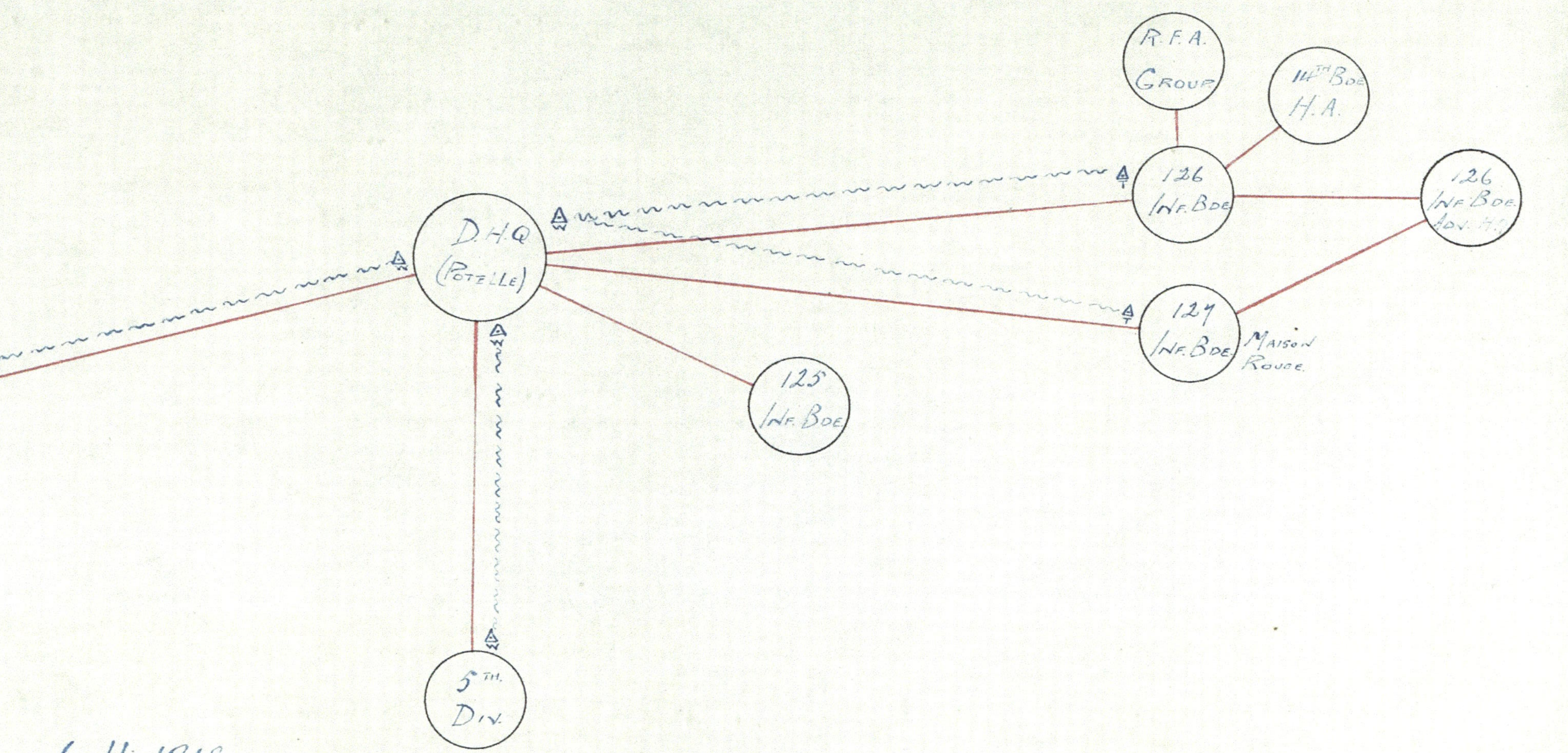

6.11.1918.

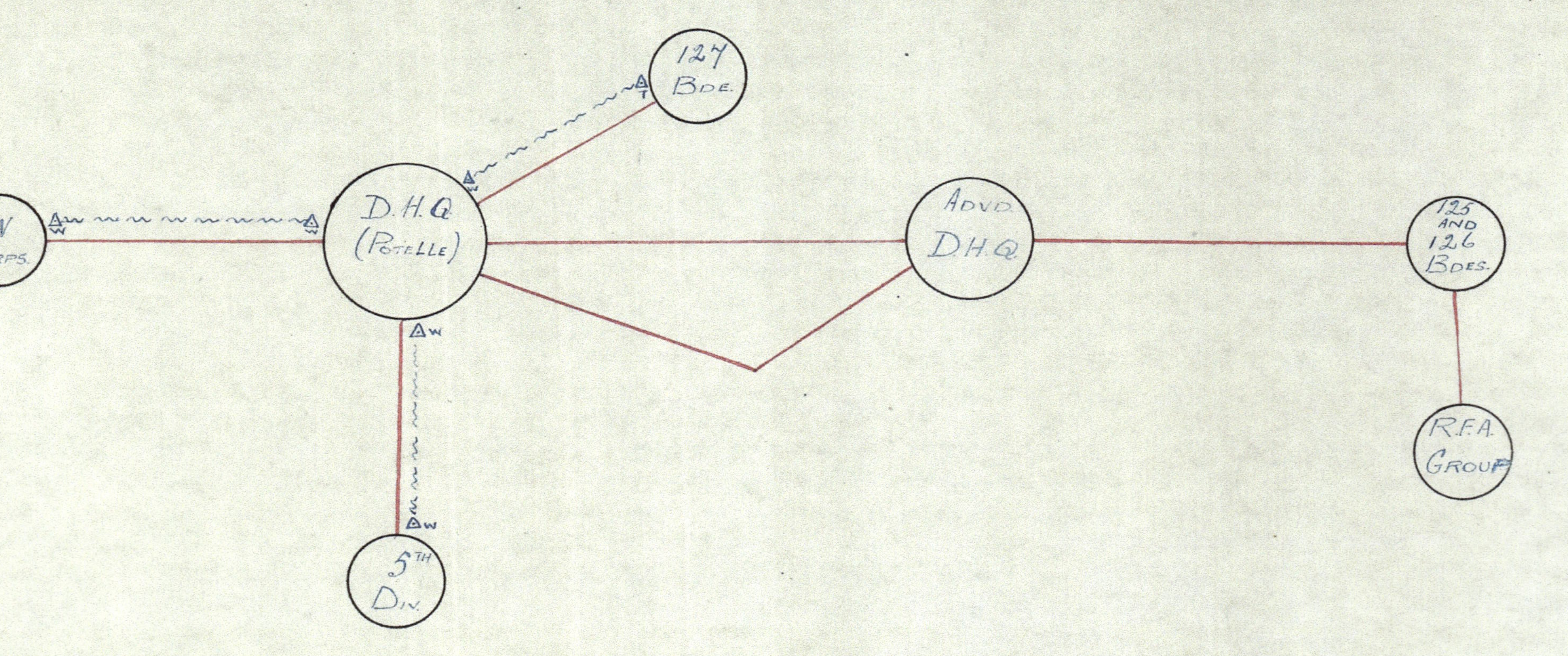
DIAGRAM 3
IV CORPS.
D.H.Q. (POTELLE)
127 BDE.
ADVD. D.H.Q.
125 AND 126 BDES.
R.F.A. GROUP
5TH DIV.
7.11.1918.

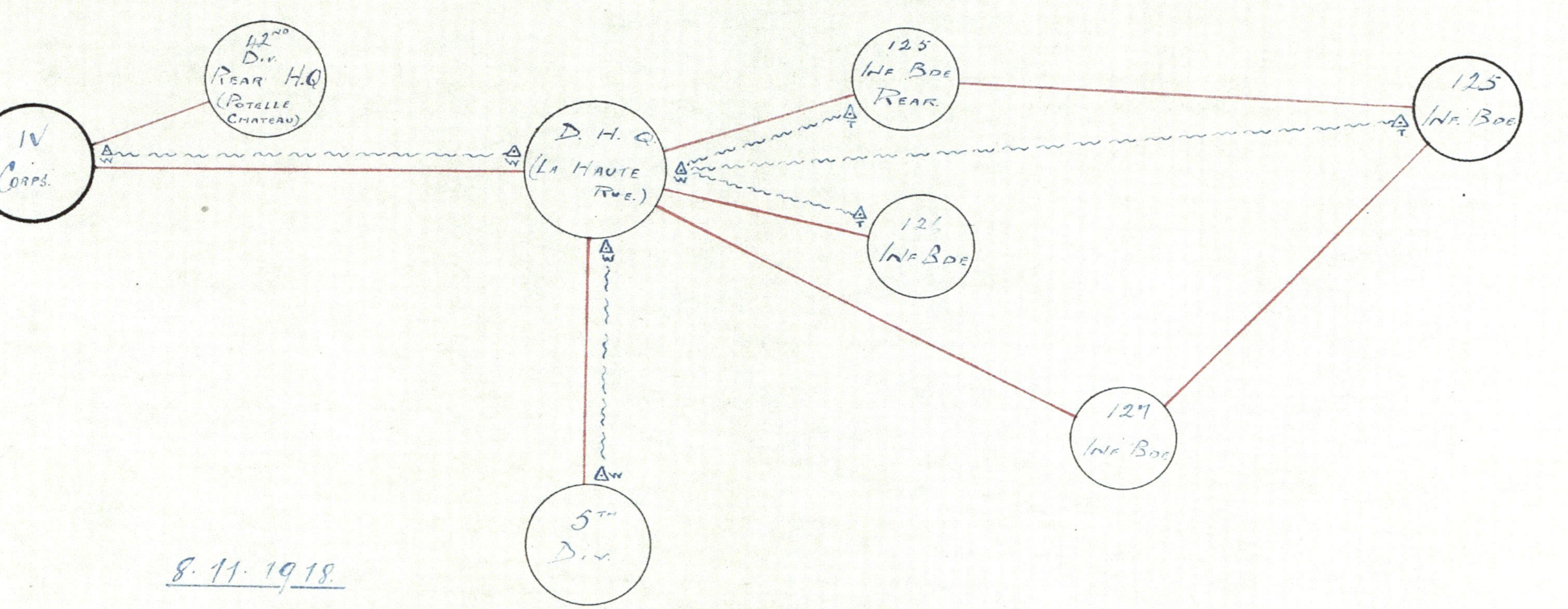
DIAGRAM 4.
IV Corps.
42ND Div. Rear H.Q (Potelle Chateau)
D. H. Q. (La Haute Rue.)
125 Inf Bde Rear.
125 Inf. Bde
126 Inf Bde
127 Inf Bde
5TH Div.
8. 11. 1918.

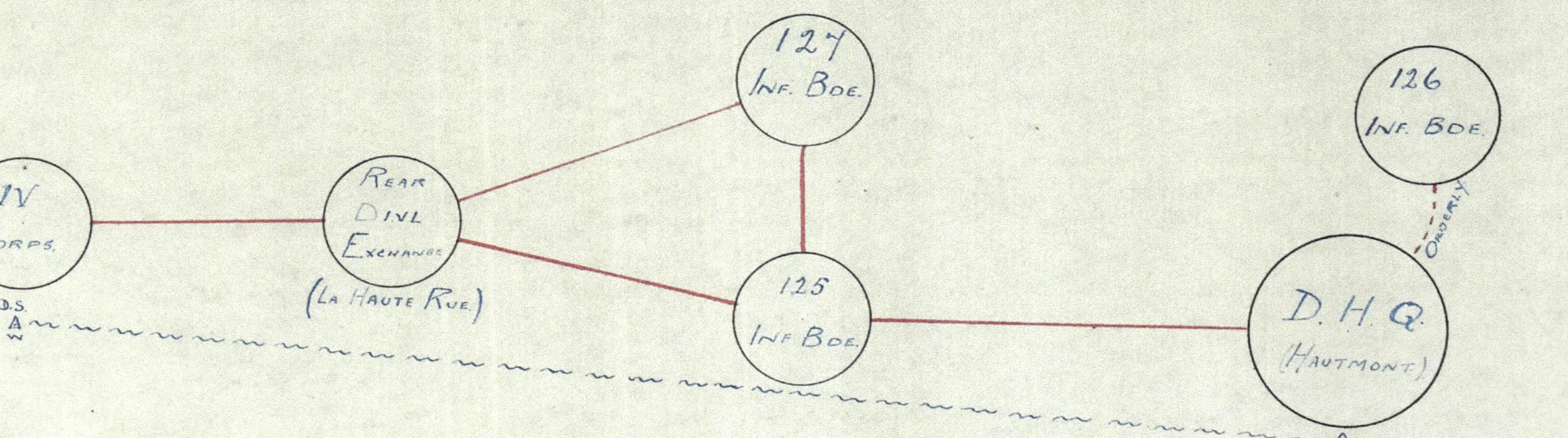
Diagram 5
IV Corps.
Rear Divl Exchange
(La Haute Rue)
127 Inf. Bde.
125 Inf Bde.
126 Inf. Bde.
Orderly
D.H.Q.
(Hautmont)
D.S.
A
W
9.11.1918

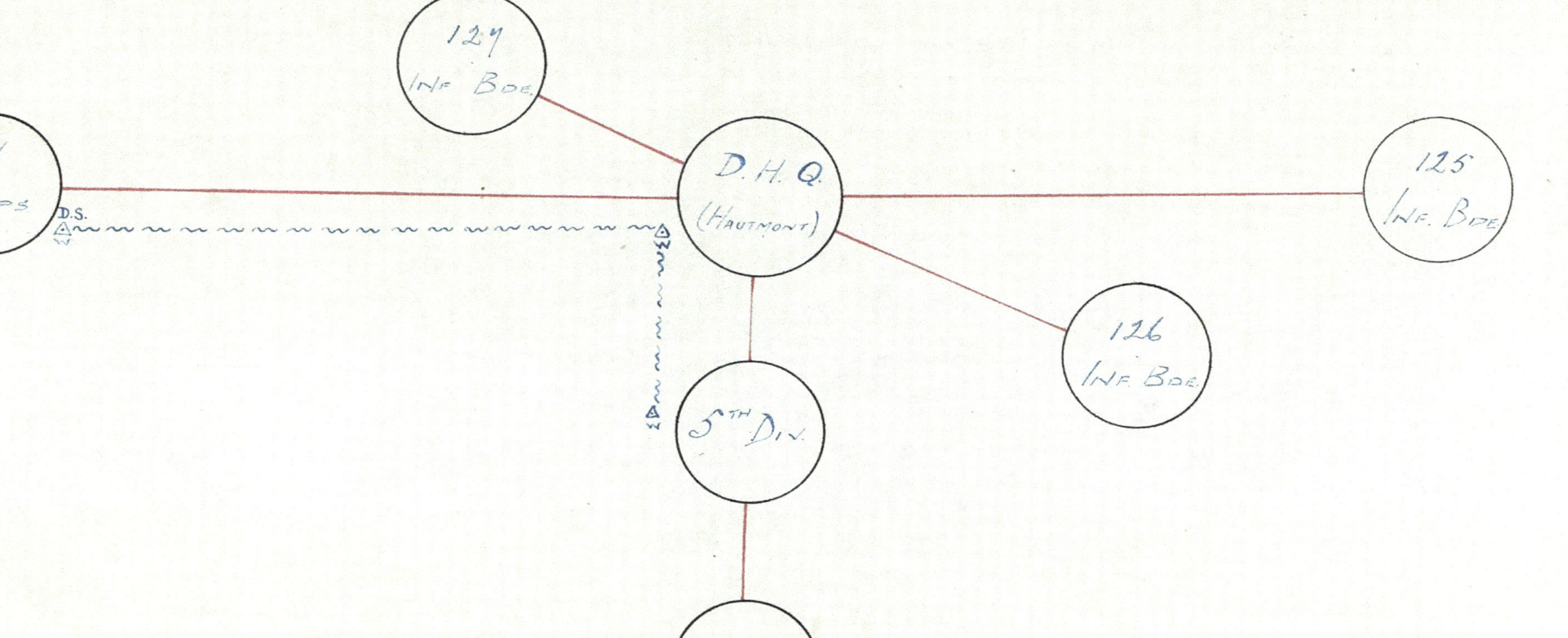
DIAGRAM 6.
127
INF BDE.
IV
CORPS
D.S.
D.H.Q.
(HAUTMONT)
125
INF. BDE.
126
INF. BDE.
5TH DIV.
14TH DIV.
10.11.1918.

APPENDIX 'A'. NOVEMBER 1918.

WAR DIARY.

HONOURS AND AWARDS.

The Corps Commander has, under authority granted by His Majesty the King, has awarded (MILITARY MEDAL) to the undermentioned N.C.O's. and men:-

No.444610 Cpl W. Williams,D.C.M.

No.439920 L/Cpl Couch,H.

No.444621 Pnr Meredew,A.

No.302195 Spr Shaw,H.

Paton.

Major. R.E.

4.12.18. O.C. 42nd Divisional Sgnal Co. R.E.

APPENDIX 'B'. NOVEMBER 1918.

WAR DIARY.

WEEKLY STRENGTHS, CASUALTIES, REINFORCEMENTS, etc.

Weekly Strengths.

	Officers.	O.R.
Week ending November 2nd.	12	299
" " " 9th.	11	268
" " " 16th	12	273
" " " 23rd.	12	275
" " " 30th	12	278

Casualties.

	Officers	O.R.
Killed.	1	-
Sick.	2	79
To Depot.	-	1
R.A.F. Cadet Unit.	-	1
Total.	3	81

Reinforcements.

	Officers	O.R.
From Hospital.	2	29
" Depot.	-	31
" Third Army Signal Co.R.E.	1	-
Total.	3	60

Paton

4.12.18. Major. R.E.
O.C. 42nd Divisional Signal Co. R.E.

APPENDIX . . D .

SECRET. Copy No 11.....

42nd Divisional Signal Company R.E. (T.F.).

Order No. 26.

1. 42nd Division will move to the BEAUDIGNIES Area on the 5th November. D.H.Q. will close down at BEAUVOIS-EN-CAMBRESIS at 12 noon and re-open at BEAUDIGNIES (R.32.d.2.7) at the same hour.

2. The Company will move under the following arrangements :-

Time.	Remarks.
0630.	Lorry with Technical, Orderly Room and Q.M. Stores, and 'C' Signal Office Relief. N.C.O - i/c - Sgt. McCarthy.
0700.	Box-car with W/T Directing Stn, Wireless and Visual Stores. N.C.O. i/c - Cpl. Hill.
0830.	All Horse Transport and personnel, less 'B' Signal Office Relief - N.C.O. i/c - Sgt. Borland.
0830.	P.E.L. Lorry with D,R's Stores.
1100.	Box-car with Officers' Kits and mess Stores - N.C.O i/c - Sgt. Blackburn.
1100.	All D.R's (Less three) will leave for BEAUDIGNIES.
1230.	Lorry with Signal Office Stores and 'B' Signal Office Relief - W.O. i/c - C.S.M. H. Willcock.

3. The C.S.M. will see that all billets and horse lines vacated by the Company are left clean. A certificate will be obtained from the Town Major.

Paton

Major, R.E.

4.11.18. O.C., 42nd Div'l Signal Coy. R.E.

Distribution:-

Copy No. 1. O.C.
2. Captain A. Roberts, M.C.
3. Lieut. A. J. Ellis, M.C.
4. 2/Lieut. H. R. Iliffe.
5. C.S.M.
6. C.Q.M.S.
7. Sgt. McCarthy.
8. Sgt. Harrison.
9. Sgt. Borland.
10. 2/Cpl. Holton.
11. War Diary.
12. File.

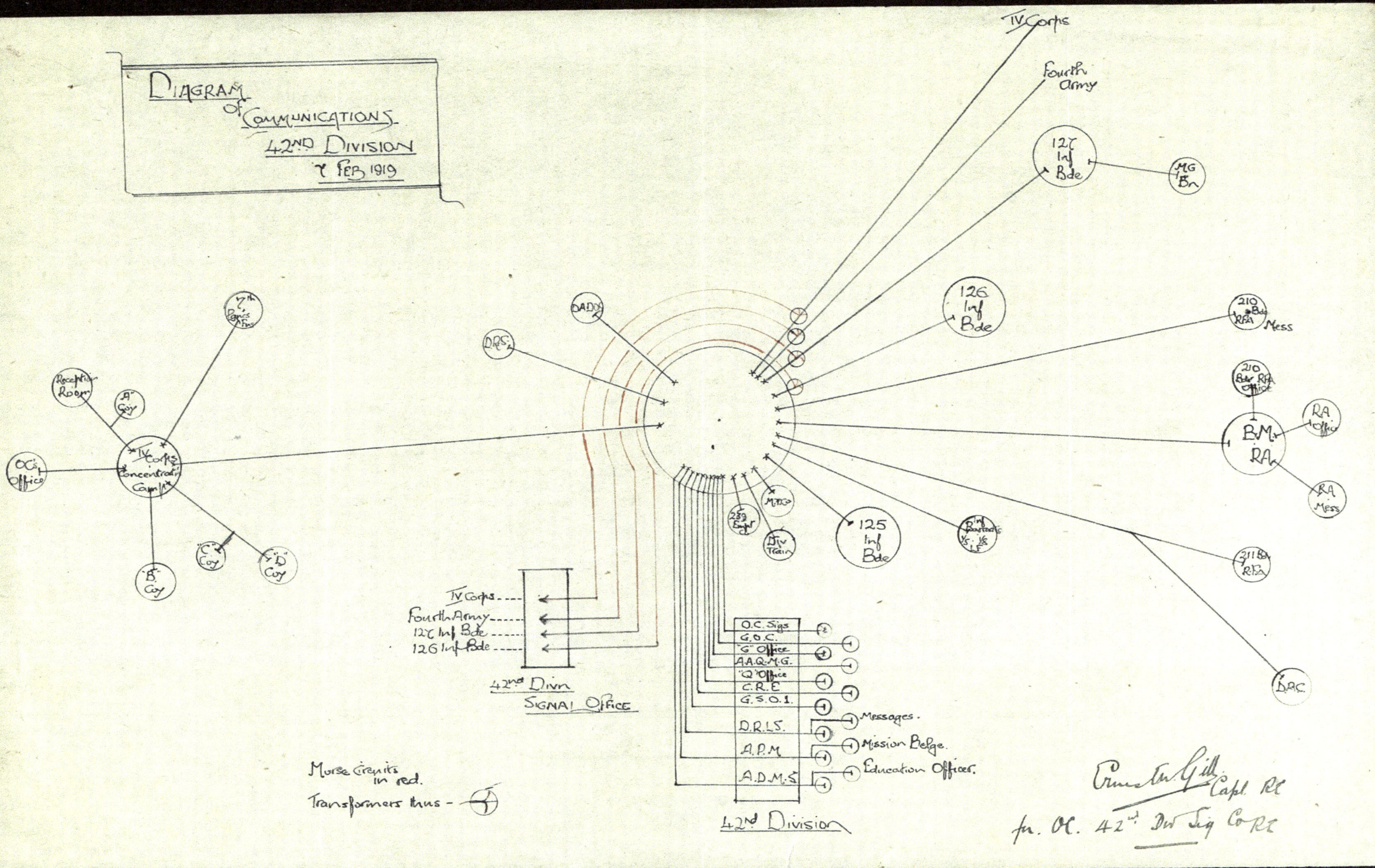
Diagram of Communications
42nd Division
7 Feb 1919
IV Corps
Fourth Army
127 Inf Bde
MG Bn
126 Inf Bde
210 Bde RFA Mess
210 Bde RFA Office
B.M. RA
RA Office
RA Mess
125 Inf Bde
211 Bde RFA
D.R.C.
DADOS
DRS
Div Train
Reception Room
'A' Coy
'B' Coy
'C' Coy
'D' Coy
OC's Office
IV Corps Concentration Camp
IV Corps
Fourth Army
127 Inf Bde
126 Inf Bde
42nd Divn Signal Office
O.C. Sigs
G.O.C.
'G' Office
A.A.Q.M.G.
'Q' Office
C.R.E.
G.S.O.1.
D.R.L.S.
A.P.M.
A.D.M.S.
Messages.
Mission Belge.
Education Officer.
42nd Division
Morse circuits in red.
Transformers thus -
Capt. RE
for. OC. 42nd Div Sig Co RE

Army Form C. 2118.

Instructions regarding War Diaries and Intelligence Summaries are contained in F. S. Regs., Part II. and the Staff Manual respectively. Title pages will be prepared in manuscript.

WAR DIARY
or
~~INTELLIGENCE SUMMARY~~.
(Erase heading not required.)

42 D Signals

98 23

Place	Date	Hour	Summary of Events and Information	Remarks and references to Appendices
CHARLEROI			January 1919. 42nd. (East Lancs) Divisional Sig. Coy. R.E.(T.F.) Reference Map BELGIUM NAMUR Sheet 8 F. 2.	
	1.1.19 to 31.1.19		The Company Headquarters remained with Divisional Headquarters in billets in the town of CHARLEROI during this period and was engaged in establishing and maintaining communication to Brigades of Infantry and Artillery and also in Educational and Recreational Training; Horse Lines being located at DAMPREMY.	
	17.1.19.		Lieutenant A.G.Smith O.i/c. 210th. Bde. R.F.A. Sub-Section proceeded to England for Demobilisation.	
	20.1.19.		Captain A.Roberts M.C., 2nd. in Command proceeded to England for Demobilisation.	
			The 15th. Course of the Divisional Signal Class opened at CHARLEROI on the 18th. January under the administration of the Reception Camp with 2nd. Lt. BERNARD 1/6th. Manchester Regiment as Officer in charge of the Signal Class.	
			During this month 65 men proceeded to England for Demobilisation.	
			APPENDIX TO THIS DIARY	
			Diagram of Communications.	
			Ernest ... Gill Captain R.E. for O.C. 42nd. Divisional Signal Company R.E.	

A7092). Wt. W12839/M1293 750,000. 1/17. D. D & L., Ltd. Forms/C2118/14.

Army Form C. 2118.

WAR DIARY
or
~~INTELLIGENCE SUMMARY.~~
(*Erase heading not required.*)

Instructions regarding War Diaries and Intelligence Summaries are contained in F. S. Regs., Part II. and the Staff Manual respectively. Title pages will be prepared in manuscript.

Place	Date	Hour	Summary of Events and Information	Remarks and references to Appendices
			42nd (East Lancs) Divisional Signal Co. R.E.(TF). Reference Map.FRANCE 1/40,000. Sheets 57B, 51A & 51.	
			CHAPTER XXV. NOVEMBER 1918.	
BEAUVOIS en CAMBRESIS.	1.11.18 - 3.11.18.		42nd Division in Fourth Corps Reserve remained in BEAUVOIS with Headquarters at I.9.d.22 (sheet 57B). Communications as at end of last month. (War Diary October Appendix A. Diagram 7).	
	3.11.18.		During day, 126th Infantry Brigade moved to SOLESMES into reserve of N.Z. Division in preparation for the next day's attack. Communication by telephone from 126th Brigade Headquarters to N.Z. Divisional Headquarters in SOLESMES established.	
	4.11.18.		Attack launched on Fourth Corps front. 42nd Division ordered to move forward in support of left (N.Z) Division. 126th Infantry Brigade moved to BEAUDIGNIES and telephone communication with advanced N.Z. Divisional Headquarters at X.2.a.65 (sheet 51A) established. 127th Infantry Brigade moved to VERTIGNEUL FARM with telephone communication with N.Z. (Rear) Headquarters at SOLESMES.	
		1000	Two complete cable Detachments moved from BEAUVOIS to SOLESMES in order to be in a position to move next day to new Headquarters of 42nd Division. Orders received in evening that Divisional Headquarters would move at 1000 from BEAUVOIS to BEAUDIGNIES.	See App^x D. (Coy. Order no. 26)
	5.11.18.	0830	Two cable Detachments moved from SOLESMES to BEAUDIGNIES. Preparations made to take over communications from N.Z. Division.	
		1100	Orders received that Divisional Headquarters would move to POTELLE CHATEAU (M.27.b.7.4. sheet 51) 126th Infantry Brigade Headquarters moved to FORRESTERS POST (N.20.c.sheet 51). 127th " " " " " HERBIGNIES. (M.30.c. " "). 125th " " " " " BEAUDIGNIES.	
POTELLE CHATEAU.			During afternoon Divisional Headquarters arrived at POTELLE CHATEAU and preparations were made to take over communications from N.Z. Divisional Signal Coy.	
		1830	G.O.C. 42nd Division took over command of Left Divisional Sector, Fourth Corps front.	

A7092). Wt. W12839/M1293 750,000. 1/17. D. D & L., Ltd. Forms/C2118/14.

Army Form C. 2118.

Instructions regarding War Diaries and Intelligence Summaries are contained in F. S. Regs., Part II. and the Staff Manual respectively. Title pages will be prepared in manuscript.

WAR DIARY

or

~~INTELLIGENCE SUMMARY.~~

(Erase heading not required.)

Place	Date	Hour	Summary of Events and Information	Remarks and references to Appendices

Night. 5/6.11.18.

The Infantry Brigades of 42nd Division relieved Brigades of N.Z.Division in the line, dispositions being as follows:-

Leading Brigade.	...	126th Infantry Brigade.
Support Brigade.	...	127th Brigade.
Reserve Brigade.	...	125th Brigade.

The Artillery under the Divisional command, consisting of three Brigades R.F.A. was formed into a single group with Group Headquarters at the Headquarters of the leading Brigade.

The communications taken over from the N.Z. Division consisted of one D.8. pair from Divisional Headquarters along main road through M.29.a & b. and HERBIGNIES to Cross Roads in N.31.a. thence N.E. along road to FORRESTER'S POST (126th Infantry Brigade and Artillery Group Headquarters). (See Diagram 1). [Remarks: DIAGRAM. 1]

One cable Detachment sent forward during the afternoon of November 5th carrying six miles D.8. cable was stationed at Headquarters of leading (126th) Infantry Brigade to lay cable forward in case of an advance of Headquarters by that Brigade.

6.11.18.

It being anticipated that the leading Infantry Brigade would that day move Headquarters to FORESTERS HOUSE (N.36.a.7.6. sheet 51),

0630

A cable Detachment was sent from Divisional Headquarters to lay a D.8. pair from POTELLE CHATEAU via HERBIGNIES, MAISON ROUGE, Cross Roads in T.3.a. thence along road in M.3.b., N.34.d., N.35.c. to FORESTERS HOUSE where the leading (126th) Infantry Brigade had established an advanced exchange and had one pair D.8. cable from their Headquarters to that Exchange.

Another Detachment was sent out to lay a single D.5. circuit from POTELLE CHATEAU by the same route to MAISON ROUGE then to go to FORESTERS POST to supply cable to the Detachment stationed there. Cable from this Detachment was also sent to complete the line mentioned above to FORESTERS HOUSE.

Owing to the very bad weather and the congested state of the roads both these Detachments were out all day before their lines could be completed.

Meanwhile owing to the state of the roads the move of the Company transport to POTELLE CHATEAU was proving very difficult. It was impossible to bring heavily loaded lorries and G.S. wagons up without considerable risk of their being bogged and the horses of the Company were very tired by the long distance and heavy work.

A7092). Wt. W12839/M1293 750,000. 1/17. D. D & L., Ltd. Forms/C2118/14.

Instructions regarding War Diaries and Intelligence Summaries are contained in F. S. Regs., Part II. and the Staff Manual respectively. Title pages will be prepared in manuscript.

WAR DIARY
or
INTELLIGENCE SUMMARY.
(Erase heading not required.)

Army Form C. 2118.

42 D Signals
Vol 25.

Place	Date	Hour	Summary of Events and Information	Remarks and references to Appendices
CHARLEROI.			February.1919. 42nd.(East Lancs)Divisional Sig. Coy.R.E.(T.F.) Reference Map Belgium Namur F.2. Sheet 8	
	1.2.19. to 28.2.19.		The Company Headquarters remained with Divisional Headquarters in billets in the town of CHARLEROI during this period and was engaged in maintaining communication to Brigades of Infantry and Artillery and also in Educational and Recreational Training. Horse Lines being located at DAMPREMY.	
	5.2.19.		The 15th.Course of the Divisional Signal Class was closed down and the men returned to their Units.	
	3.2.19.		Major.J.Parkinson.R.E. from 13th.Corps Sig.Coy. arrived to take over Command of the Company.	
	6.2.19.		Capt.R.S.Newton.M.C. 6.Batt.Lancs Fus. att.42nd. Divl.Sig.Coy. and 2/Lt.K.Wilson proceeded to England for Demobilization.	
	7.2.19.		Major P.A.Foy.M.C. proceeded to England on Demobilization and the Command of the Company was taken over by Major.J.Parkinson.	
	18.2.19.		The Telegraphy & Telephony Class was discontinued on this date owing to lack of attendance.	
	19.2.19.		2/Lt.W.McIntyre joined the Company from 4th. Army & was posted as Officer i/c.210th.Bde.R.F.A. Sub-Section.	
	21.2.19.		Lieut.J.A.Ayles Officer i/c No.4.Section proceeded to England for Demobilization.	
			During this month 70 other ranks proceeded to England for Demobilization.,29 horses and mules were sold and 7 horses proceeded to a Base Port for return to England.	
			J Parkinson Major.R.E. O.C.42nd.Divisional Signal Company.R.E.	

A7092). Wt. W12839/M1293 750,000. 1/17. D. D & L., Ltd. Forms/C2118/14.

(1)

Instructions regarding War Diaries and Intelligence Summaries are contained in F. S. Regs., Part II. and the Staff Manual respectively. Title pages will be prepared in manuscript.

Army Form C. 2118.

WAR DIARY
or
INTELLIGENCE SUMMARY.

(Erase heading not required.)

Place	Date	Hour	Summary of Events and Information	Remarks and references to Appendices
CHARLEROI.			March, 1919. 42nd.(East Lancs)Divisional Signal Co.R.E.Cadre, (T.F.)	
			Reference Map Belgium, Namur, F.2., Sheet 8.	
	1.3.19 to 31.3.19.		The Company Headquarters remained with Divisional Headqrs., in Billets, in the Town of CHARLEROI during this period.	
	5.3.19.		The Divisional Commander inspected the horses and stables at DAMPREMY and presented a Silver Cigarette Case to No. 444068 Dvr. Wright W. being the first prize for the best turned out Limber and pair of horses, at the Transport Competition held at HAUTMONT.	
	7.3.19.		The 127th. Infantry Brigade moved from FLEURUS to the CHARLEROI area, and the Brigade Headquarters was situate at No.3 RUE de PALAIS. Communication was obtained at the new Headquarters by Telephone and Morse circuit.	
	9.3.19.		The 42nd Machine Gun Battalion moved from VELAINE to the CHARLEROI area, the Headquarters being situate at RUE de TRIEUX.	
	15.3.19.		Orders were received [illegible] for the 42nd Division to reduce to Cadre strength forthwith and also that Divisional Headquarters would cease to exist as from midnight 15/16 March, and Brigadier General Fargus C.M.G., D.S.O., would take over command of all troops less R.A. Units and Machine Gun Battalion.	
	15.3.19.		Orders having been received that the 42nd Machine Gun Battn. would proceed to the Rhine, sufficient men eligible for the A. of O. and stores were transferred to No. 5 Section, to make it up to strength.	
	17.3.19.		The 42nd Machine Gun Battn. moved again to their old Headqrs. in VELAINE; Communication established.	
	17.3.19.		Orders were issued for the 42nd. Divisional Artillery to reduce to Cadre Strength.	
	18.3.19.		2/Lieut D. W. Thorpe R.E., T.C., arrived from 37th.Divl. Signal Company R.E. and was posted as Officer i/c No. 5 Section.	
	19.3.19.		2/Lieut W. McIntyre R.E., T.C., was transferred from Officer i/c 210 Brigade R.F.A. Sub-Section to "D" Corps Signal Company under orders received from Chief Signal Officer IV Corps.	

A7092). Wt. W12839/M1293 750,000. 1/17. D. D & L., Ltd. Forms/C2118/14.

Army Form C. 2118.

Instructions regarding War Diaries and Intelligence Summaries are contained in F. S. Regs., Part II. and the Staff Manual respectively. Title pages will be prepared in manuscript.

WAR DIARY (Continued)
or
INTELLIGENCE SUMMARY.

(Erase heading not required.)

Place	Date	Hour	Summary of Events and Information	Remarks and references to Appendices
	19.3.19.		Lieut. G.H. Osmaston R.E., was transferred from Officer i/c 211 Brigade R.F.A. Sub-Section, to IV Army Signal Co. under orders received from Chief Signal Officer IV Army.	
	19.3.19.		Two motor-cycles were transferred to IV Army M.T. Co.	
	20.3.19.		Lieut H.R. Iliffe, R.E., T.C., proceeded to England on Demobilization.	
	25.3.19.		Under orders received from Chief Signal Officer IV Corps, the personnel comprising No. 5 Section were transferred to "X" Corps Signal Co.	
	19.3.19.		Two Motor-cyclists and motor-cycles were transferred to IV Corps Signal Company.	
	20.3.19.		Orders were received from Chief Signal Officer that the demob--ilization of all Signal Service personnel would cease forthwith.	
	21.3.19.		IV Corps closed down at WAVRE and opened at DUREN at midnight.	
	21.3.19.		Under orders issued by Chief Signal Officer IV Army the personnel of the 93rd. Brigade A.F.A. Sub-Section, Consisting of Lieut D.M.Randell R.E., T.C., and 4 O.R's were transferred to IV Army Signal Company.	
	28.3.19.		The Cadre personnel of the 127th Inf. Brigade entrained for England and the personnel of No. 4 Section was withdrawn to the Headquarters of the Signal Company.	
	31.3.19.		The Cadre personnel of the 126th Inf. Brigade entrained for England, and the personnel of No. 3 Section was withdrawn to the Headquarters of the Signal Company.	
			During this period 50 men eligible for the A. of O. were transferred to IV Corps Signal Co., and 10 men to IV Army Signal Co., also 26 animals were sold and 26 proceeded to Base port for return to England. 55 men proceeded to England for demobilization.	

[illegible] Capt. RE
for Major R.E.
C.C.42nd.Divisional Signal Company R.E. Cadre.

A7092). Wt. W12839/M1293 750,000. 1/17. D. D & L., Ltd. Forms/C2118/14.

19

G.18/35.

D.A.G.
3rd Echelon.

Further to this office G.18/35 of 15th inst.

Herewith War Diary of Signal Coy., 42nd Div. H.Q.

[signature]

for Major General,
Commanding 42nd Division.

17th January, 1919.

APPENDIX "C"

Message Chart.

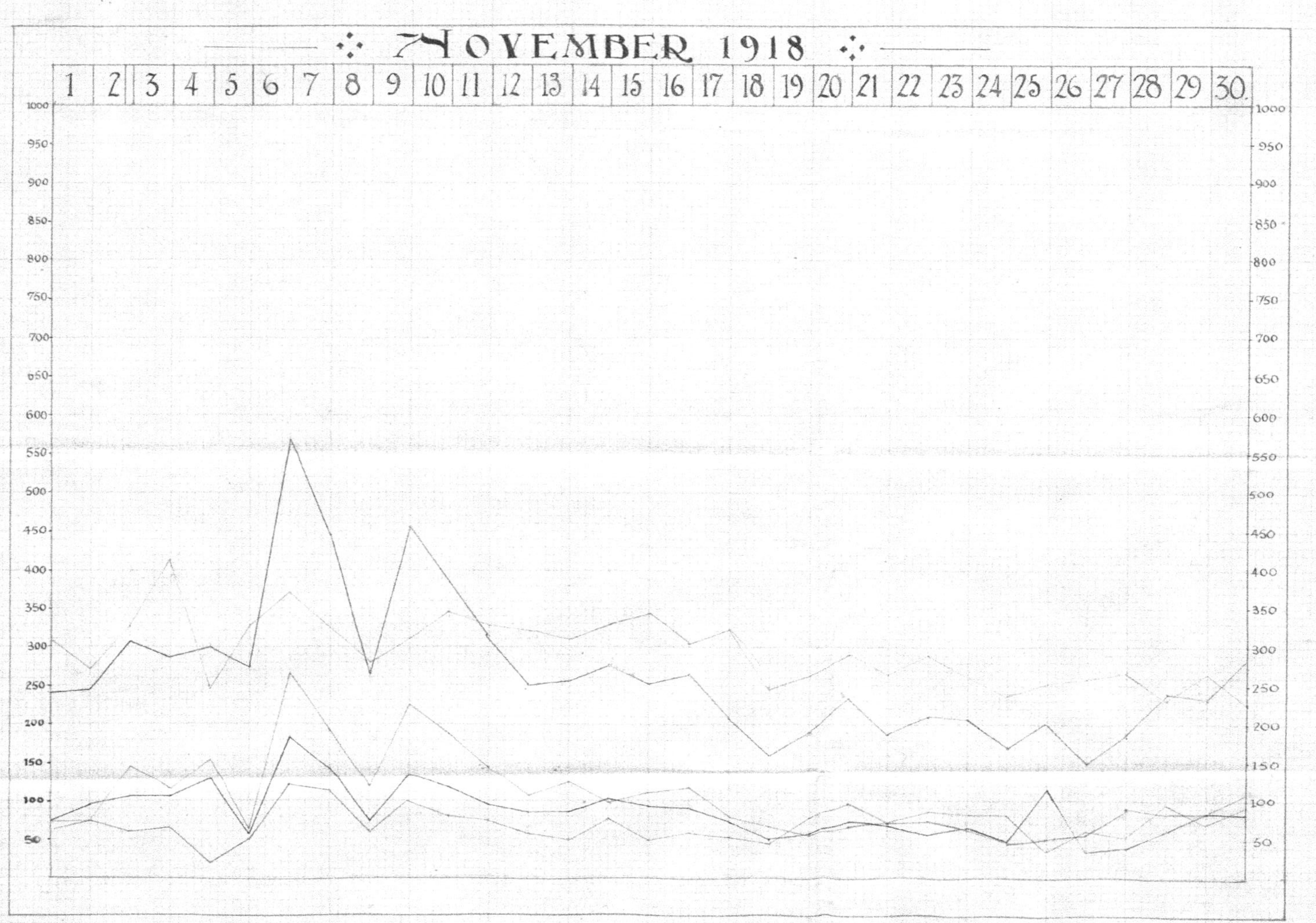

Paton
Major R.E.
OC 42nd Divl Signal Co R.E.

www.ingramcontent.com/pod-product-compliance
Lightning Source LLC
Chambersburg PA
CBHW081432300426
44108CB00016BA/2356
* 9 7 8 1 4 7 4 5 2 0 7 6 8 *